The Rise
and Fall
of Black
Slavery

D1116717

The Rise and Fall of Black Slavery

C. Duncan Rice

Picrafo

1817

HARPER & ROW, PUBLISHERS
New York, Evanston, San Francisco, London

FIRST U.S. EDITION

Library of Congress Cataloging in Publication Data
Rice, Charles Duncan, 1942–
  The rise and fall of Black slavery.
  Bibliography: p.
  Includes index.
  1. Slavery in the United States. 2. United States—
Social conditions—To 1865. I. Title.
E441.R48   301.44′93′0973   72-9149
ISBN 0-06-013552-2

75 76 77 78 10 9 8 7 6 5 4 3 2 1

for
SAMUEL WUNSCH

Contents

List of Plates

Between pages 178 *and* 179

Preface

SEVERAL years before the work on this book was completed, I delivered something vaguely similar to it as my lectures in a course at King's College, Aberdeen. The course was cavalierly entitled 'Slavery and Anti-Slavery Movements'. In the course of my teaching I discovered there was no such thing as a book which gave an introduction to the whole history of slavery, the slave trade, and the great reform movement which overthrew them both. In a fit of intellectual arrogance I set about supplying this need by converting my lecture notes into publishable form. I promptly discovered that though the absence of such a general book on slavery and abolition in the Atlantic world was indeed glaring, my poor lectures fell very far short of filling the gap. After rewriting them several times, I all but discarded them, including some splendid perorations which I dearly loved, and which cost me great emotional anguish in the scrapping. In their place, however, there grew the present great amoeba of a book. It fails to fill the gap completely, for the limitations of space and some lacunae in my own learning have left it less than fully comprehensive. As a historian of anglophonic America, too, I have tended to use more examples from the British colonies than is strictly speaking justified. I am still optimistic enough to hope that the book will be useful to anyone who wants a short introduction to the whole history of black slavery and anti-slavery in the Americas and Europe, but who shrinks both from monographs and textbooks.

This book, then, is intended for the general reader. Most publishers will agree that the general reader is as elusive as Monboddo's tailed man. I am nevertheless convinced, like my countryman Monboddo, that he exists, and that professional historians are obliged, at least sometimes, to cater to him. The book is not a work of research, although there are places in which it has been moulded by research I am doing towards other projects. I also hope that some of its ideas will be of interest to those whose business is the manufacture of monographs, even where I have made comments on fields other than my own. But the main intention is that the book will be attractive to anyone who wishes to read about slavery and abolition because they interest him, or to the student who wants a general introduction to a subject which is usually studied within its national divisions. My system of footnoting has been devised with readers of this sort in mind. I have not referred to primary sources, even for my own research area, except where I am documenting a quotation, statistic or particularly strange viewpoint. On the other hand, I have referred to secondary works not only when I am discussing or citing the thesis of a specific author, but also with the intention of guiding the reader to the works which seem to me to be the most useful in a given area, should he become interested in the material covered in any particular section of my own text. I have not cited foreign-language works except where they seem to have absolutely no equivalent in English. By and large, the footnotes are not intended to support my views, but to lead readers on to other works in areas where they wish to carry their explorations further.

A great number of men and women have given me advice and stimulation in handling the problems raised by this book. A long line of students, mentors and colleagues at Aberdeen, Edinburgh and Yale have helped mould my ideas. Among them I can name only John Hargreaves, who first interested me in slavery; George Shepperson, who first interested me in abolition; and David Brion Davis, whose influence on my conception of reform movements will be only too obvious to any scholar interested in that field. Since many of the key books in the slavery and abolition field have been written by colleagues at Yale, I should mention one of my other important advantages in working on this book. My office lies abeam of the main through route to the departmental men's room, and so it has always been easy for me to leap out on passing scholars and trap them for interrogation on their fields of specialisation whenever this seemed helpful. These influences, I hope, have always been for the good, and I am grateful for them. My errors and omissions – and I am sure they are many – are all my own fault.

I have dedicated *The Rise and Fall of Black Slavery* to my father-in-law, with my personal admiration, because he has always been deeply interested in the history of black people in

the United States. For my wife this leaves only my thanks, though
I refuse to mention her by name in case this gives satisfaction to
the many vulgar militants among our friends. Nevertheless, they
are very deep thanks.

C.D.R.

Saybrook College
Yale University

January 1973

1 Introduction

MUCH of the massive wealth of North America, of the West Indies and of Latin America was produced in the first instance by the labour of black slaves. Even an unusually ill-educated Klansman could not hide the fact that Negroes at least had something to do with the first commercial cultivation of colonial America, English, Dutch, French, Spanish and Portuguese. Most modern scholars, in Europe and America, are acutely aware of the interaction between black work and white profit. But unlike the Klansman they consider it surprising and distasteful that the opening of the New World, which represented progress, should have depended quite inconsistently on slavery, an institution which represented reaction. Most English-speaking schoolboys are familiar with *1066 and All That*, and those who are not should be. Unfortunately it is less of a parody of the historian's way of thought than he would like to think. Many scholars still write in terms of the contradiction between the colonisation of America, which was a Good Thing, and the use of slave labour in its cultivation, which was a Bad Thing. In fact this contradiction was only generally perceived long after the slave systems of the Americas had reached maturity, perhaps when they were already in decline. The New World, Catholic and Protestant, was colonised to get as much profit as possible out of it, and in the sixteenth and seventeenth centuries the most convenient and obvious way of boosting such profit was through slave labour. The conquistadores, the gentry of Virginia, even the Pilgrims and other religious refugees, all began New World cultivation for partly or predominantly commercial reasons and usually as members of commercial organisations. Confronted with a land which needed nothing but vigorous work to produce great wealth, their first concern was to find a convenient way in which this work could be provided. Owing to the expense and difficulty of the Atlantic crossing, free workmen were simply not available in sufficient numbers. It was for this reason that Emanuel Downing, of Massachusetts, made his famous comment that a successful war with the Indians would give his fellow-colonists

> men woemen and children enough to exchange for Moores, which wilbe more gaynefull pilladge for us than we conceive, for I doe not see how wee can thrive untill wee get into a stock of slaves sufficient to doe all our buisiness, for our children's children will hardly see this great Continent filled with people, soe that our servants will still desire freedome to plant for themselves, and not stay but for verie great wages. And I suppose you know verie well how wee shall mayneteyne 20 Moores cheaper than one Englishe servant.[1]

Downing exaggerated the need for labour in the small farming economy of the New England colonies, but nothing could be more natural than that he and other colonists should resort to forced labour. However much European serfdom might have weakened by the time of the American discoveries, the whole heritage of the West (and the East) sanctioned the use of unfree labour. The use of slaves to colonise the Americas was not an aberration. It is nothing like as surprising that Europe's new colonists first farmed and mined through slavery as it would have been if they had not. In a larger perspective, the real historical aberration is not the introduction of slavery into the New World in the sixteenth and seventeenth centuries. Though the Western intellectual tradition implied certain contradictions in its attitude to hereditary forced labour, whether slave or serf, nineteenth-century liberalism was rejecting institutions on which a majority of pre-industrial cultures, not least the European one, are historically based. Modern scholars have shown that individual polemicists of the sixteenth and seventeenth centuries, among them men as different as Las Casas and Walter Ralegh, had serious doubts as to the legality of enslaving their fellow-men, even if they were heathens. Such minority views represent the beginning of a historic change in European attitudes to bondage, but there is no proof that they influenced the actions of many of the men who colonised the New World.

[1] E. Downing to J. Winthrop, n.d. (1645), in E. Donnan (ed.), *Documents Illustrative of the History of the Slave Trade to America*, 4 vols (Washington, 1930–5) III 8.

What was uniquely wicked about the white colonists of the Americas was not that they enslaved their fellow-men, which was commonplace, but that they came to restrict their activities to Indians and latterly to Africans, that is to alien races who had not previously done them any harm. The construction of a slave system based so strictly on race was a new development. The use of slavery itself was not. Indeed, it was a perfectly respectable expedient, with which the colonists were familiar indirectly if not directly, and there is no reason why any historian should expect them to have been fastidious about using it. The abolitionists themselves had no illusions about slaveholding having disfigured human society since biblical times, although they took great pains to prove that Hebraic and classical servitude had been mild compared with American systems. One of the few Jewish writers on the subject was only repeating accepted abolitionist assumptions when he stated proudly (and inaccurately) that 'Palestine ... was by the Mosaic Law, three thousand years ago, what England now is – an asylum for the fugitive slaves of all nations'.[2] Even the Scottish moralist James Beattie, who was committed to anti-slavery and tried to get as much scholarly mileage as possible out of using the slavery question in his vendetta against David Hume, firmly assured his students that slavery had existed in 'many nations', although 'its forms are so various, that one cannot express its general nature in a definition, and it is utterly repugnant to every principle of reason, religion, humanity, and conscience'.[3] The authoress of the first history of the British emancipation movement, Esther Copley, admitted that 'We do not know whether it [slavery] existed before the flood; but, as the presumptuous wickedness of man had risen to such an awful height, as to call for that judgment from a righteous God, we can scarcely think that, among the monstrous evils that prevailed, the oppression of man did not hold a conspicuous place.'[4] She speculated that Nimrod, the founder of Babylon, had 'the infamous distinction of being the parent of post-diluvian slavery', and went on to describe the horrors of slave life in Egypt, Sparta, Greece,

[2] G. Gottheill, *Moses versus Slavery: Being Two Discourses on the Slave Question* (Manchester, 1861) p. 20.

[3] J. Beattie, *Elements of Moral Science*, 2 vols (Edinburgh, 1790) II 155, 156.

[4] E. Copley, *A History of Slavery and its Abolition* (London, 1839) p. 21.

Carthage and Rome. The Romans, she pointed out with some satisfaction, had themselves been enslaved in their turn by the Goths.[5] Even an American extremist like William Lloyd Garrison, who would have found Beattie's douceness and Esther Copley's orthodoxy worse than pro-slavery, never attempted to deny that slavery had always existed; he simply felt that, with other abuses, it should be abandoned at once. By his time appeals against slavery had risen to a crescendo. In 1500, or 1600, or even 1700, they were restricted to a small group of scholars. There was no good reason why the first settlers should not use slave labour whenever they could get it.

Whether they could get it turned out to be a much more vexing problem than the one of morality. The church had long pleaded against the ill treatment of serfs and slaves. There are countless examples of clerical attempts to defend the customary rights of the former against their masters. Yet the West had no fully formed religious or cultural tradition militating against slave labour itself. On the contrary, though the social structures of Europe's various regions were never uniform, and although they had gone through many stages in the thousand years before the Spanish began their ravages in the Americas, one of their constant characteristics was that they had made use, to varying extents, of unfree labour. After the collapse of the Roman Empire, no part of Europe was a 'slave society', in Finley's sense of being a society fundamentally dependent on chattel labour. The systematic marketing of slaves disappeared from northern – though not from southern or western – Europe. But this was due less to increasingly kind masters or to the pressure of the church than to the fact that the static labour demands of the feudal system seldom made the sale and resale of workmen necessary. Where this *was* necessary, for instance in servicing the plantations of Cyprus, and around the Mediterranean in general, a true chattel slave trade flourished well into the fifteenth century. Indeed the Spanish, French and Italians were still using galley slaves, latterly often white Protestants, in the reign of Louis XIV, while enslavement of Christians captured by the Barbary pirates continued until the Napoleonic wars. Medieval European serfdom, at least as it developed in France and England, did admit customary rights, including the right to property. In fact the serf's position

[5] Ibid., pp. 23, 27–46.

vis-à-vis his lord was only one of a great chain of relationships of bondage and service which extended from top to bottom of society. Yet it is still true that serfdom was designed in all its variants, like the later slavery of the black man, to get maximum output from the land by removing the labourer's power to choose the form or place of his employment. The serf's status was hereditary, his entry into it involuntary, his exit from it a cherished goal. Though it was only in isolated cases that he would ever be sold away from the village in which he had been born, it is not hard to imagine conditions in which this might be very much a mixed blessing. Again, although he seldom faced a change of his home, such as it was, like the black slave he was constantly at the mercy of a change of masters, since he changed hands as often as his estate. The great advantage of the serf was that his obligation to his land could never become a total one in time or labour, and that in general the lord's powers were much more circumscribed by custom than those of the American planter. A great deal of scholarly attention has been paid to the differences between serfdom and slavery – and they were great.[6] Yet they can have given little consolation to a serf population whose generations struggled doggedly to reduce their obligations and expand their rights, and ultimately to escape from the status altogether.

Such differences, too, were of minimal concern to the Spanish and Portuguese settlers in the Americas, and probably also to many of their would-be imitators in the Caribbean and North America. To them the main goal of serfdom and slavery alike was that the labour force should be subjected, as fully as possible, to the will of the landowner. Once ensconced in the colonies, where there were none of the bothersome community rights which the centuries had given the peasants of Europe, and where identification by skin colour gave a splendid aid to discipline, it was natural that the lords of the New World should adopt a reinforced version

[6] On true chattel slavery in medieval Europe, see C. Verlinden, *L'Esclavage dans l'Europe médiévale. Tome premier. Péninsule Ibérique – France* (Bruges, 1955) passim, and *The Beginnings of Modern Colonization: Eleven Essays*, trans. Y. Freccero (Ithaca, N.Y., 1970) pp. 33–51. Classical studies of feudal society, which carefully show the similarities and differences between slavery and serfdom, are M. Bloch, *Feudal Society*, trans. L. A. Manyon (Chicago, 1961) pp. 255–79, and J. Blum, *Lord and Peasant in Russia from the Ninth to the Nineteenth Centuries* (Princeton, 1961) pp. 49–53, 270–5.

of the labour system which had been considered most advantageous by the lords of the Old, and which in any case was most familiar to them. This was all the more so since there were parts of Europe where serfdom had not lost its vitality by 1500, or indeed 1600. Though serfdom had been abolished in the British case, its legal structure was well remembered, and in any case indentured servitude remained as a form of bondage which could readily be adapted to mould a New World slave society. Although much changed from its classical twelfth-century patterns, serfdom survived, in eastern Europe, well into the nineteenth century. In Russia, Alexander II only emancipated the serfs in 1861, the first year of the American Civil War.[7] Even in liberal, post-industrial Britain, many of the miners of south-west Scotland remained in a form of hereditary serfdom until the late eighteenth century.[8] The fact that few Europeans can have been unaware of the use of the forced labour of serfs on one side of the Atlantic is clearly one explanation of their willingness to use the forced labour of slaves on the other. This is not to mention the many colonists who must have been familiar with true chattel slavery before leaving for the Americas. We have seen that slavery survived the Middle Ages around the shores of the Mediterranean, and it is of the greatest significance that the Iberian peninsula was the area where it lingered longest. Seville had a teeming slave population throughout the sixteenth century.[9] Slavery in Sicily was abolished only in 1812. Outside Europe, Western eyes could still pick out abhorrent systems of slavery throughout Islam, and in China, Malaya, Nepal, Abyssinia and Sierra Leone well into the twentieth century; indeed, some such are still visible today.[10]

The familiarity of both Catholic and Protestant colonists with various forms of bond labour was not counteracted by any

[7] For brief comment on the parallels between Russian serfdom and slavery in the United States, see P. Dukes, *The Emergence of the Super-Powers: A Short Comparative History of the U.S.A. and the U.S.S.R.* (London, 1970) pp. 41–2, 51–2.

[8] B. F. Duckham, 'Serfdom in Eighteenth Century Scotland', *History*, LIV (1969) 178–97.

[9] R. Pike, 'Sevillan Society in the Sixteenth Century: Slaves and Freedmen', *Hispanic American Historical Review*, XLVII (1967) 344–59.

[10] G.Macmunn, *Slavery through the Ages* (London, 1938) pp. 3–16; K. Simon, *Slavery* (1929) passim; *The Anti-Slavery Society: Its Task Today* (London, 1966).

developed cultural tradition which stressed the immorality of using unfree labour. A great deal has been made of the meliorating influence of Christianity on slavery from late Roman times onwards – and indeed the influence of the church did much to improve the physical treatment of slaves, to legalise slave marriage and to regulate slave punishments. But there can be no doubt that the Christian religious tradition, like the Graeco–Roman legal one, firmly sanctioned slavery. Both traditions might place limits on the unbridled abuse of the slaveholder's power, but both fell far short of discountenancing it. Until the eighteenth century, only isolated spokesmen dreamt of breaking the bonds which held the serf or slave firmly in his place in the hierarchy. The one national exception was England, and there serfdom disappeared because of the expansion of the customary rights of the peasant, and not because of the growth of any coherent theory that the institution was 'wrong' in the sense William Wilberforce or Harriet Beecher Stowe would have understood the word. With the single exception of England, the countries of Europe received their legal system from Rome by two routes. Firstly, much of the canon law which influenced the legal systems of Europe had grown out of the civil law. Secondly, a great deal of Roman law was directly adopted throughout continental Europe, and incidentally into Scots law, in the fifteenth century. By each of these methods the West absorbed a legal code which assumed the existence of slavery and set out to regulate it with a degree of sophistication seldom equalled by the communities of the New World.

A comparison between the legal position of the Roman slave and that of the North American Negro shows close similarities.[11] Slaves were employed in a great range of occupations, many of them domestic, and even the extensive use of slave labourers in large-scale plantation agriculture and in industrial occupations was a feature of the Roman system. At least in the Republic and early Empire, the Roman slave had no positive rights which curtailed the master's power over his life and person. Again, the

[11] A. A. Sio, 'Interpretations of Slavery: The Slave Status in the Americas', *Comparative Studies in Society and History*, vii (1965) 289–308, reprinted in L. Foner and E. D. Genovese (eds.), *Slavery in the New World: A Reader in Comparative History* (Englewood Cliffs, N.J., 1969) pp. 96–112. See also M. I. Finley (ed.), *Slavery in Classical Antiquity: Views and Controversies* (Cambridge, 1960); W. L. Westermann, *The Slave Systems of Greek and Roman Antiquity* (Philadelphia, 1955).

property element in his status meant that the bondsman had no scope for participation in the life of the wider community outside the master–slave relationship. 'Of the slave's civil position,' concludes the standard authority on Roman slave law, 'it may almost be said that he had none.'[12] Certainly, all the Roman jurists admitted or implied that slavery was an institution which would not be found in a state of nature, that it was inconsistent with *ius naturalis*. But since society was not in a state of nature, and was not expected to descend to one in the foreseeable future, they saw no contradiction in assuming that slavery was upheld by *ius gentium*. Like the Greeks before them, they therefore set about elaborating a body of law which would define the slave's position. Although the contradiction between *ius naturalis* and *ius gentium* was never resolved, and its ghost would rise again to haunt the eighteenth century,[13] this gave little immediate help to the Roman slave. Even to Gaius, writing as late as A.D. 161, the slave had no rights, civil or personal. His master, on the contrary, had complete power of life and death over his slaves, as long as he did not kill them '*sine causa*' or treat them with '*maior asperitas*'. His modern editor notes that these restrictions may 'be compared with legislation against cruelty to animals'.[14] This power was gradually modified. The position of the slave had improved, particularly in respect of his opportunities for manumission, by the very late period of the Empire. Partly this was due to the tendency of Christianity to encourage better treatment of slaves, but it was also connected with fear of the massive servile population. There was also a great deal of difficulty in legislating for an increasingly diverse range of slave categories. Justinian's *Institutes*, in 533, elaborating on Constantine's reforms, gave substantial protection to slave marriages, increased the opportunities for emancipation and seriously restrained the master's power to coerce his slave. Nevertheless, these regulations, even if they were fully enforced in a rapidly disintegrating Empire, were aimed at

[12] W. W. Buckland, *The Roman Law of Slavery: The Condition of the Slave in Private Law from Augustus to Justinian* (Cambridge, 1908) p. 82.

[13] P. Gay, *The Enlightenment: An Interpretation*, 2 vols (New York, 1966, 1969) II 414–15; D. B. Davis, *The Problem of Slavery in Western Culture* (Ithaca, N.Y., 1966) pp. 391–421.

[14] F. de Zulueta (ed.), *The Institutes of Gaius*, 2 vols (Oxford, 1946) I c. 52–3; II 28.

humanising the administration of slavery, not at questioning it as an institution. It remained the bald fact that the slave had no civil rights.[15] The corpus of Roman law which was transmitted through the Middle Ages fully sanctioned slavery. Though the line between medieval slavery and serfdom is a distinct one, the gradations between the two statuses were many, and in many parts of Europe they existed side by side until early modern times. Even if slaves had completely ceased to exist, as Davis has pointed out for the special case of English villeinage, serfdom still served as the institution which passed the legal underpinning of slavery on to the sixteenth century, since medieval jurists characteristically interpreted all forced labour in terms of the Roman slave law with which they were familiar.[16] The Americas were not colonised so late that Europe's legal tradition of support for slavery had died. Moreover, this tradition was not as humane as we are led to believe by the historians who argue in favour of the benevolence of the Latin American slavemasters who inherited it.[17]

Since neither Catholic nor Protestant colonists guided their lives by what little they knew of Roman law, and many had an abiding disrespect for law in general, such a tradition might not in itself have had much effect on the ordering of society in the New World. What greatly reinforced it were the vaguer but more powerful rationalisations of slavery drawn from the great body of classical literature. Too much should not be made of isolated and eccentric protests against slavery like those of Diogenes of Sinope, or the Cynic – he of the tub. In fact the only important group of classical writers who attacked slavery were the Stoics, headed by the ex-slave Epictetus. Their speculations as to its wrongfulness presented it as an evil to be borne in this life with dignity. It left the mind of the slave unaffected, and gave him the opportunity to continue his struggle against mankind's common enslavement to its own desires, a noble but uncompelling pie-in-the-sky attitude which did little to weaken the institution.[18]

[15] J. B. Moyle (ed.), *Imperatoris Iustiniani Institutionum libri quattuor*, 2nd ed., 2 vols (Oxford, 1890) I c. 16.

[16] Davis, *Problem of Slavery*, p. 40.

[17] e.g. F. Tannenbaum, *Slave and Citizen: The Negro in the Americas* (New York, 1946).

[18] Epictetus, *Discourses*, IV i 1–177; R. D. Hicks, *Stoic and Epicurean* (New York, 1962) pp. 142–5.

Plato's *Republic* was clearly centred around slavery, as was the world of Aristotle's *Politics*.[19] The later generations of the Southern aristocracy, who saw the use of their black labour force as mirroring the arrangements of Aristotle's ideal state, were much more accurate there than in other aspects of their view of history. And aside from the great theorists, the best-known works of the classical poets, essayists and rhetoricians are strewn with references to slavery which must have familiarised the colonists with the institution even if they did not live in a part of Europe where the tradition of unfree labour had survived.[20] Cato's famous concern for justice, apart from its inconsistency with an imperialist war against Carthage, did not prevent him from writing exact instructions on the method of getting maximum labour from one's slaves, and on the need for disposing of them once they became unfit for work.[21] Cicero wrote at length on the value of liberty, but like another republican slaveholder, Thomas Jefferson, did not find this commitment a barrier to his personal use of slave labour. Juvenal could sneer at the cruelty of slave crucifixion, but his doing so made it clear to later readers that the Romans had not been noted for the kind treatment of their bondsmen.[22] Even the tolerant and jolly Horace, who con-

---

[19] 'The class which farms it [the ideal state] should ideally, and if we can choose at will, be slaves – but slaves not drawn from a single stock, or from stocks of a spirited temper. This will at once secure the advantage of a good supply of labour and eliminate any danger of revolutionary designs': *Politics*, vii x 13, trans. Ernest Barker (Oxford, 1948) p. 359. See also K. Popper, *The Open Society and its Enemies*, 5th ed., 2 vols (New York, 1967) i 224–5 (chap. iv, n. 29); R. Schlaifer, 'Greek Theories of Slavery from Homer to Aristotle', *Harvard Studies in Classical Philology*, xlvii (1936) 165–204; G. Vlastos, 'Slavery in Plato's Republic', *Philosophical Review*, l (1941) 289–304. Both the latter papers are reprinted in Finley (ed.), *Slavery in Classical Antiquity*, pp. 93–150.

[20] The best introductions to classical slavery are Westermann, *Slave Systems of Greek and Roman Antiquity*, and Finley (ed.), *Slavery in Classical Antiquity*. See also M. I. Finley, 'Between Slavery and Freedom', *Comparative Studies in Society and History*, vi (1963–4) 233–49, which specially stresses the presence of intermediate statuses between total freedom and total enslavement.

[21] Marcus Porcius Cato, *De Re Rustica*, ii 7: 'boves vetulos, armenta delicula, oves deliculas, lanam, pelles, plostrum vetus, forsamenta vetera, servum senem, servum morbosum, et siquid aliut supersit, vendat. Patrem familias vendacem, non emacem esse opportet.'

[22] *Satires*, vi 219 ff.

stantly harps on the value of the primitive patriotic virtues, implies his annoyance that Spartacus' revolt and the servile drunkenness it produced had seriously diminished the supplies of properly aged Falernian available in his lifetime.[23] Apuleius, just as witty, centred the whole tortured theme of his *Golden Ass* around the ill-luck inevitably borne by slaves. His hero's fate was to be turned into an ass not as the wages of fornication, but for the rashness of fornication with a slave girl.[24] As for the practice of slavery, all Roman treatises on agriculture, like Cato's, gave a great deal of attention to slave management. The most important of these, Columella's *De Re Rustica*, was published in A.D. 65, and was still in universal use in the late Middle Ages. It was strongly recommended in Milton's pamphlet, *On Education*, and was still being referred to with respect at the end of the nineteenth century. He gave detailed information on the correct rules to follow in purchasing, training and managing slaves.[25] It is easy to make a case for the classical writers' being aware that slavery could not be borne by those conscious of the ennobling spirit of liberty, and when later centuries began to imagine that *all* men were capable of enjoying freedom, this contradiction would seriously undermine the rationalisation for slavery. In the sixteenth and seventeenth centuries, however, the colonists, like the ancients, found slight difficulty in assuming that they themselves were earmarked for liberty, but the aliens they enslaved were not. Classical traditions, for the present, did far more to encourage the use of slavery than the opposite.

This encouragement was all the more forceful because of the absence of any firm religious disavowal of slavery. It would have been hard for an educated man living in the late fifteenth century not to have been entirely familiar with the legal and intellectual concept of slavery as well as the institution. The prevailing assumption was that forced labour had always been a part of an established mechanism of society, an assumption which the practice of the church and the prevailing interpretation of Scripture

---

[23] *Odes*, III xiv 18–20.

[24] *The Transformations of Lucius, Otherwise Known as the Golden Ass*, trans. and ed. Robert Graves (1951; reprinted New York, 1971) pp. xii–xiii.

[25] E. Hyams, *Dionysus: A Social History of the Wine Vine* (New York, 1965) pp. 106–8, 117–19. Columella's advice on slave management is in *De Re Rustica*, I viii, ix.

did little to challenge. This is not to deny that Christianity and Christian ethics had been slowly working since their inception towards mitigating the day-to-day abuses of slavery. So far, however, they had done nothing towards creating a concept of liberty as a right, or towards eroding the universal conviction that slavery was an acceptable institution. At the time when Columbus stumbled on the West Indies, neither the church nor the writings it accepted had given future settlers an indication that their use of forced labour could be considered immoral, though isolated churchmen had hinted at misgivings. The great figures of the medieval church, not to mention the Bible itself, clearly exhorted slaves to remain in the position the Divinity had chosen for them. Masters should indeed treat them well, but beyond this there was no suggestion that the institution of slavery, entwined as it was with the whole of European society, should be challenged.

Although St Augustine was probably not the greatest of all Africans, his work may be the greatest single African influence on European thought. Yet the massive strength of his *De Civitate Dei*, and the warmth of its message for the oppressed, cannot hide the way in which it argues that change of the *status quo* is irrelevant to the survival of Christianity. In effect, Christians who were in lowly and oppressed positions, that is those who were slaves or serfs, were assured that their reward for not challenging the power of those above them would be contentment and equality to be realised in the City of God. Augustine's central assumption was that the social structure, complete with unfree labour, should be maintained intact. Masters were exhorted to treat slaves well, but even if they did not, the slave's acceptance of his lot was desirable as an example of Christian humility. The reward for his suffering in an imperfect world would come only in another and perfect one.[26] This is not to deny that Augustine stressed the implicit freedom of the individual soul, or that he saw slavery as being at odds with the Law of Nature, a logical consequence of man's fall in Eden. Indeed, these aspects of his thought could be extrapolated by later writers as soon as a strong body of abolitionist opinion wished to find evidence for an intellectual tradition which challenged slavery. But for the Middle Ages, and in the first centuries of colonisation, no such body of opinion existed, and the immediate force of Augustine's plea for the unimportance

[26] *De Civitate Dei*, xix xv, xvi.

of the political and social *status quo* would be to buttress the existence of slavery and sanction its extension to the new continent. This was all the easier since the Aristotelian impact on late-medieval thought was only to provide a further justification for the enslavement of Amerindians.[27]

Few medieval writers added to Augustine's arguments for the acceptance of slavery in this life, or to his doubts and those of the classical writers as to its consistency with the natural law. There are signs of vague concern over the morality of slavery in Duns Scotus, and the sixteenth-century jurist Jean Bodin, medieval in so much of his thought, was positive in his stress on the unnaturalness of the slave relationship.[28] By and large, however, the medieval intellectual tradition which came down to the generation of Columbus did not challenge the assumption that slavery was a valuable institution in an imperfect world. The reluctance of the church to attack this attitude was clearly connected with its need to survive in a secular Europe which would not have taken kindly to interference with institutions of importance to its social system. More specifically, it is hard to see why the churchmen of the Middle Ages should have troubled to denounce slavery when the Bible, on which their moral code depended, gave them no authority for doing so. Indeed, the Bible was far and away the most influential work in framing European and American attitudes to slavery until the nineteenth century. By the late eighteenth and early nineteenth centuries, frantic attempts were being made to read binding anti-slavery principles into the Scriptures.[29] But it is of the greatest importance that neither the Old nor the New Testament says a word specifically stating the immorality of slaveholding. On the contrary, the one sets out elaborate codes of slave law, while the other exhorts

[27] L. Hanke, *Aristotle and the American Indians. A Study in Race Prejudice in the Modern World* (New York, 1959).

[28] Davis, *Problem of Slavery*, pp. 111–14.

[29] C. L. Shanks, 'The Biblical Anti-Slavery Argument of the Decade 1830–1840', *Journal of Negro History*, xvi (1930). The most influential attempt to extort abolitionism from the Bible was G. Bourne, *The Book and Slavery Irreconcileable* (1816), ed. J. W. Christie and D. L. Dumond (Wilmington, Del.: Presbyterian Historical Society, 1969). Cf. R. Harris, *Scriptural Researches on the Licitness of the Slave Trade, Showing its Conformity with the Principles of Natural and Revealed Religion, Delineated in the Sacred Writings of the Word of God* (Liverpool, 1788).

slaves to remain contented with subjection to their master. There is no need to construct an elaborate theory that African slavery followed from Ham's curse on Canaan, and that blacks were his descendants. In a post-emancipation world, at least one American rejected it because he saw that it was unnecessary to support his attitude of superiority over the black race, and because, as he logically added, 'I doubt it in the first place, because Ham's mother and father were both white folks. And I doubt it in the second place because I don't believe God would a sprung such a joke as that on the community.'[30] In fact it was easily possible to find scriptural support for the enslavement of Africans without resorting to the shakiness of the 'Cursed be Canaan' theory. The Old Testament called on the Israelites to take slaves from the surrounding tribes, and carefully regulated their conditions of labour. The New Testament, even if its spirit of love may have led to the good treatment of bondsmen, at no point denounced slavery, and on the contrary contains a crucial pro-slavery passage in which Paul orders the converted slave Philemon to return to his master Onesimus.[31] However much later abolitionists might wriggle to pervert its meaning, the Bible is manifestly a pro-slavery document. Moreover, it was pro-slavery in its effect. It was only at a later time that a body of writers accustomed to regarding the authority of Scriptures as fundamental felt obliged to reinterpret it to fit in with a series of attitudes opposed to slavery. These abolitionist attitudes were not directly biblical in origin, though they were associated with a general morality which drew its rationale from the simple message of the New Testament. The Golden Rule in itself said nothing about slavery, but its potential for underwriting social change would become revolutionary as soon as an evangelical age began to apply it as the ultimate test of all social institutions. But the first colonists were not the heirs to any intellectual or moral tradition which denied that slavery was the obvious labour system to use in the New World.

The lack of moral sanctions against slavery would have been less important if the majority of colonists had had any expertise

[30] Ozark (Alabama) *Banner-Advertiser*, 24 Oct 1895, cited in B. Palmer, 'The Rhetoric of the Southern Populists: Metaphor and Imagery in the Language of Reform', unpublished Ph.D. dissertation (Yale, 1972) p. 278.
[31] Philemon 1: 1–21.

in handling free agricultural labour, supposing there had been some miraculous way in which it had become available. Indeed, few of the Spanish or Portuguese settlers had experience in any business or agricultural enterprise other than freebooting. When the English and Dutch came to the scene they were already faced with established slave-trading routes and the example of highly profitable Iberian use of slave labour. On the other hand, apart from long-standing assumptions on serfdom, many Europeans, by the end of the fifteenth century, were familiar with standard methods of slave-trading, slave management, and even plantation agriculture. This was particularly so among the Spanish and Portuguese. Most of the techniques of the earliest slave-traders in Guinea, for instance, were perfected in the vigorous late-medieval slave trade along the routes of the Mediterranean and the Black Sea. From providing white slaves for the court market of Byzantium, or the plantation markets of Cyprus and the Atlantic islands, it was not a long step to begin shipping black slaves to meet the voracious new demands of the Americas. This Mediterranean traffic, largely in the hands of the Genoese, provided most of the techniques used in the early stages of the Atlantic trade – which, incidentally, was also heavily influenced by the Genoese. The Portuguese themselves had been shipping black slaves from West Africa to the markets of Castile and thence to other European courts fifty years before Columbus's discoveries gave them a more profitable outlet. Azurara's chronicle of the Portuguese explorations in West Africa gives a splendid account of their insistence on hunting down black slaves on horseback in much the same knightly way as they would have hunted wild boar.[32] It was only after they discovered that this lowered their chances of gathering slaves, and that African middlemen were only too glad to barter men for horses and other European merchandise, that a regular slave trade from the Coast to Portugal emerged. It was doubtless by this route that the black girl at the

[32] G. E. de Azurara, *Chronicle of the Discovery and Conquest of Guinea*, trans. and ed. C. R. Beazley and E. Prestage (London: Hakluyt Society, 1897), extracts printed in Donnan (ed.), *Documents Illustrative of the History of the Slave Trade*, 1 418–41. On the medieval antecedents of Atlantic slavery and the slave trade, see Verlinden, *L'Esclavage dans l'Europe médiévale*, and *The Beginnings of Modern Colonization*, pp. ix–xxi, 3–51. Verlinden lays particular stress on Iberian familiarity with methods of slaving and colonisation prior to the discoveries.

court of James IV of Scotland, 'my ladye with the mekle lippis', travelled to the north.[33] As for the African end of the future trade, a stream of miserable captives, at whose numbers we can hardly guess, had been shipped from the western Sudan across the Sahara to the markets of North Africa and the Levant at least since the beginning of the Islamic period – and indeed the Middle Ages had seen a trickle of them bought by Italians to be absorbed by the European luxury market for exotic court slaves. It was this trade which the Portuguese short-circuited by bringing blacks direct from Africa. In the sixteenth century it would be a very small matter to reweave all these strands of experience to create a slave trade to the Indies.

As the sixteenth century opened, then, a combination of cir-

[33] 'Of Ane Blak-Moir', in W. Mackay Mackenzie (ed.), *The Poems of William Dunbar* (1932; new ed., London, 1970) pp. 66–7:

> Lang heff I maed of ladyes quhytt,
> Nou of ane blak I will indytt,
>   That landet furth of the last schippis;
> Quhou fain wald I descryve perfytt,
>   My ladye with the mekle lippis.
>
> Quhou schou is tute mowitt lyk ane aep,
> And lyk a gangarall onto gaep;
>   And quhou hir schort catt nois up skippis;
> And quhou scho schynes lyk ony saep;
>   My ladye with the mekle lippis.
>
> Quhen schou is claid in reche apparell,
> Schou blinkis als brycht as ane tar barrell;
>   Quhen schou was born, the son tholit clippis,
> The nycht be fain faucht in hir querrell:
>   My ladye with the mekle lippis.
>
> Quhai for hir saek, with speir and scheld,
> Preiffis maest mychttelye in the feld,
>   Sall kis and withe hir go in grippis;
> And fra thyne furth hir luff sall weld:
>   My ladye with the mekle lippis.
>
> And quhai in felde receaves schaem,
> And tynis thair his knychtlie naem,
>   Sall cum behind and kis hir hippis,
> And nevir to uther confort claem:
>   My ladye with the mekle lippis.

cumstances was presenting Africa as a splendid source of labour for the colonies of the New World. Europeans had no traditions which would argue unequivocally against the use of slavery, and indeed they also had experience in managing slaves and in trading for them. The most recent area to which they had extended this trade was Africa. As soon as other sources of labour failed in the Americas, the colonists would latch on to the West African trade. This was all the easier since many West African societies were only too well able to provide the slaves which the New World required. Modern enthusiasm for things African should not be allowed to hide the cruel conditions of sixteenth-century West Africa. They were probably less cruel than conditions in Europe during the same period – but this is no reason for scholars in American history to dream up a whole pastoral scenario of Africa before the descent of the slave-hunters. The first Westerner to make the assumption that Africa had plodded on in a vice-free state of nature until the arrival of the white man was the pioneer abolitionist Anthony Benezet,[34] and a high proportion of the few Europeans and Americans who have since gone to the trouble of gathering information about Africa at all have handed on his mistakes. In fact it is impossible to make a sound analysis of the history of the slave trade without accepting the fact that it depended not only on wicked Western merchants who were prepared to buy their fellow-men, but also on African merchants who were prepared to sell them. Both groups stood to make a great deal of profit from the slave trade, and few among either had any pressing cultural reason for resisting the temptation to do so. This is not to say that African societies, prior to the era of the Atlantic slave trade, had any social institutions identical to American slavery. They did not characteristically develop a ruling class whose position depended on their distinctiveness as slaveholders, and slavery was not normally the basis of society's productive functions.[35] Moreover, slaves were seldom present as a permanent hereditary caste, and were absorbed into the ranks of freemen in a relatively small number of generations. It has

[34] A. Benezet, *Some Historical Account of Guinea, its Situation, Produce, and the General Disposition of its Inhabitants*, 2nd ed. (London, 1788).
[35] A. Norman Klein, 'West African Unfree Labour Before and After the Rise of the Atlantic Slave Trade', in Foner and Genovese (eds.), *Slavery in the New World*, pp. 87–95.

even been suggested that in some of the societies of Upper Guinea, the area from Cape Mount to the Gambia, no form of slavery existed at all until European demands produced it. 'Without a doubt,' argues one scholar, 'as far as this region is concerned, to speak of African slavery as being ancient, and to suggest that this provided the initial stimulus and early recruiting ground for slaves exported to Europe and the Americas is to stand history on its head.'[36] In other cases, however, societies not only possessed forms of chattel slavery, but an ability and willingness to adapt these forms to supply Europeans with the manpower they wanted.

It is a mistake to assume that in the sixteenth century the merchants and rulers of the Guinea Coast and its hinterland were duped by cunning Europeans, against their own good nature and better judgement, into involvement in the slave trade. This is to question their common sense, and that of Africans and the black race as a whole, and to underestimate the extent of their political and commercial sophistication. It is just as wrong to imply that the sixteenth-century West African civilisations, without the sinister influence of Europeans, would have been above the vices of greed and desire for profit. This, just as much as the old, crude accusations of their savagery, is to deny their humanity, and puts the historical African in the false position of being a mirror for modern Western morality. Both these myths, though doubtless accepted with the best of intentions, are close to the racist argument that the savages of Guinea were in a state of infancy until their fortunate 'civilisation' by the Europeans. It is this assumption which has been central to the undermining of the self-esteem of black people in the West. There is actually no reason to make the sixteenth-century African into a moral miracle. The early Atlantic slave trade was formalised in a real commercial situation, by a process of interaction between two equal parties who happened to be of different races. The Guinea states had always produced slaves, and in the sixteenth century the white newcomers began to fall over themselves to buy them. There was every reason for the African merchant to focus his great commercial skill on bartering them for Western products which could bring substantial power and status within the context of

[36] W. Rodney, 'African Slavery and Other Forms of Social Oppression on the Upper Guinea Coast in the Context of the African Slave Trade', *Journal of African History*, VII (1966) 431–3.

his own society. If there was an inequality in this unholy partnership, it worked to the disadvantage of the European, who was often powerless in the face of the African middleman's superior expertise and control over the supply of slaves. In the last resort the African merchant could do without European trade goods, but the European could hardly write off the whole investment of his voyage by leaving Africa with no slaves. It is doubtless unpleasant to explore the involvement of the African in the early stages of the slave trade, but it is less unpleasant than slipping into the patronising belief that he was an economic and cultural infant in the hands of merchants from a more advanced society.

The response of Guinea's societies to the demands of the slave-traders will be dealt with in a later chapter. For the moment, it must be pointed out that the civilisation of the great late-medieval West African states like the empires of Mali and Songhai depended centrally on the success of their trade across the Sahara to the rest of the Islamic world. The profits of their trade in gold, elephants' teeth and, not least, slaves were immense – as witness the famous effect of the fourteenth-century Mali ruler Mansa Musa's *jihad* to Mecca in 1324. During their pilgrimage he and his caravan of 60,000 followers dispensed charity (and paid for slave concubines) on such a lavish scale, and in gold, that the resulting inflation upset the rate of exchange in Egypt and Arabia for a period of years to come. The study of Songhai and Mali through the oral tradition, artifacts and Arabic manuscripts they left behind reveals an administration of high sophistication, an art and architecture of considerable beauty, and a general culture with a quality of relaxed vitality which might have been envied by Westerners in the sixteenth and seventeenth centuries and makes them appear merely vulgar in the twentieth. But it also shows a commercial life of great complexity, focused on the trade routes of the Sahara and the world of Islam.[37] When the Europeans appeared in Guinea, it was easy for a proportion of the gold, ivory, slaves and commercial expertise which had made such profits in North Africa to be diverted into the hands of rising coastal traders anxious to barter with the newcomers. European trade goods, though not indispensable enough to give their

[37] E. W. Bovill, *The Golden Trade of the Moors* (Oxford, 1958); B. Davidson, *The Lost Cities of Africa*, 2nd ed. (Boston, 1970) pp. 53–124; N. Levtzion, *Ancient Ghana and Mali* (London, 1972).

sellers a superior bargaining position, were highly attractive.
Their cloths, glasswork, metalwork, trinkets and alcohol were
sufficiently in demand to spell economic and commercial power
for the African merchant or African society which could control
their supply. It was only at a surprisingly late date, probably in
the late eighteenth or early nineteenth centuries, that firearms
became a substantial enough sector of the European export trade
to West Africa to affect its internal political balance, although
they had long given disproportionate power to the coastal traders
of the Niger Delta.[38] At this point, meeting the outside demand
for slaves came to provide the means not only to success in commercial and economic rivalries but to military supremacy as
well. Not all African states withstood, or wished to withstand,
the temptation to increase in political power, to annex their
smaller neighbours and protect themselves from their larger ones.
The wealth and strength which stemmed from the Atlantic trade
was an invaluable adjunct in such struggles, in spite of the cruel
and anti-social implications of meeting the demand for slaves. In
many cases, Africans eagerly entered into the slave trade for good
reasons of state, not because they were infantile enough to be
duped by the white man's glass beads. Though the trade at first
went on side-by-side with peaceful commerce in gum, gold, pep-
per and ivory, its profits accelerated the rise of kingdoms in the
forest belt which looked economically to the sea rather than the
desert. It was at least in part because of their success in taking
advantage of the new possibilities of the Coast trade – not always
necessarily the slave trade – that Benin, Oyo, Dahomey and
Ashanti rose successively to prominence. Especially in the case of
Benin, they too had commercial contacts to the north, but where a
state like Mali had transmitted the slaves and other wares of the
forest across the Sahara, their main concern was in shipping them
directly to the Coast in exchange for European merchandise. It
was all the easier to slip into the slave trade since many West
African societies did not consider unfree labour as abnormal, and
assumed the right of selling criminals, political enemies and
prisoners of war.[39] It was such luckless individuals who had

[38] J. F. Ade Ajayi and R. S. Smith, *Yoruba Warfare in the Nineteenth Century* (Cambridge, 1964) pp. 17–18.
[39] Although this right of sale was in most non-Islamic cases confined to the first generation of enslavement, in contrast to the American situation.

fuelled the ancient trans-Saharan slave trade, and also presumably met the first demands of the European merchants. African traders were as casual as their white brethren over the morality of slavery, and from their end they participated eagerly in launching the new Atlantic traffic. What they could not foresee was its future effect upon nineteenth-century Guinea. Her rich cultures would be brutalised as the insatiable demands for labour made slave-trading the most lucrative and eventually, in effect, the main commerce of the Coast. By then the profits of the trade became major means to political power, and some African states were locked into a vicious cycle of fighting wars to get slaves to get the means to fight more wars to get more slaves. In the sixteenth and seventeenth centuries, however, Europeans who wished to buy slaves found Africans only too willing to sell them.

There is a ghastly inevitability not only about the emergence of the Atlantic slave trade, but about the whole planting of slavery in the New World. In spite of the great differences between the Catholic and Protestant settlements of America, there is a case for seeing their adoption of the institution of black slavery as a single phenomenon. The motives of the slaveholders of all nations were similar. The Spanish and Portuguese, like the English, reconciled themselves to the pursuit of profit through the belief that they were providing bases for the spread of their respective religions in the wilderness. To use the forced labour of heathens for this purpose was not only excusable but virtuous. With unfree labour still in viable use in many of the countries of Europe, it could easily be rationalised from Christian and classical traditions which did not directly question it, and which were common to the colonists of North and South America alike. It was only in the far-distant future that slavery's relative loss of economic strength would coincide with an abolitionist attack based on the libertarian and egalitarian seed in the Christian and classical teachings. This could not happen in the world of the sixteenth and seventeenth centuries, a world of intense curiosity, of great urbanity and of rapid change – but a world which still assumed that hierarchy and subjection were natural aspects of mankind's social arrangements. As the colonists looked on their new lands, then, their first assumption was that they would be exploited by forced labour – unless, like some of the Northern colonists, they had neither the strength nor the wealth to acquire it. They were not unduly troubled over defining the position of the slave or the attributes of slavehood, although pamphleteers and jurists would later give a great deal of attention to defining an institution which in many areas had grown up within its own limits by stealth. Buckland, the great commentator on Roman slave law, who should be expected to know about the basis of definition, remarks acidly that

> The Roman law of slavery, as we know it, was developed by a series of practical lawyers who were not great philosophers, and as the main purpose of our definition is to help in the elucidation of their writings, it seems unwise to base it on a highly abstract conception which they would hardly have understood and with which they certainly never worked.[40]

If this is true of attempting to set up definitions for Roman solicitors concerned with the law of slavery, it is even more true of trying to do so for American slaveholders concerned with slavery itself. It is for this reason that the present work does not formally define the characteristics of slavery. The colonist's first concern, whatever his nationality, was to force others to do his physical work for him. His entire heritage told him that this should be done in a way which kept those others under as rigid a control as possible. It was for this reason that he adopted what we call slavery, where the labourer's status as conveyable property was hereditary, where his freedom of action was entirely destroyed by the will of the master, and where the master also gained the right to his entire output of work and its fruits. The system of slavery was by no means finalised overnight, but it eventually emerged as an extension of the old European systems of unfree labour made more efficient by the characteristics of the men who became the slaves of the New World.

The real tragedy of the Americans was not that they used slavery, which would have left no more trace today than European serfdom, but that they used black slavery. Various factors

[40] *Roman Law of Slavery*, p. 2. The most valuable modern attempts to give working definitions of various forms of unfree labour are M. I. Finley, 'Slavery', in *International Encyclopedia of the Social Sciences*, 17 vols (New York, 1968) xiv 307–13, esp. pp. 307–8; H. J. Nieboer, *Slavery as an Industrial System: Ethnological Researches* (The Hague, 1900) pp. 1–39.

made African labour the most attractive available to the colonists. The American colonist could never get enough white labour. For the Spanish and Portuguese, a small population made this an obvious impossibility, while the British, who did experiment with white indentured servants, found that they had awkward customary rights which barred total discipline. At the same time, once they were released at the end of their terms, they formed an alarming group of landless poor which presented a standing threat to the maintenance of a stable and ordered society.[41] Indians, once enslaved, had the bad taste to die off in an uneconomically short space of time. In this dilemma, the solution was to turn to Africa. Not only would it eagerly meet the demand for black slaves, but these slaves were already familiar with agricultural practices similar to those of Europeans. From a far country, black men had nowhere to appeal to in the event of maltreatment. Even better, their skin gave an aid to identification which apparently provided the perfect key to plantation discipline. It was many decades before black slavery became finalised as anything approaching a 'system', but the economic logic of colonisation decreed that the Atlantic slave trade should begin, and that America's labour force should be African. For Americans, the bane of black slavery is still with them. It was highly convenient that black slaves who escaped could be identified and brought back. But the black man, not unnaturally, has remained black, and it is less healthy that large sections of the Americas can still identify their ex-slaves as a group whom they consider separate and inferior. The reason for this tragedy is that the economic and cultural forces which shaped the colonial Americas dictated the use of slave labour. African workmen being the most suitable and the most available, the result was black slavery, and the Atlantic slave trade which fed it. The following chapters will outline the practice of the trade and its effects on Africa, and the process by which slavery came to be central to the societies of the New World.

[41] E. S. Morgan, 'Slavery and Freedom: The American Paradox' *Journal of American History*, LIX (1972) 5–29.

2 Slavery in the Early Colonies, Catholic and Protestant

By the end of the seventeenth century black slavery was accepted as a normal form of agricultural labour in substantial sectors of America, and the Atlantic slave trade had become institutionalised as an important arm of Europe's commerce. Yet neither slavery nor the slave trade emerged in its mature form overnight. Certainly, as we have seen, traditions endorsing slavery were strong. Europe and to a lesser extent Africa had long had the expertise to conduct large-scale slave-trading, and the economic demand for labour was implied in the foundation of the first New World settlements. But it took many decades for slavery to become fully established, and for the customs which regulated the sale and forced labour of Africans to be formalised. During the sixteenth and early seventeenth centuries the rising middlemen of the Guinea Coast developed the commercial practices which would govern their relationships with the Europeans, at first largely Portuguese, who came to buy the slaves they had gathered from the interior. Only a few of the sixteenth-century settlers in America, whether Spanish or Portuguese, made any bones about their willingness to use slaves to exploit their new possessions. At the outset, however, they made serious attempts to get the labour they needed from the local Indian population, either through true slavery or through the labour-tribute system of the *encomienda* and its equivalents. Only the unsuitability of the Indians as a work-force, and royal concern over their abuse, drove them towards the more costly practice of importing black labour. In the seventeenth century the English settlers in North America and the West Indies went through a similar period of experimentation, in this case principally with white indentured servants, who remained bound to their master for a period of years as a return for being brought out to the colonies at his expense.

Defoe's *Colonel Jack* gives a fine account of the adventures of one such in Virginia. The French, too, for some time made use of the similar white category of *engagés*. Both nations eventually took advantage of the superior convenience of buying African slaves. They were probably treated differently from their white fellow-servants from the outset, and eventually descended to a true chattel status where their condition was hereditary. In time this state of affairs reinforced, if it did not create, the tendency to make black people into a separate caste even when they had been emancipated, and indeed even where they had been born free.

There has been a great deal of argument over the reasons why the English did not use black slave labour from the beginning of their colonising ventures. One scholar maintains that this was a period of rationalisation during which long-held traditions of prejudice against blacks and blackness crystallised into a system of prejudice which would justify enslavement, at a time when it had been discountenanced by English law and was gradually disappearing from Europe as a whole.[1] It has also been suggested that the English quite lacked the prejudices necessary for them to isolate blacks as a slave class. They were only forced to do so by a combination of the economic demands of plantation agriculture and the relative improvement in the condition of their various classes of white labourers.[2] Various other permutations of the interaction between the desperate need for labour, the increasing temptation of plantation profits, the hardening of racial prejudice and the institutionalisation of black slavery have also been considered seriously. However, it seems unlikely that the tardiness with which the slavery of Africans emerged in the English colonies is only the reflection of a yeoman reluctance to enslave foreign races, though some English propagandists certainly saw colonisation as a means to liberate Indians from Spain. In the Carolinas the colonists were enthusiastically forcing Indians to work for them.[3] Doubtless they would have continued

[1] W. D. Jordan, *White over Black: American Attitudes toward the Negro, 1550–1812* (1968; Baltimore: Penguin Books ed., 1969) pp. 3–98.

[2] O. Handlin and M. Handlin, 'The Origins of the Southern Labor System', *William and Mary Quarterly*, 3rd ser., VII (1950) 199–222.

[3] A. W. Lauber, *Indian Slavery in Colonial Times within the Present Limits of the United States* (New York, 1913) passim; V. W. Crane, *The Southern Frontier, 1670–1732* (1929; reprinted Ann Arbor, Mich., 1956) pp. 17–18, 112–15.

to do so if it had not been for the weak social organisation of the North American Indians and the difficulty of training men and women from a Stone Age culture to perform the tasks they required. In the Virginia case, the bitter memories of the 1622 massacre left the settlers reluctant to have Indians in their midst. A major explanation for the slowness with which the institution of slavery crystallised in Barbados, Virginia and the other English colonies was that the number of blacks imported in the first forty years of settlement was too tiny to make their separation into a distinct legal category feasible. In turn, a principal reason why these blacks were initially so few was that the English settlers lacked the means to buy them. In the early seventeenth century they had no commercial contacts in West Africa, and could get blacks only by buying them at ruinous prices from Dutch merchants who had smuggled them at the expense of the Portuguese. It was principally this factor which forced the English to rely in the early stages of settlement on white indentured servants. Like Indians, these had certain disadvantages, mainly the tendencies to riot, murder their masters or run away. The English attempts to use cheap non-black labour, like the Spanish ones, came to nothing. As soon as increased capital and better commercial contacts gave them the opportunity, they too moved towards using black labour, probably spurred on by the threat to law and order posed by the growing numbers of landless and masterless whites who had served their term. They were fortunate in that this coincided with the collapse of Portuguese power and the decline of the Dutch, which enabled them to break into the Guinea trade on their own behalf. In either case, neither the Spanish nor the British used black slave labour extensively in the first stages of their settlements.

The early development of black slavery in Latin America has caused less historical controversy than in the Protestant settlements of the Caribbean and North America. This certainly does not imply any lack of complexity about the steps through which the Spanish and Portuguese colonists defined the forms of forced-labour institutions they used. Indeed, the whole subject should be approached with great caution. In the first place, it would not be easy to make simple generalisations for the whole of Latin America, even if it were not for the difference in the governmental attitudes of Spain and Portugal. Even in the Spanish dominions, settlement did not go on at the same speed or at the same time in each area, while the influence of crown, church and local landowners varied in proportion from place to place. Different mining or farming staples had different labour needs. The situation was also affected by the arrangements of the pre-Conquest rulers, as for instance in Mexico, where the Spaniards simply adopted the excellent tribute-labour system of the Aztecs. Again, the widely used labour-tribute systems of *encomienda*, *repartimiento*, *mita* and *obrajes* created categories of forced labour separate from but occasionally confused with that of true chattel slavery. Although the Latin Americanist is fortunate in having a substantial body of written sixteenth-century slave law to examine, he is hard put to determine whether such law was intended to refer only to Indian slaves or to all of them – and if the former, whether it was eventually extended to include blacks in any case. This is all the more of a complication since the slave's legal position only affected his real condition in varying degrees. In the last resort, in Latin America as in other slave societies, what really governed the slave's fate was the personality of his own master and the demands of industry and agriculture in each particular community or zone at each particular time. These affected him much more immediately than the optimistic ordinances of a distant government. Even if all the evidence needed were available, no brief outline of the early history of Spanish and Portuguese colonial slavery can take account of all these variations. What follows is an attempt, in the worst conditions possible, to give the best generalisation possible.

Full of their dignity as warrior aristocrats, the conquistadores facing the New World had no intention of gathering its wealth by the work of their own hands. The same was true of the first Portuguese settlers in Brazil. Black slaves had been common in both Spain and Portugal long before the Conquest, and there was no barrier to enslavement in the social attitudes of the colonists.[4] The first handful of Spanish conquistadores took Indian slaves

[4] C. Verlinden, *L'Esclavage dans l'Europe médiévale. Tome premier* (Bruges, 1955) passim; R. Pike, 'Sevillan Society in the Sixteenth Century: Slaves and Freedmen', *Hispanic American Historical Review*, xlvii (1967) 344–59; A. D. Ortiz, 'La esclavitud en Castilla durante la edad moderna', *Estudios de la Historia Social de España*, ii (1952) 369–428; V. Cortés, *La esclavitud en Valencia durante el reinado de los reyes católicos, 1479–1516* (Valencia, 1964).

from the outset, initially as concubines given them by their gentle hosts, or as chattels captured in war, and soon as simple conscripted labourers to act as their personal servants or help them in their feverish search for precious metals. As they settled land, their further labour needs were met by the crown's allocations on the *encomienda* system, whereby forced tribute labour became due to them from a set number of Indians, for the performance of a specific task, or from the Indians of a specific community. The first Brazilian colonists also enlisted Indian labour in their logging operations, at first in exchange for trade goods, and later through genuine chattel slavery. None of these expedients was satisfactory to the conquerors, largely because of the physical and cultural inability of the Indians to withstand their brutal tasks, and their lack of resistance to European diseases. In the Spanish case, this, together with genuine royal and clerical concern that the whole race would be exterminated instead of converted to Christianity, led to the introduction of more expensive, but more efficient, and in church eyes more expendable, West African slave labour. The Atlantic slave trade was fully under way by the 1530s, though the numbers involved were at first tiny.

It is often said that at least one of Columbus's crew on his 1492 voyage was black. Indeed, a modern handbook of black history announces proudly under the year 1493 that 'It is most probable that on Columbus' second voyage Negro slaves were brought to Jamaica, and that they took part in a revolt'.[5] Be this as it may, a small but organised traffic in African slaves was certainly under way by 1511, under a system of occasional licences granted to individuals by the Spanish crown. In this year permission was given to import fifty slaves to Hispaniola for mining work, where the need for labour was most urgent. They were quickly followed by larger consignments. Thereafter, apart from the certainty that slave-smuggling was going on in substantial volume at least from the 1520s, the number imported by royal authority increased steadily. At the same time, the sporadic permissions given to Spanish subjects in the New World to import labour widened into a system of *asientos* granted or sold to European merchants as transferable contracts enabling them to export set numbers of slaves to the Indies. One such was given in 1518 to Lorenzo de

[5] P. M. Bergman and M. N. Bergman, *The Chronological History of the Negro in America* (New York, 1969) p. 2.

Gorrevod, Governor of Bresa, although he later sold it to a Genoese merchant house. It granted him the right to carry 4,000 blacks to America for sale to the colonists, 'provided [the slaves] be Christians'. He was permitted to take them directly to the Indies instead of going through the usual commercial bottleneck of Seville, as long as he paid the usual customs duties and could prove that they had become Christians on arrival.[6] Such licences were intermittently issued until the 1580s. The crown then began the practice of vesting the *asiento* in the hands of Portuguese contractors, not only as a licence to introduce a given number of slaves, but as a monopoly right to control all slaving operations over a period of years, at a defined rate per year.

At first the slaves went not to the mainland but to the islands of the Caribbean. They were needed principally in Hispaniola or Santo Domingo, and in gold-bearing Puerto Rico, where the black population was high enough for a substantial revolt to break out in 1527. Slaves were also taken in smaller numbers to the poorer islands of Cuba and Jamaica, though the need for them there was negligible in the sixteenth century. Saco finds, in his enormous study of slavery, that in the 1530s they were employed mainly in mining, but also in domestic service, herding and arable farming. Sugar was being produced commercially in Santo Domingo from the 1520s onwards, with each successful *ingenio* using eighty or a hundred black slaves.[7] Meanwhile, slaves were also being introduced into New Spain, or Mexico, and indeed Cortés was accompanied by black servants during the Conquest. The arrival of black slaves came hard on the heels of the Spanish advance throughout the Americas – in the Isthmus, in Peru, in Rio de la Plata and in Chile. In many cases they were not taken directly across the Atlantic to the new settlements, but

[6] *Asiento* dated 18 Aug 1518, printed in E. Donnan (ed.), *Documents Illustrative of the History of the Slave Trade to America*, 4 vols (Washington, 1930–5) I 41–2. On the *asiento* system, see G. Scelle, 'The Slave Trade in the Spanish Colonies of America: The Assiento', *American Journal of International Law*, IV (1910) 612–61; idem, *La Traite négrière aux Indes de Castille. Contrats et traités d'assiento*, 2 vols (Paris, 1905, 1906). The fullest account of the early development of the trade to the sixteenth-century Spanish colonies is still J. A. Saco, *Historia de la esclavitud de la raza Africana en el Nuevo Mundo, y en especial en los países Américo-Hispanos*, 2nd ed., 3 vols (Havana, 1937–43) I 50–240.

[7] *Ibid.*, I 116 ff., 130.

were brought by masters moving lock, stock and barrel from the older colonies of the Antilles. At the same time, however, the direct trade from Africa to the Indies was increasing. The crown had originally insisted that black slaves be converted, or at least given enough exposure to Christianity to blunt their dangerous heathen influence on potential Indian converts. In effect this requirement was ignored. Although the sixteenth-century asientists were technically required to clear their cargoes through Seville, like everyone else trading to America, they were normally given specific permission not to do so. The demand for the conversion of those taken direct from Africa was observed only nominally, and had no effect in restricting the flow of slaves across the Atlantic. In the sixteenth century the numbers of blacks involved remained low: Curtin puts the total exportation up to 1595 at a little over 50,000, although he does not seem to take full account of smuggled slaves.[8] Yet it is clear that by the end of the century the trade had become the most promising solution to the colonists' problems with Indian labour.

The Spanish kings' acquiescence in black slavery cannot hide their serious efforts to protect the Indians from the rapacity of their overlords. Certainly, it is possible to see this concern as being non-idealistic. Royal interference with the Indians offered a splendid lever to counter the tendency of the New World barons to escape from crown control. On one level, too, the interest of the Catholic church in American peasants was part of its long battle over landownership with their *encomendero* masters. As total explanations of Spanish humanitarianism, however, both these theories make history into too much of a neat conspiracy. In a real sense, the motives behind attempts to regulate the treatment of Indians were genuinely benevolent. Royal attitudes underwent a major change in 1517, when the young and deeply sincere Charles V came to power after a brief regency. Where Ferdinand and his principal counsellor Juan Rodríguez de Fonseca had had little interest in the Americas or their inhabitants except as sources of wealth, the new king and his clerical advisers, the resilient Fonseca among them, found it distasteful to see Spain's converts and subjects being exterminated, especially

[8] P. Curtin, *The Atlantic Slave Trade: A Census* (Madison, Wis., 1969) pp. 21–5. This estimate is based principally on P. Chaunu and H. Chaunu, *Séville et l'Atlantique, 1504–1650*, 8 vols (Paris, 1955–60).

since the protection of the Indians in no way cut across their political needs. In either case, the most important point is not the motive behind this protection but its failure. In spite of a long series of benevolent royal decrees, the sixteenth century saw the Indian population of the Spanish Americas decimated. Government and church combined in the end proved powerless to save the Indians.

Forced Indian labour was used from the earliest stages of the Spanish Conquest. Columbus had miscalculated his distances drastically, and it soon became clear that the Indians he first met were unable to take him to the 'Great Mogul'. His next step was to organise them to look for gold. The chronicles of the conquistadores constantly mention their acquisition of Indian bondsmen and bondswomen. At first they were given concubines as chattels, gifts from the unsuspectingly friendly *caciques* themselves.[9] Although Spain's new subjects were technically freemen, taking them as slaves could be rationalised in various ways: if they were cannibals, if they were guilty of unnatural sexual practices, if they resisted Spanish authority after having the Christian faith and the authority of the crown explained to them (in Spanish), or if they were convicted of crimes by their overlords. Such unhappy exceptions to the supposed rule of Indian freedom initially became the mainstay of mining operations in the Caribbean. In the face of strong royal pressure to keep tribute labourers out of the mines, and high prices for black slaves, Indian slave captives came to fill a role complementary to that of *encomienda* Indians in the early decades of the Conquest. However, chattel slavery did not become the dominant labour system of the Spanish colonies, and it had effectively disappeared by about 1560, although it was questionable whether this made much difference to the Indians. The Spanish developed other methods of forcing the able-bodied population of whole villages and nations to work for them. The leaders and members of the various Spanish expeditions were rewarded for their services by grants under the *encomienda* system, which included rights to the labour of a sector of the native population, though not necessarily to the land they lived on. Mass Indian 'labour tribute' of this sort was quickly established in the islands and in New Spain, incidentally

9 M. Mörner, *Race Mixture in the History of Latin America* (Boston, 1967) pp. 21–5.

along lines similar to those used by Mexico's pre-Conquest rulers,
and with the co-operation of the old Indian ruling class. Technically, at least, the *encomienda* did not impair the legal freedom
of the Indians, and the crown tried sporadically to prevent their
being abused or depressed into true chattel slaves from the Laws
of Burgos of 1512 onwards. The system nevertheless made such
spectacular ravages that the Council of the Indies abolished it, at
least technically, under the *Novas Leyes de las Indias* of 1542, by
limiting all existing *encomienda* grants to one life. At the same
time, it was decreed that chattel slavery of Indians (not blacks)
should end with the release of all but those male slaves held in
bondage as criminals or war prisoners. The result was bitter discontent among the white colonists, expressed most violently in
Gonzalo Pizarro's attempted revolution in Peru. Neither ordin-
ance meant that the forced labour of Indians died out at once,
and the *encomienda* was eventually restored as a system of tribute
in produce rather than labour. The heyday of the *encomienda*
and of Indian chattel slavery was the first four decades of the
sixteenth century, before royal interference made it necessary to
find new means of dominating the miserable remnants of the
Indian population.[10] The event proved that it was effectively
impossible to extort wealth from the Americas without a mechanism to make the Indians work. In the later sixteenth century this
emerged with the institution of public rather than personal forced
labour, ironically instituted on the invitation of the crown itself.
From the 1550s the Indians just released from *encomienda*

[10] *Encomienda* is conveniently discussed in L. B. Simpson, *The Encomi-
enda in New Spain: The Beginning of Spanish Mexico* (Berkeley, 1950);
L. Hanke, *The Spanish Struggle for Justice in the Conquest of Latin
America* (Philadelphia, 1949) pp. 83–105; C. Gibson, *Spain in America*
(New York, 1967) pp. 48–67; idem, *The Aztecs under Spanish Rule: A
History of the Indians in the Valley of Mexico* (Stanford, 1964) pp. 58–97.
There is no discussion of Indian chattel slavery in English, but Silvio A.
Zavala, *New Viewpoints on the Spanish Colonization of America* (Phila-
delphia, 1943) pp. 49–68, is helpful. See also R. Konetzke, 'La esclavitud
de los Indios como elemento de la estructuración social de Hispano-
américa, *Estudios de la Historia Social de España*, I (1949) 441–79; J. A.
Saco, *Historia de la esclavitud de los Indios en el Nuevo Mundo*, 3 vols
(Havana, 1932); S. Zavala, *Los esclavos Indios en Nueva España* (Mexico
City, 1967); J. Berthe, 'Aspects de l'esclavage des Indiens en Nouvelle-
Espagne pendant la première moitié du XVIᵉ siècle', *Journal de la Société
des Américanistes*, LIV (1965) 189–209.

labour were required to work for set periods in mining operations or other public works. Each Indian community was required to provide a set number of labourers throughout the year, so that a proportion of its able-bodied males was always absent. Though such tribute was paid to the crown, the Indians involved, if not required for public works, were allocated to the service of land-owners who made the appropriate application to one or other of the colonial officials, sometimes to a *juez repartidor* appointed for the purpose. In fact the line between *repartimiento* and *encomienda* is a confused one, and the words were often used interchangeably. The wretched Indians thus had to fulfil not only the obligations in kind commuted from the old *encomienda* tribute, but also the *corvée* or public labour tribute of the *reparti-miento* system, or *mita* as it was called in Peru. Although this was not an acceptable substitute for settler exploitation of the Indians, it ensured that the Indians freed from the demands of the *encomienda* would not lapse into idleness, and in fact did little to lessen their burdens. *Repartimiento* was abolished by the crown in 1632 owing to irregularities in its administration. By this time most proprietors were relying on a combination of Indian 'free' contract labour, debt peons and black chattel slaves. The use of such a mixed labour force has been brilliantly analysed, for instance, for the sugar *haciendas* of the Cortés family.[11] For the Indians, royal intervention came too late. By the mid-1540s the impact of the Conquest and five decades of unbridled exploita-tion through the *encomienda* had brought demographic disaster to the Indian populations of Latin America.

Although *repartimiento* and *encomienda* were not systems of slavery, they had a brutal impact on the American Indians. Mass labour tribute effectively meant that the members of each *encomienda* were herded together as gang labourers. Such a tribute on the male working population left them as much dominated by the whim of their master as they would have been as true slaves, and unprotected even by the concern of the slave-

[11] W. Barrett, *The Sugar Hacienda of the Marqueses del Valle* (Min-neapolis, 1970) pp. 74–92. On *repartimiento* and its relationship to *en-comienda*, see F. A. Kirkpatrick, 'Repartimiento–Encomienda', *Hispanic American Historical Review*, XIX (1939) 372–9; Gibson, *Aztecs under Spanish Rule*, pp. 224–56; L. B. Simpson, *Studies in the Administration of the Indians of New Spain, vol.* III: *The Repartimiento System of Native Labor in New Spain and Guatemala* (Berkeley, 1938).

holder for preserving his property. Apart from the unaccustomed brutality and hardship which their new work brought, the Indians in most cases had to face the psychological disruption of losing much of the village or tribal focus which had previously been the basis of their lives. This, together with the even more crushing impact of European diseases to which it had not previously been exposed, reduced the aboriginal population drastically. Although demographers have not yet come to final conclusions on this phenomenon, and indeed may never do so, their work at least hints at the cataclysmic effect of the Conquest. For instance, two students of central Mexico, where the Indians seem to have suffered most of all, summarise a lifetime's research by estimating that the population dropped from 25·2 million in 1518 to 6·3 million in 1548 and 1·9 million in 1585. By 1605 it had reached its nadir at 1,075,000.[12] Though such a decline made it much easier for the landowners to consolidate their holdings, it brought them face to face with all but insoluble labour problems. There is an eerie symbolism in the fact that smallpox, which probably spread the worst havoc of all among the Indians, is said to have been brought to America by a black attached to Pánfilo de Narváez's 1520 expedition in Mexico.

From a Spanish point of view, then, a principal defect of using Indian labourers was that their numbers declined so swiftly. Even if the local population had remained stable, however, Indian labour was never fully satisfactory to the miners and planters of the colonies. Few Indians were as strong physically as their black successors. More important, in most cases they were unaccustomed to toiling as the mass disciplined work-force their European overlords demanded. Unlike Africans, they had little

[12] S. F. Cook and Woodrow Borah, *Essays in Population History*, vol. 1: *Mexico and the Caribbean* (Berkeley, 1971) p. viii. These estimates are drawn from a long series of studies, the most important of which are Borah and Cook, *The Population of Central Mexico in 1548* (Berkeley, 1960); Cook and Borah, *The Indian Population of Central Mexico, 1531–1610* (Berkeley, 1960); Borah and Cook, *The Aboriginal Population of Central Mexico on the Eve of the Spanish Conquest* (Berkeley, 1963). In *Essays in Population History*, 1 376–410, Cook and Borah calculate that Hispaniola's Indian population dropped from 3,770,000 in 1496 to 92,300 in 1508, 15,600 in 1518 and 125 in 1570 (summarised p. 401). On the relative effect of disease on the Indian and black populations, see P. Curtin, 'Epidemiology and the Slave Trade', *Political Science Quarterly*, LXXXIII (1968) 190–216.

experience of large-scale agriculture. The stories of Indians who pined away and died under the conquistadores' eyes, apparently from sheer perversity, are not romantic fiction. This was the response of people physically shattered by the demands of their drivers, and unable to recuperate since their culture had given them no means of coming to terms with the alien and bewildering role they were now called upon to play. Even the African, with his greater physical and cultural resilience, would be hard pressed to survive in these conditions. On the Indian the toll of enslavement was terrible. His conquerors can hardly have been expected to worry about his hardships. The supply of replacements for each dead *encomienda* Indian at first seemed inexhaustible. Their problem was a much more practical one of management. Mining and planting operations could not be carried on efficiently with a labour force which was physically weak, which acquired European skills slowly, and in which all the chastisement in the world could not produce the will to work hard.

On a smaller scale, the same process of experimentation with Indian labour, gradual exposure of its defects and drastic decline in Indian population can be seen in the case of Brazil. After its discovery in 1500 by Pedro Álvares Cabral, although it clearly belonged to the crown of Portugal under the Treaty of Tordesillas, Brazil was initially occupied only to keep other nations out, and to gather its rich timbers, its parrots and its monkeys. Mineral wealth it seemed to lack. The north-east's startling jump into large-scale sugar cultivation did not come until the late sixteenth century, although the Portuguese had already had substantial experience in sugar cultivation in Madeira and in their settlement in São Tomé in the Gulf of Guinea. However, Brazilian slaving had begun long before then. During the 1530s and 1540s a series of captaincies were established along the coast as semi-feudal communities similar to the Spanish *encomiendas*, though much larger in scale. The first Captain-General, Tomé de Sousa, was sent out to Bahia by João III in 1549. Like several of his Spanish counterparts, he was armed with royal orders to overthrow the anti-Christian practice of enslaving the Indians. He was also supported by a little band of Jesuits led by Brazil's first clerical hero, Manoel de Nobrega. As in the Spanish case, this intervention came too late. In the early stages of settlement the Portuguese had been content to extort what labour they needed from Indians through a combination of force and barter payments. As the *donatários* moved towards more substantial cultivation, they became the basis for large-scale enslavement of the Indians. This was fully established by the 1540s, carried out from the earliest stages through long-distance slave raids into the interior. In spite of the unsuitability of the primitive Brazilian Indians for the labour the Portuguese needed, this tendency became all the stronger with the impact of the Pernambuco and Bahia sugar industry, which was just getting under way at the time of Sousa's arrival.[13] The Jesuit response was to embark on a long war of attrition against the colonists by bringing as many Indians as possible into *aldeias* or mission communities which they themselves controlled directly. Yet Indian chattel slavery played a much larger part here than in the societies of Spanish America, although the barter system of labour meant that it was adopted relatively late. It was still technically based on the punishment of cannibalism, resistance to a 'just' war and other anti-social crimes. In practice the demand for Indian slaves came to be met through the slave-raiding expeditions of the *bandeirantes* from São Paulo to the interior. By another of the ironies of American history, many of the seventeenth-century *bandeirantes*, folk heroes of modern Brazil analogous to the North American trappers and *coureurs des bois*, were themselves black. In the seventeenth century an attempt at abolition in 1609 had to be hastily rescinded. It was only after the crowning of João IV, first of the Braganzas, with Portugal's return to independence, that more progress was made. Even then the triumphs of the Indians' Jesuit allies were limited, but they did manage to secure a registry of all legitimate slaves and a ban on unauthorised slave-raiding in

[13] A. Marchant, *From Barter to Slavery: The Economic Relations of Portuguese and Indians in the Settlement of Brazil, 1500–1580* (Baltimore, 1942) pp. 61 ff., 125 and passim. For brief accounts of Brazil's early development, see Caio Prado, Jr, *The Colonial Background of Modern Brazil*, trans. S. Macedo (Berkeley, 1971); C. Furtado, *The Economic Growth of Brazil: A Survey from Colonial to Modern Times*, trans. R. W. de Aguiar and E. C. Drysdale (Berkeley, 1968) pp. 1–77; and, on sugar, N. Deerr, *A History of Sugar*, 2 vols (London, 1949) I 100–11. Later royal attempts to protect the Indians are covered in M. C. Kiemen, *The Indian Policy of Portugal in the Amazon Region, 1614–1693* (Washington, 1954).

1653, and to have slavery abolished in Maranhão in 1680. But it was not until 1758 that Indian slavery was decreed ended, as an interesting side-product of the enlightened despotism of the Marquis de Pombal. Long before this, the defects of Indian slavery had become as evident in Brazil as in the Spanish colonies. Black slaves were imported by the Portuguese from the 1530s, and increased sharply in numbers with the expansion of the sugar industry in the 1570s, as a direct response to the weakness and instability of Indian labour, and with royal encouragement. By 1585 the black slaves involved in the Olinda sugar industry alone were variously estimated at 2,000 and 4,000–5,000.[14]

Though the Portuguese experiment with Indian labour was longer than the Spanish one, its eventual outcome was the resort to black slavery. By the end of the century, as in Spain, blacks were employed in a wide range of activities in Brazil – principally in the sugar industry of the Pernambuco and Bahia area, but also in domestic service, and in the ranching and grain farming of the southern captaincies. Like Indians in other parts of America, the Tupí-Guaraní, Arawak, Carib and Tapuyá peoples of Brazil lacked knowledge of iron, and had no experience of handling domestic animals; but unlike the peoples of, say, Mexico, they had no skills in regular agriculture. In fact, Brazil's Stone Age inhabitants were among the most backward in the Americas, both in terms of their weak social organisation and their sheer lack of labouring skills. The difficulties of applying them to the ranching and plantation activities for which they were needed were correspondingly great – even more so once the declining novelty of Portuguese trade goods cut back their willingness to work on the barter system. Their numbers relative to the vast size of the country were also low – something near a million to set against the teeming population of pre-Conquest Mexico. At the same time, they were equally prey to the disastrous upset caused in the American disease ecology by the arrival of the Europeans, and like their northern counterparts were devastated in the course of the sixteenth century by epidemics to which they had no resistance, principally smallpox and measles. The very attempts to protect these gentle peoples worked to destroy them, for the insistence of their Jesuit well-wishers that

[14] Marchant, *From Barter to Slavery*, pp. 131–2.

they should give up their existing hygienic habits and adopt decent post-Christian clothing provided them with new vehicles for infection.[15] Black labourers, on the other hand, though by no means immune to smallpox in particular, not only had the skills which made them splendid plantation workers, but had developed a limited resistance to Portuguese infections because of the common factors between the European and African disease environments. In Brazil, too, the Atlantic slave trade expanded and black slavery became entrenched against a background of declining native population. At the same time, the two developments were a response to the utter unsuitability of an Indian labour force for the enterprises which were to build the fantastically rich Brazil of the late seventeenth century – a result of constant planter discontent with Indians whom the Jesuits subverted, Indians who were insensible to all threats of violence, Indians who were unteachable, Indians who ran away, Indians who died on their masters' hands out of sheer spite.

Independent of outside pressures, economic logic was driving both Spanish and Portuguese settlers away from inefficient Indian labourers towards efficient African ones. What hastened the institutionalisation of the African slave trade to meet their demands, ironically, was the concern of the Catholic clergy for their Indian converts. Their only way of putting them in a position where the lords of the Americas would leave them be was by acquiescing in their drawing an alternative labour force from heathen Guinea. The salvation of the Indians, in clerical eyes, would come through swelling the trickle of black slaves who had been coming across the Atlantic since the beginning of the century. This is not to question the sincerity with which the clergy tried to solve the problems of forced labour. It is most unlikely that they thought through to the future consequences of their proposals, but there is no doubt that the connection between their crusade for the Indians and the rise of the Atlantic trade is close. At a time of extraordinary intellectualism in the Spanish church, a pressure group drawn from the clerical bureaucracy, headed by the gentle but persistent Bartolomé de las Casas, brought all its influence to bear on the crown. The series of edicts

[15] G. Freyre, *The Masters and the Slaves: A Study in the Development of Brazilian Civilization*, 2nd English-language ed., trans. S. Putnam (New York, 1956) pp. 112, 81–184.

protecting the legal status of Spain's Indian subjects, culminating in the *Novas Leyes* of 1542, was a response to their agitation. Although the crown itself was not unsympathetic, the vested interests (and intellectual traditions) which stood in the way of interference with settler control over their Indians were strong. Las Casas and the humanitarian party by no means represented the whole spectrum of Spanish intellectual opinion on Indian servitude, and their debate with their rivals is a fascinating one. Their arguments, which absorbed the Spanish church during the first half of the sixteenth century, laid down the lines for controversies on the basis of race which have continued down to our time.

It is essential to understand, however, that these arguments, and the relatively benevolent legislation with which they were connected, were concerned with the position of the Indians, not of the Negro. This point is important because the case of those historians who argue for the relatively happy lot of the black slave in Latin America is based, among other misconceptions, on the idea that laws designed to protect *encomienda* or chattel Indians were applied to black slaves as well.[16] In a sense this is academic, since it is optimistic to assume that legislation can prevent any slaveholder from bashing his slaves quietly on his own premises if he chooses to do so, but it does bear on a heated historical controversy. In either case, the sixteenth-century debates show a real element of idealism at the Spanish court. They also formulated a number of concepts and arguments on race which could subsequently be applied to the Negro as well as the Indian, and which came to provide much of the stock-in-trade of propagandists for and against white supremacy in later years. The controversy is also an early example of the oppression of a subject race being attacked by third parties for political reasons overlaid with the rhetoric of honest moral rage. The question of who should rule the Indians, it has often been said, was itself part of the larger question of who should rule the Indies. There were certainly many bureaucrats at the Spanish court and in the *Consejo de las Indias* for whom the abuse of the Indians was a fine stick with which to beat the American barons whom it was

---

[16] e.g. F. Tannenbaum, *Slave and Citizen: The Negro in the Americas* (New York, 1946). cf. D. B. Davis, *The Problem of Slavery in Western Culture* (Ithaca, N.Y., 1966) pp. 224–5 n.

their task to control. As for its origins, the whole series of debates culminating at Valladolid in 1550 has been carefully charted and set in the context of late-medieval assumptions on equality and subjection by Lewis Hanke.[17]

The Spanish church had shown concern over the position of the Indian, and clearly set out its responsibility to save savage souls, at the time of the discovery. From 1514 onwards, leaders of expeditions to the New World were ordered to preface hostilities against the Indians they encountered by reading them a manifesto probably composed by the Jesuit theologian Palacios Rubios. This *Requirimiento*, as it was called, briefly explained the Spanish claim to the Americas, and the essentials of the Christian faith, and warned the Indians of enslavement or death which would follow if they rejected them. It had little impact on the Indians, since they had not enough of the gift of tongues to understand a language they had never heard. But though the *Requirimiento* was a formality both for the conquerors and the Indians, it is a pointer to the depth of clerical consternation over the justice of Spain's position *vis-à-vis* her new American subjects. Spanish churchmen were by no means united in their views. When their arguments on the Indian question were finally fought out at the Valladolid debates, the two principal contenders were the greatest churchmen, perhaps the greatest clerical intellectuals, of Spain's sixteenth century, the century of her Golden Age. On the side of the Indian, denying the justice of conquest by force, and arguing against the excuses of the *encomenderos*, was the Bishop of Chiapas, Bartolomé de las Casas. The case for the justice of war against infidels, and incidentally their enslavement, was represented equally ably by the Aristotelian scholar Juan Ginés de Sepúlveda. Although the *encomenderos* seized upon Sepúlveda as the defender of their interests, neither man was prepared to accept unbridled exploitation of the Indians. Las Casas in particular, however, with his long experience in America, was spurred on by a deep personal horror of the atrocities committed by the colonists. His *Brevísima Relación de la destrucción de las Indias*, published at Seville in 1552, summarised the worst

[17] *Aristotle and the American Indians: A Study in Race Prejudice in the Modern World* (New York, 1959) passim; *Spanish Struggle for Justice*, passim. See also J. Friede and B. Keen (eds.), *Bartolomé de las Casas in History* (DeKalb, Ill., 1971).

excesses he had observed in a lifetime spent campaigning to save the Indians for conversion. It contains a catalogue of barbarities extraordinary even for the sixteenth century, as moving as the title of its best-known English edition, *The Tears of the Indians.*[18] As far as the problem of black slavery is concerned, his propaganda was only too successful. The *Brevísima Relación*'s tale of the miseries of the Indians became one of the main rationalisations for replacing them with hardier labourers uprooted from the Guinea Coast. Though it would have come to the New World even if Las Casas had never been born, black slavery did not have to make headway against a clerical campaign of the sort fought for the Indians. Having reached heights of concern over the Indian question, Las Casas's generation of the Spanish intelligentsia easily lapsed into ignoring the sufferings of the black slaves who now began to pour into the Americas.

Though Sepúlveda lacked Las Casas's American experience, he too was aware of the devastation caused by the Conquest. But his solution was as different from Las Casas's as their political philosophies. Las Casas's warm Christian egalitarianism drove him to assume responsibility for the direct protection and conversion of each individual Indian by the church. Sepúlveda's paradoxically more modern vision embraced a hierarchy between the races drawn from the Aristotelian theories then fashionable among the *avant-garde* of European scholarship, and which he himself had done much to popularise through his translation of the *Politics.* Conquest of an infidel and barbarous race with a view to their future conversion he thought fully justified. The Indians he saw as being naturally inferior, the conquistadores as naturally superior and fitted to guide them from barbarism to civilisation and Christianity. The church certainly had a responsibility to protect and teach the lower race, but it would do this indirectly, using the white colonists as intermediaries. It was only through these colonists that the church would exert its influence -- not by taking the Indians directly under crown/church protection, as Las Casas wished. Sepúlveda missed what Las Casas saw, that the conquistadores had so far made a bloodily sorry job of the whole business of protecting the Indians, and he did not

[18] *The Tears of the Indians: Being an Historical and True Account of the Cruel Massacres and Slaughters of Above Twenty Millions of Innocent People* (n.p., 1656).

shrink from the use of force against them. But the responsibility and sincerity of his conception of stewardship over the Indians was none the less real. Like Las Casas, he was supported by some of the leading minds of sixteenth-century Spain.

The Valladolid debates, called at Sepúlveda's instigation in 1550 and 1551, marked a turning-point in Spanish colonial policy. During their course all licences for expeditions of conquest in the Indies were suspended, until the justice of the Spanish advance could be confirmed. Both Las Casas and Sepúlveda presented their cases at length before a panel of fourteen judges in August and September 1550. After a gap of four months during which the controversy was canvassed further, they reconvened for further sessions. Owing to the absence of full records of the debates, it is still not quite clear what the judges' verdict was. Both Las Casas and Sepúlveda considered himself the victor. Yet it is unrealistic to assume that the debates could have resulted in the triumph of Sepúlveda's justification for conquest and denigration of Indian abilities, which the *encomenderos* had already seized upon avidly as mandates for their power. Royal responsibility for the Indians, and opposition to their exploitation by the conquerors, had been set policy since the early part of the century. Though the debates showed the genuine sensitivity of Charles V in matters of faith, and created the impression of impartiality, they could have done nothing to check or turn back the prohibition of slavery and erosion of *encomienda* which had arisen from the *Novas Leyes* of 1542. Eventually the body of statute law protecting the Indians and curbing the powers of the colonists was confirmed and codified in the *Recopilación de las Leyes de las Indias* in 1680. At the same time, Spanish law came to accept the Church of Rome's attitude to the Conquest. Five years before the *Novas Leyes*, fourteen before Valladolid, Pope Paul III had promulgated the Bull *Veritas ipsa*, which denounced enslavement of Indians, except for criminal offences. In the same year, 1537, the Bull *Sublimis Deus* had not only supported the case for the Indians being rational beings, but defined the opposite opinion as a heresy. These too worked in the same direction as the arguments of Las Casas. But the royal insistence on the rights of non-hostile Indians as subjects of Spain written into the *Recopilación* of 1680 was part of a tradition which had been a constant in policy from the outset. For most

Indians freedom was only the freedom to die, but at least the Spanish authorities strove valiantly to ensure them this.

This tradition of responsibility was very far from the attitudes of the *encomenderos* to the Indian population. By mid-century their own depredations and the ravages of disease had already reduced the Indians to a fraction of their original numbers. At the same time, the royal assault on slavery and the *encomienda* was seriously impairing their powers over the remainder. Though it is hard to believe that Spanish law had any effect in checking brutalities the colonists chose to commit in the privacy of their households, the outlawing of the *encomienda* labour tribute through the *Novas Leyes* made their sources of labour even more unstable. At the same time, the drastic inflation of the sixteenth century soon made the non-labour tributes assessed on the Indians a nominal source of income. The *mita* and *repartimiento* systems guaranteed labour for public works and enterprises of national interest like the excavation of the mountain of silver at Potosí, but they fell short of meeting the demands of the land-owner who needed a continuous, stable and teachable labour force – and complete power over it. It was not only in a figurative sense that the tide of conquest carried the filth of Europe along with it. European infection, together with the impact of the colonists' beasts, whose grazing upset the delicate agricultural balance which supported the New World population, would eventually have decimated the Indian labour pool without royal interference. But it was because the *Novas Leyes* removed what was then their only possible labour force that the *encomendero* response was so violent. Neither their revolt in Peru, nor their dogged resistance elsewhere, could bring back the *encomienda* in its original form. In this sense, the royal concern for the Indians forced the colonists, sooner than might otherwise have been the case, into a radical rethinking of their economic practices. At the same time, population decline among the Indians put more land at the colonists' disposal.[19]

Faced with a fixed income declining rapidly in real value, with a diminishing supply of Indian labour, with cheap land and with royal restrictions preventing its unbridled exploitation, the Spanish colonists at mid-century moved further towards the importation of black slaves.

[19] Barrett, *Sugar Hacienda of the Marqueses del Valle*, pp. 5, 25–39.

In a very real sense, they had no alternative. This is not to say that the later arguments that white men cannot work in the tropics are anything better than nonsense. But there is no historical example of a warrior caste which has conquered a land by brute strength and then rejected the temptation to force others to cultivate it for them. There is no reason to expect the Portuguese and Spanish to have been the first. Of course, they *could* have cultivated the Americas themselves, if their numbers had been increased a thousandfold, thus leaving the Iberian peninsula empty, and if their entire cultural and psychological background had been different – in which case they would not have tried to take land away from the Indians in the first place. As it was, the Spanish and Portuguese tried Indian labour first. Finding that it could not be exploited as efficiently as they wished, and in any case under pressure from their governments to leave the Indian alone, they turned to importing blacks. With experience in slave management and contacts in slave-trading – particularly in the case of the Portuguese – they bought black slaves instead of trying to contract black or other wage-earners, which they could not have done even if they had wished to. Their economic needs, cultural background and personal experience, together with the devastation of the Indian population, had all pushed them towards black slavery. It may not be of much importance whether the emergence of African slaveholding in Latin America was 'inevitable'. But given the cultural background of the conquerors, whose ethic excluded the possibility of doing non-military work themselves, it is hard to see how else they could have found the labour to reap riches from the land they had seized.

The Whigs among American historians would have us believe that the English colonies in the New World were settled peaceably by freedom-loving yeomen, men to whom the rapacious behaviour of the Spanish and Portuguese was quite alien. In fact the English were as aggressive as anyone else. Their colonies were in the first instance based on force, however much they may later have come to depend on commerce which was at least overtly peaceful. Because English colonisation was carried out with less cataclysmic speed than the Spaniards', and because there were more colonists among whom land had to be distributed, smaller units give the appearance of relatively greater democracy; but

English colonists, in spite of common law traditions of equality, would also use forced labour when the opportunity and need arose. Like the Spaniards, after a period of experimentation with various forms of non-black labour, they turned to investing the money they had accumulated in black slaves from whom they hoped to draw attractive dividends. The English first made do with white indentured servants or convicts and confessedly second-choice makeshifts like the occasional enslavement of Indians. As a rough rule of thumb, the speed with which each English colony turned to buying blacks was directly proportional to the speed with which it or its London backers could accumulate the capital this required. The use of white servants instead of the hopeless Indians does not reflect any credit on the English. They were much poorer and much weaker than the Spanish, had learned from the South American example, and in any case had fewer but more formidable Indians to kill, though it is true that in the end they too did a pretty good job of annihilating them. Land was parcelled out in small units, and white indentured servants used in the early settlements, not only because of the need for accommodating small shareholders, but also because in the first instance there was no other way of getting the land cultivated. The Spanish flirtation with Indian labour, and the English use of whites, were two aspects of the same process. In each case a period of experimentation with relatively cheap sources of labour was followed by a move towards buying black slaves.

England, again like Spain, expanded into the New World at the end of a prolonged period of warfare. The conquest of Granada and the end of the Moorish wars loosed on the New World a group of ruthless and impoverished mercenaries, accustomed to living by the sword. In the same way, the Stuart conclusion of the long and now aimless war with Spain released numbers of energetic soldiers and seamen who had learned ways of violence in Flanders, or on the seas as privateers. From making a living off preying directly on the Spanish, they turned to doing so indirectly by competing with them in wringing out the wealth of the Americas. More important, the interruption of privateering removed the main available area for high-risk, high-return investment, and the obvious alternative was to sink the funds thus released into the equally risky business of colonisation. Ireland, although it gave the English much of their early experience in labour management and in settlements of virgin land, had largely been exhausted as a field for speculation by the end of the sixteenth century. The new American ventures were to absorb the same kinds of men and money as the wars of Ireland and Flanders and their ancillary investments. This certainly does not exclude the strong religious motives behind much English colonisation. Colonies were attractive for evangelist as well as strategic reasons, as the propaganda of Hakluyt and Purchas, the promoters of the Virginia Company, and a host of other polemicists makes clear. The hope of building a godly city on a hill in the New World was by no means confined to the New England Puritans, and all the settlers shared religious traditions which associated true slavery with punishment for crime or participation in unjust war. But these doubts could be rationalised away where necessary. The background of the men involved and the raw profit motive which inspired them left only a few with serious scruples against the use of forced labour in their ventures. The English had followed their queen in exulting at the profits of Sir John Hawkins's pioneer slave-trade voyages in the 1560s. Though it took them a long time to gather as much experience with Indians and Africans as the Spanish and Portuguese had, most of the seventeenth-century settlers were enough offspring of their times to see little inconsistency between being a Christian and enslaving heathens.[20] War against the heathen, at least the heathen who had deliberately rejected missionary initiatives, was by definition just, the heathen's bondage the legitimate outcome of unbelief.

This moral insensitivity was not confined to the Caribbean or to the Southern mainland colonies. The weakness of slavery in the Northern colonies stemmed more from different economic

[20] Cf. E. S. Morgan, 'Slavery and Freedom: The American Paradox', *Journal of American History*, LIX (1972) 5–29, which documents late sixteenth-century distrust of enslavement, and positive intentions of liberating those blacks and Indians owned by the Spanish. This is principally based, however, on the cases of Ralegh and Hakluyt, and on views which may well have been moulded by the expediency of war against Spain. On the striking similarities between the labour problems attached to British and Portuguese colonisation alike, see R. R. Beeman, 'Labor Forces and Race Relations: A Comparative View of the Colonization of Brazil and Virginia', *Political Science Quarterly*, LXXXVI (1971) 609–36.

needs than a higher level of concern for other races. The differences between the ethics accepted by Northern and Southern
settlers were less in reality than they seem on the surface. All paid
at least lip-service to the glorification of hard work, and the
undesirableness of dishonesty, indolence and debauchery. If these
ideals were not always practically implemented in the Caribbean
and the South, this was also the case in New England. Even the
separatist Pilgrims in Plymouth Colony, and the Puritans in
Massachusetts Bay, were not always scrupulous over day-to-day
morality. They took pains to suppress flagrant and God-provok-
ing excesses in their own midst and among their neighbours. This
is what Miles Standish was doing when he destroyed Thomas
Morton's charming English enclave at Merrymount, where
festivities around the pagan maypole were leading to mass fornication and drunkenness. In his *History*, Governor Bradford
recounted that

> Morton became Lord of Misrule and maintained . . . a School
> of Atheism . . . quaffing and drinking, both wine and strong
> waters in great excess (and, as some reported) £10 worth in a
> morning. They also set up a maypole, drinking and dancing
> about it many days together, inviting the Indian women for
> their consorts, dancing and frisking together like so many
> fairies, or furies, rather; and worse practices. As if they had
> anew revived and celebrated the feasts of the Roman goddess
> Flora, or the beastly practices of the mad Bacchanalians.[21]

Yet the leadership of the New England colonies, like that of the
Southern ones, assumed and to some extent tolerated manageable
levels of immorality among rank-and-file settlers. 'The Puritans',
concludes one of their most sensitive historians, 'became inured
to sexual offences because there were so many.'[22] At the same
time, their acceptance of the work ethic did not prevent them
from wishing to acquire slaves. After the Pequot war of 1637
they experimented with Indian slaves taken as captives in the
hostilities. Later they began to acquire small numbers of black

[21] W. Bradford, *Of Plymouth Plantation, 1620–1647*, ed. S. E. Morison
(New York, 1952) pp. 205–6.
[22] E. S. Morgan, 'The Puritans and Sex', *New England Quarterly*, xv
(1942) 595.

slaves in exchange for Indians shipped south to the West Indies because of the risk of keeping them close to their own people. The enslavement of Indians did bring serious conscientious scruples, and Puritan preachers and writers channelled a great deal of energy into trying to reconcile it with Scripture. The assumption that it was only hostile or criminal Indians who could legally be made slaves was never abandoned. The 1641 Laws and Liberties of Massachusetts stated firmly that there should be no 'bond slavery' in the colony,

> unlesse it be lawfull captives taken in just warrs, and such strangers as willingly sell themselves, or are solde to us: and such shall have the libertyes and christian usages which the law of God established in Israell concerning such persons doth morally require, *provided, this exempts none from servitude who shall be judged thereto by Authoritie.*[23]

Even these strictures did not entirely prevent black slavery from emerging in Massachusetts. Africans brought from Barbados, New Providence or Guinea itself could conveniently fall into the category of those sold by others, presumably enslaved because of prior crime or defeat in war. There was certainly a black in Massachusetts by 1638, and possibly earlier. The numbers of blacks rose very slowly, and they never became a major sector of Massachusetts population – no more than 2·2 per cent in the eighteenth century, and this only for the brief peak period of the 1760s. In the seventeenth century the numbers involved were tiny – as late as 1708 probably only 550. Black population was even lower to the north of Massachusetts, but somewhat higher in Rhode Island and Connecticut. Although their seventeenth-century black population was less than that of Massachusetts, the balance had changed by 1774. Rhode Island then had 3,761 black inhabitants, 6·3 per cent of its total population. For Connecticut the corresponding figures were 6,464 and 3·2 per cent. New Englanders of the revolutionary generation were still overwhelmingly white, with a small black minority of 2·4 per cent, or a little over 16,000, in their midst.[24] This was obviously

[23] M. Farrand (ed.), *The Laws and Liberties of Colonial Massachusetts* (Cambridge, Mass., 1929) p. 4. My italics.

[24] Figures from L. J. Greene, *The Negro in Colonial New England* (New York, 1942) pp. 72–99.

a much smaller contingent than the black population of the South, but it was also lower than that of the Mid-Atlantic states. Of these, the rich coastal area of New Jersey had the largest proportion of blacks. A tiny handful of their descendants, in fact, were still technically slaves at the outbreak of the Civil War. One historian finds that East Jersey had a 12 per cent black minority. West Jersey was much less tainted with slaveholding, so that for the two colonies taken together the figure was only 8 per cent.[25] The most acceptable estimates for New York and Pennsylvania, in 1770, are 12·5 per cent and 2·5 per cent respectively – 19,112 and 5,761.[26] These percentages had remained more or less constant since the late seventeenth century, and were high enough except in the case of Pennsylvania for the status of black people to be a major problem in the middle colonies. The solution was the gradual crystallisation of slavery through the emergence of a body of disciplinary law which set even free blacks apart from their counterparts in the white population.

It is more surprising that there were similar developments in Massachusetts and the New England colonies generally, where the black population was so tiny. Indeed, the insignificance of black numbers in Massachusetts does seem to have delayed the demarcation of the slave's status from that of the white labourer. Although men and women bought as chattels, unlike English or even Irish servants, presumably lacked the guarantee that their servitude would be terminated at a set date, the earliest black servants in Massachusetts seem to have been given the same civil and legal rights as white subjects. In trials for arson, murder, manslaughter and sexual offences, at least, Massachusetts justice was dispensed regardless of skin colour, though this does not prove that personal prejudice did not exist. In either case, neither Puritan rectitude nor the tiny number of blacks prevented their gradual setting apart as a legally separate caste. Whether because of increasing prejudice spreading from the other colonies, or because of the slight rise in black population, legislation in this direction began in the 1680s with attempts to ban the sale of liquor to servants and slave *or free* blacks. In 1703 a curfew was

[25] A. Zilversmit, *The First Emancipation: The Abolition of Slavery in the North* (Chicago, 1967) pp. 4–5.
[26] U.S. Bureau of the Census, *Historical Statistics of the United States: Colonial Times to 1957* (Washington, 1960) p. 756.

imposed on all blacks, and their manumission without their master's posting a bond curtailed. Two years later sexual contact between the races, in or out of wedlock, was singled out in 'An Act for the Better Preventing of a Spurious and Mixt Issue'.[27] The bonds had finally tightened. Puritan ethic or no, the Negro, slave or free, was now in a position set apart from those of other races. His status hardened similarly in the other New England colonies with any appreciable black population. Yet although such a response expressed fear and distrust of blacks, it reinforced the structure of black slavery, ironically at a time when it was becoming clear that the great bulk of New England had no pressing need for slave labour. If it had not been that their relatively infertile land turned them towards mixed farming and maritime commerce, where capital accumulation was slow and labour needs low, it is unlikely that the New England colonies would have stood aloof from the large-scale slaveholding of their richer brothers in the South and the West Indies.

The British colonies were not founded at the same time, and the form of agriculture from which they made money or failed to make it differed widely. Apart from Sir Walter Ralegh's ill-fated Roanoke experiment in 1584, the English annexation was a movement purely of the seventeenth century. The Virginia colony of 1607 was the first on the mainland, and it was quickly followed by the Plymouth Colony, the Massachusetts Bay Colony, Connecticut, and Maryland, founded in 1632. The Carolinas, New York, Pennsylvania and the Jerseys were not settled until the second half of the century, although New York had, of course, initially been established by the Dutch. Georgia was founded as late as the 1730s. In the Caribbean, Barbados was the second earliest and the most successful of the West Indian sugar islands, soon joined by others of the Lesser Antilles. Jamaica was annexed by Oliver Cromwell's generals in 1655 only after their dismal failure to seize Hispaniola from the Spaniards, and did not become a stable plantation colony until after the Glorious Revolution. The Bahamas, although Eleuthera was colonised in 1647, remained a relatively sparsely settled group and in Spanish hands until the British annexation in 1670. As for the rest of the

[27] See R. C. Twombley and R. H. Moore, 'Black Puritan: The Negro in Seventeenth Century Massachusetts', *William and Mary Quarterly*, 3rd ser., xxiv (1967) 224–42.

Caribbean, Puerto Rico and Cuba remained Spanish until they became informal American colonies after the Spanish–American War of 1898. Part of Hispaniola, or Santo Domingo, was seized from them in 1665 by the French, who finally acquired it as Saint-Domingue at the Peace of Ryswick in 1697, and who had held the equally rich islands of Guadeloupe and Martinique since 1635. As early as 1687 Saint-Domingue, the French section of Hispaniola, had 7,000 slaves. Even after the tide of their onslaught against the Spanish and Portuguese receded, the Dutch retained the islands of Curaçao, Bonaire, Aruba, St Eustatius and St Martin, as well as mainland Essequibo, Berbice and Demerara, the territories whose slaveholders eventually attained a more sinister reputation than any other in the New World. Until Sweden's acquisition of St Bartélemy, the only other power in the West Indies was Denmark. In 1670 she acquired the island of St Thomas and other minor possessions in the Virgin Islands group, which were later sold to the United States in 1917. To return to the English, they did not acquire Essequibo, Berbice and Demerara, eventually British Guiana, or modern Guyana, from the Dutch until 1814, though they held these areas by force for most of the Napoleonic Wars. This was only a fraction of the Caribbean territory seized by Britain during the second half of the eighteenth century. She acquired Grenada, St Vincent, Dominica and Tobago in 1763, and during the Napoleonic wars added Trinidad and St Lucia. She also held the little colony of Bermuda, originally named the Somers Islands, since 1612. It was thus the earliest successful English settlement, though it became prosperous only in the eighteenth century. It had a complex network of trade links with the mainland, as well as with the Bahamas and the Caribbean islands to the south. The mutual influences between Bermuda and South Carolina were particularly strong.[28]

[28] Bermuda is nevertheless a special case, most fully treated in H. C. Wilkinson, *Bermuda in the Old Empire* (Oxford, 1950). The only acceptable English history of the West Indies is J. H. Parry and P. M. Sherlock, *A Short History of the West Indies*, 2nd ed. (London, 1963). The fullest and most exciting study of the English Caribbean, R. S. Dunn, *Sugar and Slaves: The Rise of the Planter Class in the English West Indies, 1624–1713* (Williamsburg, Va., 1972), did not become available until this book was essentially completed. See also A. P. Newton, *The European Nations in the West Indies, 1493–1688* (London, 1935); and J. H. Rose, A. P.

All the earlier colonies had labour difficulties from the outset. The case of Virginia on the North American mainland usefully illustrates the slow evolution of the black slave system. The first shipment of '20. and odd Negros' arrived in Virginia in 1619. They were carried by a Dutch vessel which had evidently captured them in a privateering action on the Spanish Main. There is a common assumption that this event represented the beginning of slavery in the colonies which in time became the United States. Certainly, it is the point at which the trickle of black immigration which later became a flood began. Yet the numbers of blacks in the colony remained tiny until the eighteenth century, never more than a few hundred until 1660. But they were higher than in any other part of the English mainland: 3,000 or $6\frac{1}{4}$ per cent of the population in 1680, 9,345 or $15\frac{2}{3}$ per cent ten years later, 16,390 or 26 per cent in 1700, 220,582 or 41 per cent in 1780.[29] For the whole of the seventeenth century, Virginia's labour force was predominantly made up of indentured servants who secured their passage to the colonies by agreeing, if they had not been kidnapped, to work for the master who brought them there. Their periods of work ran for four, five, seven or eight years, and their contracts were similar to those by which apprentices tied themselves to their masters in Europe. Although the twenty 'negars' and the other blacks who followed them had clearly not been in a position to decide whether or not they

Newton and E. A. Benians (eds.), *The Cambridge History of the British Empire*, vol. 1: *The Old Empire from the Beginnings to 1783* (Cambridge, 1929) pp. 1–329. Britain's seventeenth-century mainland colonies are fully treated in C. M. Andrews, *The Colonial Period of American History*, 4 vols (New Haven, 1934–8) vol. 1, and the island ones in W. L. Burn, *The British West Indies* (London, 1951); A. C. Burns, *The History of the British West Indies* (London, 1954); C. Bridenbaugh, *No Peace beyond the Line: The English in the Caribbean, 1624–1690* (New York, 1972). On the French colonies there is no full work in English, but see the relevant material in G. Hanotaux and A. Martineau (eds.), *Histoire des colonies françaises et l'expansion de la France dans le monde*, 6 vols (Paris, 1929–33).

[29] *Historical Statistics of the United States*, p. 756. The first three estimates may well be high. W. F. Craven, *White, Red, and Black: The Seventeenth Century Virginian* (Charlottesville, Va., 1971) pp. 73–109, calculates from headrights issued in recognition of black servants brought to the colony that the really sharp rise in black population did not come until the decade 1700–10, and that the total number of blacks in the colony in 1700 was not much above 6,000. In either case, this is a sharp rise from the handful of the period prior to 1660, or even 1680.

wished to come to Jamestown, on arrival they seem to have been treated at law in much the same way as white indentured servants. Their period of service was longer, but the expectation at first seems to have been that there was little impetus towards giving them a special institutional position, and certainly no need for translating any differences in status into law. This is not to accept the theory that until their natural goodwill was soured by the economic pressure of the institution of slavery, the two peoples shared none of the mutual distrust which has dominated American history ever since. The English, like other Europeans, had long considered the black peoples as being apart from themselves, an alien race to whose skin colour a whole series of symbolic and psychological connotations of inferiority were attached. These seventeenth-century attitudes have been splendidly analysed by Jordan, who has also suggested that in the New World context they were reinforced by the strain of preserving a cultural identity in an alien environment.[30] By way of negative self-identification, English settlers began to reinforce their faith in their own culture by emphasising the separateness and inferiority of black people. This theory is not absolutely watertight. It does not, for instance, explain wherein lies the difference between colonial distrust of the blacks and of the Irish. Nor does it take account of the extent to which stereotypes of 'blackness' or 'darkness' have been applied to white peasant classes (including the Irish) throughout the history of the West. Nevertheless, if historians ever agree to accept an explanation of the emergence of prejudice and slavery in colonial America, it will probably be an explanation very similar to Jordan's. This does not mean that white men and black did not do the same jobs or work together. White indentured servants and the new black arrivals worked side by side in the fields of seventeenth-century Virginia, in much the same way as later Southern yeomen and their few slaves worked together on the smaller farms of the nineteenth-century South. The colony's rigid class divisions often overrode racial ones. During Bacon's rebellion, for instance, white and black rebels fought side by side, and there is no evidence that the ruling class saw any reason to differentiate between insurgents from the two races. Conditions were appalling for white servants, and it

[30] Jordan, *White over Black*, pp. 3–98. Cf. Handlin and Handlin, in *W.M.Q.*, 3rd ser., VII 199–222.

may even be the case that blacks were better off because their longer service gave masters a greater incentive to treat them well. In other directions, there is plenty of evidence that from the outset blacks in Virginia at least were given treatment inferior even to the harsh lot of white labourers. For instance, their punishment for the petty everyday crimes, particularly sexual ones, were more severe than for whites.[31] The very length of their period of indentured service suggests discrimination. By 1661 the legislature decreed special punishments in cases involving blacks, whose service was now assumed to last throughout their lives, so that they could not be disciplined simply by extending their indentures. All unfree labour was treated in this way, though there was clearly also special prejudice against Scots and Irish servants, presumably because they too represented outside elements who might be considered to endanger the safety of the colony – and presumably also because of the same long-term traditions of negative self-identification and cultural distrust which Jordan has outlined for the black–white relationship.[32]

After about 1680, such informal discrimination became more than a flexible barrier to everyday social equality. In the eighteenth century it came to form the underpinning of the great legal machinery of slavery, which in turn ironically worked to reinforce it. There were many reasons why men who began as a somewhat distrusted out-group ended up as chattel slaves. All of them were compelling for the landowners who lived off their labour. The laws of the last part of the century which formalised the slave status were undoubtedly sanctioning existing practice. Uniquely defenceless, of all the poor and weak elements in Virginia, the Negro was the most convenient victim for planters in search of a labour force. Unlike white indentured servants,

[31] C. N. Degler, 'Slavery and the Genesis of American Race Prejudice', *Comparative Studies in Society and History*, II (1959) 49–66; idem, *Out of our Past*, 2nd ed. (New York, 1970) pp. 26–36. On indentured servitude, the most useful works are A. E. Smith, *Colonists in Bondage: White Servitude and Convict Labor in America, 1607–1776* (Chapel Hill, N.C., 1947); C. Bridenbaugh, *Vexed and Troubled Englishmen, 1590–1642* (New York, 1969); R. B. Morris, *Government and Labor in Early America* (New York, 1946) pp. 310–512; M. Campbell, 'Social Origins of Some Early Americans', in J. M. Smith (ed.), *Seventeenth Century America Essays in Colonial History* (Chapel Hill, N.C., 1959) pp. 63–89.

[32] Jordan, *White over Black*, pp. 3–98.

even Irish or Scottish ones, blacks had no one in England or America to whom they could appeal for redress if their liberties were curtailed or if they were generally maltreated. White servants were also abused by their masters, and landless white freemen feared, but the blacks as a group were the only one which, by definition, neither had friends in government nor understood the right of appeal to it – the more so since the British authorities, unlike the Spanish, followed a policy of decentralisation. They were unlikely to interfere with the powers of the merchants and planters to whom they had delegated control for the sake of a few heathen servants.

This was not the only way in which the sheer convenience of black slavery led to its adoption as the dominant labour device of Virginia and the other planting colonies. Another was the corresponding inconvenience and worry of using white indentured servants. The late Elizabethan and early Stuart polemicists and officials had been obsessed by the fear of overpopulation. By the last decades of the century, however, this had changed into a concern over the drain of national manpower to the New World. This concern was actually a mistaken one. The alarming amount of land going out of cultivation was not a symptom of the ills of emigration, but a result of the Elizabethan enclosures and the growing movement of population to the cities. Nevertheless, the Restoration government could see men of definite ability – and, even worse, men of capital – leaving England. At the same time, they tried to clamp down on the 'spirits' responsible for illegal shipments of servants. The result was that they discouraged the exodus of indentured servants, both the poorest and those who came of substantial family, where their predecessors had encouraged it. This in itself might have had little effect on the determined emigrant, but it cut the labour supply drastically when it came on top of unpleasant reports of the hardship and savagery of colonial existence which began to filter back to Britain in the 1620s and 1630s. The New World paradise described by Purchas or John Smith of Virginia, or in the propaganda of the Virginia Company and the other organisations determined to promote emigration, had never materialised. It had turned out to be a bitter land where a livelihood, indeed life itself, could be eked out only by incessant hard work in miserable conditions. The flow of white labour to the Americas was thus seriously impeded. Although Cromwell had begun the practice of sending convicts, criminals, traitors, heretics and Scots overseas, these went mainly to the newly acquired Jamaica and Britain's other Caribbean possessions. In any case, they did very little to make up for the fluctuations in the voluntary signing of indentures. The island legislatures in particular began to complain bitterly about the slackness of white emigration.[33] At the same time, in spite of constant complaints about shortage of good labourers, the paradox in Virginia was that masters began to have new doubts over the suitability of a white labour force. Improving longevity of immigrants meant that more of them survived their servitude. After their indentures expired, these servants passed out of the control of their employers, and came to form the great mass of landless and masterless men who were the worst nightmare of Tudor and Stuart polemicists. Continual deliberations and ordinances from the Assembly failed to bring them under control. The spectre of anarchy raised in 1676 by Bacon's rebellion, supported by this very element, increased such fears, and spurred the semi-conscious decisions which set the Negro slave apart as the main labourer in the colony's future.[34] Earlier English distrust of blacks had brought informal but not institutional discrimination against them – and it had not prevented situations in which the two races might co-operate as equals. By the end of the century, fear of *whites*, together with the ease of controlling blacks, had prompted the Assembly to define black subordination through legislation against their bearing of arms and illegal assembly, and in favour of their lifetime and hereditary servitude.

Black labour also became attractive once it was possible for the colonists to buy it, which had not been the case at the time of Virginia's foundation. The continued decline of the Portuguese in the seventeenth century meant that the lines of slave supply gradually fell into Protestant hands, at first those of the Dutch. After 1672, however, the foundation of the Royal African Company brought a reasonably stable supply of slaves into English hands. Where slaves had previously been scarce, they were now

---

[33] Smith, *Colonists in Bondage*, pp. 31–5.

[34] Morgan, in *J.A.H.*, LIX 5–29; forthcoming paper by Timothy Breen on 'A Changing Labor Force and the Problem of Internal Security: Virginia, 1660–1710', kindly made available to me by the author.

relatively more available for those who could afford to buy them, though few English Guineamen came direct to Virginia, and the majority of the colonies' slaves were probably bought as re-exports from the islands. As the little black community of Virginia grew, and was increasingly set aside in a position inferior to the rest of the labouring class, the profitability of investing in black labour became greater. The fiction of the black's 'indenture' was abandoned, and his period of service extended throughout life – and in the last resort to dictate the condition of his offspring as well. Investment in a black slave thus brought the return of his services for life, and hopefully the services of his or her children as well. Indentured servants, on the other hand, were entitled to freedom after their period of indenture was up. If cheated, they could appeal to the authorities at home. In a country where land was so plentiful, at least on the frontier, that few had to work on someone else's farm for want of their own – the classic example of Nieboer's 'open resources' case[35] – there was little hope that a servant would continue to work for his master for wages when he was no longer under indenture, even if time and money had been invested in teaching him specific skills. He might also claim a severance payment in land when he had completed his part of the contract. This was a simple case where every penny invested in the labour of a black slave brought a return at least until his death, while control over an indentured servant was a wasting asset. Again, indentured servants posed appalling problems of discipline in a form of agriculture where mechanical obedience in monotonous tasks was essential to the plantation-owner's success. Since they had troublesome European notions of their rights, whites were often unruly when maltreated, overworked or kept in bondage for illegally long periods. Nor, as Bacon's rebellion demonstrates, did these dangers to security end with freedom. Problems of brawling, drunkenness, violence and escape were as rife among white servants as black, but they did not have the compensating advantage that they could be easily suppressed. Black servants expressed their objections to their position in the same ways: sporadic violence, theft, passive resistance and escape. But their tragedy was that if they resisted and were brutally punished, there was nowhere for them to go for

[35] H. J. Nieboer, *Slavery as an Industrial System: Ethnological Researches* (The Hague, 1900).

redress, and no communal sympathy for the wrongs of an alien element in society. Long-standing prejudices did make blacks easy victims, but the governing factor in the situation was their complete aloneness. They were the only element who could be reduced to the total discipline the planters considered essential to raise their crops and to protect their investments – that is, to hereditary chattel slavery.

The final strand in the black man's doom was the distinctiveness of his skin colour. No doubt the legacy of prejudice against his race, colour and religion was a factor in easing him towards slavery. It is much more important that the logic of control over the labour force made him an ideal slave. The white indentured servant could run away, and escape into the anonymity of being white like all other freemen. The Negro could not, or at least if and when he did could readily be distinguished by colour from the dominant free population, and returned to bondage. Carrying this to its logical conclusion eventually came to mean not only that all slaves must be black, but that all blacks must be slaves. In the nineteenth century the mature slave systems of the United States, though they never entirely succeeded, would aim at enslaving or removing all free blacks. In the planters' ideal society, the man who invested in a black slave and woke up next morning to find him gone could expect the escapee to be impounded automatically on the assumption that he *could not* be free. As it was, in early eighteenth-century Virginia the escaping black could only go to join the Indians, and not even to them as the coastal nations declined in power. The other irony of the black man's position in the colonies was that though it was his unique helplessness and lack of allies which initially made him the victim of enslavement, it was his terrifying potential for resistance which made his condition progressively harsher. Slavery emerged in Virginia because of the greed of the planters, and it was formalised because of their fear. As more and more Africans came to the colony, they replaced white servants and freedmen as the largest recognisable group which endangered its security. By the early 1700s the status of black slavery had emerged in Virginia from the logic of the planters' economic ambition, black population had soared, and the need for its legal regulation became urgent. The colony's Assembly not only recognised the status of hereditary chattel slavery, but placed a series of security restrictions against blacks gathering in groups, carrying arms, moving at night and intermarrying with whites. These laws protected not only the investments of those who used the labour force, but also transposed the class system to a caste system drawn along the line of colour, which naturally had the effect of compounding existing prejudices. This legal crystallisation of the Virginia slave system will be discussed in detail in a future chapter. For the moment it should be seen as the culmination of a long process by which the colonial planters discarded other forms of labour and adopted the system which gave them the best possible work-force, the best possible protection for their investments and the best possible internal security.

Though this process took different lengths of time in the other colonies, it can be seen in all the settlements of the seventeenth century. By and large, the slave system formalised more quickly in those colonies which were founded latest, and in those where tropical agriculture brought such fabulous returns that black slaves could be bought immediately. Barbados is a splendid example which shows exactly the same process as Virginia in much shorter compass. Settled in 1627 by the English, it was at first parcelled out in relatively small lots, to farmers who might use a handful of indentured servants to help them. The high profitability of sugar cultivation, together with the high costs of buying plant for boiling and reducing cane, meant that a few large producers quickly drove the small ones into inferior highland holdings – or completely out of business. All the cultivable land in the small colony was quickly taken up, and just as news of this situation checked the flow of indentured servants, blacks were becoming readily available and the larger farmers were accumulating enough capital to buy them. In 1650 the island's population of 30,000 included 6,000 blacks. By 1653 there were 20,000 blacks to 26,000 whites. By 1690 the proportion was 20,000 whites to 60,000 blacks.[36] At first supplied by the Dutch,

[36] V. T. Harlow, *A History of Barbados, 1625–1685* (Oxford, 1926) pp. 292–330; Bridenbaugh, *No Peace beyond the Line*, pp. 195–266; Dunn, *Sugar and Slaves*, pp. 46–116. The central source on early Barbadian history is still R. Ligon, *A True and Exact History of the Island of Barbados* (London, 1657). See also Deerr, *History of Sugar*, 1 160–6. These figures for Barbados population growth are taken from Bridenbaugh, p. 226. Dunn, *Sugar and Slaves*, pp. 75–6, 84–116, suggests that this rise in black population is exaggerated, and the white decline underestimated,

it was also Barbados and its neighbours which absorbed the first importations of the Royal African Company. In the most important French possessions of the Lesser Antilles, Martinique and Guadeloupe, though sugar was not fully established there until the 1670s, and in Saint-Domingue, the demands of the sugar revolution pushed white population down and black population up in exactly the same way. *Engagés* were gradually replaced with black slaves, though royal policy favoured white emigration at least until the 1680s. The change apparently met with only one protest, and this based on security fears rather than distrust of slavery.[37] In Jamaica the process was slightly different. Plantations were large and land plentiful from the outset, and sugar profits were high, but it was not until the late 1680s that cane became the principal crop. Convict labour was extensively used for some time after the island's capture from the Spanish under the Protectorate, together with highly unsatisfactory voluntary indentured labour. But it was difficult to tempt slavers, or indeed any traders, to sail through the extra thousand miles of waters beyond Barbados and the Leewards, and only the expulsion of the buccaneers made the Jamaican market attractive enough to bring an adequate supply of labour. Thereafter black population soared and sugar production expanded dramatically, at the expense of the cotton, indigo and cocoa with which the earlier planters had experimented.[38] In the Northern British colonies, in the absence of the commitment to cane, black slaves always remained a small minority. Yet they were by no means a negligible minority, as we have already seen, particularly since local concentrations, as in the Narragansett area of Rhode Island,

though he still finds more than three blacks for every white on the island by the end of the century.

[37] Deerr, *History of Sugar*, I 218–36. On indentured servitude in the French islands, see G. Debien, 'Les Engagés pour les Antilles, 1634–1715', *Revue d'Histoire des Colonies*, xxxviii (1951) 7–279; L. Vignole, 'L'Institution des engagés, 1626–1774', *Revue d'Histoire Économique et Sociale*, xvi (1928) 12–45. On slavery and its origins, the best work is still L. Peytraud, *Histoire de l'esclavage dans les colonies françaises avant 1789* (Paris, 1897). See also S. T. McLoy, *The Negro in the French West Indies* (Lexington, Ky., 1966) pp. 2–14.

[38] H. O. Patterson, *The Sociology of Slavery: An Analysis of the Origins, Development and Structure of Negro Slave Society in Jamaica* (London, 1967) pp. 16–23; E. Long, *The History of Jamaica*, 3 vols (London, 1774) I 375–8; Dunn, *Sugar and Slaves*, pp. 149–87.

were often higher than the population percentages of complete colonies. The Northern colonies also complained about the lack of indentured servants and their unruliness, and they too made good the deficiencies in white labourers by importing slaves wherever farm businesses were large enough to make the employment of a sizeable labour force possible or necessary. The same was true of the Hudson valley and the rich seaboard farms of New Jersey, which began with the usual indentured labour force – much of it white but non-British, including a large element of Finns in the Jerseys – but by the early eighteenth century they too had enough black slaves to be paranoid about the problem of security. Certainly, there were exceptions where this process of experimentation did not appear. The planters of Dutch Surinam, for instance, with characteristic Flemish practicality, simply purchased a full force of black slaves and set about whipping them into carving out sugar plantations from scratch. By and large, however, the seventeenth-century settlements, like the Spaniards, adopted black slavery only after they had made attempts to use other and cheaper sources of labour, and there are even traces of this process in the Dutch colonies.

It would be quite wrong to assume that this time-lag was caused by moral scruples, though these may have been present in isolated cases. But it is nevertheless important that black slavery did not emerge as the standard labour system immediately settlement was begun, either in the Spanish and Portuguese colonies or the others. Few sixteenth- or seventeenth-century settlers had any intention of doing physical work themselves if they could avoid it, while they wished to make as much money as possible. At the same time, however, they did not set out with the intention of founding societies based on black slave labour. One of the common factors between Spanish and Portuguese, and the predominantly Protestant settlers in the West Indies and North America, is that they set out to try all available forms of labour, beginning with the cheapest. The Spanish found Indian labour ineffective, and the British and French found their *engagés* and indentured servants unsuitable, dangerous, and in any case not always available. Both finally settled on the form of labour which was dearest, that is, the imported black slave. It also proved to be the most efficient. Again, because the black had no allies in the Americas, his form of forced labour in both cases became harsher than others. Systems of slave law of varying rigidity were formulated throughout the Americas to define the status of the slave after the fact. They also set up a communal system of discipline so that the planter could protect his investments in the black labour force and ensure that slaves would not endanger his own physical security. The relative harshness of these systems is very much under debate by historians. For the moment, however, it is enough to note that black slavery in both Catholic and Protestant America seems to have arisen from similar motives and by a similar process.

3 The Establishment of Slavery in Law and Practice, to about 1700

As a general rule, then, black slavery was not transplanted to the New World as a formed institution. This does not deny that the Europeans who settled the Americas shared the assumption that they would exploit their new possessions through unfree labour. Again, whatever their nationality, they had common notions, however vague, as to the barbarity of those races whose skin colour was different from their own, particularly when the peoples they confronted were also heathens.[1] Except in Canada and the Northern English colonies, they turned to blacks as a source of labour as soon as they found other workers unavailable or unsuitable, and as soon as they could afford them. This process was common to all the tropical colonies of Spain, Portugal, Holland, England and France. Yet though all depended on black slavery until the nineteenth century, the form and conditions of that slavery varied greatly from settlement to settlement, and indeed within each settlement. Slavery became more or less feasible and more or less harsh according to the pressures, economic or other, which the times brought to bear on each generation of slaveholders. Cultural differences between the various colonies also had some effect on the lot of the slave. Nevertheless, the extent to which the legal expression of these differences really affected day-to-day life is probably less significant than the extent to which they have interested comparative-minded historians.[2]

[1] W. D. Jordan, *White over Black: American Attitudes toward the Negro, 1550–1812* (1968);(Baltimore: Penguin Books ed., 1969) pp. 3–43.

[2] The finest introduction to their controversies is L. Foner and E. D. Genovese (eds.), *Slavery in the New World: A Reader in Comparative History* (Englewood Cliffs, N.J., 1969) esp. Genovese, 'The Treatment of Slaves in Different Countries: Problems in the Applications of the Comparative Method', pp. 202–10.

In an age of slow communications, slaveholders safe on their own plantations were unlikely to be affected in the way they treated their slaves by the pious edicts of a distant and often rickety central government. The law which mattered was that which formalised existing customs of authority, not that which, as in the Spanish case, attempted to undercut them.

Yet a substantial amount of slave law emerged in Latin America by the end of the sixteenth century, and elsewhere in the colonies by the end of the seventeenth. For both areas of America it gives a great deal of information on the formal status and day-to-day discipline over the slave labour force. It is unwise, however, to accept such law as giving an exact picture of the way in which slaves were treated. The few measures designed to protect them are interesting as an expression of intent, but it is not clear that they were ever enforceable. Conversely, those provisions designed to discipline and punish them were so dramatically barbaric that they must often have been deterrent in intention, although they sanctioned a severity of discipline to which masters certainly proceeded on occasion. Neither the letter of the law nor the culture from which it arose governed the reality of the slave's existence. Even the master's personal whim was more important. A more central governing factor was the extent to which economic pressures added force to the already harsh discipline required to keep slavery viable at all. Because of such variables, it is a mistake to think of slave 'systems'. The slave condition varies from place to place and from time to time, along lines a great deal more complex than the one between Protestant and Catholic America. This chapter will close by examining the different positions of the slaves in the eighteenth-century tobacco and sugar industries of the English colonies, but will first describe their delineation of a body of written slave law. The importance of this law is not its impact on slavery itself, but the light it sheds on the preconceptions and economic needs with which the English approached the problems arising from the possession of black slaves.

It is in this context, too, that the differences in the legal expression of slavery in the Americas are of great importance. In spite of the strength of European legal traditions dealing with slavery, none of the main colonising nations came to the New World with a formal corpus of slave law by which the position of its labour force was to be regulated. In the case of the Spanish, recurrent attempts were made by the crown to impose such legislation throughout the sixteenth century, though its concern was centrally for Indians. Comparable law was not developed for the blacks in the English and French colonies until the end of the next century, and in the case of some individual settlements well into the early 1700s. Portugal never evolved anything more than a few piece-meal ordinances dealing with black slavery. The assumptions of the chattel status of the Negro and his general rightlessness were accepted by Portuguese masters in the Americas as sufficient justification for slavery, if it ever occurred to them that one was needed at all.[3] This tardiness of legal development has been explained in various ways.[4] All are agreed that the relationship between the legal expression of slavery and the growth of pre-judice was close, although there is still hopeless disagreement as to which was cause and which effect. No one, however, has simply suggested that in both North and South America the first decades of settlement were a period of experimentation when labour devices other than black slavery were tried out. The legacy of distrust of black peoples meant it was always possible that they could be enslaved. It was at the point where the other experi-ments had failed that this was done, and the customary accept-ance of various aspects of slavery was subsequently crystallised in law.

Because this historical process was not a neat one, slave law showed varying degrees of concern for the physical and spiritual welfare of the slaves. But these differences frequently fall along lines other than the one between Catholic and Protestant. For instance, the slave legislation of the French, who were a Catholic nation, was not strikingly different from that of the Protestant English. As in the Spanish case, French colonists were not left to work out the law of slavery for themselves. This did not prevent

[3] C. R. Boxer, *The Golden Age of Brazil, 1695–1750: Growing Pains of a Colonial Society* (1962; reprinted Berkeley, 1969) pp. 138–9.

[4] O. Handlin and M. Handlin, 'The Origins of the Southern Labor System', *William and Mary Quarterly*, 3rd ser., VII (1950) 199–222; M. Harris, *Patterns of Race in the Americas* (New York, 1964) pp. 69–70; C. N. Degler, 'Slavery and the Genesis of American Race Prejudice', *Comparative Studies in Society and History*, II (1959) 49–66; idem, *Out of our Past*, 2nd ed. (New York, 1970) pp. 26–36; Jordan, *White over Black*, pp. 3–98.

their assuming the hereditary chattel nature of black service, or of working out by custom aspects of the slave's work conditions and discipline. Moreover, when Louis XIV's officials finally compiled a slave code, as the *Code Noir* of 1685, it was remarkably similar to law meanwhile being written in Virginia and the other English colonies – not only in its practice but also in its formal provisions.[5] As for the Catholic Portuguese, they made no systematic attempt to regulate slavery beyond isolated and certainly ineffective edicts intended to protect the slave from the most extreme physical excesses.[6] It is equally difficult to generalise about the law of the Protestant colonising nations. The extent to which the personality of the slave was recognised by each of the English and other colonies, in the islands and on the mainland, varied widely. At the most vicious end of the scale, it is difficult to find a connection between the conduct of the Dutch planters of Surinam and any rule of law whatsoever. But the same was true of the more capitalistic coffee-planters of Brazil or the sugar magnates of Cuba in the nineteenth century. In the same period, the discipline of declining Virginia, or of Bermuda, was as lax as anything in the Latin American world.

Apart from such difficulties of generalisation, there are doubts over the extent to which Spanish slaves really were protected by law. The thirteenth-century *Siete Partidas* of Alfonso the Wise admittedly expressed a regard for the personality of the slave which was enshrined in the sixteenth-century royal ordinances intended to protect the Indians. When the *Recopilación* or Digest of colonial laws was compiled in 1680, its slave provisions were clearly aimed at blacks, but it laid as much stress on police regu-

[5] E. V. Goveia, 'The West Indian Slave Laws of the Eighteenth Century', *Revista de Ciencias Sociales*, IV (1960) 75–105; S. T. McLoy, *The Negro in the French West Indies* (Lexington, Ky., 1966) pp. 15–34. The case for the principal factor behind the differing severity of slavery being religious is made in F. Tannenbaum, *Slave and the Citizen: The Negro in the Americas* (New York, 1946). See also S. Elkins, *Slavery: A Problem in American Institutional and Intellectual Life*, 2nd ed. (Chicago, 1969) pp. 27–80; essays in A. J. Lane (ed.), *The Debate over 'Slavery': Stanley Elkins and his Critics* (Urbana, Ill., 1971) pp. 111–209; H. S. Klein, *Slavery in the Americas: A Comparative Study of Virginia and Cuba* (Chicago, 1967). Cf. C. N. Degler, *Neither Black nor White: Slavery and Race Relations in Brazil and the United States* (New York, 1971); Harris, *Patterns of Race in the Americas*, pp. 44–94 and passim.

[6] Boxer, *Golden Age of Brazil*, pp. 138–40.

lations to keep them under control as on their protection. Their right of assembly, freedom of movement and bearing of arms were all regulated. Although baptism and religious instruction were demanded, manumission praised and the destruction of slave marriages deplored, the core of the Digest was its *restriction* of black freedoms. The distinctiveness of the slave caste was confirmed in exactly the same way as in the English colonies – by discrimination against even the free members of the subject race. Free blacks, for instance, though their initial manumission was seen as a laudable act, were required to have a white patron who would answer for their good behaviour. This is not far removed from later North American laws which stipulated that freed slaves should be removed from the state, or at least that their ex-masters should give security to prevent their becoming a charge on the community. As always, it was the provisions strengthening the masters' power which were the enforceable ones. In the realities of the colonial situation, law aimed at the spiritual or physical well-being of the slave could safely be ignored. There are no studies of the actual operation of the *Recopilación*, but there is little evidence of the conviction of masters under its provisions. The much more liberal 1789 *Real Cédula*, in which Madrid again tried to produce an up-to-date slave code, was similarly inoperative. Standards of dress and maintenance were laid down, though vaguely, and punishments limited, though only to twenty-five lashes at any one time. A series of fines were stipulated for masters who abused their slaves, and a 'protector' appointed to ensure enforcement. The only problem about this great edifice of humanitarianism was that any hope of its being implemented was visionary. In fact the experiment of enforcement was never tried, for the Captains-General of the various colonies, under severe pressure from local slave-owners, refused to publish it for fear the very *idea* of such laxity would ruin discipline. If Spanish slave law is stripped of its inoperative provisions, it becomes very similar to that of the colonies of other powers. The workable core of slave law everywhere confirmed and defined the authority of the master over the slave, rather than the rights of the slave against the master.[7]

[7] The most convenient English introduction to Spanish slave law is F. W. Knight, *Slave Society in Cuba during the Nineteenth Century* (Madison, Wis., 1970) pp. 121–36. There is no English source on Brazil,

The written law of the English and French colonies, too, butt-ressed the abolute power of the master over his slave. In the case of the English possessions, which will now be examined more closely, much legislation was connected with dangers posed by the over-large black population, or with the state of panic pro-duced by real or imagined slave insurrection. Slave law stemmed from a wish to define the position of the bondsman, already accepted in custom, as a means of guaranteeing discipline. In this sense it was often aimed less at the blacks themselves than at masters who might endanger the safety of the community and its ruling class by treating their slaves too laxly.

Most of the early slave law of the English settlements was enacted piecemeal by the legislatures of the individual colonies, to cover immediate problems of controlling the black labour force. In the last decades of the seventeenth century, however, a number of the colonies summarised and restated their legislation in an attempt to provide coherent local slave codes. A fine example of such a code was Barbados's one, drafted in 1688 as 'An Act for the Governing of Negroes'.[8] Like other colonists, the Barbadian assemblymen felt that separate black law was necessary 'forasmuch as the said Negroes and other Slaves brought unto the People of this Island . . . are of barbarous, wild, and savage Natures, and such as renders them wholly unqualified to be governed by the Laws, Customs, and Practices of our Nation'. The code was aimed – and in this it was typical – both at restraining the blacks and punishing those whites who endangered the colony through

where the standard work is still A. M. P. Malheiro, *A escravidão no Brasil. Ensaio histórico-jurídico-social*, 2 vols (São Paulo, 1944). Still useful for the law of the English colonies, in spite of a strong abolitionist bias, is J. Stephen, *The Slavery of the British West India Colonies Delineated, as it Exists Both in Law and Practice*, 2 vols (London, 1824, 1830). See also E. V. Goveia, *Slave Society in the British Leeward Islands* (New Haven, 1965) pp. 152–202. On the French colonies, see Goveia, in *Revista de Ciencias Sociales*, IV 75–105; A. Gisler, *L'Esclavage aux Antilles françaises (XVIIᵉ–XIXᵉ siècle). Contribution au problème de l'esclavage* (Freiburg, 1965) pp. 19–33; L. Peytraud, *Histoire de l'esclavage dans les colonies françaises avant 1789* (Paris, 1897).

[8] *Acts of Assembly Passed in the Island of Barbadoes, from 1648 to 1718* (London, 1738) p. 160. On the slave law of Barbados, Jamaica and the English Leewards, see R. S. Dunn, *Sugar and Slaves: The Rise of the Planter Class in the English West Indies, 1624–1713* (Williamsburg, Va., 1972) pp. 238–46.

the laxity of their discipline. No slave could leave his plantation without a pass. Since it was 'absolutely necessary to the Safety of this Place, that all due care be taken to restrain the Wanderings and Meetings of Negroes', any white was authorised to capture and whip any slave abroad without a pass or with weapons, horns or drums. Masters who did not periodically search for weapons and musical instruments were to be fined. If a slave offered 'any Violence to any Christian', he was to be whipped for a first offence, branded for a second, punished more severely for a third. A reward of 10s. was given to anyone seizing a runaway slave. For arson, murder, burglary, robbery, and stealing or maiming of livestock, slaves could be sentenced to death by two justices with three co-opted freeholders, without benefit of jury trial. Petty theft brought forty lashes for a first offence, branding on the forehead for a second, death for a third. Those guilty of insurrection were to suffer 'Death or other Pains, as their Crimes shall deserve', at the discretion of the commanders who caught them, with compensation for the master if he could prove it was not he who had driven his people to revolt. To keep down the dangers of a large servile population, buying them just to hire out was forbidden, with specific mention of owners of 'the *Hebrew* Nation'. Any white who killed his own slave 'of Wantonness, or only of Bloody-mindedness' was to pay a fine of £15; if someone else's, a fine of £25, and double his value to the injured master. Finally, it was enacted

That all the Slaves within this Island shall have Clothes once every year (that is to say) Drawers and Caps for Men, and Petticoats and Caps for Women, upon pain of forfeiting Five Shillings for every slave that shall not be clothed, as aforesaid, One Third to the Informer, the other Two Thirds to His Majesty, for the Use of the Poor of the Parish where the Offender liveth.

By the time of Barbados's 1688 legislation, slavery was fully accepted in custom in a number of the English colonies. As early as 1669 the proprietors of Carolina felt obliged to assure prospective emigrants from the various West Indian colonies that they would not be subject to any encroachment on the powers they already held over their servants, even if converted to Christianity, and would continue to enjoy 'absolute Power and Authority over

his Negro Slaves'.[9] But Barbados was the first English colony to
import African slaves in numbers large enough to form its main
labour force. Actually, ten blacks were among the first contingent
of its settlers, who had captured them from a hostile ship they
seized as a prize on their voyage to America.[10] Slavery as it
developed there became the example for most of the other
English colonies. Barbados was the central possession in the
'Caribbee Isles', and it also provided a large number of emigrants
who later settled the Leeward and Windward Islands, and in
time Jamaica. On the mainland, South Carolina was colonised
directly by a group of businessmen and planters who had gained
their experience in Barbados.[11] The Barbadian system, in fact, is
the key to the form slavery took in the English Caribbean and
North America. In this context, to return to comparisons, it is
significant that there is a definite continuity between slavery in
Latin America and in Barbados, which was settled by English
Anglican businessmen, closely advised by Dutch Calvinist and
Jewish managers. They themselves had in turn learned the art of
slave management as planters in Catholic Brazil during the short
period of the Netherlands' occupation of the northern sugar-
growing area. The first Barbadian slaveholders, in fact, did not
model a new English slave system for themselves, but drew indirectly on the experience of their Catholic neighbours on the
South American mainland. Even so, slave labour was not used
extensively in the first years of settlement. The paradox of
Barbados's early history is that a colony divided into small yeoman holdings was quickly transformed, through the agency of
sugar, into a disturbingly small island carved up among a small
number of estate-owners whose black slaves brought them great
riches. The British first took possession of Barbados in 1627 – the
second island acquisition after St Kitts. As a business venture the
settlement was organised by a London group headed by the great

[9] E. E. Parker (ed.), *North Carolina Charters and Constitutions, 1578–
1698* (Raleigh, N. C., 1963) pp. 150, 164, 183.
[10] V. T. Harlow, *A History of Barbados, 1625–1685* (Oxford, 1926) p. 4.
[11] W. F. Craven, *The Southern Colonies in the Seventeenth Century,
1607–1689* (Baton Rouge, La., 1969) pp. 329–34; M. E. Sirmans, 'The
Legal Status of the Slave in South Carolina, 1670–1740', *Journal of
Southern History*, XXVIII (1962) 462–6; C. Bridenbaugh, *No Peace beyond
the Line: The English in the Caribbean, 1624–1690* (New York, 1972) pp.
195–229; Dunn, *Sugar and Slaves*, pp. 110–16.

Anglo–Dutch merchant Sir William Courteen. It was then taken over by the Earl of Carlisle as Lord Proprietor of the Caribbee Islands, and its land distributed in small units by those who leased the proprietor's rights to sell land-tenure patents. Apart from its distinctive beauty, Barbados had other natural advantages. Great fertility it shared with many of the West Indian islands, but unlike others, for instance French Martinique and Guadeloupe, it was not already occupied by strong groups of hostile Amerindians. The Barbadian settlers had no need to fight bitterly with the Caribs before agriculture could become established, and the development of their colony was correspondingly quick. The earliest Barbadian farms concentrated on ensuring subsistence by growing food crops locally, mainly sweet corn. Only a little tropical produce was grown for export on the early smallholdings, and such as it was it was tobacco and cotton rather than sugar. With the average landholding well below 30 acres, the need for labour was not great, but what there was was provided by white indentured servants rather than African slaves. By 1640, when sugar had not yet made its mark, the island's white population was well into the 30,000s.

The modest success of Barbados and its neighbours St Kitts and Nevis could last only as long as tobacco prices remained high. As soon as expanding production in Virginia removed the demand for their tobacco, which was in any case of inferior quality, the Barbadian planters were left with nothing to sell. It was at this time, probably about 1645, that the possibility of planting sugar as an alternative crop was first considered. Capital, equipment and credit were provided by Amsterdam, while technical advice and the first sugar canes themselves were brought in by Dutch refugees from the sugar-growing areas around Pernambuco, now under severe counter-attack from the Portuguese. Charles Andrews has called the Dutch 'the foster-fathers of the early colonies, some of which could hardly have grown to maturity without them'.[12] Barbadian skill in sugar production increased in the late 1640s. When Richard Ligon visited the island in 1647, he was told that

[12] C. M. Andrews, *The Colonial Period of American History*, 4 vols (New Haven, 1934–8) IV 9. See also Bridenbaugh, *No Peace beyond the Line*, pp. 63–72, and, on the earlier Dutch experience in Brazil, C. R. Boxer, *The Dutch in Brazil, 1624–1654* (Oxford, 1957).

the great work of Sugar-making, was but newly practised by the inhabitants there. Some of the most industrial men, having gotten plants from *Pernambock*, a place in *Brasill*, and made tryall of them at the *Barbadoes*; and finding them to grow, they planted more and more, as they grew and multiplied on the place, till they had such a considerable number, as they were worth the while to set up a very small *Ingenio*, and so make tryall what Sugar could be made upon that soyl. But, the secrets of the work not being well understood, the Sugars they made were very inconsiderable, and of little worth, for two or three years. But they finding their errours by their daily practice, began a little to mend; and, by new directions from *Brasil*, sometimes by strangers, and now and then by their own people, (who . . . were content sometimes to make a voyage thither, to improve their knowledge in a thing they so much desired [)]. . . . At the time of our arrival there, we found many sugar works set up, and at work.[13]

The initial difficulties were well on the way to being overcome when Ligon went home in 1650, and by the time his *True and Exact History of the Island of Barbados* was published in 1657, sugar had swept out tobacco throughout the island. Even currency was now expressed in terms of pounds of sugar, where the early settlers had reckoned prices in pounds of tobacco. The most obvious group to suffer from this agricultural change were the miserable Negro slaves whom the most successful planters brought into Barbados to cultivate the cane. Sugar also brought disaster for the great majority of white settlers. Since cane must be crushed and boiled on the plantation where it is grown, its cultivation requires heavy investment. To get maximum return on capital, the equipment used for this process had to be kept fully employed throughout the harvest period, so that the acreage required for a viable sugar plantation was much greater than for a tobacco one. Even more capital was therefore required to purchase large units of land. Only a few planters were wealthy enough to be able to move into sugar cultivation. Their returns were so great that they were able to start buying up the small-

[13] R. Ligon, *A True and Exact History of the Island of Barbados* (London, 1657) p. 85.

holdings of neighbours who were falling on hard times as tobacco prices fell. The result was a general consolidation of plantations. Plantations larger than 200 acres were atypical, but the change was none the less radical. From being a society of modest yeomen farmers, Barbados came to be the preserve of a relatively small number of forceful magnates concentrating exclusively on sugar production. Their less successful fellows emigrated to other parts of the West Indies and to the mainland colonies. The white population of the island fell, even in absolute terms, from 26,000 in 1653 to 19,568 in 1684.[14]

At the same time, black immigration to Barbados soared, for the other characteristic of large-scale sugar cultivation was that it required a labour force of a size which the small farmers of previous decades could never have afforded. To them that have shall be given, was the story of Barbadian sugar-planting. Only wealth could buy equipment and slaves to grow cane, and wealth could come only from growing cane. The supply of white indentured labour dried up as it became clear that the small units of land granted after working out indentures were useless under the new dispensation of sugar. Even where force replaced persuasion – and indeed, 'barbadoing' or transportation to the island was a standard penalty in the courts until the end of the century – white servants came nowhere near to being as plentiful or stable a labour force as the planters needed. At the same time, the income which came to those who succeeded in sugar made it possible for them to buy slaves. Their potential for earning even more increased accordingly. More slaves meant more sugar cultivation, and more sugar cultivation meant more slaves. The white servants who had worked in the fields along with the first Negroes in the early stages of the sugar boom were replaced by the more easily disciplined blacks. By the early Restoration years, Barbados society was dominated by several hundred planters in charge of a vast slave labour force. Between them there was only the miserable remnant of poor whites – failed small farmers, a handful of wretched indentured servants and a growing group of unruly transported convicts. In 1650 the island's black population was 6,000, in 1690 about 60,000. The racial mix of roughly

[14] Bridenbaugh, *No Peace beyond the Line*, pp. 226, 69–101, 195–229; Harlow, *History of Barbados*, pp. 292–328. On methods of sugar production, see also N. Deerr, *A History of Sugar*, 2 vols (London, 1949).

three blacks to each white was maintained from the beginning of the eighteenth century until emancipation.[15]

The growing disproportion between black and white population in Barbados gave rise to a chronic fear of servile rebellion, especially in view of the irresponsibility of the poor whites. In fact the racial imbalance in Barbados was mirrored in all the islands colonised and put under sugar at this time – in French Guadeloupe, Martinique and Saint-Domingue, in British Antigua, Montserrat, St Kitts and Nevis. Where whites had outnumbered blacks in the early years of settlement, the last quarter of the eighteenth century saw the British Leewards with only 8,000 whites to 91,000 black slaves. Guadeloupe had 3,083 whites to 4,267 blacks in 1671, 13,712 to 89,523 in 1789. Martinique's white population increased only from 5,019 to 11,619 from 1686 to 1776; the corresponding black figures were 11,101 and 71,268. Exactly the same process took place in Jamaica, though there the trend was even faster. In the heyday of Jamaica's sugar cultivation, its whites were outnumbered by their own slaves in a ratio higher than 10 to 1. Local concentrations were even higher. By 1794 St David's Parish had 92 whites to 2,685 blacks, a ratio of about 29 to 1.[16] As for the white reaction to this situation, Barbados, as in so many other ways, was typical of the other sugar islands. Its response was one of stark fear. As black population rose, so rose the possibility of successful insurrection, a correlation of which master and slave were equally aware. Though there was a rising in the Puritan colony of Old Providence in 1638, the first major revolt in the British West Indies came in Barbados in 1675. The savagery of its suppression gives a hint that white Barbadians, like their successors in the Southern United States, were already obsessed with the terror of being murdered in their beds by the alien slaves who surrounded them. Physical repression and savage punishment of the ringleaders was

---

[15] Bridenbaugh, *No Peace beyond the Line*, p. 226. Cf. the slightly slower rise in seventeenth-century black population suggested in Deerr, *History of Sugar*, ii 278, and Harlow, *History of Barbados*, p. 339, adopted by P. Curtin, *The Atlantic Slave Trade: A Census* (Madison, Wis., 1969) p. 59.

[16] H. O. Patterson, *The Sociology of Slavery: An Analysis of the Origin, Development and Structure of Negro Slave Society in Jamaica* (London, 1967) p. 56; Goveia, *Slave Society in the British Leeward Islands*, p. 85; Deerr, *History of Sugar*, i 278–81.

accompanied by legislation aimed at tightening control over the slave population.[17] The connection between fear of black resistance and the strengthening of regulations to keep the slaves under control is a theme which runs right through the history of American plantation slavery. In the seventeenth century, as the sugar revolution went on, British island colonists also made frantic attempts to restore a safe balance between black and white population. In 1677, for instance, the Assembly of Antigua enacted a law compelling each planter to keep one white worker for every ten (black) slaves. Two years later a similar law was adopted by St Kitts, with the additional provision that the French planters who still remained on the island should not be allowed to employ French servants outnumbering their British ones. The Jamaican Assembly similarly insisted on the employment of two whites for every ten blacks. Difficulties with labour supply meant that legislation demanding employment of white servants was unenforceable, but its enactment points to the constant preoccupation of the sugar-planters with the danger of slave disorder.

In both the British and the French possessions, then, this concern had produced a somewhat disordered corpus of slave law by the beginning of the eighteenth century, some of it summarised in codes similar to the Barbadian one we have already discussed. In the English case, this was promulgated by the colonial legislatures. In the French colonies, tht *Code Noir* was the work of the metropolitan government. Because it was intended to secure an existing situation, such legislation was not concerned with the moral justification of slaveholding, but primarily aimed to strengthen discipline by defining the power of the master and the white community over black slave labourers. Central to all legislation, of course, was the assumption that the slave was property. Although this did not remove the possibility of ambiguity in cases where his human nature emerged, it was from the slave's position *qua* chattel that the master's all but limitless power over him arose. For instance, no English colony admitted the slave's status as a legal agent. Whatever his suffering, he could never sue for redress against any man at all, far less against his own master. Custom also denied him the right to appear as a witness, except against one of his fellow-slaves, although it was only in the late

[17] Harlow, *History of Barbados*, pp. 326–7.

1780s that this was formally enacted in Barbados and elsewhere. In another direction, the slave never had legal protection for whatever little property he might amass, or even redress if his family bonds should be broken by the action of his master. His children, too, were inevitably placed within the slave status by the confirmation that the slave offspring followed the condition of the mother. Even slave life was left unprotected by law. Differential penalties for the murder or injury of slaves were reconfirmed by most of the English colonial legislatures in the late eighteenth century as 'meliorating' legislation designed to *improve* the status of the slave.[18] In no case were these penalties remotely similar in severity to those for killing a white freeman. Although it remains to be seen how far the severity of law might be eased by custom and daily usage, the British West Indian slave was effectively without rights.

For the safety of the planting community, however, colonial law confirmed that the rights of the master over his slave were all but boundless. In many ways, however, it did so by *refusing* to define the rights and obligations of bondsman and owner. Naturally, the master's right to sell a man designated as his chattel went unchallenged, irrespective of the family ties or personal preference of the slave. The right of punishment was restricted only by minor fines for murder and mayhem – and this only in so far as there was any probability of masters and overseers who proceeded to these lengths of brutality being convicted. As for the less extreme chastisement of whipping, it was only with the comparative enlightenment of the late eighteenth and early nineteenth centuries that the individual colonies restricted the number of lashes legal for punishment. An example of the new dispensation was the Grenada law of 1804 which generously cut the admitted maximum punishment given *at any one time* to thirty-nine strokes of the cart-whip.[19] The enforceability of such restrictions is doubtful, and in any case earlier slave law made no suggestion that the power of unlimited whipping should be curtailed. Because the physical power of the master or his overseer over the slave was unlimited in the custom of the seventeenth century, it remained unchecked by law then or in the heyday of British

[18] Stephen, *Slavery of the British West India Colonies Delineated*, 1 18–19.
[19] Cited ibid., 1 18 n.

West Indian slavery in the eighteenth century. Nor was there any attempt to curb the extent to which the master might make unreasonable demands on the work and time of his slave, though the need to have slaves raise adequate food in their own time prevented many from doing so. Yet rest was only a discretionary boon. It was only in the phase of 'meliorating' legislation in the early nineteenth century that some of the island assemblies agreed to the protection of the slave's right to work on his own behalf on Sundays. During the life of slavery, no attempt was ever made to put limits on the number of hours per day which the slave could be forced to labour in the fields. In fact the slaves of the English islands suffered as much for the areas where the law was silent about the planter's rights as they did from the positive legislation which tried to define their relationship with him.

The legislation of the late seventeenth century itself did much to restrict the liberties of the slave, and to set the seal on his depressed position. Aside from the relationship between the slave and his own individual master, where, as we have seen, colonial law, by default, left the former effectively without rights, the legislatures further cut back his liberty by a sharp definition of his relationship with white society as a whole. It was in this direction that the fear of slave insurrection became most clear. One clause of Jamaica's 'Consolidation Act' of 1788, summarising previous legislation, carefully proscribed black drunkenness, drumming, music and gathering for dances, which were all considered conducive to rebellion. It forbade slaves possessing powder or firearms, and specified a death penalty for any slave who struck a white person, 'provided such striking or conflict be not by command of his or their owners . . . or in the lawful defence of their owners' persons or goods'.[20] In the seventeenth century the law had in some ways been more severe: for the first blow, a sound whipping, followed for the second offence by having 'his or her Nose slit, and Face burnt in some Place'; for the third offence, death.[21] Though so essential for the maintenance of slave discipline, this denial of what they considered the natural right of

[20] *The Code of Laws for the Government of the Negro Slaves in the Island of Jamaica* (London, 1789) cc. xix–xxiii.

[21] *An Abridgement of the Laws in Force and Use in Her Majesty's Plantations* (London, 1704) p. 144.

self-defence was particularly horrifying to the abolitionists of the eighteenth and nineteenth centuries.[22] Nevertheless, the penalties even for resisting attack by a white person were re-enacted in the colonial meliorating laws of the decades before emancipation. The slave's helplessness on this level was not merely a matter of the total power of his own master. He was equally at the mercy of the whole white caste, since these penalties applied to the first white stranger whom he might be provoked to strike. As the abolitionist scholar James Stephen concluded, 'the negro . . . is in some respects a slave to every white man in the community'.[23]

In other ways, too, any vestige of liberty he might have had was narrowed still further for the benefit of the white community at large. Although the Barbados Assembly was denouncing Quaker attempts to evangelise Negroes as early as 1676, the British West India planters never went so far as later slaveholders in the United States in penalising those who attempted to teach slaves to read and write, or to understand Scripture, though this liberalism did not extend to welcoming the anti-slavery Baptist and Methodist missionaries of the nineteenth century. However, they were quick to emphasise that conversion to Christianity did not imply any right to emancipation. The Jamaica Assembly did this in 1696, as a step essential to ensure the permanence of the black slave's servitude.[24] Beyond this, the slave's condition was defined by a penal code which tried to secure his docility by stipulating much greater punishments than for the same crime committed by free men. Differential legislation emerged early in the history of slavery in the sugar islands. In 1688, for instance, Barbados, in 'An Act for the Governing of Negroes', announced that felonies of 'Negroes and other slaves' should be punished without the benefit of a jury, which 'being brutish Slaves, [they] deserve not, for the Baseness of their Condition'.[25] Where indentured servants who escaped were normally whipped if recaptured, most of the islands adopted legislation permitting the death penalty for runaway slaves and those who harboured them, though it is not clear how often this was enforced. Jamaica's 'Act for the More Effectual Punishing of Crimes Committed by

[22] Stephen, *Slavery of the British West India Colonies Delineated*, 1 187 ff.   [23] Ibid., p. 192.
[24] *An Abridgement of the Laws . . . in H. M. Plantations*, p. 144.
[25] *Acts of Assembly . . . Barbadoes*, p. 122.

Slaves', of 1717, stipulated that escaped slaves who remained away from their masters for more than thirty days should be punished by having one of their feet cut off.[26] No monstrosities of this sort had ever been used, even as a threat, in disciplining white servants. Petty restrictions were placed on the liberty of blacks to grow whatever they wished in any spare time at their disposal, to prevent their crops competing with those of the masters. In this way the little island of Montserrat, in 1736, called on its masters to prevent their slaves from cultivating indigo, cotton, ginger, cocoa and coffee.[27] Again, no such attempt was made, in law at least, to prevent white indentured servants from growing whatever they wished if they had the opportunity. In these ways, the condition of the slave was set apart even more sharply from that of the white inhabitants of the sugar islands.

Above all, however, the colonial legislatures concerned themselves with removing all opportunities for the slave population to plan or launch the servile rebellion which was the planters' constant and most harrowing fear. The right of assembly without permission was curtailed in all the islands, even where such assembly was for the purposes of amusement or worship. Dancing and excessive drinking were of particular concern to the legislatures, presumably because the excitement they generated could so easily be channelled into aggression against whites. Drumming and the sounding or possession of horns were also prohibited, because of the recognition that their potential in signalling would be so useful in case of a co-ordinated revolt. The planters were also aware of the importance of African religious cults as a basis for slave resistance. By 1760 Jamaica, for one, specified a death penalty for the observance of *obeah*, a cult as dangerous as voodoo.[28] Even certain punishments given to slaves were reserved for them alone, and unknown to the law of England as it applied to free white persons. For assault on whites, rape and rebellion, Barbadian and Jamaican history has no shortage of examples of court sentences involving burning alive, or gibbeting in chains.[29]

[26] *Acts of Assembly Passed in the Island of Jamaica, from 1681 to 1737* (London, 1738) p. 160.

[27] *Acts of Assembly Passed in the Island of Montserrat, from 1668 to 1740* (London, 1740) pp. 110–12.

[28] E. Long, *The History of Jamaica*, 3 vols (London, 1774) II 489.

[29] Patterson, *Sociology of Slavery*, p. 272; Harlow, *History of Barbados*, p. 326.

As a legal entity, the West Indian slave came to be firmly differentiated from the free population, though it should certainly not be assumed that all laws aimed at controlling slaves were consistently enforced. Indeed, one of the legislators' most pressing problems was to devise ways of preventing masters from allowing their slaves to endanger community security.

The similarities between the slave's status in the English North American and Caribbean colonies are more striking than the differences. The mainland and island colonists came from the same stock and shared common national preconceptions. Equally important, however, was the broad similarity in the economic history of all the English tropical colonies. Sugar dominated the islands in the seventeenth and eighteenth centuries, but this was also the great age of tobacco on the English mainland. The amount of capital required to equip a tobacco plantation was never as great as that required for sugar production, and the tobacco labour force was smaller. The demographic impact of tobacco cultivation in distorting the ratio between black and white population was never as great as that of sugar. Yet the demands of the two staples for land and labour were similar, qualitatively if not in degree. On the mainland, as in the Caribbean, one colony was the pioneer in defining the slave status in law and practice. In this sense, Virginia is the mainland equivalent of Barbados. Both emerged from the difficulties of settlement by finding a cash crop which ensured their stability by the 1640s – sugar in the one case, tobacco in the other. Both crops, with their vast profits, produced a pressing demand for labour. In both cases the result was the emergence of a black slavery which was accepted in custom and crystallising in law by the end of the seventeenth century. Their comparison gives little support to the Cuban essayist who has represented sugar as the feminine principle, or tobacco as the masculine, in the history of the Americas.[30] The relationship between Barbados and Virginia was not a contrapuntal but a parallel one.

Virginia's early troubles were not caused solely by shortage of labour. Its first successful settlement, planted by the London Company at Jamestown in 1607, very nearly foundered owing to the poor calibre of the colonists, their total incomprehension of

[30] F. D. Ortiz, *Cuban Counterpoint: Tobacco and Sugar*, trans. H. de Onís (1947; reprinted New York, 1970) pp. 3–93.

the difficulties of wilderness life, and poor lines of supply between England and the colony. In spite of the company reorganisation of 1609, it was only through the imposition of martial law that it succeeded in weathering the 'starving time' of 1609 to 1612. Even then the future was highly uncertain. No cash crop had been found to exchange for the necessities which the young colony required from Europe.[31] Virginia was simply a determined but struggling group of subsistence farmers with unenthusiastic London backers until the first planting of tobacco and the first arrival of Negro servants. Although it had been bedevilled by get-rich-quick gold-seekers in the early years of settlement, the granting of private ownership of 50 acres of land to each subscriber of £12 10s. after 1616, and the subsequent introduction of the headright system, produced a large number of men prepared to farm their own land, and to cast around for new expedients and crops to make it pay.[32] John Rolfe, the husband of the Pocahontas who we are told had saved John Smith's life from her father Powhatan, had first experimented with the growing of tobacco in Virginia in 1612. Incidentally, he used *Nicotianum tabacum*, a strain imported from Spanish Trinidad, not the coarse *Nicotiana rustica* of the Indians. His first shipment, grown without the aid of black slave labour, was sent off to London two years later. Tobacco cultivation came to be more and more attractive as the new fad caught on in England and prices rose.[33] It was increasing rapidly when the development of the colony was checked by the Indian massacre of 1622 directed by Powhatan's successor, Opechancanough, the uncle of Pocahontas. Meanwhile, James VI's early distrust of tobacco had been lessened by the delightful possibility of taxing it. One sideproduct of the massacre had been the death of the craftsmen whom the Virginia Company had employed to introduce new enterprises like glass-blowing and silk-raising into the colony, and the great profits to be made increasingly committed Virginia to tobacco cultivation. Prices were all the higher since Virginia's

[31] Andrews, *Colonial Period of American History*, 1 98 ff.; Craven, *Southern Colonies in the Seventeenth Century*, pp. 60–182.

[32] Andrews, *Colonial Period of American History*, 1 124–5. Cf. E. S. Morgan, 'The First American Boom: Virginia, 1618 to 1630', *William and Mary Quarterly*, 3rd ser., xxviii (1971) 169–98.

[33] J. C. Robert, *The Story of Tobacco in America* (1949; reprinted Chapel Hill, N.C., 1967) pp. 3–16.

climate made it possible to produce a quality of leaf much higher than the sodden and bitter crop of island competitors like Barbados. In spite of its doubts about pinning the colony to a single-crop cultivation, the company was able to improve its market in 1619 when the crown banned all production of tobacco within England and Wales. Even this did not break the competition of more skilled tobacco-growers. Though the Virginians could command better prices than the other English colonists, it took some time before they could produce a leaf as attractive to seasoned smokers as the Spanish. Even once the early experiments of drying leaves by spreading them on the ground were abandoned in favour of drying them on lines, imperfectly cured cargoes often spoiled before reaching the English consumer. Duties against superior Spanish tobacco could not quite push it out of the market, and indeed much of Virginia's coarse early crop was re-exported from England.

Nevertheless, the production of tobacco expanded apace – though certainly not at the spectacular growth rate of sugar cultivation in Barbados. Tobacco was the ideal staple for a colony intent on quick profits but without the skill or capital to embark on sugar cultivation. In the fertile Virginian soil its yield per acre was high. Its weight in proportion to value was low, which made for great convenience at a time when ships were small and shipping costs high.[34] In 1619 Virginia exported 20,000 lb.; the next year 40,000 lb.; in 1621, 55,000 lb.; in 1628, 500,000 lb.; in 1639 its production, together with that of the infant Maryland colony, amounted to 1·5 million lb. By 1688 the two colonies were exporting something over 18 million lb. of leaf.[35] This boom in tobacco provided the labour demand which brought black slaves pouring into the country – and at the same time it provided the capital which made it possible for the colonists to buy them. Although the process was slower, the result was the same as in Barbados and the other sugar islands. White indentured servants were gradually replaced by black slaves.

---

[34] A. O. Craven, *Soil Exhaustion as a Factor in the Agricultural History of Virginia and Maryland, 1606–1860* (Urbana, Ill., 1926) pp. 29–32. See also M. Jacobstein, *The Tobacco Industry in the United States* (New York, 1907) pp. 12–19; L. C. Gray, *History of Agriculture in the Southern United States to 1860*, 2 vols (Washington, 1933) I 223.

[35] Jacobstein, *Tobacco Industry in the U.S.*, p. 23.

Perhaps because tobacco-planters accumulated capital less rapidly than their brethren in the sugar business, Virginia's black population remained low in the early decades of settlement. Indeed, the colony's importations were restricted to small lots of black servants re-exported from the West Indies until the end of the seventeenth century.[36] Yet in the long run tobacco made the same labour demands as sugar. One authority computes that Virginia imported 53,500 black slaves from 1710 to 1769. They were carried in 889 ships, of which only 134 had sailed directly from Africa carrying complete cargoes of slaves. However, the proportion of black people carried by the latter group was high – a little over 45,000 in all. The black population of Virginia, unlike that of the West Indian islands, rose not only owing to the upward curve of importations, but also through its own natural increase. In 1715 Virginia's total population of 95,000 included 23,000, or 24·2 per cent, Negroes. In 1754 it supported 168,000 souls, of whom about 69,000, or 40·9 per cent, were black. A similar increase took place in the black population of Maryland, the neighbouring colony which was chartered in 1632. It had a 30 per cent black population at the Revolution, though only the southern or Eastern Shore part of the colony developed a plantation economy.[37] In fact, black population rose in all the mainland colonies throughout the seventeenth and eighteenth centuries at a rate out of all proportion to the numbers of men and women brought to North America by the slave-ships. It had just passed the half-million mark at the time of the Revolution, though the number of blacks who landed in all of English-speaking North America up to 1780 seems to have been under 200,000, and probably well under it.

This rise in black population was not as striking as that of the Caribbean colonies, and it did not involve so total an imbalance between blacks and whites as, say, eighteenth-century Jamaica. Nevertheless, it was accompanied by a similar hardening of the Negroes' position as servant to that of slave, and by the drafting of a body of law designed to ensure the discipline of the dangerous and terrifying servile class. In Virginia, as in the islands, it

[36] Curtin, *Atlantic Slave Trade*, pp. 118–19.
[37] Figures from ibid., pp. 118–19, 142; *Historical Statistics of the United States*, p. 756; E. Donnan (ed.), *Documents Illustrative of the History of the Slave Trade to America*, 4 vols (Washington, 1930–5) IV 175–234.

was the colonists themselves who defined the status of the black slave. At first they drifted towards the assumption that he should have the hereditary status of a chattel, and laid down the parameters of his treatment by custom. They also developed a body of written law on slavery. Nevertheless, as the rise in black population was slower here, so the emergence of a rigid slave status took longer on the mainland. There is little doubt that the cultural background of the Virginian colonists provided all the preconditions for discrimination, and that this emerged as soon as the twenty 'negars' arrived in Jamestown in 1619. Doubtless, they and other early black arrivals were treated worse than other servants who happened to be white, had worse terms of service, and were generally regarded with distrust by English settlers, whether bond or free.[38] For instance, the Virginia law of 1662 which imposed twice as big a fine for fornication between blacks and whites as for fornication between two whites shows the depth of the legislators' pre-existing prejudice. This is all the more striking since the Assembly had been punishing miscegenation long before this, as it did in 1630 when it sentenced a hapless colonist to be 'soundly whipped' for 'defiling his body in lying with a negro'.[39] Before he became a slave, the Negro in the British mainland colonies was treated as an inferior, from his first arrival in Virginia and from their inception in the others. By mid-century, moreover, the mainland settlers had had plenty of opportunity to adopt the prejudices and fears of their countrymen in Bermuda and the West Indies.[40] This prejudice certainly made it possible for the colonists to accept the economically convenient transition of black servants to the status of slaves, and eventually to confirm this transition by law.

[38] Degler, in *C.S.S.H.*, II 49–66. The following examples are drawn largely from the citations in this paper. The best authority on North American slave law as a whole is still J. C. Hurd, *The Law of Freedom and Bondage in the United States*, 2 vols (Boston, 1858), though this does not deal fully with the colonial period. Court decisions on American slavery are collected in H. T. Catterall, *Judicial Cases Concerning American Slavery and the Negro*, 5 vols (Washington, 1926–37).

[39] W. W. Hening, *The Statutes at Large: Being a Collection of All the Laws of Virginia*, 13 vols (Richmond, Va., 1809–23) II 170; I 146.

[40] Degler, in *C.S.S.H.*, II 53–6. See also W. D. Jordan, 'The Influence of the West Indies on the Origins of New England Slavery', *William and Mary Quarterly*, 3rd ser., XVIII (1961) 243–50; S. Ames, *Studies of the Virginia Eastern Shore in the Seventeenth Century* (Richmond, Va., 1940) pp. 101–10.

This process was not a speedy one – nothing like so much so as in the islands. As early as 1636, that is, nine years after the first settlement, the Governor of Barbados had provided that Negroes should serve their masters for life unless a specific agreement was made to the contrary. The earliest date at which there is evidence for lifetime servitude in Virginia is 1640, and even this is indirect. Lifetime service is not mentioned directly in Virginia statutes until 1660, that is, forty-one years after the arrival of the first blacks in Jamestown. This slowness of development tells nothing about the absence of prejudice, and it is closely related to the relatively small black population. But it is nevertheless an important point that it was perfectly possible, at least for a limited time, for blacks to work in Virginia tobacco cultivation without being formally reduced to the status of chattel slaves. Exactly the same was true of Maryland, where the first black immigrants came to the colony in 1642. The first oblique reference to their serving for life was not until 1663, and a year later the Assembly produced 'An Act Concerning Negroes and other Slaves', declaring that Negroes should serve *durante vita*.[41]

The position of the black slaves of Virginia was formally defined in the code of slave law promulgated in 1705.[42] Much of this, however, was simply summarising and strengthening the piecemeal legislation of the previous century. For instance, it had soon become clear not only that the black servant would remain in bondage throughout his life, but also that his status as a slave should be hereditary. This heritage was to be passed down through the mother, thus ensuring that even children of a free father, whether black or white, would remain in slavery. There are definite examples of black servants being sold with their posterity in the 1640s and 1650s. It is clear that by 1660 it was accepted that the children of blacks bound to serve for life should become the property of their parents' master. The Virginia law of 1662 concerning descent of status did not trouble to confirm that the offspring of a slave retained the slave status. Its

[41] J. R. Brackett, *The Negro in Maryland* (Baltimore, 1889) p. 26; *Maryland Archives*, I 489, 533–4. The slow legal and judicial development of slavery in Virginia and Maryland does not imply acceptance of the position that anti-black prejudice was absent until it was created by slavery. Cf. Handlin and Handlin, in *W.M.Q.*, 3rd ser., VII 199–222.

[42] Hening, *Statutes at Large*, III 447–62.

concern was with attempting to prevent fornication between the races, and with specifying the status of infants who were born of one free and one unfree parent. It declared that the offspring should always follow the status of the mother, the provision that Roman law had passed on to the Spanish and Portuguese empires. This became the general rule in the English colonies, and it ensured that not only blacks but also mulattoes and the descendants of mulattoes should remain in slavery.[43] Though Virginia's blacks were few until the end of the century, their freedom was also circumscribed by measures similar to those of the sugar islands, designed to minimise the risk of rebellion and general indiscipline. In the matter of bearing arms, a Virginia law of 1640 exhorted heads of households to find weapons for themselves and their dependants, but specifically stated that this did not apply to Negroes.[44] It may be suggested, however, that this is not a case where custom was being confirmed by law, but rather one where legislators felt called upon to deplore the *opposite* custom for the sake of the colony's security. The conclusion may actually be that in many families, and undoubtedly in some families, blacks were still being allowed to carry weapons in 1640.[45] In 1680, however, the legislature made a more systematic attempt to preserve the colony from slave revolt. Strict punishments were prescribed for any Negro, whether free or unfree, found carrying any sort of weapon. The black slave was also forbidden to leave his master's plantation without a pass, and above all to 'lift his hand' against any 'Christian'. Power over the slave was no longer confined to the master, but extended to the whole white community, free and indentured. Finally, the law authorised anyone who met with resistance in trying to recapture a fugitive slave to kill him.[46] In this last provision, the 1680 law was continuing the trend towards total power of the master over the slave, at the same time as the slave himself was descending into a condition of rightlessness. In 1669 the Assembly had effectively given the master *carte blanche* to murder his slaves. They blandly remarked that the black slave's transgressions

---

[43] Ibid., II 170.

[44] 'Acts of General Assembly, Jan. 6, 1639–40', *William and Mary Quarterly*, 2nd ser., IV (1924) 147.

[45] Cf. Degler, in *C.S.S.H.*, II 49–66.

[46] Hening, *Statutes at Large*, II 481–2.

could not be punished by extension of his term, which was already lifelong. Only 'violent meanes' could be used to curb their 'obstinacy'. Accordingly, they observed that it should not be a case of felony if a master should accidentally kill his slave or, as they put it, if the slave 'by the extremity of his correction should chance to die'.[47] This law capped the totality of the master's power over his slave, though in fairness to the Virginians it should be mentioned that it was not as sweeping as the corresponding enactment in the newer colony of South Carolina. Probably under Barbadian influence, its Fundamental Constitutions announced that every free master should have 'absolute power and authority over his negro slaves'.

As a response to increasing numbers of slaves arriving in Virginia at the beginning of the eighteenth century, the great slave code of 1705 restated the police regulations against illegal assembly, travelling without a pass, escape, and striking white persons, though a recent masterly study implies that the colony felt sufficiently secure from the 'inward-directed' resistance of unassimilated slaves not to enforce these regulations fully.[48] The code went on to attack the civil rights of free Negroes. They were denied the right to bear witness in court proceedings against any but other blacks, and it was announced, perhaps somewhat unnecessarily, that 'no Negro, molatto, or Indian shall presume to take upon him, act in or exercise any office, ecclesiastic, civil, or military'. Virginia had now formally defined the relationship between the races and the relationship between master and slave. Her slave code was not markedly different from the contemporaneous laws of Barbados or Jamaica, or from the nineteenth-century codes of Black Belt cotton states like Alabama. If there was a difference, it was in the absence of the later insistence that the slaves should be denied tuition in the Gospel and in reading and writing, and in the absence of the more lurid punishments specified elsewhere for indiscipline.

England's other North American colonies built their slave systems in much the same way as Virginia. In the neighbouring tobacco colony of Maryland slavery developed at a comparable pace, though black population was lower and concentrated in the

[47] Ibid., II 270.
[48] Ibid., III 447–62. Cf. G. W. Mullin, *Flight and Rebellion: Slave Resistance in Eighteenth Century Virginia* (New York, 1972).

Eastern Shore area. For a short period slavery was recognised in custom alone, it was then referred to obliquely in casual and piecemeal legislation, and in the end was defined by a series of formal statutes passed at the very end of the seventeenth century. In New York evolution was similar, although the earliest contacts between the races there took place in the period when the colony was in the possession of the Dutch. Its slave law was summarised in 1712 in what is certainly the most brutal of the Northern colonial codes, drawn up as a panic reaction to a major slave revolt which led to the death of nine whites – and incidentally to the execution of twenty-one blacks, by burning, breaking on the wheel or gibbeting.[49] In East and West Jersey development was also relatively slow, partly because of the disorganised nature of the early settlements there. However, the Jerseys eventually came to have a higher black population than any other Northern colony, and they adopted a slave code similar to the New York one in 1714, again in response to fears of insurrection. In the colonies founded at later dates the delineation of the slave's status was more abrupt. In South Carolina, for instance, the London and Barbadian businessmen behind the settlement intended from the first to import blacks as slaves in the Barbadian sense. Black population rose sharply – it almost equalled white population by 1708 – and in its early years the colony produced written laws defining their position along the usual lines, but more stringently than in any of the other colonies. In 1722 this law was summarised to become the most severe of all the colonial slave codes. As in the islands, legislators were obsessed with the danger of a large black labour force. In North Carolina, where there was no boom in rice cultivation, poverty prevented the planters moving on to slave labour at once. Negroes there did not pass through any transitional period when their status was uncertain, and they were also judged by the 1722 code until and probably even after the colonies separated in 1729.[50] In Georgia, not founded until 1732, slavery was introduced gradually but in its mature form by hard-headed settlers unwilling to abstain from slave-holding as their directors in London wished. As for Pennsylvania, Massachusetts and Connecticut, though none of them had any-

---

[49] K. Scott, 'The Slave Insurrection in New York in 1712', *New York Historical Quarterly*, XLV (1961).

[50] Sirmans, in *J.S.H.*, XXVIII 466–73.

thing like the number of slaves held in New York, the Jerseys or the Southern colonies, development was again slow, and laws adopting many of the features of the Southern ones appeared at the end of the seventeenth and the beginning of the eighteenth centuries. For instance, Massachusetts announced in 1703 that after nine at night no Negro or mulatto servant or slave should be out in the streets without specific permission from his master, as part of its increasing discrimination against a group hitherto treated relatively well.[51] Little Rhode Island, which would eventually use genuine gang slavery in the farms around Narrangansett Bay, in spite of its early prohibition of slaveholding, also established curfew for Negroes and Indians in 1703.[52] In Pennsylvania the legal provisions defining the position of the slave were not completed until 1726. Prior to that there had been more concern with keeping down Negro population by putting prohibitive duties on the slave trade to the colony – primarily as a security measure, not a humanitarian one.[53] Like New Jersey, New York and Delaware, Pennsylvania adopted separate courts to try Negroes, so that they did not have the benefit of regular jury trial. By the first quarter of the eighteenth century, black slavery had been defined in law as well as accepted in custom throughout the English colonies.

In none of these settlements did the slaves themselves leave any written record of their reaction to slavery. We know far too little about the extent to which these early black Americans retained the language, religion and culture of their native Africa. For the seventeenth and part of the eighteenth century the answer to this question depends in a great degree on inference from the later cultural history of black people, together with the deduction

[51] R. C. Twombley and R. H. Moore, 'Black Puritan: The Negro in Seventeenth Century Massachusetts', *William and Mary Quarterly*, 3rd ser., XXIV (1967) 224–42; L. J. Greene, *The Negro in Colonial New England* (New York, 1942) pp. 125–41. There is also a convenient summary of Northern slave law in A. Zilversmit, *The First Emancipation: The Abolition of Slavery in the North* (Chicago, 1967) pp. 12–24.

[52] *Records of the Colony of Rhode Island and Providence Plantations*, 10 vols (Providence, R.I., 1856–62) III 492.

[53] W. E. B. DuBois, *The Suppression of the African Slave Trade to the United States of America, 1638–1870* (1896; reprinted New York, 1969) pp. 22–3. The general thesis of this work is that the motive behind all colonial attempts to restrict the slave trade was fear of the insecurity of control over a large servile population.

which can be made from the study of the West African cultures themselves.[54] Again, beyond the fact that they loathed slavery and resisted it whenever they could, it is difficult to chart the first slaves' exact impressions of the new world to which they came and the white society into which they were thrust. Not a great deal is known about the thought of American Negroes until the late eighteenth and nineteenth centuries, and by that time acculturation had gone a long way, and African 'survivals' were undoubtedly fewer and weaker than at times when the proportion of slaves actually born in Africa was higher. Until the nineteenth century, too, apart from tangential evidence, the history of the black slaves must regrettably be reconstructed from sources written by members of the dominant white master class or their sympathisers. Even for the seventeenth century it is possible to paint a tolerably accurate picture of the tasks of black people, and also of some aspects of their day-to-day lives. The greatest danger here is not in lack of evidence but in over-generalisation. In the last resort the slave's life was governed by the completely individual interaction between the way in which his master chose to treat him and his own reaction to this treatment. But there were also differences in the lot of groups of slaves along broad regional lines. With the exceptions of the few areas like Narragansett Bay where they were present in large numbers, slaves in the Northern mainland colonies were in a different position from their fellows in the South and in the Caribbean. This does not spring from any difference in the cultural matrix of slave societies. It is linked with the differences in the function of labourers in a mixed economy and in a plantation economy producing a single tropical staple – and no less with the scale of discipline problems caused by the size of the servile population. By the same token, it is clear that population level affected the strength of black culture, which depended for its vitality on the presence of substantial numbers of blacks frequently in touch with one another. In this way the number of Africanisms still

[54] We do not yet have as full a study of eighteenth-century slave life as the principally nineteenth-century work of J. Blassingame, *The Slave Community: Plantation Life in the Ante-Bellum South* (New York, 1972), though many of its brilliant insights apply to the slave experience from the seventeenth century onwards. See also Mullin, *Flight and Rebellion*, pp. 34–47.

central to black life – and these would provide much of the basis for resistance to whites, as masters throughout the Americas recognised in their obsession with stamping out *obeah* and voodoo – were fewer in South Carolina than in Jamaica, fewer in Virginia than in South Carolina, and fewer still in New England than in Virginia. It was because of his very cultural loneliness that the slave in the Northern colonies clung less to the heritage of Africa than his fellows in, say, the Sea Islands of South Carolina or, to take a non-English example, in Haiti. Again, the economic roles he was called to play were much more varied than in the plantation colonies.[55] As a free man in eighteenth-century Boston, New York or Philadelphia, the Negro might and did achieve success on his own behalf as a craftsman or shopkeeper, or in country areas as a small farmer. As a slave also, he had a great range of tasks and duties. In effect he might do any work done by a white servant – most often as farm labourer, artisan or domestic, but in many cases also as a highly skilled craftsman. Benjamin Banneker, the black Philadelphia clockmaker, happened to be free, but he was doing work which could equally well have been open to substantial numbers of blacks held in slavery in the North. The kind of diversified occupations open to Northern slaves brought them constant white contacts, to an extent which eroded cultural differences much faster than the experience of plantation field slaves whose relations with the white world were minimal. The Northern slave shared the central experience of discrimination and of submission to the absolute will of the master, but his case was one very much apart from the men and women in thrall to the plantations. In fact, plantation cultivation is central to the black history of the Americas. The difference between the slave experience in England's Northern and Southern mainland colonies is much greater than that between these Southern colonies and other plantation colonies anywhere else in the New World.

There is a core of similarity in the lives of the slaves in the mainland and island colonies of the English. Such differences as there are again lead back to the economic function of the plantations in each individual colony, and to the demographic balance between black and white. Indeed, the latter was one of the main factors which moulded the characteristics of slavery in each part

[55] Greene, *The Negro in Colonial New England*, pp. 100–23.

of the Americas. It was because of the enormously high, and correspondingly dangerous, black population of the English sugar islands that slave discipline there was even more savage than on the mainland, and that slave culture remained stronger. In most of the colonies the routine of plantation life was astonishingly quick in the laying down. This is not to say, however, that by any means all slaves worked on large farms, or as members of large work-forces, even in the so-called plantation colonies. Particularly in the British mainland, some were held as city slaves, hired out as craftsmen or domestics. By the nineteenth century, slaves were filling an enormous range of industrial and commercial occupations in the American South.[56] A much more important group in the eighteenth century were the numbers of blacks who did not work on true plantations, but belonged to small planters or yeomen owning anything from one to a dozen slaves. Such minor slaveholders were scattered throughout the South. In Virginia, excluded from the economies of scale which would bring self-sufficiency and success, they drew their supplies and sold their crop through the small élite of large-scale plantation-owners on the tidewater. Even as late as 1860, when holdings had if anything consolidated more than in the previous century, one in four of America's slaves lived on plantations employing ten slaves or fewer. At the 1790 census the average holding of slaves in the principal plantation counties of Virginia and Maryland, where holdings were presumably largest, was only between 8·5 and 13.[57] Small farms were less plentiful on the English islands, but they were present even there, wherever smallholders had managed to hold out against the sugar frontier. The same was true of the French islands, though there many of the smaller landowners tended to be Creoles rather than Frenchmen. Being in so small a group had incalculable effects on slave personality and the development of black culture, but even there the life of the slave

[56] T. W. Tate, Jr, *The Negro in Eighteenth Century Williamsburg* (Charlottesville, Va., 1965) pp. 56–78; R. C. Wade, *Slavery in the Cities* (New York, 1964); R. S. Starobin, *Industrial Slavery in the Old South* (New York, 1970); Mullin, *Flight and Rebellion*, pp. 83–123.

[57] K. M. Stampp, *The Peculiar Institution: Slavery in the Ante-Bellum South* (New York, 1956) p. 31; U. B. Phillips, *American Negro Slavery* (1918; reprinted Baton Rouge, La., 1966, with an Introduction by E. D. Genovese) p. 84. On the special characteristics of eighteenth-century Virginia, see Mullin, *Flight and Rebellion*, passim.

was dominated by the same body of law and by the same rhythms of the agricultural year. For the majority of slaves, daily work had great similarities in all the colonies. On small farms, though the slave was likely to become a jack-of-all-trades and general dog's-body, his principal tasks were connected with raising crops. From the earliest times, whenever slaves were employed in large numbers, there appeared a division between those slaves who had domestic tasks and the field-workers. This tendency was no less marked in England's island colonies, where domestic servants multiplied, although absentee ownership should have meant there was less need for servants to look after a great house of the sort which emerged on the larger estates of the mainland.[58] Very large plantations also had their own specialist craftsmen – smiths, carpenters, boilermen and the like. As for the field slaves, whatever the staple, they were organised for gang cultivation, often in separate groups according to age, strength and labour needed. Their tasks were of necessity simple, boring and repetitive. Beyond this, however, the uniformity of slave routine depended on the staple under cultivation. For the English colonies of the seventeenth and eighteenth centuries the great dividing line was between the tobacco estates of Virginia, Maryland and North Carolina, and the rice and indigo plantations of South Carolina and the sugar plantations of the islands.

The care of tobacco was a year-round engagement. After sowing in carefully prepared beds in the late winter, the little plants were normally transplanted in May, to newly hoed land – and about a quarter of it newly cleared and broken. It then had to be hoed and weeded constantly until maturity, and it also required topping of surplus leaves and constant vigilance against insects, particularly hornworm. The crop was cut in August, and dried for some six weeks before being laboriously packed into hogsheads and transported to the waterfront for collection by English ships. Slaves were also used extensively in the constant work of transportation and estate maintenance. It was normally calculated that a prime slave was required for the cultivation of each

[58] Patterson, *Sociology of Slavery*, p. 58. On plantation organisation in the United States, the best introduction is Stampp, *The Peculiar Institution*, though this generalises from the nineteenth century. See also Gray, *History of Agriculture in the Southern United States*, I 462–80, 529–67; Phillips, *American Negro Slavery*, pp. 228–343.

three acres of tobacco plants, a lower figure than the slave per two acres needed for sugar. As prices boomed, masters added to their slaves and brought new land under cultivation, thus sealing their own eventual doom by worsening over-production and exhausting the land at their disposal, which they seldom troubled to fertilise properly, at least until the nineteenth century.[59] Since each plantation at least aimed at self-sufficiency, any time remaining to slaves was spent in raising crops and livestock for subsistence, either for the collective use of the plantation or, less often, on little plots assigned to each slave family. The privileges allowed to the slaves within the limits set by the hectic labouring routine of the tobacco year depended primarily on their individual master, though he too was influenced by the custom of neighbouring plantations and his slaves' perceptions of them.

For the seventeenth century, when so many of the workers on the mainland colonies, even Virginia and Maryland, were white indentured servants, it is difficult to separate the treatment and working conditions of blacks from those of the whole society.[60] The picture of slave life is very hazy until black population rises. Living conditions naturally varied according to the size of farm owned by the master – from the tiny holding with one slave on the piedmont to the great plantations of the tidewater. The smaller unit was unlikely to create the conditions for black servants to be separated in diet and accommodation from other servants or even from the master's family. Accommodation was spartan, work hard and diet coarse for all.[61] Early slaves, like the early white settlers, suffered severely from unbalanced diet and the ravages of malaria and typhoid. Even on the largest plantations it was only in the eighteenth century – sometimes not even then – that the concept of the 'quarters' emerged, as the numbers of slaves rose and they were more completely separated from other servants. Prior to the influx of black population after 1700, there must have been very few slaves who did not eat and live with unfree whites, or even with free ones. Thereafter, however,

[59] Gray, *History of Agriculture in the Southern United States*, I 213–35.

[60] A. E. Smith, *Colonists in Bondage: White Servitude and Convict Labor in America, 1607–1776* (Chapel Hill, N.C., 1947); R. B. Morris, *Government and Labor in Early America* (New York, 1946).

[61] See E. S. Morgan, *Virginians at Home: Family Life in the Eighteenth Century* (Williamsburg, Va., 1952) pp. 51–72; Mullin, *Flight and Rebellion*, pp. 34–82.

the larger estates did move on to the practice already adopted in the sugar colonies, of having their slaves live in cabins separate from the white household. Then, too, it became customary for them to supplement the rations issued from the plantation's common stocks, and its imports from outside, by growing vegetables on their personal plots – sometimes with such success as to be able to make a modest profit by selling produce in the nearest community. Economies of scale also dictated the buying of coarse food in bulk for the slaves as a whole. While white diet by and large improved, the slave's food eventually became fixed on maize, beans and the cheapest cuts of pork, supplemented by the few vegetables the slaves grew themselves. Alcohol, the principal tonic of the white colonists, was a holiday pleasure or a forbidden one for the blacks. The natural results were dietetic deficiencies worse than those of the white population, and a resulting proneness to disease.

Yet dismal diet, appalling housing and crushing labour never entirely eradicated the slave's personality. Much of his own black culture remained to him. In the eighteenth-century tobacco colonies, such holidays as there were were times at which the slave population gathered for recreation and religious observance which was partly and sometimes wholly of African origin. By the time separate slave quarters emerged, the same was true of the talk and general social life which went on among the slaves in what time was left after the working day.[62] This side of slave life the master class could not touch and, as we shall see, it became the basis for vigorous resistance, direct and indirect, active and passive, to the plantation regime. Nevertheless, liberal romantics to the contrary, it may be that the sheer physical hardship of the slave's existence was a much greater burden than the formal loss of liberty itself. Concern over liberty, except for exceptional persons, is very much a luxury for men and women who are on the verge of starvation.

In South Carolina, as in the sugar islands, the development of a separate slave society came faster. The colony was founded with the stated intention of using slave labour. As we have seen,

[62] See M. J. Herskovits, *The Myth of the Negro Past*, 2nd ed. (Boston, 1958). On the problem of African survivals in the New World as a whole, see also R. Bastide, *African Civilizations in the New World*, trans. P. Green (New York, 1972).

its charter specifically reassured immigrants from the West Indies that their power over their servants would be left unchallenged. Hopeful settlers did come to South Carolina, mainly pushed out by the expansion of large-scale sugar production in Barbados. Their influence on the colony was great, but it nevertheless became very much a special case among England's tropical possessions, similar in the provisions of its slave law to the islands, but different in the work routine and structure of its slave society. The individualism of its development was increased by its isolation, bounded as it was by swamp and forest to the north and the threat of the Spanish and Indians to the south. Its crops, too, were different. Although founded in 1670, low population, difficult terrain and conservative proprietary government gave Carolina little real prosperity until the 1730s. At this point the colony went over to the large-scale production of rice and indigo, then the principal source for blue dyestuffs. Success with these crops brought for South Carolina and its central port, Charleston, riches much greater even than those of successful Virginia tobacco dynasties like the Byrds and the Carters. During the period from 1740 to the Revolution, rice exports grew threefold, indigo exports fourfold. Units of production were moderate in size. A prime field-hand farming rice was expected to produce about 2,250 lb. of rice per season, and a suitable working size for a plantation was anything between ten and twenty slaves. However, it was possible to operate large numbers of such small plantations, and some of the greatest magnates had enormous holdings where rice farming was by no means the only activity. By the Revolution, the élite of Charleston was the richest in North America, with huge personal fortunes like that of Henry Middleton, who died with total holdings of 50,000 acres and 800 slaves.[63]

[63] On the colonial history of South Carolina, see C. Bridenbaugh, *Myths and Realities: Societies of the Colonial South* (1952; reprinted New York, 1970) pp. 54–118; Craven, *Southern Colonies in the Seventeenth Century*, pp. 310–59; F. J. Klingberg, *An Appraisal of the Negro in Colonial South Carolina* (Washington, 1941). Slavery in rice and indigo cultivation is also covered in Phillips, *American Negro Slavery*, pp. 87–97; Gray, *History of Agriculture in the Southern United States*, I 277–97. There is a good sketch of this society as it had emerged in the early nineteenth century in W. W. Frehling, *Prelude to Civil War: The Nullification Controversy in South Carolina, 1816–1836* (1965; reprinted New York, 1968) pp. 7–24.

One reason for the accumulation of such wealth was the extent to which the cultivation of indigo and rice complemented one another. On a large estate it was possible to get maximum return on investment by growing both. Where rice grew on swampy, low ground, indigo throve on light upland soils which would otherwise have been useless. In the early spring, when the rice had been flooded for the first time and was left to take care of itself, slaves could be employed tending indigo, or in gathering the pitch, timber and other naval supplies which the colony also exported from its highland areas. For the rest of the year, it is true, they were principally occupied with the rice crop. Raking and removing old stubble was done in the winter, sowing early in the year. After the first flooding was drained at the beginning of the summer, the young plants had to be constantly weeded and hoed during their second and third floodings, until cropping in September. After the harvest the slaves were also responsible for threshing, cleaning and drying the rice, and packing it in barrels for shipment to England. These tasks were seasonally more varied than in the tobacco or sugar colonies, but there were compensating disadvantages for the Carolina rice slaves. Rice was cultivated in hot, swampy lowlands where they were constantly exposed to infection with malaria and other tropical fevers. Again, it required extensive work standing knee-deep in water, which brought constant risk of chills, inflammation and circulatory diseases. The housing and dietetic conditions of slavery were not markedly different in Carolina from the islands: they too had the monotonous diet of salt fish, corn and occasionally fat pork, but discipline was probably harsher. The severity of the Carolina slave code, and its similarity to that of Barbados, has already been noted. This was closely connected to the density of black population in the colony's rural areas. In 1750 it had a total ratio of 39,000 blacks to 25,000 whites; in 1780, 97,000 to 83,000; and in the rice-growing areas of the coast and on the Sea Islands, local concentrations of black population were much higher.[64] This in itself explains the Carolinian horror of revolts, and the correspondingly harsh treatment of slaves in law and practice. However, though large plantations were the exception rather than the rule, the high slave population also had important results for black communal life. In South Carolina and the nearby

[64] *Historical Statistics of the United States*, p. 756.

areas of Georgia, particularly on the Sea Islands, survivals in African folklore, music, religion and sculpture are commoner than in any other part of North America. The same was true as late as the Civil War, when Northern missionaries flooded into the Sea Islands of South Carolina to begin work with the freedmen. They found their charges had an almost total lack of links with their own Western culture, a patois of their own almost unintelligible to New Englanders, and a series of African beliefs and habits which they regrettably dismissed as collective superstition, childishness or brutalisation.[65]

In the sugar islands also, black population was higher and the period between the arrival of the first blacks and their becoming the dominant labour force as slaves was shorter than in the tobacco colonies. In spite of this difference, however, the legal basis of slavery was dissimilar only in degree in the various British colonies. What gave slave life in the islands its characteristics were the requirements of sugar. First, it absorbed land with a totality which left little space for local raising of provisions, though other cash crops, like cotton, indigo and coffee, were grown on a small scale throughout the colonial period. The staple imports for slave consumption were peas, beans and salt fish from New England. Plantains and yams were grown locally, but the sugar structure removed the possibility of any but the most efficient master's growing adequate crops for his own slaves. They were thus left to grow fresh provisions as best they might – which effectively meant giving over Sunday or any other leisure time to gardening – or, more commonly, to do without them. The regular work of sugar-planting – hoeing, weeding and ratooning, especially the first – was physically shattering. Again, the yearly routine of sugar cultivation was as busy as that for tobacco, but the demand for labour at cropping time much greater. It was not unusual for blacks to work an eighteen-hour day over the harvest, because of the pressure to boil cane before it dried – and much of this labour involved tending sugar vats and their fires in tropical heat. The gathering and processing of the crop is vividly described in Grainger's heroic poem, 'The Sugar Cane', in spite of its Augustan detachment from the brutal treatment of blacks:

[65] W. L. Rose, *Rehearsal for Reconstruction: The Port Royal Experiment* (1964; reprinted New York, 1967) pp. 91–101.

The Negro-train, with placid looks, survey
Thy fields, which full perfection have attain'd,
And pant to wield the bill.[66]

Apart from the danger to health involved in this itself, industrial injuries were frequent in accidents with the boiling and
crushing machinery. With a working day of this length, given the
fact that the slave was often expected to prepare his own food,
the tendency was to skimp on cooking which in turn resulted in
further malnutrition and increased ease of infection. Certainly,
the large black population of the sugar islands meant that the
slave's culture retained more strength than on the mainland, but
then again, the sugar routine and generally larger plantation
units increased regimentation and left less time for him to live
any life of his own. Family life was less strong than on the mainland, owing among other things to the high mortality of males
and the low proportion of female slaves brought to the islands.
The rapid advance of the sugar frontier increased the chance of
being arbitrarily sold to another plantation or another island. In
the boom sugar economy, the psychological oppression of the
slave was probably much greater than on the tobacco estates,
quite apart from physical hardship. Added to this was the West
Indian practice of absentee ownership, which meant that blacks
were often directly under the control of an overseer whose only
concern was to present a good crop return to his employer in
England, often irrespective of the cost in slave life and health or
long-term investment prospects. There is little profit in deciding
whether slavery in one place is 'worse' than slavery in another,
but the very form of the society geared to producing sugar goes
far to explain the reason why the slaveowners of Jamaica or
Martinique, unlike those of Virginia or even South Carolina,
could not maintain the population of their bondsmen. Given
roughly similar legal codes and cultural backgrounds, even given

[66] J. Grainger, 'The Sugar Cane', III 96–8. On methods of sugar cultivation, see Deerr, *History of Sugar;* B. Edwards, *The History, Civil and
Commercial, of the British Colonies in the West Indies*, 2 vols (Dublin,
1793) II 195–296; F. W. Pitman, 'Slavery on British West India Plantations
in the Eighteenth Century', *Journal of Negro History*, XI (1926) 584–668;
M. Craton and J. Walvin, *A Jamaica Plantation: The History of Worthy
Park, 1670–1970* (London, 1970). Jamaican cultivation is concisely covered
in Patterson, *Sociology of Slavery*, pp. 52–69, 216–83.

similar boom conditions, the human wastage of sugar cultivation was simply greater than that of tobacco. This was true not only of the English colonies but also of the French, where the sugar boom not only kept slave population static, but actually brought a net annual decrease.[67]

The connection between the booming of market demand and the hardship of the slave is a constant one in the history of the black Americas. The legal structure of slavery in the various parts of the New World does not seem to have made much difference to the day-to-day lot of the Negro. In the last resort his treatment was dictated by the interaction between the discipline problems created by the black–white population ratio, and the conditions of life and labour created by the staple he cultivated. Whatever the staple, the load of work demanded of him became more crushing as market demand increased, and the prospect of quick profits to be made by over-exploitation of his slaves became more attractive to the master. His demands were not dictated by culture, religion or law. They were more persistent, and the slave's hardship correspondingly greater, when the market for the staple of each colony was expansive. In this way there are similarities between slave societies at similar boom stages of economic development: between the mining slavery of sixteenth-century Spanish America; the sugar slavery of eighteenth-century Jamaica and Martinique, or nineteenth-century Cuba; the coffee slavery of nineteenth-century Brazil; and the cotton slavery of the nineteenth-century United States. Slavery was moulded much more by the function it fulfilled than by the national peculiarities of its slaveholders, and it is much easier to compare different slave societies by grouping them functionally or demographically than along the lines between the rule of different countries or religions.

In this sense, black slavery in the Americas can be seen as a single institution. By the early eighteenth century it had been formalised in the possessions of all the major colonising powers. Its detailed legal underpinning varied from colony to colony, but in all cases it ensured the master's complete and absolute power over the slave, at least in circumstances where he chose to use it. In this common power lay the potential for a common

[67] Curtin, *Atlantic Slave Trade*, pp. 75–82; Pitman, in *J.N.H.*, xi 629–649.

development. From the eighteenth century onwards, the evolution of slavery would depend on the rise and fall of demand for the staples being produced in each colony. Rising demand normally meant rising slave population, and a cumulative depression of the slave's condition. At the same time, the profits spawned by mature slavery revolutionised society throughout the Atlantic world. Slaveholding and slave-trading not only produced new élites in the Americas, but also in the Old World and in the African societies of the Guinea Coast.

4 Slave-Trading, Slaveholding, and Atlantic Society

ONE day George III, taking the air at Weymouth with his Prime Minister, passed a West Indian planter driven in a coach and six of considerably greater magnificence than his own. In a fit of envy, he is said to have turned to his companion and snarled: 'All *that* sugar! How are the duties, eh, Pitt. . . ?'[1] The stereotype of the rich and usually vulgar West Indian is a well-known one in English literature. No novelist ever produced a West Indian anti-hero to equal the seedy East Indian magnificence of Thackeray's Josh Sedley. Yet *Vanity Fair* itself presents Becky Sharp's strident mulatto schoolfellow not as the product of black West Indian inadequacy but as the spawn of *white* West Indian vulgarity; though a more sensitive Jane Austen, in *Mansfield Park*, had already pointed to the responsible stewardship with which some of the absentee planters used their wealth. It is not generally realised, however, how fundamentally the profits from the sale and labour of slaves altered the society of Old and New World both. Africa itself clearly suffered from an endless drain on her manpower for nearly four centuries of the trade, but on the Guinea Coast the rise of new classes and new nations to prominence was in some cases accelerated by its profits. In North America it was not only the tobacco- and rice-planters of the Southern colonies who were thrown to the top of a new society based on slavery. Indirectly, many New England merchants rose on the profits of provisioning the slave colonies, apart from the relatively few who had a stake in the African trade itself. Brazilian slavery, too, produced not only its great coffee barons and sugar magnates, but also the merchant princes of Bahia, Rio and São

[1] Cited in B. Davidson, *The African Slave Trade: Precolonial History, 1450–1850*, 2nd ed., previously published as *Black Mother* (Boston, 1961) p. 62.

Paulo, who provided the country with slaves or sold its produce to Europe. Other forms of labour coercion were too important in the Spanish possessions for Negro slavery to have so direct an effect on the development of early colonial society, but by the nineteenth century slavery was underwritten by the vested interests of Cuban sugar-planters, as well as merchants of Havana and their colleagues in Madrid and behind the teeming wharves of Seville.

As for the British, the *nouveaux riches* planters who came home to try to worm their way into polite society were only one group whom slavery thrust to the fore. This was just the garish tip of the iceberg. Modern scholarship suggests that the yield on the slave trade itself, and even the general plantation trade, was much less spectacular than has traditionally been supposed, but it is still fair to say that not only some families, but whole cities, first Bristol and then Liverpool, owed their prosperity to them. It is no coincidence that the cornices of the Liverpool Exchange were decorated with a Negro's head motif. Nantes and La Rochelle reaped a similar harvest from the Atlantic trade, which also had more marginal effects on the prosperity of Bordeaux, Saint-Malo and Cherbourg. The fortunes of Nantes in particular were linked with its clique of *négriers*, though the trade goods they used came not from France but through Amsterdam from the manufacturers of the Netherlands and Germany. In Scotland, much of Glasgow's early wealth was built on shipping to the Southern mainland colonies and the yield from the tobacco trade. It is now clear that the slave trade in itself did not bring such striking economic growth for these parts. But it is still true that it depended on the entire complex of the plantation world's economic activities, and thus indirectly on black slavery.

Nevertheless, Eric Williams's claim, in *Capitalism and Slavery*, that enormous plantation profits were the central factor in bringing about European and specifically British industrialisation, must now be treated with caution.[2] These profits were simply not large enough. It is true that it was not only the slave-traders and planters themselves, or even those with New World investments, who grew rich from the sale of black men and women or their labour. For every person directly involved in the British and French Atlantic trade there were many whose business was to

[2] E. Williams, *Capitalism and Slavery*, 2nd ed. (London, 1964).

provide Guineamen and West Indiamen with provisions, equipment and trade goods. This applied to the main trading nations themselves, and also to the Swedish, German and Dutch manufacturers who throve particularly on the French and Portuguese demand for metalwork, glassware and, later, cheap gin. The Atlantic trade, then, clearly gave a boost to the European economy as a whole. But its profits were simply not large enough to become a key factor in industrialisation. Even the strong prima facie case for a close connection between Liverpool slaving and Lancashire prosperity weakens before the recent calculation that slave-trade profits in the latter half of the eighteenth century averaged some 7·5 per cent, and that even if *all* British slave-trade profits had been reinvested, they would have represented only 1·51 per cent of total national investment. If an average proportion was reinvested, this figure shrinks to 0·11 per cent of the total national investment, a derisory proportion of the whole.[2a] In France, yields were similarly low, and it is now clear that the profits brought from the slave and plantation trades alike were simply reinvested in other commercial schemes rather than going back into industry.[2b] Most striking of all, the genuine triangular trade of the Dutch Middleburg Company, in the four decades from 1761 to 1800, averaged a tiny profit of 1·43 per cent.[2c] Aside from the occasional bonanza voyage, slave-trade profits were too low to have injected any substantial amount of capital into new industrial ventures. Even going beyond the slave trade,

[2a] R. Anstey, 'The Volume and Profitability of the British Slave Trade, 1761–1807', unpublished paper originally read at the Comparative Systems of Slavery Conference (Rochester, N.Y., 1972), kindly made available to me by Mr. Anstey in its revised form. See also F. E. Hyde, B. B. Parkinson and S. Marriner, 'The Nature and Profitability of the Liverpool Slave Trade', *Economic History Review*, 2nd ser., v (1953) 368–77; S. L. Engerman, 'The Slave Trade and British Capital Formation in the Eighteenth Century: A Comment on the Williams Thesis,' *Business History Review*, XLVI (1972) 430–43.

[2b] Unpublished paper by Professor Perry Viles, 'The Slaving Interest in the Atlantic Ports, 1763–1792'. I am most obliged to Professor Viles for allowing me to cite this paper, prior to its appearance in *French Studies*, XXVI (1972).

[2c] Information from W. S. Unger, 'Bijdragen tot de Geschiedenis van de Nederlandse Slavenhandel: 2. De Slavenhandel der Middleburgsche Commercie Compagnie, 1732–1808', in *Economisch-Historisch Jaarboek* (1958) pp. 87–91, tabulated by Anstey, loc. cit.

it is not clear that West Indian investment considered as a whole was profitable enough relative to total national income to have much reinvestment effect. Even then, it is likely that much of its dividend went into land or else commercial rather than industrial enterprises. In any case, it has recently been argued that the total British return on capital invested in West Indian ventures was less than it would have earned if put to work at home.[2d]

The link between capitalism and slavery in the eighteenth century no longer seems an obvious one. Where the link does exist is in the nineteenth, when the Lancashire factories which provided the whole world with cotton goods depended almost entirely on the slave population of the Black Belt of the United States. In time, even after slavery had gone, these cottons became the trading staples most important in keeping Europe's commercial supremacy over Africa and the Far East. Black labour was the motive force behind the colossal change of which industrial Manchester was the symbol. Even in the eighteenth century, the effect of the Atlantic trade on British society was a great one. 'Are we not indebted', asked Malachy Postlethwayt, the mercantilist pamphleteer, 'to those valuable people, the *Africans*, for our *Sugars, Tobaccos, Rice, Rum,* and all other *Plantation Produce*?'[2e] He would have been wrong to go on to draw an anachronistic link between the Africans and industrialisation, but he might have added that the profits from 'plantation produce' had made many English fortunes. Those who did not promptly squander them, and their descendants, went on to play important roles in politics, as gentry and in commerce. Plantation trade and its ancillary activities, in fact, was one of many activities by which Englishmen could haul themselves into the landed class. Its impact there was part of a broad pattern by which slavery and the slave trade affected the societies of France, New England, parts of West Africa and all the tropical Americas.

In spite of its value, the slave trade was never as rigidly formalised as the triangle to which it has been compared. More

[2d] See R. P. Thomas, 'The Sugar Colonies of the Old Empire: Profit or Loss for Great Britain?', *Economic History Review*, 2nd ser., xxi (1968) 30–45. Cf. R. B. Sheridan, 'The Wealth of Jamaica in the Eighteenth Century', ibid., 2nd ser., xviii (1965) 292–311.

[2e] M. Postlethwayt, *The African Trade, the Great Pillar and Support of the British Plantation Trade in America* (London, 1748) p. 6.

accurately, it may be said that there was never *a* triangular trade, but that it was made up of many triangles, the apex of which varied according to market conditions in Africa and the New World. Not only this, but variations in the demand for slaves and the availability of tropical produce meant that permutations of ports of call constantly varied. By the latter half of the eighteenth century, in fact, few vessels made genuine triangular voyages. Many ships were being forced to sail back to England from the West Indies in ballast, taking their payment in discounted bills of exchange, since the sugar crop was being shipped by commission merchants trading directly with the islands. The same was true of the French colonies, much of whose produce was latterly taken back to the mother country in bottoms sailing out of Nantes or Bordeaux but not directly involved in the slave trade at all. In fact the only fixed point in the trading pattern was usually the port from which each vessel sailed. This is not to deny that in the early eighteenth century there was a broad pattern in which ships sailed from Europe to Africa to America and back home. This emerged as soon as the first *asientos* were granted to Genoese merchants by the Spanish in the early sixteenth century. But the possible permutations of ports of call in each continent were innumerable. A 'typical' slaver might sail from Bristol carrying trade goods, barter for a full cargo of slaves, carry its slaves to Barbados, exchange them for a cargo of coarsely refined sugar, and thence return directly to England. However, the captain of such a voyage would either be extraordinarily lucky, or else employed by an unusually well-organised mercantile house. On the Coast, even in areas where factors supposedly gathered slaves to wait for the arrival of their companies, the supply of slaves was always uncertain, while prices fluctuated markedly according to local conditions – and also the bargaining skill of the African middleman. Individual traders who could not rely on the protection of company posts or the aid of factors who would gather slaves for them, would spend months peddling their wares up and down the Coast before they could amass a full cargo. To some extent this might be done by all traders, and certainly all of them frequently had to lie at anchor for prolonged periods while their allies on shore gathered the slaves they needed. For instance, in 1699 James Barbot recorded that the *Albion-Frigate*, out of London, after trading sporadically down the Gold

Coast for a few slaves, some elephants' teeth, provisions and gold, arrived at New Calabar only to find that their contact, King William of Bonny, 'objected much against our basons, tankards, yellow beads, and some other merchandize, as of little or no demand there at that time'.[3] Even once his permission to trade was bought, it took the *Albion-Frigate* eight weeks to make up its full complement of 648 slaves. This was not by any means an unlucky or particularly tortuous voyage. At the West Indies end the situation was similarly flexible. Most British ships probably anchored first in Barbados, or at a later period in Jamaica, but they could also unload at other islands, and a far smaller group sailed direct to Charleston, fewer still to Virginia.

In the seventeenth century, patterns of trade had been even less formal. Many merchants looked for other trade goods as well as slaves on the Guinea Coast. This was certainly so in the case of the Royal African Company. From 1672 to 1713 the Royal Mint coined 548,327 guineas from gold imported by the company. It brought 17,113 cwt. of ivory home during the same period.[4] But whether they belonged to chartered companies, or to individual merchant ships visiting Africa illegally, they were as anxious to buy gold, gum and ivory as slaves, until soaring slave prices made other forms of commerce less attractive; and even then other merchandise was never entirely forgotten. By the early eighteenth century, too, the rising merchants of New England had become involved in the plantation trade. Because of the time required to build up contacts and credit, they were slow to enter the Atlantic slave trade themselves, and at first contented themselves with buying molasses and re-exported slaves from the West Indies, in exchange for pipe-staves, fish and horses, and in turn selling their purchases in the Southern mainland colonies. The first African

[3] James Barbot, 'An Abstract of a Voyage to New Calabar River or Rio Real', in John Churchill, *A Collection of Voyages and Travels*, 3rd ed., 6 vols (London, 1746) v 455–66, partly reprinted in E. Donnan (ed.), *Documents Illustrative of the History of the Slave Trade to America*, 4 vols (Washington, 1930–5) I 430–5, and in G. F. Dow, *Slave Ships and Slaving* (Salem, Mass., 1927) pp. 73–87. On the general structure of the trade, see R. B. Sheridan, 'The Commercial and Financial Organisation of the British Slave Trade, 1750–1807', *Economic History Review*, 2nd ser., XI (1958) 249–63.

[4] K. G. Davies, *The Royal African Company* (London, 1957; reprinted New York, 1970) p. 360.

voyage from New England does not seem to have occurred until 1645, when a Boston ship returned across the Atlantic with a mixed cargo of slaves for Barbados and madeira for Massachusetts. Yankee ingenuity suggested many combinations of cargoes and ports of call, but a common run was to sail from Boston to Madeira to exchange pipe-staves and salt fish for wine. A few ships went further south, to buy slaves and assorted non-human produce in Guinea, after which they could return to the Americas. On the way home they might call at the islands to trade slaves for sugar and molasses, or less frequently sail direct to the mainland colonies. Such a full commitment to slaving was abnormal in the seventeenth century, but increasingly common in the eighteenth, especially since the abundance of cheap colonial rum lessened the need for British trade goods and gave important advantages on the Coast. The American slave trade gradually came to be focused on Newport, Rhode Island, which in the final years almost monopolised it. Between 1804 and 1808 Charleston, the principal Southern port to which slaves were introduced directly, unloaded fifty-nine Rhode Island ships, and only one from Massachusetts.[5] By the nineteenth century, owing to the strenuous efforts of the British to suppress the trade, and the lack of facilities for known slavers in European ports, the concept of a triangular trade, long a hazy one, had gone completely.

Much as the patterns of trade varied owing to different market conditions and at different points in time, its continuing impact on Africa was similar over the years. It cost the continent a total loss in population of something over 8 million men and women. However, it is questionable whether the effect of this drain, in a purely numerical sense, was as great as the effect of the restructuring of traditional African societies, and the changing balance of their relative power, brought about in part by the demands of white traders for slaves. This was not related in any sense to Europe's inventing slavery and the buying and selling of black people. Various forms of bondage and dependence were central to many though not all African societies prior to the sixteenth century. Although the central 'slave' relationship of traditional society was that of a client or dependant, and did not have a chattel component, the categories of prisoners of war and in some

[5] S. E. Morison, *The Maritime History of Massachusetts, 1783–1860* (1921; reprinted Boston, 1961) p. 35.

cases convicts and debt slaves created a pool of slaves who could be transferred on the open market. Even here, there are few African societies where slaves did not become parts of established lineage groups, and cease to be transferable, after one or at most three generations. Nevertheless, it was probably from the prisoners of war and convict categories that the resources for the medieval Islamic trade came. Later they could be artificially increased in numbers to meet the demands of the Atlantic traders.[6] Africa had been providing streams of captives for the markets of North Africa and the Levant for many centuries, chiefly in exchange for salt. At least since the rise of Islam, slaves had been carried north from West Africa via the trans-Saharan route, and from East Africa via Zanzibar and the Red Sea – not to mention the smaller and more exotic trade across the Indian Ocean.[7] There was nothing new about the provision of huge numbers of slaves for alien powers. This is not to say that Africa's political history was moulded solely, or even fundamentally, by outside influences. The most modern African historians, who have escaped from the Western perspective of their predecessors, have made it clear that the demands of the trade were seldom the only determinant of the internal developments of the Guinea states. Their success or failure, their rise and fall, was not dictated by their slaving concerns, but primarily – sometimes even wholly – by internal stresses and conflicts purely African in origin. Yet it would be a

[6] Here and in my other comments on African slavery I am heavily indebted to the unpublished work of Mr Frederick Cooper of Yale University, though he would disagree with many of the comments I have made here. There is no adequate published study of African slavery, although there is some introductory material in A. G. B. Fisher and H. J. Fisher, *Slavery and Muslim Society in Africa* (New York, 1971), a frankly mistitled volume based on the observations of the German explorer Gustav Nachtigal. See also M. G. Smith, 'Slavery and Emancipation in Two Societies', *Social and Economic Studies*, III (1954) 239–90, which compares Jamaica and Zaria, a Hausa society of northern Nigeria, and J. D. Fage, 'Slavery and the Slave Trade in the Context of West African History', *Journal of African History*, x (1969) 393–404. Note that it is important, both in East Africa and in Guinea, not to confuse forms of bondage which are genuinely African and those which are Islamic in origin.

[7] E. W. Bovill, *The Golden Trade of the Moors* (Oxford, 1958) pp. 23–4, 244–5. For a superb discussion of prejudice against the black slaves brought into the Islamic world, see B. Lewis, *Race and Color in Islam* (New York, 1971).

mistake to carry this kind of argument too far. It is illogical to take the position that a trade of this magnitude could have been carried on so long without having marked effects on the societies involved in it. We now know that a state like Benin could rise to greatness and subsequently collapse for reasons other than the pressures of slaving, but Benin was atypical in that it was never heavily involved in the trade, and in any case declined partly because of the success of its vassals in getting European arms in exchange for slaves. It is hard to generalise for so vast an area comprising so many diverse societies, but the most accurate conclusion is probably close to Professor Fage's that the European demand 'accentuated and expanded the internal growth of slavery and the slave trade.... West African rulers and merchants reacted to the demand with economic reasoning, and used it to strengthen streams of economic and political developments that were already current before the Atlantic slave trade began.'[8]

The coming of the European traders altered the structure of many West African societies. In the first place, it meant that the commercial balance of Guinea was now weighted towards the Atlantic instead of the Sahara. Even Benin traded extensively with the Europeans, though not necessarily in slaves or to the exclusion of its northern trade. Those states with access to the sea henceforth had major commercial advantages over those which faced on to the desert. By the nineteenth century this became all the more dramatic since the Atlantic trade brought the firearms which became the basis of each state's hegemony, and which in turn made it possible to find more slaves to buy more firearms. Even states like Dahomey, which may at first have shrunk from slaving because of the weakness it might bring, were inevitably drawn in because of the obverse fear that lack of access to European goods would destroy their strength even more surely, and the lack of viable alternatives.[9] At the same time, within some West African societies, disproportionate power moved to the

[8] Fage, in *J.Af.H.*, x 404. Cf. C. C. Wrigley, 'Historicism in Africa: Slavery and State Formation', *African Affairs*, LXX (1971) 113–24. On the Benin case I have relied on A. F. C. Ryder, *Benin and the Europeans, 1485–1897* (New York, 1969), which clearly demonstrates Benin's diverse interests and relative abstinence from slaving, without demonstrating that we can extrapolate from this for West Africa as a whole.

[9] I. A. Akinjogbin, *Dahomey and its Neighbours, 1708–1818* (Cambridge, 1967).

middlemen and merchants on whom success in the Atlantic trade depended. The depredations of the white slavers were not new, except perhaps in scale, but in this way the slave trade to the Americas strengthened some African nations and weakened others, as well as bringing a new black bourgeoisie to prominence.

The effect of the slave trade on African history was thus greater than the simple loss of 8 million people. It changed the political development of large parts of the continent. At the same time, however, the early development of the Atlantic slave trade was moulded not by the whims of the first European adventurers, but by the political structure of West Africa. This bore little resemblance to the anarchy from which later apologists of slavery and the slave trade liked to argue they had rescued the fortunate Africans who were taken to the New World. One such writer stressed the benefit of the learning of Christianity, but also remarked that the blacks were being taken from a harsh servitude to 'une autre incomparablement plus douce et plus tolérable'.[10] Another argued that all African social organisation and civilisation was similar to that of the Hottentots.[11] A third, who appeared to imagine that the Hottentots lived in Guinea, described West Africans in their natural state as 'the most stupid, beastly race of animals in human shape, of any in the whole world'.[12] Yet another remarked on the luck of the 'stupid and unenlightened Hordes, immersed in the most gross and impenetrable glooms of barbarism', in being taken to the blessings of West Indian plantation life.[13] The cultural vision of such writers and their age

[10] [B. de Saint-Quentin], *Dissertation sur la traite et le commerce des Nègres* (Paris, 1764) p. 22.

[11] [R. Nesbit], *Slavery not Forbidden by Scripture, or a Defence of the West India Planters, from the Aspersions Thrown out against them, etc.* (Philadelphia, 1773) pp. 20–2.

[12] *Personal Slavery Established, by the Suffrages of Custom and Right Reason: Being a Short Answer to the Gloomy and Visionary Reveries, of all the fanatical and enthusiastical Writers on the Subject* (Philadelphia, 1773) p. 15. This extraordinary pamphlet may be a parody, though the abolitionists took it seriously enough.

[13] *Slavery no Oppression; or, Some New Arguments against the Idea of African Liberty* (London, n.d. [c. 1791]) p. 12. For the history of changing Western attitudes to Africa and Africans, see W. D. Jordan, *White over Black: American Attitudes toward the Negro, 1550–1812* (1968; Baltimore: Penguin Books ed., 1969) pp. 3–42; P. Curtin, *The Image of Africa: British Ideas and Action, 1780–1850* (Madison, Wis., 1966).

produced a nearly complete incomprehension of the power and stability of the kingdoms of West Africa. They were unable to equate with European states units like the great empires of Mali in the fourteenth century, of Songhai in the sixteenth, of Bornu in the seventeenth, of Benin, Oyo, Dahomey and Ashanti in the eighteenth and nineteenth centuries.[14] It is important that this last group of states were based on the forest, while the Sudanese empires which preceded them were based on the savannah. It was the power of such new states in some areas, its absence in others, and in some cases the conflicts between them, which dictated the trading conditions for the first Europeans who came to Guinea in search of slaves. This influenced the supply of slaves from the interior, and also the facilities given to traders on the seaboard.

It was because of local political conditions, too, that the methods of slave-trading varied so much from one part of the Coast to another. Wherever the power of the African authorities was great, they resisted giving the Europeans any foothold on shore at all, or, in some cases, did so only under their own conditions and in return for set rents and customs duties. Even within the spheres of influence of the great territorial empires, each followed different conventions in dealing with the foreigners. In some cases, too, trade remained a royal monopoly, whereas in others, most notably the small states of the Niger Delta, it fell into the hands of strong groups of African businessmen. Broadly speaking, European traders divided the Coast into several main sections.[15] The first division was the one between the Windward Coast, to the north and west of Cape Palmas, and the Leeward Coast to its south and east, but this was only one way of referring to the various trading areas. North of Cape Mount lay Upper Guinea, including the heavily-indented coast beyond Sherbro Island in Sierra Leone. Further north still were the Senegal and Gambia rivers with their major European settlements, first Portuguese and later French and British. East of Sierra Leone lay the

[14] The most comprehensive work on West Africa is J. F. A. Ajayi and M. Crowder (eds), *History of West Africa*, vol. 1 (New York, 1972). See also B. Davidson, *Lost Cities of Africa*, 2nd ed. (Boston, 1970) pp. 71–147; N. Levtzion, *Ancient Ghana and Mali* (London, 1972); D. Forde and P. M. Kaberry (eds), *West African Kingdoms in the Nineteenth Century* (London, 1967).

[15] Davies, *Royal African Company*, pp. 213 ff.

Grain Coast, roughly corresponding to modern Liberia. Beyond this, to the east of Cape Palmas, came the great sweep of the Leeward Coast, in turn subdivided according to regional staples. The first area after Cape Palmas, where the African coastline turns inwards to run eastwards, was the Ivory Coast. Both here and in the Grain Coast, though no central power protected the country from the Europeans, slave-trading remained relatively low in volume. Vicious tides and currents made it difficult for sailing-ships to stand offshore for periods long enough to load slaves, which in any case were an unwieldy cargo for which to carry out long lighterage operations in heavy surf. This was less of a problem in the Gold Coast, running along the shore of present-day Ghana, where anchorages were available and the Portuguese were, in the fifteenth and sixteenth centuries, able to found their great trading forts of Elmina and Axim. From the Volta eastwards, round the Bight of Benin to the far side of the Niger Delta and the Bight of Biafra, lay the Slave Coast. According to Curtin's calculations, this area provided 39·6 per cent of the slaves carried from Africa by the French and English from 1715 to 1810. Of the remainder, 35·7 per cent came from the rest of West Africa, and 24·7 per cent from Central and East Africa.[16]

Penetration to the interior was difficult for Europeans in all parts of the Coast. This was partly due to the hazards of heat, fever and the terrain itself, but also to the resistance of African nations. Even in the Gold Coast, in spite of the strength of the forts built by the Portuguese – initially to trade for gold dust, not slaves – local rule firmly and successfully denied access to the forest hinterland and the sources of the merchandise the Europeans wanted. Portugal was more successful in pushing into the interior in Senegambia, and indeed right along the Coast from the Senegal to Sherbro Island. The great waterways of the Senegal, the Gambia and the Corubal (Rio Grande) offered them a great advantage, but it was more important that they had no strongly organised state which could check their advance. Though the Portuguese forts in Upper Guinea were overwhelmed by the

[16] P. Curtin, *The Atlantic Slave Trade: A Census* (Madison, Wis., 1969) p. 221. There is a convenient map of West Africa during the slave-trade period in J. D. Fage, *An Introduction to the History of West Africa*, 3rd ed. (Cambridge, 1962) p. 66.

Dutch in the 1630s, they had little time to take advantage of the web of commercial contacts in the interior before being ousted in their turn by the French. France swept the Dutch out of the area, and took the forts at Arguim and Gorée, in the Franco-Dutch war of 1672–8. In the eighteenth century the two bases of Saint-Louis and Gorée were the centre of a substantial trade down the Coast, and as far up the Senegal as the junction with the Falémé, where it ran into serious opposition from Arab traders buying slaves, gum and ivory for the trans-Saharan route. Although French trade depended largely on contacts with local Moslem entrepreneurs, as with the Portuguese their success was due to the weakness of local states.[17] It was only with the nineteenth century that the great *jihads* of Al 'Haj 'Omar, Samori and other Islamic rulers created a sphere of influence which seriously hampered the penetration of the Europeans. This affected equally the French on the Senegal, the British on the Gambia, and the traders of mixed nationality operating between the Gambia and Sierra Leone.

In other parts of the Coast this process was reversed. Resistance to the extension of European influence inland did not simply stiffen in the nineteenth century, but was a constant factor from the earliest period of European commerce. The only other areas which did not fall within the orbit of any major African power were the Grain and Ivory Coasts. Although here there was no outstanding political opposition to the entrenchment of European traders, they were prevented from setting up permanent bases by difficult sailing conditions and the lack of safe anchorages. On the Gold Coast and the Slave Coast, however, the situation was quite different, and the local authorities were able to prevent Europeans from trading anywhere except on the coast itself, and even here trade went on in strictly African terms. In this way the profits of African middlemen – and African rulers – were boosted, and the possibility of any major political threat removed, at least until the power of the forest states collapsed in the nineteenth century. For instance, the Portuguese found that they were able to seize the offshore islands of Fernando Póo, Príncipe and São Tomé, in the Bight of Biafra, and they were permitted to build their forts at Elmina and Axim on the Gold Coast. But it was

[17] J. D. Hargreaves, *West Africa: The Former French States* (Englewood Cliffs, N.J., 1967) pp. 59 ff.

made clear from the outset that the land for these forts was in effect leased from the local rulers, and their construction did not imply any right to operate inland. They were aimed at protecting the goods of Portuguese traders from seaborne attacks by other powers, not from the onslaught of Africans, whom the tiny European garrisons could have done little to withstand had they decided to push them into the sea overnight. This remained the situation when the forts were captured by the Dutch, and others, most important Cape Coast Castle, built by the English. Until the late nineteenth century the strength of Dahomey and the Ashanti Union prevented the British from seizing the lines of commerce which brought merchandise, primarily slaves, to their forts and to other outposts on the Gold Coast.

The influence of African nations on the patterns of slave-trading was most marked on the Slave Coast and the Niger Delta, or the Oil Rivers as it was originally called. The most modern studies suggest that it was not purely due to the pressure of the slave trade that Benin and Oyo collapsed, or that bitter fighting broke out between the successor states. In this sense it seems that the impact of the Europeans on eighteenth or even nineteenth-century politics was considerably less than the abolitionists thought, or than modern scholars like Professor Fage have argued.[18] In either case, they had little success in enlarging their power on the Bights of Benin and Biafra in the sixteenth, seventeenth and eighteenth centuries. In the Bight of Benin, the normal policy was for 'factors' to be left on shore by the various trading companies, in the hope that they would be able to gather cargoes of slaves against the arrival of ships from the home country. However, their trading was done strictly through African middlemen, usually after payment of fat customs duties, and was not always successful. The factories were small and normally squalid. In 1694, for instance, the establishment of the Royal African Company at the key port of Whydah stood

low near the marshes, which renders it a very unhealthy place

[18] J. D. Graham, 'The Slave Trade, Depopulation, and Human Sacrifice in Benin History', *Cahiers d'Études Africaines*, v (1965) 317–34; Ryder, *Benin and the Europeans*, pp. 196–238; J. F. Ade Ajayi and R. S. Smith, *Yoruba Warfare in the Nineteenth Century* (Cambridge, 1964) pp. 123–8. Cf. Fage, *Introduction to the History of West Africa*, pp. 87 ff.

to live in; the white men the *African* company send there, seldom returning to tell their tale; 'tis compass'd round with a mud wall, about six foot high, and on the south-side is the gate; within is a large yard, a mud thatch'd house, where the factor lives, with the white men; also a store-house, a trunk [*tronco* or stocks] for slaves, and a place where they bury their dead white men, call'd, very improperly, the hog-yard.[19]

Gathering of slaves by the factors remained a chancy business, and ships were seldom able to avoid waiting offshore to fill up their slave decks. In the Oil Rivers, on the various mouths of the Niger, small trading states like Bonny and Brass, which grew up specifically in response to the demand for slaves, were even more jealous of the extension of European influence. The operations of the few factors there were confined to hulks anchored in the rivers. It was in these unsavoury and unsafe bases that they attempted to gather cargoes of slaves prior to the arrival of ships from Britain or France. Overcrowding and filth, consequently disease and mortality, were even worse here than in the barracoons set up by African rulers on the Grain and Ivory Coasts, where European traders had no permanent establishment and slaves were herded together to await a purchaser. This method was also used in some areas of the Oil Rivers.

Keeping the European traders physically at bay did not prevent their having a significant effect on some of the traditional societies of the Coast. Apart from anything else, the slave trade was a great source of income for African rulers. As Fage suggests, if the Atlantic trade did nothing else, it gave African rulers the option of selling slaves in their possession for imported merchandise, instead of retaining them for productive use within their own societies.[20] Even those who did not retain the trade in their own hands were quick to impose heavy customs duties on Europeans before giving them permission to buy slaves. Complaints against their conditions appear again and again in the narratives

[19] T. Phillips, 'A Journal of a Voyage Made in the *Hannibal* of London, Ann. 1693, 1694 to Cape Monseradoe, in Africa; and ... to Barbadoes', in Churchill, *Voyages*, VI 231, reprinted in Donnan (ed.), *Documents Illustrative of the History of the Slave Trade*, I 399. The whole of Phillips's account is in Churchill, VI 189–255.

[20] Fage, in *J.Af.H.*, X 393–404.

of the men who sailed to the Coast. During his 1694 voyage, Thomas Phillips, on the *Hannibal* out of London, apart from his distress at the prices asked by the king of Whydah – 'he and his cappasheirs exacted very high' – described his practice of taking a proportion of the price paid to the 'cappasheirs' or nobles for slaves they tried to sell on their own behalf. In addition to this, each ship was required, 'for leave to trade, protection, and justice', to pay six slaves' worth of cowries to the king and two slaves' worth to each of his officials, and a total of five and a half slaves' worth to various local officials who supervised or assisted in the trading process.[21] In 1699 James Barbot noted that the *Albion-Frigate* paid the king of Bonny, in the Niger Delta, two copper rings for every slave she took on board, apart from informal but clearly obligatory 'presents'.[22] A year later, sailing as supercargo on the *Don Carlos* of London, Barbot had to pay duties of 47 pieces of assorted goods to the king of Cabinda and $82\frac{1}{2}$ more to sundry other officials, by way of customs duties. At the court of Sony, or Songo, which they had first visited, it was also obligatory to visit the resident Portuguese chaplain before reaching an agreement on trade conditions.[23] Often African rulers and merchants withheld slaves from factors on the spot, in the full realisation that the arrival of a ship and its natural wish to get off the Coast as quickly as possible would push prices up. One luckless factor at Fort Commenda recorded plaintively in his report to the Royal African Company that 'it's with great difficulty I can gett any [slaves] at the Comp'ys price and I have been Bargaining for this last slave above a Month before I cou'd come to an agreement, so hard are the Traders to deal with.'[24] Aside from tribulations of this sort, and the levy of formal customs, the European traders were normally expected to provide gifts and entertainment for their African contacts. 'If you look strange and are niggardly of your Drams,' wrote John Atkins, 'you frighten him; *Sambo* is gone, . . . he never cares to treat with dry Lips, and as the Expence is in English Spirits of two Shillings a Gallon, brought partly for that purpose; the good

---

[21] Phillips, loc. cit., VI 233, 242–3, reprinted in Donnan, I 403–4.

[22] Barbot, loc. cit., V 460, reprinted in Donnan, I 434.

[23] James Barbot, 'An Abstract of a Voyage to Congo River on the Zair', in Churchill, *Voyages*, V 497–522, partly reprinted in Donnan, I 451–65.

[24] Report dated 23 Oct. 1714, printed in Donnan, II 186–7.

Humour it brings them into, is found discounted in the Sale of Goods.'[25]

On the Slave Coast itself, the trade strengthened a number of small states which prospered by acting as intermediaries between the Europeans and the slave markets of the interior. All were chiefdoms whose heads gained strength from their control over the slave trade, and the most important in the early eighteenth century were Great Ardra, Jacquin and, above all, Whydah or Fida, the king of which, it was once remarked, was as 'absolute as a Boar'.[26] From the 1720s, however, these states were coming under increasing pressure from the expansion of Dahomey. One of Dahomey's primary objectives was to secure an outlet to the sea. Success came in 1727, when King Agaja rolled up Whydah itself. Although the first intention of the Dahomeyans was probably to create an empire without the incubus of perpetual slaving around its neck, the eighteenth century made it painfully clear that there was no other stable economic base on which the state could maintain itself. Dahomeyan officials dealt directly with the British and French in Whydah, exchanging the slaves gained in Dahomey's numerous imperialist wars against her inland neighbours for Europeans' trade goods – foremost among them the weapons necessary to fight further imperialist wars. Locked into this activity, Dahomey eventually became one of the greatest slaving machines on the Coast.[27] Its rise not only crushed the power of the small Aja kingdoms of the coast, but threatened the trade routes of its overlord, the Alafin of Oyo. Much of Oyo's greatness in the seventeenth century had been built on its commanding position, with a combination of easy routes to the sea and access to the savannah cities of the western Sudan. From the seventeenth century Oyo shipped substantial numbers of slaves through Whydah. It was only once the growing strength of Dahomey made the port unsafe, though she was forced to pay tribute to Oyo from 1730 to the 1820s, that Oyo found new out-

[25] J. Atkins, *A Voyage to Guinea, Brasil, and the West-Indies, in His Majesty's Ships, the Swallow and Weymouth... with Remarks on the Gold, Ivory, and Slave-Trade* (London, 1735) pp. 170–1.

[26] Ibid., p. 172.

[27] Akinjogbin, *Dahomey and its Neighbours.* On the society and growth of old Dahomey, see M. J. Herskovits, *Dahomey: An Ancient West African Kingdom*, 2 vols (New York, 1938); R. Cornevin, *Histoire du Dahomey* (Paris, 1962) pp. 10–364.

lets in Badagry and Porto Novo. This shift notwithstanding, the European trade was central to Oyo's power, though it is not entirely clear that wars were ever fought by her specifically to seize slaves for sale on the Coast – or that this was done even in the years of disorder which followed her collapse in the nineteenth century.[28] The first of the great forest states, Benin, also gained from the European trade, in spite of the recent suggestion that cloth and ivory exports were as important to her economy and her strength as slaves.[29] Her drive to the coast in the seventeenth century, which extended Benin power as far as Lagos, also involved selling the slaves captured in war to the Europeans. It may well be, in fact, that the way in which the Oba of Benin kept the nobility under control was by allowing them to occupy themselves with expeditions of their own to the interior. The fruit of such conquests was slaves, drawn mainly from the luckless Ibo, with the resulting ultimate reward of success in the Coast trade. In Benin's decline, too, a principal problem was controlling vassals whose strength was based on arms drawn from the slave trade. There is no doubt that the expansion of the last of the forest empires to emerge, the Ashanti Union, was closely linked with its attempts to crush the small coastal kingdoms which had previously acted as middlemen in the Atlantic trade in gold and slaves. Even under the great Asantahene Osei Tuta it had taken the port of Appolonia in 1715. By the reign of Osei Bonsu (1800–24) the Ashanti Union, like Dahomey, had been a major power on the Coast for over half a century.[30] This is still not to insist that wars were specifically fought to gather slaves for the Europeans. But although the forest states maintained northern commercial contacts, their political development would have been entirely different if West Africa's commerce had remained centred purely on the desert and the north. These states were neither created nor made into slaving machines by the West, but they were drawn to expand towards the coast by the economic and military gains to be made by trading with the Europeans, primarily in slaves.

Whatever the implications of the slave trade for Benin, Oyo,

---

[28] R. S. Smith, *Kingdoms of the Yoruba* (London, 1969) pp. 45–6, 157.

[29] Ryder, *Benin and the Europeans.*

[30] C. W. Newbury, *The Western Slave Coast and its Rulers* (Oxford, (1961).

Dahomey and Ashanti, it did not revolutionise the fundamental structure of their society. In Senegal and Gambia, and along the whole coastline of Upper Guinea, north of Cape Mount, the absence in many areas of strong royal authorities who would take control of the trade left its profits to be engrossed by Portuguese half-castes and Islamic merchants, neither of whom fitted into traditional African society. These not only maintained establishments on the Coast, but also became involved in the lines of supply from the interior. In the Cape Verde Islands, in São Tomé and Príncipe, there developed a new society dominated by the Portuguese and Portuguese-speaking mulattoes. New elements also appeared in the shadow of the great European forts, around British Elmina and Cape Coast Castle, or Anomabu, or French Saint-Louis in Senegal. There a polyglot population was drawn together by the prospects of wealth offered by constant trading activity, and the needs of ocean-going ships for skilled craftsmen and assistants. Though there was not yet anything so dramatic as the racial mixture of Sierra Leone,[31] these areas saw a breakdown of the barriers between African cultures and the emergence of small enclaves of society dependent on the activities of the African and European traders.

However, this kind of development, confined to very small areas as it was, was nothing like so far-reaching as the change brought about by the slave trade in the societies of the Niger Delta. Here success in the Atlantic trade brought new classes into control of the body politic. Prior to the seventeenth century, Bonny, Nembe (Brass), Kalabari, Okrika and New Calabar had been organised as primitive tribal societies subsisting on fishing and salt-panning. No other activities were open to them, since their country was predominantly mangrove swamp. In response to the commercial demands of the Europeans, they began to use their great war canoes to seize slaves from the hinterland. In turn, to meet the organisational needs of crewing their canoes, they developed a complex set of social regulations referred to as the 'house system'. Each house was dominated by a 'father' whose 'family' included the dependants in varying degrees of freedom and unfreedom who made up the complement of each trading canoe. Slaves were obtained from the Ibo and Ijo hinterland,

[31] See A. T. Porter, *Creoledom: A Study of the Development of Free-town Society* (Oxford, 1963).

many of them through the Aro oracle or Long Juju on the Niger. The Aro oracle spoke from a cave supposed to be the residence of the divinity Chuku, and its role was the settlement of disputes among those who accepted its cult. In each dispute one party was drawn into the cave to be eaten by the god, but was promptly removed by the Aro priesthood by another exit, whence he and other victims were distributed to the traders of the city-states on the Delta. This did not prevent or replace the absorption of slaves from the normal groups of prisoners of war, convicts and debtors, but it provided the most consistent element in the resources of the Delta traders, especially in Bonny. The exact way in which the Aro people master-minded the great system on which their oracle depended is obscure, and we know too little about the position of the Aro as an élite within the Ibo people as a whole. However, it was doubtless because of the Long Juju's great appetite that the Oil Rivers were able to provide a more stable supply of slaves than parts of the Coast where European purchasers were at the mercy of variables like war or peace in the interior.[32]

There is no area where traditional African society altered so markedly in direct response to the slave trade as the city-states of the Delta. In Angola and the Congo, however, they absorbed aspects of European culture to an extent quite foreign to Guinea except in the offshore Portuguese islands of the Bights. Diego Cão, the discoverer of the Congo river, or Zaïre, left four Franciscan friars at the estuary of the river in 1483 and took a group of Congolese back to Portugal. On a third voyage, provided with what was effectively a complete mission, he travelled to the court of the king of Congo. From this point on, the kingdoms of Portugal and Congo treated with one another as allies, on an equal basis. Naturally, the long intercourse between the two had an enormous effect on the history of the Congo. Much of the foundation of the relationship was built in the reign of

[32] K. O. Dike, *Trade and Politics in the Niger Delta* (Oxford, 1957) pp. 30–41; D. C. Forde (ed.), *Efik Traders of Old Calabar* (London, 1956) passim; M. Crowder, *The Story of Nigeria*, 2nd ed. (London, 1962) pp. 79–89; G. I. Jones, *The Trading States of the Oil Rivers* (London, 1963); E. J. Alagoa, 'The Niger Delta States and their Neighbours, 1600–1800', in Ajayi and Crowder (eds), *History of West Africa*, 1 269–303; K. K. Nair, *Politics and Society in South Eastern Nigeria, 1841–1906* (London, 1972) pp. 1–35; A. J. H. Latham, *Old Calabar, 1600–1891* (London, 1973).

Nzinga Mbemba, or Dom Affonso I, from 1506 to 1543.[33] It was during this reign that Congo sent a substantial mission to Rome, which ordained the king's son Prince Henry as the first Bishop of Congo. Yet the forms of Christianity and European civilisation held few benefits for Congo, since whatever benevolent implications they may have had were washed out by the trading requirements of the Portuguese. The partnership rapidly came to be an unequal one where Portugal began to drain Congo and its neighbouring kingdoms of slaves, shutting out contact with other European nations and giving little or nothing in return. Above all, the Portuguese authorities allowed traders based on São Tomé to trade directly with Loanga and the other vassals of Congo, thus undermining the power of Dom Affonso and the Mani-Congos who succeeded him. Not only this, but the Portuguese began to try to destroy the power of the Mani-Congo completely through alliance with his rebellious southern vassal, the Ngola or king of Ndonga, or Angola.

Although the Portuguese connection remained, Congo had been weakened to an extent where it could do little to withstand the attacks of powerful Jaga raiders from the west – who began in turn to trade in slaves with the Europeans. Congo never recovered from their crushing invasion in 1568, though its monarchy technically survived until the nineteenth century. Meanwhile the Portuguese began a century of warfare with Ndonga, which they eventually reduced to become their colony of Angola. Its political structure also was smashed, in spite of bitter resistance to Portugal and her puppets.[34] From then on, with the cohesiveness of the Congolese and Angolan states broken, and impressive religious establishments at their forts in Benguela, Luanda and other out-

[33] J. Vansina, *Kingdoms of the Savanna* (Madison, Wis., 1966) pp. 41–69; C. R. Boxer, *The Portuguese Seaborne Empire, 1415–1825* (New York, 1969) pp. 96–103; W. G. L. Randles, *L'Ancien Royaume du Congo des origines à la fin du XIXe siècle* (Paris, 1968) pp. 97–104; G. Balandier, *La vie quotidienne au royaume du Congo du XVIe au XVIIIe siècle* (Paris, 1965).

[34] Vansina, *Kingdoms of the Savanna*, pp. 124–54; C. R. Boxer, *Salvador da Sá and the Struggle for Brazil and Angola* (London, 1952) pp. 223–92; D. Birmingham, *Trade and Conflict in Angola: The Mbundu and their Neighbours under the Influence of the Portuguese* (New York, 1966). The standard study is O. da Cadornega, *Historia geral das guerras Angolanas*, 3 vols (Lisbon, 1940–2).

posts on the Coast, the Portuguese were able to pour slaves across the Atlantic on their own terms. Christianisation had made remarkable progress among Africans, or at least among their rulers, but it had done nothing to prevent the gearing of what had been a stable and prosperous society to the single activity of providing slaves for the New World. Slaves were gathered by great trading caravans led to the interior by black, mulatto or, very occasionally, Portuguese *pombeiros* – a method similar to the one used by the Arab and Portuguese slave-raiders in East Africa. As in the societies of Upper Guinea, the trade produced a group of petty coastal chieftains whose main interest was in selling slaves and distributing European merchandise to the interior. Such Portuguese civilisation as there was in the coastal ports certainly affected the African commercial classes in language and life-style, usually for the worse, since any Portuguese prepared to live in tropical Africa was likely to be drawn from the scum of the empire. Though the early fervour of the missions soon waned, they did affect African religious belief, and the superb copper and bronze sculpture of the Congo turned partly towards Christian objects. Yet the trading cities of Congo and Angola soon degenerated into squalid outposts, epitomising the bastardisation of human society created by the slave trade, and quite lacking the brilliance of Goa, Bahia and the towns in more fortunate parts of the Portuguese empire.

Congo and Angola were examples of societies which reduced themselves to ruins by trying to meet the insistent demands of the Portuguese for slaves. Yet neither was unfamiliar with various forms of bondage prior to the arrival of the Europeans. The latter was also true of the forest kingdoms and the societies of the Gold Coast, the Slave Coast and the Oil Rivers, though none paid as bitter a price for their Atlantic trade as Congo and Angola. In some parts of Upper Guinea, however, the slave trade had even more extraordinary results. Along the coast to the north of Sherbro Island, prior to the arrival of the Europeans, there had been a chain of small stateless societies in which every individual had a relationship to his lineage group effectively excluding any form of unfree labour. With the Atlantic demand for slaves, however, such societies not only began to transmit men and women from the hinterland to the slave-ships, but also to keep them in bondage for their own use in imitation of the Westerners' chattel relationship with their slaves.[35] It would be unwise to generalise from the work done by Rodney in this area to the whole of West Africa. Still, it is clear that however much the traders elsewhere were expanding the potential and hardening the terms of an existing African institution, in this substantial part of Upper Guinea they were creating a new one.

As for East Africa, the impact of the Portuguese there was in the long run no more impressive than in Congo and Angola. Their ventures severely damaged an African–Islamic society of great wealth and substantial culture. However, slaving was not a dominant factor in the history of great trading city-states like Kilwa, Mombasa, Malindi and Pate, though the numbers of slaves carried across the Atlantic from East Africa after 1500 were gigantic: even for the short period from 1817 to 1843 Curtin calculates, working only from knowledge available to the British Foreign Office, that Brazil imported 116,000 slaves from Mozambique and Madagascar alone.[36] Though this process of leeching manpower from East Africa goes back to the arrival of the Europeans and beyond, the worst ravages of the slavers in the Indian Ocean came in the boom years of nineteenth-century Brazil and Cuba. From the fifteenth to the eighteenth century the Portuguese in East Africa behaved in the simple role of thugs, without particular specialisation in slaving, which probably brought them little profit in the sixteenth and seventeenth centuries. Barbarians as they were, their great advantage in firepower gave them the capability to meet and overcome the Eastern sultanates – through sheer physical destruction and looting, through cutting the trade routes across the Indian Ocean on which these civilisations depended. The city-states were either destroyed by bombardment, as was Kilwa in 1505, or agreed to pay crushing tributes as Zanzibar did in 1503. Again, the European impact was confined largely to the coast. Although they were able to seize the gold trade of the Monomatapa in the seventeenth century, it was only in the nineteenth that large-scale raiding far into the interior began, in Arab and Portuguese hands. The slave coffles noted with horror by Livingstone and Kirk were, relatively speaking, a

[35] W. Rodney, 'African Slavery and Other Forms of Social Oppression on the Upper Guinea Coast in the Context of the African Slave Trade', *Journal of African History*, VII (1966) 431–43.

[36] Curtin, *Atlantic Slave Trade*, p. 240.

new phenomenon. By this time, the city-states of the coast had recovered with the decline of Portuguese power. Yet they provided no protection against these ravages, and indeed came to be distribution points for slaves systematically captured far inland. They themselves used slave labour extensively in farming, especially in Zanzibari, clove-growing, and in domestic service. Indeed it was a major diplomatic conundrum for the British to secure their co-operation in suppressing the trade. But the societies which suffered from it, and which were drastically changed by slavery itself, were those of Central Africa.[37]

The effect of the trade on Africa as a whole was drastic, not only in terms of simple loss of manpower. It brought sweeping changes in some African societies, altered their internal politics and their international relations in others. It is not true that African nations were peaceful and uniformly prosperous until they felt the impact of the Atlantic trade. With a few exceptions, too, slaving was not a new enterprise for them, nor did it become their only activity. Slave-trading for most African states was one economic activity among others, but its intensity increased sharply with the arrival of the Europeans. The importance of contacts with them and the goods they brought unquestionably altered the history of Africa's great Bronze Age cultures.

Drastic though they were, these changes in African society were only part of a wider process by which the slave trade and slavery produced new élites throughout the Atlantic world. Of such groups, the most obvious were the planters of the Americas, men who themselves owned slaves and made their fortunes

[37] The nineteenth-century East African trade is discussed briefly below, pp. 366–9. For background on the earlier period, see E. Axelson, *The Portuguese in South-East Africa, 1600–1700* (Johannesburg, 1960); C. R. Boxer and C. de Azevedo, *Fort Jesus and the Portuguese in Mombasa, 1593–1729* (London, 1960); J. Strandes, *The Portuguese Period in Africa*, trans. J. Wallwork and J. S. Kirkman (Nairobi, 1961); G. S. P. Freeman-Grenville, 'The Coast, 1498–1840', in R. Oliver and G. Mathew (eds), *History of East Africa*, vol. 1 (Oxford, 1963) pp. 129–68. On the pre-European civilisations, see G. Mathew, 'The East African Coast until the Coming of the Portuguese', ibid., pp. 94–128; G. S. P. Freeman-Grenville, *The Medieval History of the Coast of Tanganyika* (Oxford, 1962). A good introduction to the history of Africa's indigenous trading patterns, and incidentally to the slave trade, is R. Gray and D. Birmingham (eds), *Pre-Colonial African Trade: Essays on Trade in Central and Eastern Africa before 1900* (London, 1970).

directly from their labour. By the late seventeenth century, for instance, the Brazilian sugar industry had spawned an American aristocracy of enormous wealth, living in splendour on their own estates and in the rich colonial towns of São Paulo, Rio de Janeiro, Bahia and Pernambuco. The Spanish colonies, too, had thrown up their own Creole élite of successful miners, ranchers and planters, many of whose enterprises had depended on slaves. In the eighteenth century the French sugar islands also produced enormous local wealth. In Martinique, Guadeloupe and Saint-Domingue, though absenteeism was common, many of the sugar barons remained in the West Indies to form a Creole aristocracy sharply differentiated from the parallel society of free people of colour. However, the slaveowning aristocracy most firmly wedded to its American existence was the one of England's Southern mainland colonies. The successful planters of eighteenth-century Virginia and South Carolina, unlike their countrymen in the sugar islands, seldom returned to Britain once they made their fortunes. Instead they began to ape the manners of English country gentlemen, in their dress, their reading, their recreation. Their sons they sent occasionally to Oxford, Edinburgh or to the Inns of Court, though such young men were very much a minority. Even the careers of the foreign-educated remained focused on their American estates and on their political activities as legislators in Williamsburg or Charleston. In spite of the ethos of aristocracy, only a tiny minority had come from anything higher than yeomen or artisan stock in England. Many, at least in Virginia, had arrived as indentured servants. Yet in a space of two or three generations from settlement, the profits from slave-grown tobacco, rice and indigo had brought them to positions of leadership in the plantation colonies. William Byrd of Westover is one example of this group. His level of culture and education was uncommon in Virginia – uncommon enough to bring frequent comment – but his *Diary* shows the combination of the instinct to work hard, indifference to the hardships of his slaves, and genuine if intermittent piety, which were the standard attributes of those men who succeeded with him.[38]

[38] L. B. Wright and M. Tinling (eds), *The Secret Diary of William Byrd of Westover, 1700–1712* (Richmond, Va., 1941). A fine introduction to this period is C. Bridenbaugh, *Myths and Realities: Societies of the Colonial South* (1952); reprinted New York, 1970). See also L. Morton, *Robert*

In many ways Virginia and Carolina produced leaders more American than any other New World slave societies, men who saw their future as being colonial rather than pinned to a return to the mother country at some hopeful date in the future. This was different from the case of the English sugar islands, where the planter's first response to success was to endanger it by becoming an absentee. Those who made the greatest West India fortunes – Beckford, Modyford, Jeaffreson, Pinney – returned to England, where they prospered or otherwise by diversifying their investments and by extorting the maximum wealth from their estates through· overseers. Yet absenteeism was not a universal rule. All the British islands had many planter families who had been born in the West Indies and stayed there permanently. The romantic riches of the returned West Indians cannot hide the fact that they were only a few of the tens of thousands who had sought their fortunes in the Antilles, indeed only a small fraction of those who had survived as planters. Those who remained formed a rough and turbulent local ruling class, seldom well educated, permanently in debt, but inordinately tough and hospitable to the point of profligacy. Sugar society also produced a white colonial superstructure composed of commission agents, merchants, managers, soldiers and privateer captains. The ties between these whites were close, and their social life vigorous. At least one visitor to St Kitts, for instance, was uniformly charmed by her hosts, but half dismayed by the social whirl into which they drew her:

> We live in constant fear of the arrival of our ship, which will hurry us away, and we have not less than twenty invitations, and we dance every night for several hours, from which no person is exempted. All dance from fifteen to four score, and we are to have a fine ball here a few days hence, where the whole Island are to be.[39]

Carter of Nomini Hall: A Virginia Tobacco Planter of the Eighteenth Century (1941; reprinted Charlottesville, Va., 1964); Jack P. Greene (ed.), *The Diary of Colonel Landon Carter of Sabine Hall, 1752–1778*, vol. 1 (Charlottesville, Va., 1965); G. W. Mullin, *Flight and Rebellion: Slave Resistance in Eighteenth Century Virginia* (New York, 1972).

[39] J. Schaw, *Journal of a Lady of Quality: Being the Narrative of a Journey from Scotland to the West Indies, North Carolina, and Portugal, in the Years 1774–1776*, ed. E. W. Andrews and C. M. Andrews (New Haven, 1922) p. 125. The white groups not directly connected with agricul-

What Janet Schaw did not see outside the ballroom was the
section of the white English Caribbean which was not part of
'society' – the wretched remnants of the white servants who had
gone to Barbados, the Leewards and Jamaica, hopefully or under
duress, in the first fifty years of settlement. If it was from them
that the buccaneers drew their recruits, they also provided the
down-and-outs, whores and general riff-raff who gave colour to
the seaports of the islands. Bridgetown at least, and Port Royal
until the great earthquake of 1692, Kingston thereafter, were
entrepôts as busy and sordid as any of the cities of England's
mainland colonies. Black slavery was the edifice around which
the interests and activities of a complete white Caribbean world
were constructed.

The influence of the slave system went much further than this,
for large sectors of the European business community were
closely concerned with slavery and the slave trade. Apart from
the African and Guinea merchants themselves, the cheap trade
goods required for the Coast trade opened a market for embryo
industries in Holland, Germany and Scandinavia, as well as in
England. In the British case, although the Royal African Company dealt mainly in re-exported cotton from India and copper
and iron goods from Sweden or Germany, the traders of the
eighteenth century concentrated more on colonial rum and the
manufactures of England.[40] The success of merchants using these
wares was a factor in the collapse of the old chartered companies
with which England had first approached the Guinea trade.
There is little doubt that their monopolies had raised prices to a
point which slowed colonial development, and generally hampered
national success in slaving and in slave agriculture. 'The names
of old *Empson* and *Dudley* are infamous and odious to this day',
remarked a Barbadian planter in 1689, 'and they were hang'd
for their Villanies. Yet they ruin'd men but singly, and one by
one. How much higher Gibbets, and how much greater detesta-

---

ture are well described in C. Bridenbaugh, *No Peace beyond the Line: The
English in the Caribbean, 1624–1690* (New York, 1972) pp. 364–411; E.
Brathwaite, *The Development of Creole Society in Jamaica, 1770–1820*
(Oxford, 1970) pp. 135–50; R. S. Dunn, *Sugar and Slaves: The Rise of the
Planter Class in the English West Indies* (Williamsburg, Va., 1972).

[40] Williams, *Capitalism and Slavery*, pp. 65–84. All references are to the
second (1964) edition.

tion, do these men deserve, that have destroyed whole Countrys?'[41]

The merchants of the Royal African Company did not end their careers on the gallows, but they were not successful in maintaining their monopoly. The opposition they faced arose not from a national love of democracy in commerce. The main complaint against them was that they represented London merchants, to the exclusion of those in the provincial seaports or 'outports'. This was quite apart from their exclusion of merchants from Ireland and Scotland, who were to be kept outside the mercantilist structure. The Scots had little success with their own ventures, the short-lived Company of Scotland Trading to Africa and the Indies, and the disastrous Darien scheme.[42] The attack on the Royal African Company was launched by English provincial merchants eager to share the profits of the Guinea trade, and justly critical of the hampering effect of the monopoly on national success. London was never the greatest English slaving port. In its early decades British slaving was dominated by Bristol, with its long traditions as an international port and its obviously favourable geographical position. Even in the years from 1730 to 1739, 387 vessels, or 38·7 per cent of all British ships in the Guinea trade, cleared from Bristol, although the city's share dropped to 199 ships or 22·1 per cent in the following decade.[43] Until the rise of Liverpool, Bristol controlled by far the largest sector of the slave trade. Even once it was knocked out of the Guinea market it continued to prosper on importing sugar from the Caribbean in exchange for manufactured goods. During the long struggle between the Royal African Company and the out-

[41] [E. Littleton], *The Groans of the Plantations; or, a True Account of their Grievous and Extreme Sufferings by the Heavy Impositions upon Sugar, and Other Hardships, Relating More Particularly to the Island of Barbados* (1689; reprinted London, 1698) p. 19.

[42] G. P. Insh, *The Company of Scotland Trading to Africa and the Indies* (London, 1932); J. Prebble, *The Darien Disaster: A Scots Colony in the New World* (New York, 1969); T. C. Smout, *Scottish Trade on the Eve of the Union, 1660–1707* (Edinburgh, 1963) pp. 250–3.

[43] Figures quoted, with the author's kind permission, from unpublished paper by W. E. Minchinton, 'Bristol in the Eighteenth Century', delivered at the 86th Annual Meeting of the American Historical Association, New York, Dec 1971. See also Professor Minchinton's published studies, *The Trade of Bristol in the Eighteenth Century* (Bristol, 1957); *The Port of Bristol in the Eighteenth Century* (Bristol, 1962).

ports, the merchants of Bristol prospered as 'separate traders'. One of their principal complaints against the company was that, apart from its monopoly, it was too weak to keep out foreigners in the period of savage international competition which followed the decline of Portuguese power on the Coast.

The history of the Royal African Company has been superbly written by Kenneth Davies.[44] By the time it came into being in 1672, England and most of the other European nations had long used the device of the chartered company to carry out enterprises which involved large and long-term investment, high risk and the hope of great profit. The Muscovy and Levant Companies were such ones, as were the Virginia and Massachusetts Bay Companies. The Compagnie du Sénégal, the Dutch West India Company, the Danish West India Company and the Swedish African Company were foreign equivalents. The Company of Scotland Trading to Africa was an attempted Scottish imitation.[45] The Royal African Company itself was the successor of a 'Company of Adventurers of London Trading to Gynney and Bynney [Benin]', founded as early as 1618, and the Royal Adventurers into Africa formed at the Restoration. It was in desperate straits by 1672. From then until 1698 the Royal African Company was able to keep its legal monopoly, although this did not prevent the incursions of interlopers. Their competition, together with the high overheads of defence on the Coast and the debt service made necessary by inadequate capitalisation from the outset, meant that its shareholders drew no real profits. It was in serious financial difficulties by the time the charter was lost. It also suffered from the insistence of its captains, agents and factors on trading on their own account in the company's ships.

The company's decline did not affect the success of the private traders. Their overheads were low and their mobility greater. The exhorbitant level of company prices for slaves meant that they were welcomed in the West Indies. This gave them a market for their own wares, but also prevented the company from getting any legal redress for its grievances in colonial courts, which were

[44] Davies, *Royal African Company*.
[45] The various forms of company organisation used in the English colonisation are conveniently discussed in C. M. Andrews, *The Colonial Period of American History*, 4 vols (New Haven, 1934–8) I 28–45; Davies, *Royal African Company*, pp. 16–38.

more than ready to award damages to traders quite justly seized for infringing the monopoly.[46] The very complexity of routes in the Atlantic trade made systematic policing for interlopers impracticable, even if the money had been available for it. After the exile of the Stuarts the company's position became even weaker, since it no longer had members of the royal family among its shareholders. It could now expect little support from an unsympathetic government. In 1698 it was accepted that private traders could work the Guinea Coast after paying dues of 10 per cent off their profits to the company. A proportion of them did so, sailing as 'ten per cent men' instead of ignoring the official licence system. But the company's impotence to enforce its monopoly soon made even this gesture superfluous, and the trade was formally thrown open by Act of Parliament in 1712. Although the company was only reorganised belatedly in 1750, it had abandoned slaving in 1731. In effect, however, its monopoly had become meaningless by the end of the eighteenth century, if not by the end of the Stuart period.

The fortunes made by the merchants who took over the trade from the Royal African Company went not to London but to the outports, principally Bristol and Liverpool. Bristol, although its fishing and trading had made it a major port in the late Middle Ages, rose on the profits of the African trade to be England's second city. The initial success of its merchants was due partly to its geographical position, but also to the fact that, unlike the predominantly London-based traders of the Royal African Company, they had complete flexibility in their operations on the Guinea Coast. They also avoided the high overheads of debt service and the upkeep of expensive and unnecessary forts. Besides, they did not suffer to the same extent from the dishonesty and carelessness of the network of officials maintained by the African Company. In the period of Bristol's greatest prosperity, few of its citizens did not have some connection, direct or indirect, with slaving ventures. The profits of general New World shipping, together with the great scale of the interloper trade to Guinea and the Antilles, meant that Bristol's heyday had begun before the Royal African Company was defunct. The throwing open of the Guinea trade, and the city's almost total absorption in slaving, set the seal on its prosperity. Even after being pushed

[46] Ibid., pp. 116 ff.

out of this activity by the more efficient methods of the Liverpool traders, it continued to make enormous profits from trading directly in West Indian sugar, and from the refining industry which grew up around the city. The slave trade and the plantation trade out of Bristol between them bred several of the great families of the West of England.

Few such families made their fortunes directly in slaving. Most were brought to prosperity by young men who went out to the West Indian colonies as factors of one or other of Bristol's mercantile houses, acting as their agents in handling their sales of slaves or their purchases of sugar. If successful, they might move into trade on their own account or, more attractively, become planters themselves. Either course could produce a fortune with outrageous speed. At this point the emigrant would return to the West Country. There he would either continue in trade as a Bristol merchant, or put his money into the respectability of becoming a landowner, from which distant standpoint he would run his West Indian estates. If his shortcomings as a *nouveau riche* could be ignored or blustered away, and if absenteeism did not wreck his West Indian affairs or extravagance his English ones, he might then hope to be absorbed into the squirearchy.

In time the returned colonist or his sons might buy a seat in Parliament, at which point he had become an established member of the landed ruling class. Indeed, the extraordinary sums which status-hungry West Indians were prepared to pay for Commons seats inflated their prices to an extent which seriously upset the balance of English political power. It was no longer possible for the old-established but impecunious squirearchy to buy parliamentary seats in competition with ex-planters to whom money was no object.[47] An obvious corollary was that it became more difficult for those who had made relatively modest fortunes in mere trade to buy their way into the charmed circle of parliamentary privilege. One of the qualities of the unreformed House of Commons, often missed by modern historians, was that it worked splendidly, at least until the rise in the price of seats caused by vulgar and unscrupulous West Indians. Ironically, it

[47] On the West India interest in English politics, see L. Penson, 'The London West India Interest in the Eighteenth Century', *English Historical Review*, XXXVI (1921) 373–92; idem, *The Colonial Agents of the British West Indies* (London, 1924).

may partly have been this price rise which eventually pushed the successful commercial classes towards clamouring for electoral reform, where before they too had been able to purchase their privileges in an orderly manner which left the system unharmed. In either case, there is no doubt that the West Indians were able to get the seats they wanted – varying in numbers and loyalty, but able to raise fifty or sixty votes at times of crisis, and always enough to form a substantial and cohesive lobby – by the middle of the eighteenth century. At first this hung on the network of profit centred on Bristol, but later also on Liverpool and, to a lesser extent, Glasgow. This lobby retained some of its power into the 1830s and beyond, though it had shrunk grievously by the time of the Napoleonic wars. Naturally, it led the defence against abolition of the slave trade and slavery. More generally, since its vested interest in the unreformed Parliament was so great, and it was tied to the landed interest into which it had bought an entrée, it was a staunch opponent of electoral reform and the repeal of the Corn Laws. Eric Williams's theory that the attack on West Indian slavery was part of a middle-class free-trade conspiracy is crude. However, the strength and characteristics of the West Indian lobby produced a logic of power which ensured that slavery, protection and the unreformed Parliament would rise or fall together. The West Indians in the nineteenth century thus became one of the vociferous pressure groups in defence of an eighteenth-century *status quo*. Their emergence is one of the most striking side-products of the Atlantic slave trade.

The Bristol trade produced several of the most important families of the West India interest. The rise and fall of their individual fortunes can well be traced through the records left behind by their businesses. Many such studies remain to be done, but the outline of the rise of the groups who depended on Bristol sugar and Bristol slaves can already be traced. Few of the men involved came from backgrounds of genuine poverty, and the story of the great magnate Richard Miles who first came to Bristol with three-halfpence in his pocket is atypical. If for no other reason, rags-to-riches careers were few because of the costly level of education required to prosper in trade by the late seventeenth or early eighteenth century. For instance, one family of Bristol West Indian merchants which has been thoroughly studied, and whose story I outline as an example of a typical Bristol fortune, were the Pinneys of Somerton Erleigh in Somerset. They were descended from a Dorset clergyman with comfortable interests in lacemaking and land.[48] Indeed, it stood to reason that those most likely to succeed in the West Indian and African trade were men with the great advantage of having a small operating capital to begin with. Though Bristol and Liverpool both developed a mythology of the tattered apprentice who rose to become a merchant on 'Change, slaves and sugar seldom made poor men prosperous. What they did do in a great number of cases was make comfortable men extremely rich.

This the Bristol trade certainly did for the Pinneys. The first Pinney to make money in the West Indies was Azariah, who was compelled by his part in Monmouth's rebellion of 1685 to take up sugar-planting in Nevis, in the Leeward Islands. Yet even as a political fugitive, cut off from his father, beginning life in the New World on a modest scale, he required £35 to equip himself for his voyage, and took a further £15 with him for future investment. He was able to gather more money by acting as a factor in selling lace and other goods sent out by his family. From here he moved to working as a general factor or commission agent for English merchants, and began trading on his own account. Finally he bought land to become a planter and proprietor himself. His son John went to Pembroke College, Oxford, and added to the Nevis estates by marriage. Azariah's grandson John Frederick in turn rose to become M.P. for the West Country town of Bridgeport – and at the same time, though seldom in Nevis, was able to add slightly to the family holdings there. Yet his attitude to his West Indian holdings was that they provided a convenient source of income to support his position as a Dorset squire. It was probably because of this attitude that he died in 1762 leaving both his British and Caribbean estates encumbered with debt. He was succeeded by a distant cousin, John Pinney, who was able to reorganise the family's West India interests. Its landholdings were actually reduced, but consolidated to make the largest single plantation in Nevis.

The family fortune, by the end of John Pinney's life, had become one of the greatest in the West Country. The Pinney sugar exported was handled through Bristol, so that the factorage

---

[48] R. Pares, *A West India Fortune* (London, 1950) pp. 3–5 and passim. The following account of the Pinney family is taken wholly from this work.

operations begun by the founder of the dynasty were never entirely given up. John Pinney also invested heavily in lending to planters. He sold the last of his own land in Nevis in 1808, incidentally to one Edward Huggins, whose flogging and murder of his slaves were mentioned in most later abolitionist propaganda. But John Pinney still had almost £130,000 lent out against West Indian property at the end of his life in 1818, though he had lived primarily in Britain since 1783. His main business since then, in fact, had not been in his plantations, but in his Bristol merchant house. It was while building this business that he was able to entrench himself even more firmly among the gentry by expanding his landholdings in Dorset. Though John's elder sons were not successful in business, the youngest became Mayor of Bristol in 1831. He continued the affairs of his father's sugar-factors' house until it was wound up in 1850. The bulk of family income, however, by this time came not from sugar brokerage commissions, certainly not from actual West Indian landholding, but from their investment in West India shipping and in West India mortgages and finance. Few families had such splendid good fortune as the Pinneys, though enough did so to keep envy of the West Indians alive. One other example was the great Jamaica fortune founded by Peter Beckford, whose descendants included a Lord Mayor of London and the eccentric scholar-millionaire William Beckford, whose *Vathek* is one of our finest short Gothic novels. Another West Indian with a taste for the Gothic was the Jamaica absentee Matthew G. ('Monk') Lewis, whose *The Monk* was one of the most successful of its kind – one of the 'horrid novels' which Jane Austen parodied in *Northanger Abbey*.[49] By an extraordinary coincidence, Beckford and Lewis not only shared their interest in Gothic writing, but were both homosexuals and both sat in the Commons at separate times for the same constituency of Hindon.

Nevertheless, partly because of extravagance, partly because of reductions in income caused by absenteeism, partly because the movement of the sugar frontier constantly brought new competition for the older islands, the generality of the planters

[49] On the Beckfords, see B. Alexander, *England's Wealthiest Son* (London, 1962). Lewis, in later life, published a perceptive *Journal of a West India Proprietor, Kept during a Residence in the Island of Jamaica* (London, 1834).

formed a class of chronic debtors. At the time of old John Pinney's death, in fact, he was drawing personal income from some £200,000 worth of investments in the West Indies, independent of the more modest operations of the family house. This figure included only one small plantation, Richland Park in St Vincent. It was only with the collapse of sugar prices after the Napoleonic wars that they began to try to take their capital home as far as this was in their power. They were not entirely successful, and they suffered with the planters and other West India merchants from the collapse of sugar cultivation and land values brought about by the Emancipation Act of 1833. The family fortune declined slowly from the time of John Pinney's death in 1818. When the house of Pinney was wound up in 1857, John Pinney's two sons, Charles and John Frederick, were living as substantial English gentlemen from capital they had reinvested in land and on the stock market. By and large, they and their families were now indistinguishable from the other gentry of the West Country, but the basis of their position was the exertions of their father and grandfather in Bristol's West India trade.

The Pinneys were only one of many families who joined the English ruling class with the help of Bristol slaves and Bristol sugar. The city had been beginning to gain wealth from shipping to the new colonies and from the early Virginia tobacco trade in the mid-seventeenth century.[50] Its great fortunes, however, were made after the beginning of the sugar boom, either by selling slaves to or buying sugar from the early British planters, or both. One of the great Bristol houses which began in this way and then went on, like the Pinneys, to become a general broker and rentier in West Indian investments was Protheroe & Claxton; another was Evan Baillie & Sons. Some Bristol-owned ships sailed the triangular run. Others, an increasing proportion as the volume of Liverpool slaving swelled, plied directly between Bristol and the West Indies. One modern historian of Bristol announces apologetically that the latter were the majority, and that it is to them rather than the slavers that 'one must look for the essence and beauty of Bristol's westward faring'.[51] Yet sugar profits depended as fully as the slave-ships themselves on the Atlantic slave trade,

[50] B. Little, *The City and County of Bristol* (London, 1954) p. 141.

[51] Ibid., p. 160. See also Minchinton, *Trade of Bristol in the Eighteenth Century*, and *Port of Bristol in the Eighteenth Century*.

which was the main lever by which the Bristol merchants rose in the world. Atlantic profits may have helped the 'industries' of the surrounding area: coal-mining, sugar-refining, glassmaking and brassfounding became the staple industries of Bristol and its hinterland during the first sixty years of the eighteenth century. Yet the connection between this flourishing of industry and the slave trade was not absolute. Bristol's position as England's main western port gave it a great deal of wealth from other sources, and in any case local industry, especially in metal and glasswork, had been growing before the major impact of profits from the slave trade and slave sugar.[52] Some of the most important mercantile families who put their profits into local industry, notably the Champion family, were engaged not in the tropical trade but in trade with the English colonies in New York and New England. The importance of slaves and sugar for Bristol was enormous; but it was already a great city before English slave cultivation began, and in any case had other interests. The triangular trade and the direct West Indian trade accelerated its rise to greatness, but they alone did not cause it.

The case for Liverpool's prosperity being founded solely on the direct and indirect profits of slavery is much clearer. Unlike Bristol, which had been England's second port since the Middle Ages, Liverpool was little more than a fishing village until it began sending out slave-ships. It was perhaps because of their being latecomers with relatively little capital that the Liverpool traders were forced to rationalise this trade as a way of smashing Bristol and London competition.

Indeed, Liverpool engrossed its enormous share of the Atlantic slave trade at Bristol's expense. It had several natural advantages over its rival. One of them was its closeness to the growing industries of Manchester and Birmingham, from which cheap trade goods for Guinea could be drawn with minimum transportation costs. Manchester cotton checks could be sold much more cheaply in Guinea than the 'osnaburgs' from Europe on which Bristol depended. Another advantage came to be of greater importance as the century went on. With war very close to being a permanent condition, ships grew larger for economies of scale and self-protection. Vessels of 400 or 500 tons, in Liverpool's great deep-

[52] J. Latimer, *The Annals of Bristol in the Eighteenth Century* (London, 1893) pp. 7, 66 ff.

water harbour, could be directly loaded and unloaded at the quayside. In Bristol, if used at all, they involved their owners in expensive lighterage operations because of the muddy and relatively shallow estuaries of the Avon and the Troom. Again, loss in warfare was less – and insurance rates a little lower – because ships in and out of Liverpool beat up the Irish Channel instead of making their way through the mouth of the English Channel and across the regular beats of French or Spanish privateers. Bristol's only geographical advantage was the closeness of the Welsh coalfields, which gave a cheap product to sell to the West Indian planters once they began to use steam engines for crushing cane; but this only affected the direct trade, and in any case came far too late to have any effect on British slaving. Once Liverpool entered the slave trade as a serious competitor of Bristol, she had all the advantages, especially given her concentration, forced by lack of contacts and lack of capital, on the slave trade itself instead of the complex network of West Indian involvement which was the fortune but at the same time the bugbear of so many of the Bristol houses.

The economical practices of the Lancashire slavers may have been even more important than their natural advantages. If the unattractive cheese-paring aspects of the work ethic appear anywhere in the history of the Atlantic trade, it was among the Liverpudlians. Bristol merchants, in fact, had earned from the outset a reputation for personal extravagance which, assuming it was an extension of their business practices, makes it only too clear why it was so easy to push them out of the slave trade. In retrospect, the defeat of the Bristol merchants in Guinea, like the outbreak of the American Civil War or the failure of the '45, has a sort of ghastly inevitability about it. For instance, there is something ominous in the enthusiasm of this group of provincial businessmen for splendidly extravagant funerals.[53] Perhaps Bristol had succeeded too well. Its claim to be the second city in the land, with its undoubted position as the capital of the West Country, had given its traders the illusion of being an aristocracy who had stepped outside the merchants' obligation to make ends meet. This is one conclusion which can be drawn from a comparison between the running of Bristol and Liverpool slavers. The principal difference was that where Bristol employees had

[53] Ibid., pp. 9–10.

been paid commission on their business, those of Liverpool –
captains, agents and factors – were restricted to a salary and
nothing more. Other employees were dispensed with, and a
greater number of apprentices put in their places. Minor overheads were also cut, for instance by removing the captain's
privileges to a wine allowance while at sea and a dining allowance
while in port. Captains from Bristol and London, notes a
nineteenth-century historian, could 'occasionally eat on shore,
and drink their bottle of Madeira, whereas, the poor Liverpool
shipper was obliged to repair on board to his piece of salt beef
and biscuit, and bowl of new rum punch, sweetened with rum
sugar'.[54] Bristol was never pushed entirely out of African trade,
and her interests were still great enough in 1750 for her council
and corporation to petition repeatedly against the African Company in the debate leading to the removal of its charter and the
organisation of the open corporation called the Company of
Merchants Trading to Africa.[55] Yet all the advantages were on
Liverpool's side, and by this time she had engrossed the bulk of
the slave trade. By the end of the century Bristol was confined
almost wholly to the direct sugar trade, while Liverpool ships
were doing well enough in slaving to deliver their slaves and
return from the West Indies in ballast, leaving much of the sugar-
shipping to direct Bristol traders. Where 387 ships in the British
African trade had come from Bristol to Liverpool's 210 from
1730 to 1739, the ratio for 1764–75 was 276 to 983. In 1764, in
fact, Liverpool sent out half of all Britain's African shipping.[56]
This share increased during the remaining years of the century.
As for Bristol, it is significant that although its corporation
remained firm in support of the slave trade to the last, the first
provincial committee to promote abolition was formed there in
1788.

Before its slaveholding years, Liverpool had only come to
national prominence once, when besieged by the Roundheads
during the Civil War. It had no fortunes like those of Champion
from brass, zinc and china, or Abraham Elton in copper, which

---

[54] G. Williams, *The Liverpool Privateers, with an Account of the Liverpool Slave Trade* (London, 1897) p. 471.

[55] Latimer, *Annals of Bristol*, pp. 270–1.

[56] Williams, *Liverpool Privateers*, p. 495. Clearing figures from unpublished paper by Minchinton, 'Bristol in the Eighteenth Century', loc. cit.

antedated those made by the slavers. Its ventures in Africa, like Bristol's, were floated by sharing capital. Again, few citizens in the port had no interest in the trade. This was true not only of slaving but also of privateering. One survivor of the eighteenth century recorded that these occupations were not regarded as derogatory because so many people there were 'tarred with the same brush'.[57] Privateering and slaving were overwhelmingly Liverpool's central economic activities. It was also the practice to convert slave-ships into privateers when the Atlantic trade routes were disrupted by war and the profits from prizes became attractive. There is a whiff of illegitimacy about all Liverpool's early commerce. Not only did the port start off in the Atlantic trade by infringing the African Company's monopoly and by smuggling to the Spanish Indies, but her prosperity, unlike Bristol's, was based wholly on the marginal activities of legalised piracy and legalised kidnapping.

The rewards for these activities were great, but it is perhaps because Liverpool had no older merchant élite that its atmosphere in the eighteenth century was much cruder and less genteel than that of Bristol. Wealth it did acquire, but one of the few ways in which it was ploughed back into civic improvement was the decoration of the Liverpool Exchange with a frieze of elephants' and Negroes' heads. Otherwise Liverpool remained a mean and hard-headed town. Few provincial cities of the late eighteenth century, with the possible exceptions of Bath, Bristol and Edinburgh, could boast much elegance, but Liverpool seems to have remained at a level of outstanding squalor and barbarism. Even Samuel Curwen, the American loyalist, who was accustomed to primitive colonial communities and had seen other European cities, was appalled by Liverpool:

Streets long, narrow, crooked, and dirty in an eminent degree . . . we scarcely saw a well-dressed person, nor half a dozen gentlemen's carriages; few of the shops appear so well as in other great towns; dress and looks more like the inhabitants of Wapping, Shadwell, and Rotherhithe, than in the neighbourhood of the Exchange, or any part of London above the Tower. The whole complexion nautical, and so infinitely

[57] [J. Stonehouse], *Recollections of Old Liverpool, by a Nonagenarian* (Liverpool, 1863) p. 10.

below all our expectations, that naught but the thoughts of the few hours we had to pass here rendered it tolerable. The docks however are stupendously grand.[58]

It is pretty clear that the profits of the city were being ploughed back into further investments, rather than spent on conspicuous display. It was obviously because of the centrality of slaving to Liverpool's prosperity that its opposition to abolition was all but complete. Where Thomas Clarkson found a substantial number of allies in Bristol, he met few friends in Liverpool apart from the Quaker William Rathbone, who had already shown his opposition to slaving by refusing to provide timbers for ships to be used in the trade. The Liverpool families not directly concerned in slave-trading were often deeply involved in West Indian brokerage and real estate. The Gladstones, who were members of the large group of Scottish immigrants to Liverpool, are a splendid example.[59]

The relevance of this wealth for British industrial development was relatively slight. This was not because the fabled extravagance of the West Indians meant that their fortunes were squandered instead of being put back into making investments. Ostentation and debauchery characterised many if not most returned planters, but it was foreign to the sober merchants who drew their wealth from trading itself and from money-lending and brokerage in the sugar islands. However, we have seen that though some of their profits may well have been reinvested in industry, and though we do not yet have enough detailed studies to say exactly how much reinvestment took place, or exactly where it was lodged, the volume of such reinvestment cannot have been enough to affect the overall development of British industry to any appreciable extent. The impact of mercantile prosperity was even less in the case of Bristol than Liverpool, for there the ostentatious habits of an established merchant élite worked against careful reinvestment

[58] S. Curwen, *Journal and Letters*, ed. G. A. Ward, 3rd ed. (New York, 1845) p. 246, quoted in Williams, *Liverpool Privateers*, pp. 281–2.

[59] T. Clarkson, *The History of the Rise, Progress, and Accomplishment of the Abolition of the African Slave-Trade by the British Parliament*, 2 vols. (London, 1808) I 371–2; S. Checkland, *The Gladstones: A Family Biography* (Cambridge, 1971) pp. 185–200 and passim. On Liverpool's response to the abolitionists, see also A. Mackenzie-Grieve, *The Last Years of the English Slave Trade: Liverpool, 1750–1807* (London, 1941).

of profits. Again, the West Country's lack of plentiful water power, and its relatively inaccessible coal supplies, made it less suitable for development than Lancashire. The industrial development of Bristol's hinterland before and during the eighteenth century, though substantial, never equalled the dramatic growth of Midlands manufacturers. On the face of it, the case for a connection between the rise of Liverpool and industrialisation in the Black Country looks stronger. However, it is impossible to get round the fact that slaving and plantation profits were never *consistently* large enough to have been even a significant enabling factor in Lancashire's industrial revolution. Liverpool's most careful nineteenth-century historian, by averaging the profits per share of six representative slaving voyages and multiplying this figure by the number of slaves landed by Liverpool ships from 1783 to 1793, calculated that the net annual profit of the city's merchants was £1,187,335 11s. This is not a large figure given the fact that merchant families had to live, and that they were constantly drawn to reinvest in other shipping and colonial ventures, and in any case it is now clear that it must be revised substantially downwards.[60] It is true that crude profit figures on slave-shipping are often misleading because of the close interaction of slaving *per se* with other speculation in Caribbean money-lending, mortgages and real estate. But even the most modern studies of the total investment in the sugar colonies as a whole suggest that its averaged profits, if indeed they were reinvested in industry at all, were not substantial enough to have had real impact. Though Eric Williams's arguments in *Capitalism and Slavery* are logically persuasive, the real evidence for them is no longer acceptable.[61]

It seems probable, then, that there was not much connection between slavery and industrialisation. This does not mean that there was no connection between slavery and industry. British manufacturers cannot have been unaffected by the demand for the exports used to buy slaves in Guinea, and for the rudimentary tools and machinery needed for the plantations. The trade goods used on the Coast were enormously varied. Apart from foreign cloths, mainly German, the Bristol Guineamen had traded

[60] Cf. unpublished paper by Anstey, loc. cit.
[61] Williams, *Capitalism and Slavery*, pp. 98–107. Cf. Thomas, in *Econ.H.R.*, 2nd ser., xxi 30–45.

primarily in cheap metal and glass goods from their English industries. Once it became available to replace French brandy and
Dutch or German gin, they joined the American colonists in
flooding West Africa with rum from their own distilleries. The
Liverpool slavers were able to give the growing metallurgical
industry of the Midlands orders for the same brass and iron trade
goods. More important, however, they began to have outstanding
success in West Africa selling locally produced and printed cotton
and linen, mainly in simple red and white or blue and white
checks and stripes. Highly attractive in the Guinea market
because of their similarity to locally produced cloth, these fabrics
almost completely ousted the European 'osnaburgs' and expensive Indian calicoes so far used in the trade. Since there was little
British market for Lancashire cloth at this time, and it had not
yet reached the point of being able to compete with East India
cotton on its own territory, the slave-traders' demand for them
was crucial to the growth of the textile industry. One of the
arguments used against abolition in 1788 was that Manchester
alone was exporting to Africa goods to the annual value of half a
million pounds. Of this sum, £200,000 was accounted for by
textiles.[62] The cloth industry was very much an advance sector of
the industrial revolution, and its importance in the eighteenth
century lies not only in its own advances but in the stimulus it
gave to associated industries like the production of weaving and
spinning machinery, and thus indirectly to iron- and steelfounding
and the mining industries. The scale of Manchester's cloth
exports to Africa is a fine indication of the importance of Liverpool's Guinea trade in stimulating new manufactures. Liverpool
above all is the port which bears out the neat conclusion of Basil
Davidson that it was out of the expansion of trade in the tropical
Atlantic that 'there flowed the circumstances that enabled England
to achieve an industrial revolution'.[63] But this was so only in so
far as mercantile demands for manufactured goods created new
markets, and not in the sense that substantial plantation profits
were injected into industrial expansion.

There is no British, or indeed European, city where the link
between slaving and industry was so obvious as Liverpool, but it
is none the less there in several other cases. The connection

[62] Williams, *Capitalism and Slavery*, p. 70.
[63] Davidson, *African Slave Trade*, p. 63.

between Bristol's port business and the metallurgical and distilling industries of the West Country has already been noted. London itself, however, should not be forgotten in the West Indian and African trades. In the first instance the Royal African Company had provided its African clients with European spirits and textiles instead of the British articles, and they had also re-exported a great deal of Swedish copper and iron instead of using metalwork produced in England. However much demand for various items varied on the Coast, they were pretty constant in selling iron bars and copper and brass rings, as well as finished metal goods like basins, knives, swords, guns and hatchets. Such goods, as well as glasswork for the African trade, were at first bought in Amsterdam, though the growing success of London as an entrepôt meant that by the end of the seventeenth century her merchants were going directly to the countries of origin to get their goods for re-export to Africa. An even more important trend during the first thirty years of the company's existence, however, was the movement from re-exports to exports. Although it does not appear to have taken advantage of the output from Bristol's expanding glassworks, it began increasingly to use English knives, swords, guns and metalwork. By the late 1680s its buying of European cloth had shrunk, and it was sending substantial amounts of English-manufactured 'annabasses' and perpetuanos out to Africa.[64] It is difficult to trace the fortunes made directly in London's African trade to specific investors, since those London merchants who invested in the African and West Indian trade were normally men who had already made their fortunes in other areas of commerce, and London was already so well established as the first seaport of the kingdom prior to the opening of the Atlantic slave trade. Nevertheless, it is clear that a stimulus was given to British manufacture by the volume of manufactures exported to Africa from London, apart from the substantial share of the trade to the West Indies in cloth and plantation supplies. London's share of the slave trade itself declined in the eighteenth century, but it was never wiped out by competition from Liverpool in the same way as Bristol. The 104 ships it sent to Guinea in 1701 had fallen to 30 by 1707, but the total was back up to 87

[64] Davies, *Royal African Company*, pp. 165–79. London's share of the financial and insurance sectors of the West India trade is stressed by Sheridan, in *Econ.H.R.*, 2nd ser., XI 249–51.

by 1725, to Bristol's 63. She still sent out 389 ships from 1764 to 1775, to Bristol's 276 and Liverpool's 983.[65] Apart from this, the West India trade continued and even grew, though the slave trade itself slackened. Obviously, London's prosperity did not depend on the African and West Indian trades in the same way as Bristol or Liverpool, but its importance to British industry as a channel for selling manufactures in the tropics was nevertheless great.

In the eighteenth century the enormous bulk of the British slave trade was handled by Liverpool, London and Bristol, but lesser towns also had minor stakes in the African trade and occasionally sent ships to Guinea. Some now seem absurdly small ports – Exeter, Plymouth, Chester, Whitehaven. The Scottish ports were not admitted to England's trading monopolies until after the Act of Union in 1707. The attempt of the Company of Scotland Trading to Africa to set up a Scottish settlement in Darien was a catastrophe, as we have seen, and any small profits the Scots made off the Guinea and West Indian trades of the seventeenth century were illicit ones. After 1707, however, Glasgow became a serious competitor of Bristol and London. Only the occasional slaver left the port, but many of its merchants waxed fat on the direct trades in sugar and tobacco. Some made fortunes directly by becoming planters in the West Indies. The Mac-Dowalls and the Oswalds were two families who did so, though in their cases the family estates were founded the easy way, by marrying a West India heiress. The story of both dynasties closely parallels that of the Pinney family of Bristol. As in Bristol, the most important wealth came not from those sons of the city who became planters, but from those who became brokers and importers in tropical produce. It is a commonplace that Glasgow was built on tobacco, through her own imports from Virginia and through the fortunes Scots made as factors in the Bristol trade before launching out on their own account. What is less well known is Glasgow's importance in the direct carrying trade in sugar. Like Bristol, it spawned a network of refineries in the towns near it, stretching up the Clyde valley and along the coast. Greenock is still a great centre of sugar-refining, but the industry became central to the economy of south-west Scotland in the last quarter of the eighteenth century. Where Glasgow had been a

[65] Figures from Minchinton, 'Bristol in the Eighteenth Century', loc. cit.

peaceful country village with no distinction but its cathedral before the Union, it was catching up on Edinburgh in size and had far outstripped it in industrial importance by the beginning of the nineteenth century. Once again, the groundwork for this remarkable expansion was the tropical produce cultivated by black slaves.[66]

For British politics, the result of the inflow of wealth from Africa and the West Indies was startling. Apart from the ministerial placemen and the country members themselves, with whom indeed they often voted, the West Indians became the largest recognisable lobby in the unreformed House of Commons. Even so, they were surprisingly few in numbers, but the power given to them by their group discipline was enormous. They might occasionally differ, and vote separately, since they represented different elements within the West India interest: some were simple ex-planters, others the representatives of ports whose interests were in the shipping and money-lending networks of which the planters constantly complained. However, by and large they voted as a powerful bloc which represented planters as well as the three great seaports, and which would vote together on any issue which affected the general welfare of the trade in slaves, sugar and tobacco, and the financial world which depended on it. In foreign policy, too, they constantly fought against any plan which might endanger the frail security of the sugar islands. It was only their decline in the latter part of the eighteenth century which made the attack on the slave trade and slavery possible, though it would be a mistake to underestimate the bitterness of their resistance.[67] British politics, like the British economy, was deeply affected by the needs of slave agriculture and the slave trade.

The case of the French, the second most important of the slave-carrying nations in the eighteenth century, was rather different. The French commitment in the Caribbean was as great as if not greater than the English. They too were constantly

[66] R. Renwick, J. Lindsay and J. Eyre-Todd, *History of Glasgow*, 3 vols (Glasgow, 1921–34) III 257–64, 295–302; W. Ferguson, *Scotland: 1689 to the Present* (Edinburgh, 1968) pp. 182–5.

[67] L. J. Ragatz, *The Fall of the Planter Class in the British Caribbean, 1763–1833* (New York, 1928) passim. See also Penson, in *E.H.R.*, xxxvi 373–92.

concerned with promoting the supply of slaves for their plantations, and with the protection of their sources of sugar in the West Indies. However, they never managed to engross a substantial share of the trade in carrying slaves for other nations. As for the effect of the African and West Indian trades on France's seaports, it was as great as that on the British ones. Gaston Martin, historian of the French trade, records that most of France's ports had a stake in the slave trade and, less convincingly, that there were few great merchant families which did not share in its profits or those of the direct trade to the islands. The most enormous fortunes were made after the seizure of Saint-Domingue from the Spanish, when the opening of its great new sugar estates brought a spurt in its demand for labour. It has been calculated that from 1748 to 1792, 246,800 slaves were carried to the Caribbean in Nantois ships alone. Of these, 181,000 were taken to Saint-Domingue.[68] Apart from the slave trade itself, the Caribbean was centrally important to French commerce. Before the Revolution the plantations and slave-traders together accounted for approximately a quarter of France's overseas trade.

Nantes was the Liverpool of France, pulling far ahead of lesser slaving ports in the latter part of the eighteenth century. Here, as in Bordeaux, Le Havre and La Rochelle, the labour demands of the planters brought striking wealth to the great dynasties of *négriers*, families like the Nairacs, de Luynes, Montaudouins, de Guests and van Alsteins. Yet the position of these families was not quite the same as that of their British counterparts. To begin with, in Nantes and in most other French slaving ports they were predominantly Huguenots. As such, except in La Rochelle, they were excluded from membership of dominant city merchant corporations and their political power was correspondingly weak. They formed a separate élite closely connected among themselves by marriage and the community of business interests. Again, in the latter part of the eighteenth century the average profits on the slave trade itself declined – one student puts them at between 1 and 6 per cent.[69] What kept the Nantois *négriers* in the trade

[68] D. Rinchon, *Le Trafic négrier, d'après les livres de commerce du capitaine nantois Pierre-Ignace-Liévin van Alstein. Tome Ie* (Paris, 1938) pp. 247–305. See also Curtin, *Atlantic Slave Trade*, pp. 163–203.

[69] Viles, 'The Slaving Interest in the Atlantic Ports, 1763–1792', to be published in *French Studies*, xxvi (1972). Cf. Jean Meyer, 'Le Commerce

was the effective exclusion of private shippers, that is those of the outports, from the East India and China trade and a continued government concern for the sugar islands which induced them to maintain a system of bounties on occasion amounting to a quarter of the investment in a voyage. Profitability could thus be maintained and, as in Bristol and Liverpool, the *négriers* boosted their fortunes through investment in direct trading, in insurance and in West Indian mortgages.

The wealth of the *négriers* certainly went back into the French economy. But the relationship between capitalism and slavery here is again quite different from the one Williams suggests for Liverpool. The reinvestments and exports associated with the French slave trade had a slighter effect on industrialism than in England. The common practice for French slave merchants was not to put their profits into industry, but to reinvest them in other maritime schemes. Even the stimulus given by the demand of the Guineamen for trade goods was less than in the Lancashire case. By and large, owing to the relatively underdeveloped state of French manufactures, the *négriers* shipped a higher proportion of re-exports than their British counterparts. Their manufactured goods came principally from Amsterdam or directly from Germany, even in the years immediately before the Revolution. The impact on the French economy must have been correspondingly less, though substantial amounts of light French textiles were exported to Africa. A proportion of the capital in the French trade came not from France itself but from Amsterdam, and indeed several of the families were Huguenots of Dutch extraction. A corresponding share of the trade's profits presumably returned to Holland, to be reinvested as the Dutch saw fit; though this too, like the use of re-exported Swedish, Dutch and German manufactures by the British and French Guineamen, must have had a stimulating effect on European industry in general. Some of the

---

négrier nantais (1774–1792), *Annales: Économies, Sociétés, Civilisations,* xv (1960) 120–30, which demonstrates the great expansion of the French trade in the years 1783–92, though it does not deal with the problem of profit levels, and points to many bankruptcies just before then. In his *L'Armement nantais dans la deuxième moitié du XVIIIe siècle* (Paris, 1969) pp. 205–48, however, Meyer shows that apparently large profits were in reality small owing to the tardiness of payments from the Antilles. On the merchant families, see also G. Martin, *Nantes au XVIIIe siècle L'Ère des négriers* (Paris, 1931).

French profits from the trade may also have been absorbed in money-lending to the aristocracy and the crown. French industrialisation was notoriously retarded in the mid-eighteenth century, too much so to be an attractive area of reinvestment for commercial houses accustomed to placing spare capital in more traditional enterprise.

In fact the link between slavery and industrialisation is everywhere less plausible than in Britain, if only because the preconditions for full industrialisation had not emerged in other countries at times when the major profits from the slave trade were coming in. Nevertheless, the demands of the slave trade affected the economic life of Europe as a whole. The earliest fortunes to be made from the slave trade were those of the Genoese and Spanish asientists, and the slave trade in the seventeenth century, as part of its great carrying trade, laid part of the foundation of Amsterdam's commercial hegemony. We have already seen how the French and, to a lesser extent, the British bought many of their African trade goods from German and Swedish manufactories, so that they too were affected by the conditions of trade in Guinea – quite apart from the impact of minor ventures like the voyages made by the Danes, Swedes and Brandenburgers on their own account. In this way the Atlantic slave trade had an effect on economic life throughout Europe, even on powers which were not themselves committed to the African trade.

Nor was the impact of the traffic confined to the Old World. After independence, Brazil would produce its own caste of merchants whose prosperity depended on slaving; but the close commercial link between England's rising Northern colonies and the slave societies of the Caribbean emerges in the seventeenth century. Again, the permutations of trading patterns involved were endless, and the most important factor in the equation was not the slave trade. Indeed, the involvement of New York, Pennsylvania and the New England colonies in slaving as such was never great, though there were isolated exceptions. The most important Northern fortunes were made in the trade in plantation supplies. It was primarily from the North that the British planters, both in the Caribbean and on the mainland, drew the food for their slaves, much of their livestock and the packing materials for their own produce. By the late seventeenth century, merchants from the mainland were trading along a flexible and bewildering complex of routes – to England, Madeira, the Canaries and, very occasionally, Africa. Furs were the richest of their exports, but their most consistent profits came from selling salt fish to the Catholics of Europe and the Negroes of the Caribbean, and pipe-staves to the wine-growers of the Atlantic islands and the sugar-planters of the West Indies – to whom they also sent salt beef, pork and livestock. In return they brought home Canary and Madeira to satisfy the extraordinary thirst of the mainland colonies, and molasses which could in turn be made into rum. In time this rum became the staple for direct slave-trading. Philadelphia, New York, Boston and, most of all, Newport, Rhode Island, were involved in the direct slave trade by the late eighteenth century. Charleston also, as the principal mainland port to which slaves were brought directly from Africa, became implicated. Yet the overall involvement of the colonial ports remained small, kept so by the great capital required to stock ships with adequate trade goods, by the competition of British ports and by the limited ability of the mainland colonies to absorb complete cargoes of slaves. Any true American slaving ran from the colonies to Africa – sometimes via England – and thence along the standard run to the islands, to Charleston or Virginia, where slaves were sold for cash, bills of exchange, or produce to be brought home to Newport or elsewhere. Other slavers became involved in the re-export trade, selling plantation supplies for seasoned island slaves, who were sold on the mainland for tobacco or indigo which could be brought to the North. Both in Charleston and on the Chesapeake, incidentally, bitter experience had shown planters that re-exported slaves were less satisfactory than new ones, and slave prices and import duties varied accordingly. In neither case, however, was this trade the true basis of the wealth of the Northern seaports. They did indeed depend on slavery, but their dependence was indirect. Without the opportunity to sell their wares as supplies for the Caribbean slaveowners, it is hard to imagine the rise of New England or New York commerce. Actual slaving did indeed play a great role in the mainland ports, especially Newport and Charleston, but the real growth of colonial commerce and of colonial commercial élites depended not on supplying slaves but on maintaining West Indian slave society. It was from the latter that the great trading dynasties of the New England and Mid-Atlantic colonies made their fortunes – and these were the men who became the ruling class of the new republic after the Revolution.[70]

Directly or indirectly, the demands of the West Indian slave system changed the development of society all around the shores of the Atlantic – in Africa, North America and Europe, quite apart from the impact of slavery itself on Latin America and Britain's Southern colonies. The relative power of African societies, and in some cases their actual structure, changed to meet the demands of the slavers. In North America the trade of the plantation colonies made the fortunes of the cities from which the Revolution would be fought. In Britain and France it brought new ports into prominence, and created new political pressure groups. Most strikingly in England, and to some extent in other European countries, though plantation profits did not finance industrialisation, the demand of slavers and planters for new manufactured goods inevitably stimulated industry. The rise of sugar and tobacco cultivation in the seventeenth and eighteenth centuries, and the slave trade which fed them, had effects much more complex than the depopulation of West Africa and the enrichment of the American slaveholders. Even in the nineteenth century, the period of illicit slaving, the colourful renegade Captain Canot could sneer at the hypocrisy of ignoring the network of European interests which depended on the slave-ships:

> England, today, with all her philanthropy, sends, under the cross of St George, to convenient magazines of *lawful commerce* on the coast, her Birmingham muskets, Manchester cottons, and Liverpool lead, all of which are righteously swapped at Sierra Leone, Acra [*sic*], and on the Gold coast, for Spanish or Brazilian bills on London. Yet, what British merchant does not know the traffic on which those bills are founded... ? France, with her *bonnet rouge* and fraternity, dispatches her Rouen cottons, Marseilles brandies, flimsy taffetas,

---

[70] B. Bailyn, *The New England Merchants in the Seventeenth Century* (Cambridge, Mass., 1955); S. E. Morison, *Builders of the Bay Colony*, 2nd ed. (Boston, 1962) pp. 143–5, 172–6. On Rhode Island slaving, see P. J. Coleman, *The Transformation of Rhode Island* (Providence, R.I., 1963) pp. 51–8, chap. ii passim. A useful introduction to early American economic history is S. Bruchey, *The Roots of American Economic Growth, 1607–1861* (London, 1965).

and indescribable variety of tinsel gewgaws. Philosophic Germany demands a slice for her looking-glasses and beads; while multitudes of our worthy [American] traders, who would hang a slaver as a pirate *when caught*, do not hesitate to supply him indirectly with tobacco, powder, cotton, Yankee rum, and New England notions, in order to bait the trap in which he *may* be caught.[71]

Even in the days of its decline, the web of the slave trade's interests was spun throughout the Atlantic economy.

[71] B. Mayer (ed.), *Captain Canot: or, Twenty Years of an African Slaver* (New York, 1954) p. 127.

5 The Flaws in Slave Society and the First Abolitionist Ideas

SLAVERY was overthrown when its profitability declined and when the classes who supported it themselves began to lose strength. This is not the same as saying that abolition was nothing but a product of changes in the economic needs of the class structure of western Europe.[1] An abolitionist movement was produced by the interaction between such economic and social change, and a complex series of intellectual developments, philosophical, literary and religious. Occasionally the abolitionists might have an aristocratic ally, much more occasionally a working-class one. But they were overwhelmingly drawn from the ranks of the solid businessmen of a rapidly industrialising world, or the lawyers, clergymen and other professionals who were their servants. There had been little reason for the traditional groups of pre-industrial society to query the viability of making slaves of black men and women. This was why it was so easy for the first colonists and slave-traders to slip into a relationship which now seems morally so repulsive. Those who later turned against slavery had been born into a more modern world in which it was an anomaly. This was so not only because it was cruel, though this did suddenly dawn on its critics, but because it now seemed less efficient. In any case, it was less important to the economies of the European countries. By the late eighteenth century, sugar-growing was simply a less important part of national effort. Many of those who had originally prospered in it had moved on to other activities. The British and French were also facing increasing competition from the virgin soils of Cuba and Brazil. It was against this background that there came the

[1] Cf. E. Williams, *Capitalism and Slavery*, 2nd ed. (London, 1964).

genuine intellectual changes which revolutionised the attitudes of the West to slavery, the Negro and the slave trade.

The potential for such changes became clear at an early stage. There is a substantial scattering of articles and pamphlets attacking slavery from the end of the seventeenth century onwards, starting with the so-called Germantown Protest of 1688. The importance of this and other documents, together with the pamphlets of anti-slavery pioneers like Sewall, Hepburn, Sandiford and Lay, will be discussed in the next chapter. Together they represent a comprehensive series of arguments against slavery, which made a great deal of progress towards the abolitionist standpoints of the later eighteenth and even nineteenth centuries. Nevertheless, these first voices against slavery cried in the wilderness. It is wrong to think of any kind of anti-slavery 'movement' in the first half of the eighteenth century. Protests against slavery there certainly were, but their writers had no substantial following. In some cases they were at best eccentrics, whose extraordinary comments on slavery only added to their reputation for being unbalanced. A small number of Europeans had always campaigned for the Christianisation of black slaves. One Archbishop of Seville, for instance, complained bitterly of those missionaries in Africa and America who gave the sacrament of baptism to blacks without their understanding its importance, and published elaborate instructions for ministering to them more conscientiously.[2] A later English example was the plea of the Welsh Anglican clergyman Morgan Godwyn, published as *The Negro's and Indian's Advocate*.[3] But all the writers who produced polemics specifically attacking slavery as an enormity in itself lived in the colonies. The majority of them, though by no means all, were Quakers. The importance of early anti-slavery protests has been exaggerated, first by abolitionists trying to find a respectable tradition for their ideas, and later by American historians determined to demonstrate that slavery had been a ghastly aberration from America's more usual enthusiasm for

[2] Pedro de Castro y Quiñones, *Instrucción para remediar y assegurar quanto con la divina gracia fuere possible, que ninguno de los Negros, q. vienen de Guinea, Angola, y otras provincias de aquella costa de Africa, carezca del sagrado baptismo* (Seville, 1614).

[3] M. Godwyn, *The Negro's and Indian's Advocate, Suing for their Admission into the Church, etc.* (London, 1680).

liberty and equality. Actually the truth is quite different. Early anti-slavery literature is highly important, but it represents a pointer to the trends of the future rather than any widespread societal doubt about the validity of slavery.

At least until the 1760s there was almost total white acceptance of the use of black men and women as slaves. Protests against this prevailing assumption were individual ones. Precious few were found to disagree with the colonial pamphleteer who remarked that 'Of all the things we have occasion for, *Negroes* are the most necessary, and the most valuable'.[4] The vested interest in slavery, real or imagined, was simply too great to assess the institution on the hazy level of morality. For isolated protests to become either a general questioning of the justification for slavery, or a real organised movement aimed at its overthrow, major changes had to take place. The first was the weakening of the very vested interest in slavery itself. The second was an intellectual revolution which made the holding of fellow-men as chattels seem revolting, a revolution furthered by eighteenth-century writers in philosophy, religion, poetry and belles-lettres. The economic change did not 'cause' the intellectual one, or vice versa. However, the two developments are closely interconnected. It was the weakening of the economic buttresses of the plantation regime which allowed the change in Western attitudes towards slavery to take effect, first in abolition of the slave trade and then in emancipation.

The viability of slavery, at least in some parts of the world, was weakening in various ways by the latter half of the eighteenth century. Tropical agriculture in any given colony was never consistently prosperous or consistently poor. The major tropical crops grown by slave labour, sugar and tobacco, quickly exhausted the soil. Fresh and fertile new lands were constantly being opened. Slavery became more profitable in some areas as it became less so in others. In Britain's mainland colonies, for instance, soil exhaustion in Virginia and Maryland pushed them away from tobacco cultivation towards mixed agriculture in

---

[4] [E. Littleton], *The Groans of the Plantations; or, a True Account of their Grievous and Extreme Sufferings by the Heavy Impositions upon Sugar, and Other Hardships. Relating More Particularly to the Island of Barbados* (1689; reprinted London, 1698) p. 7.

which the gang labour of slaves was unnecessary. This trend was most marked in the nineteenth century, but even at the Revolution it was becoming increasingly difficult to grow tobacco profitably in the tidewater colonies. The heyday of magnates like William Byrd of Westover was over before the Revolution. Tobacco could no longer bring the quick profits on which his success had been built. The successors of his class, the great Virginians of the revolutionary generation and the young republic, were men who had the status of a hereditary aristocracy but who could maintain their prosperity only through a willingness to adapt to declining tobacco yields.[5] On the other hand, the newer lands of Georgia and South Carolina had not yet come to difficulties. In the United States of the nineteenth century, with the invention of the cotton gin, the virgin soil of these states, and of Alabama, Mississippi and Louisiana, would give them a prosperity based on slave-grown cotton quite in contrast to the decay of the tobacco tidewater. Meanwhile the concentration of the Northern colonies on commerce rather than large-scale agriculture made the buying of slaves anomalous as soon as a supply of free white labour was available.

In the Caribbean, different sugar islands gave the most attractive returns at different periods. Barbados began the boom, and it was soon joined in its prosperity by St Kitts, Nevis, Montserrat and Antigua. By the early eighteenth century, however, the most expansive of the English sugar islands was Jamaica. Jamaica in turn was challenged first by the possessions seized by the British at the peace of 1763, especially Trinidad, and in the nineteenth century by the mainland plantation settlements of modern Guyana – Demerara, Essequibo and Berbice. More serious, however, as the latter half of the century progressed and the available sugar soil of Jamaica was used up, was the competition of the fertile islands belonging to the French. It is not as amusing as it sounds that the British seriously considered taking Guadeloupe and Martinique instead of Canada from the French at the end of the Seven Years War. By all the normal canons of the commercial thought of 1763, the decision was preposterous. Few would have been found to quarrel with Voltaire's sneer at those northern

---

[5] A. O. Craven, *Soil Exhaustion as a Factor in the Agricultural History of Virginia and Maryland, 1606–1860* (Urbana, Ill., 1926) pp. 11–121; idem, *Edmund Ruffin, Southerner* (Baton Rouge, La., 1966) pp. 49–72.

possessions as 'a few acres of snow'.[6] The sugar-producing potential of the two tiny islands, on the other hand, made them the richest possessions in the tropical world. Ironically, some of the pressure for refusing to take them came from the West India lobby themselves, who were reluctant to compete within their protected English market with floods of cheaply produced sugars from Guadeloupe and Martinique. The problem of competition from French possessions had become even worse with the opening of Saint-Domingue. It was producing sugar as a serious competitor to the English in world markets by the 1760s, and it absorbed the vast majority of the slaves carried across the Atlantic by the French in the last twenty years before 1789. Only the collapse of Haitian sugar culture with Toussaint l'Ouverture's revolution temporarily released the British from this threat. The problem of competition, given their own exhausted soil, need for dunging and high selling prices, had two effects on the aims of Britain's West India interest. Firstly, it intensified their opposition to free trade, and their determination to protect their own expensive sugars with high tariff walls. Secondly, for those planters and West Indian merchants who had eyes to see, it became clear that the continuation of the slave trade was simply giving the French, and ultimately the Cubans and Brazilians, more strong arms to produce enough sugar to destroy the world market for English produce altogether. This conception, though it by no means removed resistance to the abolition of the slave trade, at least made that resistance less determined. By the same token, of course, the slave trade was of greater importance than ever before to the French in the period between the Seven Years War and the Revolution, when they owned the most fertile sugar-growing soil in the world, but never had enough labour to exploit it fully. It was this situation which the French government was recognising in the elaborate bounties it paid to maintain mercantile interest in a slave trade which was not in itself particularly profitable.

In the latter half of the eighteenth century, three powerful English-speaking groups which had previously supported slavery and the slave trade began to turn away from them. At least some of those who saw the preservation of the West India interest as a national priority came to the conclusion that it was illogical to continue the slave trade for the benefit of their competitors. At

[6] *Candide*, trans. and ed. John Butt (London, 1947) p. 110.

the same time, the Northern mainland colonies had less and less use for slaves as their interests focused increasingly on commerce and manufacture. Tidewater planters, too, who were in any case having difficulties with plantation tobacco cultivation, could afford to be critical of slavery if the fancy took them. Taking 1763, the end of the Seven Years War, as a rough starting-point on this shift in economic interest, we can see some of Britain's most powerful elements of support for slavery and the slave trade becoming apathetic. This weakening of the forces they were opposed to was central in making possible the early triumphs of the English and American abolitionists, though it did not *cause* them. There is also *some* truth in the theory that the abolitionists were members of the rising middle class resentful of the social and political supremacy of the conservative landed interest with which the West Indians were identified. According to this argument, the attack on slavery and the slave trade was used as a tool to discredit a backward-looking group whose opposition to free trade seriously threatened industrial development. Along the same lines, it has been argued that the American abolitionists, right up to the Civil War, picked up slavery as a useful staff with which to beat quasi-feudal planters. The latter were dangerous in that they demanded free trade at a time when protection was required to encourage infant American industries. They generally stood for an archaic social order at odds with the conditions required for the triumph of Northern capitalism.

Such economic interpretations should not be dismissed out of hand. The process of industrial change forms the backdrop for the attack on slavery and the slave trade. Again, the success of the abolitionists would have been impossible if the enormous change in society's economic balance had not made those classes with a direct vested interest in slavery proportionately weaker and less important. The economic interpretation also contains the truth that it made abolitionist rhetoric more effective. The luxury of testing an institution by morality could only be afforded on a large scale once the anti-slavery audience had come to consider it unprofitable or at least irrelevant. Finally, the consciousness of their difference in economic world-picture made sections in America and interest groups in Europe readier to formulate different moral and intellectual positions on slavery. In all these senses, economic change made the task of the abolitionist movement easier. However, the economic interpretation is absolutely irrelevant in answering the questions of why abolitionist ideas emerged and why the anti-slavery ranks swelled to the proportion of a full-scale movement in the last part of the eighteenth and the nineteenth centuries. The root of this problem lies with the abolitionists themselves. Few scholars would now put their concern over slavery, or even all their success, down to sinister self-interest. Even the great Trinidadian pan-Africanist George Padmore, whose effect on his countryman Eric Williams was so great, describes the British abolitionists of 1807 and 1833 as 'these noble and selfless fighters for right against wrong, for freedom and justice for the black man'.[7] The economic interpretation has little to do with the abolitionists, though it has a great deal of relevance to the way in which society responded to them. The emergence of the European anti-slavery movement in the 1760s was not just the product of lessening enthusiasm for sugar and tobacco – the demand for both has continued to rise steadily until the present day – but of radical changes in the intellectual and religious assumptions of the West.

These changes should not be over-simplified. It is tempting to conclude that if the eighteenth-century revulsion against slavery and the slave trade was not a factor of economics, it was produced by the combination of the ideas of the European Enlightenment with the evangelical movement, by a genuine moral revolution. Sir Reginald Coupland, quoting Lecky, once announced firmly that the British campaign for the abolition of the slave trade was 'among the three or four perfectly virtuous pages comprised in the history of nations'. The simplicity of this dictum has been scathingly attacked.[8] Coupland and his school have been less savagely handled for their allied assumption that the writing of these 'perfectly virtuous pages' was stimulated by the meeting of evangelicalism and the Enlightenment. To men deeply

[7] G. Padmore, *Pan-Africanism or Communism?* (New York, 1956) p. 37.

[8] R. Coupland, *The British Anti-Slavery Movement* (Oxford, 1933) p. 251. Coupland's view is supported, at least with qualifications, in idem, *Wilberforce: A Narrative* (Oxford, 1923); F. J. Klingberg, *The Anti-Slavery Movement: A Study in English Humanitarianism* (New Haven, 1926); G. R. Mellor, *British Imperial Trusteeship, 1783–1850* (London, 1951) pp. 31–127. Cf. Williams, *Capitalism and Slavery*. A recent attempt to synthesise the two views of the British case is D. H. Porter, *The Abolition of the Slave Trade in England, 1784–1807* (Hamden, Conn., 1970).

influenced by the benevolence of John Wesley and the egalitarianism of the Age of Reason, it was supposed, black chattel slavery
had become morally outrageous. The relative importance of the
two influences might differ for different men. The concern of
Wilberforce, for instance, was a Christian one, whereas that of
Charles James Fox was secular. But all eighteenth- and early
nineteenth-century abolitionists are presented as children of an
age of benevolence itself born from the union of reason and
evangelicalism. Within this standard interpretation of the influences on the abolitionists, little attempt is made to trace either
stream of thought to its origins. The Christian influence is
assumed to rise with the emergence of Methodists inside the
Church of England, oddly promoted by Quaker intermediaries.
The influence of the Age of Reason is seen as stemming directly
from the European Enlightenment, primarily the French one. In
fact none of this interpretation is accurate as it stands. What is
certainly true is that all abolitionists were aware of, and were
influenced by, the problems raised by the writers of the Enlightenment and by the increasingly evangelical Christianity of their
age.

The nature of the abolitionist impulse was intensely complex.
It is simply not an adequate explanation to say that it proceeded
from the two groups of potentially revolutionary ideas. The anti-
slavery movement arose at a point when a series of contradictions
in both the secular and religious thought of the West on slavery
became unmanageable. This did bring a tendency towards
egalitarianism – though certainly not equality; certainly, too, it
brought an increase in benevolence towards the poor and the
oppressed, and even in one or two eccentric cases towards
animals. Behind these manifestations, however, lies a ferment of
tortured reconsideration of the religious and intellectual underpinning of slavery, and indeed of hierarchy in general. Unravel-
ling the various influences in play is the more difficult since they
were seldom transmitted directly. They do not proceed in an
orderly manner from the Continent to England and thence to the
American colonies and the young United States. The germ of the
intellectual attack on slavery was taken from Montesquieu by
the scholars of the Scottish Enlightenment. It was they who perfected most of the eighteenth century's rational arguments against
slavery. The ideas of Hutcheson, Wallace and Millar did not go

direct to the English abolitionists. Instead they were first adopted by American pamphleteers, particularly the Philadelphia Quaker Anthony Benezet, whose work in turn passed on the anti-slavery legacy of the Scottish (and French) Enlightenment to England. Not only this, but it also appears that the French were themselves influenced by this dog-leg transfer of ideas. French abolitionists like Brissot de Warville, too, were confessedly inspired by colonial Quakers. As for the evangelical influence on the English abolitionists, it was not just produced by the levelling impact of Wesley's thought within the Church of England. The most important godly impulse towards British abolition of slavery and the slave trade came from the Quakers, who had been influenced partly by changes in the attitudes of colonial Friends with whom they were closely in contact. Even Wilberforce and the evangelicals themselves adopted ideas formed partly by colonial influences, for the individual who did most of all to draw them to the cause was the London ordnance clerk Granville Sharp. He in turn had drawn his assumptions from extensive contacts with American Quakers. Revivalism itself, and its impact on benevolence, was certainly not confined to England. The American abolitionists who were so central in their influence in England had changed their attitudes to slavery not only under the impact of the Scottish Enlightenment, but also because of the changing conceptions of sin introduced by their own Great Awakening and the revivals which followed it. Thus the process was not one where a total abolitionist message born in the meeting of English evangelicalism and the ideas of the European Enlightenment was received by English reformers and then passed on to the colonies. Anti-slavery grew out of an extraordinarily complex interplay between the ideas of the European continent, America, Scotland and England. Until very recently the importance of the Edinburgh philosophers and the Philadelphia Quakers has been missed by historians, and the sheer complexity of eighteenth-century abolitionist thought accordingly underestimated.[9]

---

[9] This problem is brilliantly treated in D. B. Davis, *The Problem of Slavery in Western Culture* (Ithaca, N.Y., 1966), to which my own interpretation and the following account are deeply indebted. See also M. Kraus, *The Atlantic Civilization: Eighteenth Century Origins* (1949; reprinted Ithaca, N.Y., 1966) pp. 144 ff. and passim; idem, 'Slavery Reform in the Eighteenth Century: An Aspect of Transatlantic Intellectual

The two constants which appear throughout the whole web of intellectual change are the thought of Montesquieu and the synthesising of the French–American Quaker Anthony Benezet. A startling number of eighteenth-century polemics on slavery, especially in the American colonies and in Scotland, quote or mention the famous book xv, chapter v, of *L'Esprit des Lois*, published in 1748. The following wording is that of a widely circulated English translation of the eighteenth century:

Were I to vindicate our right to make slaves of the Negroes, these should be my arguments.

The Europeans, having extirpated the Americans, were obliged to make slaves of the Africans for clearing such vast tracts of land.

Sugar would be too dear, if the plants which produce it were cultivated by any other than slaves.

These creatures are all over black, and with such a flat nose, that they can scarcely be pitied.

It is hardly to be believed that God, who is a wise Being, should place a soul, especially a good soul, in such a black ugly body.

It is so natural to look upon colour as the criterion of human nature, that the Asiatics, among whom eunuchs are employed, always deprive the *Blacks* of their resemblance to us, by a more opprobrious distinction.

The colour of the skin may be determined by that of the hair, which among the Ægyptians, the best philosophers in the world, was of such importance, that they put to death all the red-haired who fell into their hands.

The Negroes prefer a glass necklace to that gold, which polite nations so highly value: can there be a greater proof of their wanting common sense?

It is impossible for us to suppose these creatures to be men, because allowing them to be men, a suspicion would follow, that we ourselves are not Christians.

Weak minds exaggerate too much the wrong done to the Africans. For were the case as they state it, would the European powers, who make so many needless conventions among themselves, have failed to make a general one, in behalf of humanity and compassion?"[10]

The danger of this form of satire, given Montesquieu's relative conservatism on other issues, was that it could be taken literally. The British lecturer and pamphleteer William Dickson, an abolitionist friend of the philosopher James Beattie of Aberdeen, thought it worth writing a lengthy passage proving that Montesquieu's disparaging comments on the Negro were not to be accepted seriously.[11] In general, however, a much neglected book by one of Montesquieu's commentators has made it clear that his influence in the English-speaking world was even greater than the extent to which he himself was influenced by British institutions.[12] On slavery at least, his furthest-reaching influence was on the writers of the Scottish Enlightenment. Among the abolitionists themselves, it was the early colonial pamphleteers who absorbed Montesquieu most fully, though they seem to have done so second-hand, through the writing of Ferguson, Hutcheson, Wallace and Beattie.

No one has yet given a full explanation for the extraordinary flowering of Scottish thought in the latter half of the eighteenth century.[13] The focus of the Scottish Enlightenment was Edinburgh, but a number of its most important writers belonged to the two other universities of Glasgow and Aberdeen. This does not imply that the Enlightenment, here or in Europe, was confined to university towns. The writers of the Scottish Enlightenment came from many backgrounds – ministers, academics,

[10] *The Spirit of Laws*, trans. T. Nugent, 2nd ed., 2 vols (London, 1752) II 341–2.

[11] W. Dickson, *Letters on Slavery* (London, 1789) pp. 81–5.

[12] F. T. H. Fletcher, *Montesquieu and English Politics, 1750–1800* (London, 1939); idem, 'Montesquieu's Influence on Anti-Slavery Opinion in England', *Journal of Negro History*, XVIII (1933) 414–25. See also R. P. Jameson, *Montesquieu et l'esclavage. Étude sur les origines de l'opinion antiesclavagiste en France au XVIIIe siècle* (Paris, 1911).

[13] G. Bryson, *Man and Society: The Scottish Inquiry of the Eighteenth Century* (Princeton, 1945); N. T. Phillipson and R. Mitchison (eds), *Scotland in the Age of Improvement* (Edinburgh, 1970); W. Ferguson, *Scotland: 1689 to the Present* (Edinburgh, 1968) pp. 198–225; C. Robbins, *The Eighteenth Century Commonwealthman* (1959; reprinted New York, 1968) pp. 177–220. On the American impact, see S. E. Ahlstrom, 'The Scottish Philosophy and American Theology', *Church History*, XXIV (1955) 257–72.

gentry and, above all, lawyers. Boswell records his own and
Johnson's discussion in Skye with an obscure Highland clergyman who announced belligerently that 'The world . . . takes us
to be credulous men in a remote corner. We will shew them that
we are more enlightened than they think.'[14] The Scottish
Enlightenment, then, had an impact along an extraordinarily
broad front. Its writers were prophets who had the unusual
experience of being honoured not only in their own generation
but also in their own country. Outside Scotland the picture is
somewhat more surprising. There is no doubt that the work of
these men was known in England. Hume became one of the
luminaries of London, Paris or whichever cities he visited on his
extensive travels from London. Hutcheson, Ferguson, Beattie
and others had London publishers and were men of note in
English intellectual life. But in London eyes, the Scots philosophers, with the exception of the acerbic and urbane Hume,
found it difficult to step outside the depressing category of provincial intellectuals. They were handicapped when met in the
flesh by abrasive Scottish accents, and even suspect for the
'Scotticisms' which they found it so hard to eradicate from their
prose. It is a measure of their relatively low intellectual status
that the best-known northern writer after Hume in the London
world of the 1760s and 1770s was 'Corsica' Boswell, arguably the
most delightful but certainly not the cleverest Scot of the century.[15] The Scottish Enlightenment did not have its most important effect in England, perhaps not even in Scotland itself, but in
the American colonies. It was there that the Enlightenment
philosophers were considered most deeply. This was not simply a
function of the circulation of Scottish works in the colonies,
though this was wide. The intellectual community of the colonies
and Britain formed an organic whole, but when Americans
looked towards the British universities and the British world of
authorship, their focus most often was not on London but on
Edinburgh. The negative side of this connection was the extent
to which Scotland and the colonies shared a status as 'cultural
provinces'. The seldom admitted resentment of London superiority

[14] J. Boswell, *The Journal of a Tour to the Hebrides with Samuel Johnson, Ll.D.* (London: Everyman ed., 1909) p. 214.

[15] F. A. Pottle, *James Boswell: The Earlier Years, 1740–1769* (New York, 1966) pp. 356–68.

brought a conscious sense of community between America and the eighteenth-century British provinces – and indeed the same is true of the Atlantic connection in the nineteenth and twentieth centuries. One of the most striking things about Boswell's *London Journal*, for instance, is the similarity of his love–hate response to the capital to that of the Virginian William Byrd forty years before.[16] In the second half of the eighteenth century, on a more positive level, Edinburgh had the finest medical school in the world. Out of a series of very small graduating classes from 1749 to 1800, it gave out a total of 117 medical degrees to Americans, and of these, 76 were granted after the Revolution.[17] Hume, Ferguson and Hutcheson, in spite of the diversity of their ideas, were alike admired in America. At a time when Oxford and Cambridge were sunk in Anglican apathy, colonists admired Edinburgh as the intellectual capital of their world. This relationship was furthered by institutional contacts, by the number of Scots clergymen who were called to take positions among Presbyterians in the New World, and above all by the role of Edinburgh University in founding the College of New Jersey. Princeton's early history was dominated by graduates of the Scottish colleges, most notably one of its greatest presidents, John Witherspoon. To a lesser extent this was also true of the Philadelphia medical school, organised under the aegis of Benjamin Rush. At first it was staffed predominantly by doctors who had studied, like him, under the great William Cullen at Edinburgh. Such contacts could not fail to have an influence outside the simple practising of medicine. When he announced that 'Methinks I see the place of my nativity becoming the *Edinburgh of America*', Rush was preaching his vision of a city in a state of complete cultural regeneration.[18]

Given the extent to which the colonial intellectual looked towards Edinburgh, it is of the utmost importance that the writers of the Scottish Enlightenment adopted Montesquieu's standpoint

[16] B. Bailyn and J. Clive, 'England's Cultural Provinces: Scotland and America', *William and Mary Quarterly*, 3rd ser., xi (1954) 200–13; J. Boswell, *The London Journal, 1760–63*, ed. F. A. Pottle (New York, 1950); L. B. Wright and M. Tinling (eds), *William Byrd of Westover: The London Diary (1717–1721) and Other Writings* (New York, 1958).

[17] Kraus, *Atlantic Civilization*, pp. 192–3.

[18] B. Rush to J. Morgan, 16 Nov 1766, in L. H. Butterfield (ed.), *Letters of Benjamin Rush*, 2 vols (Princeton, 1951) i 28–9.

on slavery. This is not to say that Montesquieu was not absorbed and adapted by Americans in other ways. The work on law and politics most widely read in the colonies was Blackstone's *Commentaries*, which had been deeply influenced by Montesquieu's argument that slavery was forbidden by natural law.[19] Again, Montesquieu was read in the original in English America, though probably not very extensively. The French patriot Brissot de Warville, himself an abolitionist and a founder of the Société des Amis des Noirs, was enthralled in his Gallic way by the library of Harvard College: 'The heart of a Frenchman beats faster to find Racine, Montesquieu, and the Encyclopedia in a place where a century and a half ago the Indians smoked their calumets.'[20] To an extraordinary degree, however, the conceptions of the Enlightenment came to the English-speaking colonies through the Scottish philosophers.[21] All of them, with the possible exception of David Hume and the very definite exception of Henry Home, Lord Kames, at one time or another took standpoints which had an impact on and could be turned to good use in the campaign against slavery. Hume's paternalistic comments on Negro inferiority were squashed by another of America's more popular authors, James Beattie of Aberdeen, while Kames' painstaking four-volume monograph, *Sketches in the History of Man*, became the butt of a great Princeton scholar, later its President, Samuel Stanhope Smith.[22] The other Scots *philosophes*

[19] W. Blackstone, *Commentaries on the Laws of England*, new rev. ed., 4 vols (London, 1813) I 426–9. See also Fletcher, *Montesquieu and English Politics*, p. 29.

[20] J. P. Brissot de Warville, *New Travels in the United States of America*, ed. D. Echeverria (Cambridge, Mass., 1964) p. 95.

[21] Ahlstrom, in *Church History*, xxiv 257–72; Robbins, *Eighteenth Century Commonwealthman*, pp. 177–220.

[22] J. Beattie, *Elements of Moral Science*, 2 vols (Edinburgh, 1790) II 199 ff.; idem, *An Essay on the Nature and Immutability of Truth, in Opposition to Sophistry and Scepticism*, 6th ed. (Edinburgh, 1805) p. 310; S. S. Smith, *An Essay on the Causes of the Variety of Complexion and Figure in the Human Species. To which are Added Strictures on Lord Kaim's Discourse, on the Original Diversity of Mankind* (Philadelphia, 1787). Cf. Henry Home, Lord Kames, *Sketches in the History of Man*, 2nd ed., 4 vols (Edinburgh, 1778); D. Hume, 'Of National Characters', revised version (1756), in T. H. Green and T. H. Grose (eds), *Essays Moral, Literary and Political*, 2 vols (London, 1875) I 244–52: 'In JAMAICA indeed they talk of one negroe as a man of parts and learning; but 'tis likely he is admired

uniformly deplored the brutality of slavery – even Hume, in spite of his assumption of Negro inability. Their attacks were absorbed in the colonies, and returned to the Old World in the form of the early pamphlet polemics of the American abolitionists. These in turn had an extraordinary impact in Europe. Davis has recently made the fascinating discovery that de Jaucourt wrote the formative *Encyclopédie* passage on slavery simply by lifting it from the work of the obscure Scots jurist George Wallace, one of Montesquieu's most avid British followers and the author of the first volume of a *System of the Principles of the Law of Scotland.* The same passage was simultaneously used by Anthony Benezet in his *Short Account of that Part of Africa, Inhabited by the Negroes* (1762).[23] Wallace was thus absorbed by Europe via de Jaucourt, and by the English via Benezet, Granville Sharp, and finally Wilberforce and the Clapham Sect whom Sharp influenced so deeply. In the latter half of the eighteenth century the anti-slavery idea ran along all the filaments of an Atlantic intellectual web, at the centre of which sat the philosophers of the Scottish Enlightenment.

Perhaps the most significant of all these men was Francis Hutcheson. His work, though deeply influenced by Anthony Ashley Cooper, Lord Shaftesbury, was formative to the evolution of the Scottish Enlightenment, and indeed to the European Enlightenment in general. He held the chair of moral science and natural philosophy at Glasgow University, and his *Inquiry into the Original of our Ideas of Beauty and Virtue* was published in 1725. Later its ideas were expanded in the *System of Moral Philosophy.* This work demolished the classical assumption that the structure of morality was dictated by reason. Instead, like the structure of aesthetics, it was a function of an inner and essentially non-rational sense. This could override the claims of the 'rational' organisation of society, and even ultimately the demands of Christian revelation. This is not to say that the rational element in human organisation was to be abandoned. Quite the contrary, but the 'utility' of each institution or practice was to be tested against the hardship which the sense of benevolence

---

for very slender accomplishments, like a parrot, who speaks a few words plainly' (II 252 n).

[23] D. B. Davis, 'New Sidelights on Early Anti-Slavery Radicalism', *William and Mary Quarterly*, 3rd ser., xxviii (1971) 585–94.

told humanity it caused. Society, like the individual, would constantly strive to balance the twin principles of 'benevolence' and 'utility'. Yet the potential of 'benevolism' as a criterion in subverting accepted notions of hierarchy in society is clear. Hutcheson's work removed the 'classical' rationalisation for slavery. It was thus possible for his disciples, principally Ferguson and Adam Smith, to approach and test the problem of slavery untrammelled by the assumption that the morality which upheld it was immutable. In short, Hutcheson opened the way to testing social institutions, including slavery, by 'romantic' or humanitarian ethics based on the non-rational sensation of 'benevolism'. 'The natural sense of justice and humanity', wrote Hutcheson in his *System of Moral Philosophy*, 'abhors the thought' of inequality, even that based on superior education. Wisdom in itself gave no automatic right to govern, 'since it may be employed by a selfish corrupt temper to the worst purposes, even the general misery of the community'.[24] This completely removed the need to accept the Aristotelian theory of 'natural' slavery. Hutcheson briefly but specifically attacked hereditary enslavement of Africans, though not by name, in the second volume of the *System of Moral Philosophy*. His remedy was the vague one that they would only be freed after working long enough to repay their masters for carrying them from Africa and thus, by implication, saving their lives. He went on at greater length to demolish the traditional justifications for the enslavement of captives taken in war:

No damage done or crime committed can change a rational creature into a piece of goods devoid of all right, and incapable of acquiring any, or of receiving any injury from the proprietor; unless one should maintain that doing useless mischief, and creating excessive misery unnecessarily, can tend to the general good; and occasion no diminution of the happiness in the system, which is so contradictory in the very terms.[25]

The Hutchesonian notions of justice and morality were most directly adopted by Adam Smith, his successor in the chair of

[24] F. Hutcheson, *A System of Moral Philosophy*, 2 vols (London, 1755) I 302–3. This thesis is brilliantly set out in W. Sypher, 'Hutcheson and the Classical Theory of Slavery', *Journal of Negro History*, XXIV (1939) 263–80.   [25] *System of Moral Philosophy*, II 84–5, 202–3, 199–212.

moral philosophy at Edinburgh. Smith's lectures on political economy, known to us as *The Wealth of Nations*, do contain a condemnation of slavery and the slave trade. But they were less important for his eighteenth-century reputation than his *Theory of Moral Sentiments*. This was published in 1759, and it built on the work of his teacher Francis Hutcheson in rejecting a 'natural' basis for hierarchy. In terms of the intellectual origins of anti-slavery, this standpoint was as influential as the argument of *The Wealth of Nations* that slavery and the slave trade were economically inexpedient. Yet the latter assumption was central to abolitionist thought.[26] Since the Hutchesonian tests for human institutions were the twin ones of benevolence and utility, Smith undercut the case for African slavery by demonstrating that it was not only repugnant to human feelings but also unnecessary to promote the happiness (or prosperity) of society at large. Certainly, Hutcheson's conception of benevolence was built on the ideas of Shaftesbury, and certainly Smith's conception of utility had been hinted at by Hume and was elaborated by his pupil John Millar, of the chair of civil law at Glasgow, in his *Observations Concerning the Distinction of Ranks*. However, it was from the writing of these two Glasgow professors, Hutcheson and Smith, that the West drew its twin secular indictment of slavery. Its brutality outraged human benevolence, while its inefficiency and unprofitability outraged the societal principle of utility. The latter point was to become a stock shot in the abolitionists' propaganda locker. Slavery retarded progress, slavery created an idleness unproductive to society. 'The experience of all ages and nations', claimed *The Wealth of Nations*, 'demonstrates that the work done by slaves, though it appears to cost only their maintenance, is in the end dearest of all'.[27]

Smith was not the only British moralist who expanded on Hutcheson. Two other influential writers who did so were the dissenting minister James Foster, and later the episcopalian Archdeacon of Carlisle, William Paley. As important in terms of their international appeal, however, were the other writers of the

[26] A. Smith, *The Theory of Moral Sentiments*, 10th ed. (London, 1804) 1 97–129; idem, *An Inquiry into the Nature and Causes of the Wealth of Nations*, 2 vols (London: Everyman ed., 1933) 1 344–6.

[27] Ibid., 1 345. On Millar's thought, see W. C. Lehmann, *John Millar of Glasgow, 1735–1801: His Life and Thought and Contributions to Sociological Analysis* (New York, 1960).

Scottish school. This is not to say that the specific concern of the Scottish Enlightenment was with slavery. Its really important effect on the growth of abolitionist ideas came through the wide reading of its general works on morals and society, all of which *incidentally* stated or at the very least implied a position on slavery. This was so in the cases of Hutcheson and Adam Smith, and also of other eighteenth-century Scottish writers. Of these the most important in terms of international influence was the Edinburgh sociologist Adam Ferguson. Just as Adam Smith is known, somewhat glibly, as the father of political economy, Ferguson has been described as a pioneer of modern sociology.[28] His *Essay on the History of Civil Society* first appeared in 1767. In many ways it was a pioneering work, for instance in rejecting the theory of social contract and stipulating that man had been living in a full state of society from the outset. Ferguson is also unusual among the *philosophes*, though less so among the Scottish ones, in seeing conflict as natural and as essential to human progress. Most important, however, was his insistence on a rigorous empirical study of the structure, origin and goals of society, in place of the abstract speculation which he considered was the weakness of his predecessors and fellow-scholars, even the exacting David Hume.[29] It was on the empirical basis set out by Ferguson that the abolitionists were later able to dismiss slavery as being ahistorical as well as immoral. Though the great *Essay on the History of Civil Society* said little specifically on slavery, the importance of his method for testing the expediency of the institution of slavery cannot be exaggerated. Benjamin Rush, for instance, though horrified by the 'moderation' of Ferguson, was not prevented from absorbing his rationalistic science while a student at Edinburgh. He 'assimilated the new rationalistic science, improved it by his future work and thought, and employed it to give his version of Christianity a scientific plausibility'.[30]

[28] P. Hazard, *European Thought in the Eighteenth Century*, trans. J. L. May (London, 1965) p. 232.

[29] A. Ferguson, *An Essay on the History of Civil Society*, ed. Duncan Forbes (Edinburgh, 1966) pp. xiii–xli. See also Bryson, *Man and Society*, pp. 30–52; W. C. Lehmann, *Adam Ferguson and the Beginning of Modern Sociology* (New York, 1930); D. Kettler, *The Social and Political Thought of Adam Ferguson* (Columbus, Ohio, 1965).

[30] D. J. D'Elia, 'The Republican Theology of Benjamin Rush', *Pennsylvania History*, XXXIII (1966) 193.

The general standpoint of Ferguson, like that of Hutcheson and Smith, was central in forming the ideas of the abolitionists.

Others among Scottish writers focused their thought more directly on slavery and even on the wider problem of race. A recent commentator on the Enlightenment has concluded that its responses to slavery were 'predictable and anything but systematic . . . generally exclamations, rarely thoroughgoing analyses'.[31] While this is certainly true of the continental philosophers, it does not apply to all the Scottish school. Hutcheson, Ferguson and Smith wrote only incidentally on slavery, but some other Scottish moralists produced sections on slavery long enough to imply thorough and systematic thought on the subject. Still, few of the *illuminati* of late eighteenth-century Glasgow and Edinburgh were concerned with the problem of slavery as their primary study. Nor did all of them come to benevolent conclusions. For instance, Henry Home, Lord Kames, built on David Hume in his pseudo-scientific *Sketches in the History of Man* (1774). This purported to prove that the Negro was naturally inferior and next in level of intelligence and ability to the apes. He made this point, incidentally, with the help of the advanced and anti-scriptural argument that there had been separate re-creations of the various races in the time after the building of the Tower of Babel. The other Scottish scholar deeply concerned with questions of race, also a Law Lord, was James Burnett, Lord Monboddo. He buttressed his pleas for the ending of slavery and the good treatment of Negroes with a theory of the total unity not only of all mankind but of all primates. This he supported with his famous and presumably spurious evidence on tailed men, which he saw no reason to suspect. 'Other people', remarked Dr Johnson, 'have strange notions; but they conceal them. If they have tails, they hide them; but Monboddo is as jealous of his tail as a squirrel.'[32] On the other hand, James Boswell, the most colourful figure of eighteenth-century Edinburgh, was categorically opposed to all forms of visionary tampering with slavery.

[31] P. Gay, *The Enlightenment: An Interpretation*, vol. II: *The Science of Freedom* (New York, 1969) p. 410.

[32] Boswell, *Journal of a Tour to the Hebrides*, p. 93; Kames, *Sketches in the History of Man;* Bryson, *Man and Society*, pp. 62–77. On Kames, see also W. C. Lehmann, *Henry Home, Lord Kames, and the Scottish Enlightenment: A Study in National Character and in the History of Ideas* (The Hague, 1971).

Dr Johnson's morbid fascination with the woes of the Negroes he put down, with his habitual dogged respect for all forms of hierarchy other than the Corsican one, to simple ignorance of the facts.[33]

Neither the Boswellian and Kamesian reactions, nor the oblique approach of a Hutcheson or a Smith, should be allowed to hide the contributions to the study of slavery made quite deliberately by other figures of the Scottish Enlightenment. Of these the most important were John Millar, of the chair of civil law at Glasgow University; James Beattie, professor of moral philosophy and belles-lettres at King's College in Aberdeen; and George Wallace, an obscure Edinburgh lawyer whose influence on de Jaucourt and Benezet has already been mentioned. Beattie, alone among the theorists of the Enlightenment, was himself an active abolitionist, a friend of Wilberforce and a correspondent of Benjamin Rush. Little is known about the circulation of Millar's work outside Scotland, but Beattie and Wallace at least appear to have been read in the English-speaking colonies. It was there that their message was adapted to create an abolitionist propaganda which in turn was to be transmitted back to Europe.

John Millar, as a student at Glasgow, had originally been taught by Adam Smith. The first version of his *Observations Concerning the Distinction of Ranks* was published in 1771, five years before *The Wealth of Nations*, but well after its ideas had been formulated in Smith's undergraduate lectures. Millar's long chapter on slavery was an elaboration of his essential though briefly expressed point on the inutility of slave labour. Here too slavery was described not only as being unprofitable, but also as a system which encouraged laziness among the working population, irresponsibility and luxury among the ruling class, and the risk of rebellion and unrest in society at large. Millar might well have been looking forward to Thomas Jefferson's 'With the morals of the people, their industry is also destroyed'.[34] His main indictment, like that of his mentor Adam Smith, was the utilitarian one that, whatever its cash profits in special situations, forced labour did not promote the welfare of society as a whole.

---

[33] J. Boswell, *Life of Johnson* (New York: Modern Library Edition, 1931) entry for 23 Sep 1777, p. 749.

[34] J. Millar, *Observations Concerning the Distinction of Ranks in Society*, 2nd ed. (London, 1773) pp. 251–312.

Millar's brilliant writing looks forward to Marx in suggesting an economic base for the power of the ruling class at each of several stages of history. Yet he remains very much an obscure figure of the Enlightenment. *The Distinction of Ranks* went through three editions, and it clearly contributed to the expediency argument later used by English and Scottish abolitionists. But it had no colonial edition, and there is at present no indication that it had any substantial impact outside Britain. This is entirely different from the history of the work of the Edinburgh lawyer George Wallace, which had an ironically slight impact within Scotland. We know very little about his personal life. His father, Robert, was a Church of Scotland minister, and an authority on population with a modest but genuine European reputation. The younger Wallace went to the Scots Bar but apparently ruined his career in his late twenties by antagonising Henry Dundas and his family, then the principal fountainhead of Scottish patronage. There is little information on Wallace's later career. He wrote only one volume of what was intended as a full jurisprudential study of Scots law. Volume I of his *System of the Principles of the Law of Scotland* appeared in 1760. A huge, erudite and expensive book, it was presumably intended, at least by Wallace's publisher, to sell among practising Scots lawyers as a reference work. Since no second volume appeared, it seems likely that they refused to buy it, and that the whole project was commercially a failure. However, the first volume contained a systematic assessment of the legal basis of slavery. Indeed, it was probably because of this kind of digression that the working Scots solicitor was less than enthusiastic about putting the book on his shelves. None the less, Wallace's argument on the incompatibility of slavery with natural law was more forceful than that of Montesquieu, upon whom he had closely drawn. As we have seen, it had a remarkable influence outside Scotland.[35] The right of liberty, wrote Wallace, was legally inalienable, since the Law 'would presume, *praesumptione juris et de jure*, that he who had alienated such an invaluable possession, either was deprived of the use of his reason, or was circumvented, and, for one or other of these reasons, would restore him against the alienation'.

[35] Davis, in *W.M.Q.*, 3rd ser., XXVIII 585–94. These comments on Wallace rely heavily on this paper and on information supplied by Mr Nicholas Phillipson of the University of Edinburgh.

Slavery was not only 'banished' by Scots law, but was legally indefensible in America. Any commercial transaction involving the loss of personal liberty was '*ipso jure* void. This right he [the slave] carries about with him, and is entitled every where to get it declared'.[36] This was the most uncompromising statement that slavery was illegal, and from it could be deduced the 'immediatist' standpoint that slavery must be abolished at once. The *System of the Principles of the Law of Scotland* shared the position of Hutcheson and Smith that the abolition of slavery could be justified on grounds of utility. Though it might cause a temporary interruption of trade, it would bring immense commercial blessings in the long run. More advanced, however, was its radical restatement of Montesquieu's position on the relationship between natural law and slavery. Wallace argued that all inequality not absolutely necessary to society's welfare was unnatural, that slavery was unnecessary, and that it should therefore be abolished at once as a step towards the complete equality which would be attained in a more perfect state of society. Potentially this was more extreme than any other statement of the sort made in the eighteenth century. Indeed, it was not until 1824 that any British abolitionist progressed to making the demand for immediate abolition, far less to presenting abolition as an instalment in full societal equality. Wallace's work was apparently less horrifying in the colonies, at least to Anthony Benezet, an endlessly humane but not particularly radical man.

The writing of James Beattie did not have the same spectacular international influence as the *System of the Principles of the Law of Scotland*. Nevertheless, Beattie had an enormous reputation in his day. This was chiefly because of his imagined success in demolishing Hume, in the somewhat immodestly entitled *Essay on the Nature and Immutability of Truth, in Opposition to Sophistry and Scepticism* (1769). The extraordinary allegorical painting of Beattie by his acquaintance Reynolds simply summed up a public assumption when he showed a somewhat anaemic philosopher, with a wave of his copy of the *Essay on Truth*, and only one angelic ally, sending a triumvirate of demons shrieking back to the pit.[37] Beattie was greatly respected and admired by

---

[36] G. Wallace, *A System of the Principles of the Law of Scotland*, vol. 1 (Edinburgh, 1760) pp. 94, 88, 95.

[37] This painting is in the possession of Aberdeen University. It is repro-

scholars as diverse as John Wilkes and Samuel Johnson. After first being introduced to him by Boswell, another of Beattie's friends, Johnson had written that 'Of Dr Beattie I should have thought much but that his lady puts him out of my head; she is a very lovely woman'.[38] Actually, Beattie's reputation extended far outside Britain, in spite of the shoddiness of his *Essay* and his almost complete misunderstanding of Hume. In France the Abbé Grégoire approvingly cited his attack on Hume's anti-scriptural comments on Negro inferiority. He was widely read in America. When he was made a member of the American Philosophical Society on the nomination of Benjamin Rush, this was in recognition of his supposed success in overthrowing Voltaire and Hume rather than because of his anti-slavery contributions. To Rush he was 'The David who slew that giant of infidelity'.[39] Nevertheless, Beattie's impact on anti-slavery thought was great, much more so than any permanent effect he may have had on checking the bane of scepticism. There is some reference to the problem of the Negro's inherent inferiority in the *Essay on Truth*, but this is less extensive and was probably less influential than the long passage on slavery in the lectures Beattie gave during his many years in the Marischal College chair of moral philosophy, which he took over at the age of twenty-five. These were published in 1790 as *Elements of Moral Science*, one of the most popular philosophical works to be written in English in the late stages of the Enlightenment. A long part of the section on 'Economicks' was devoted to slavery, with special reference to the slavery of Africans. Lacking both the dangerous radicalism of Wallace and the coldness of Ferguson, it was more likely than they to have an appeal to the general reader on moral subjects. It is of the greatest importance, then, that its position summarised, even popularised, the Enlightenment's indictment:

---

duced as the frontispiece of M. Forbes, *Beattie and his Friends* (London, 1904).

[38] Ibid., p. 35. Mrs Mary Beattie was the daughter of James Dun, the prominent northern educationalist and Rector of Aberdeen Grammar School.

[39] H. Grégoire, *De la littérature des Nègres* (Paris, 1808) p. 37; Beattie to Rush, 12 Dec 1786, in L. H. Butterfield, 'A Survey of Benjamin Rush Papers', *Pennsylvania Magazine of History and Biography*, LXX (1946) 97–8; Rush to J. Kidd, 13 May 1794, in Butterfield (ed.), *Letters of Benjamin Rush*, II 748.

... that slavery is inconsistent with the dearest and most essential rights of man's nature; that it is detrimental to virtue and industry; that it hardens the heart to those tender sympathies, which form the most lovely part of the human character; that it involves the innocent in hopeless misery, in order to procure wealth and pleasure for the author of that misery; that it seeks to degrade into brutes, beings whom the Lord of heaven and earth endowed with rational souls, and created for immortality; in short, that it is utterly repugnant to every principle of reason, religion, humanity, and conscience.[40]

Beattie, born later than the better-known *philosophes*, shows a concern for the slave's soul which is evangelical rather than utilitarian or merely benevolent, but the main lines of the Scottish Enlightenment's anti-slavery argument are here.

The reason why the Scottish Enlightenment is discussed so extensively here is its centrality as a clearing-house for Enlightenment ideas on slavery. Slavery was discussed at greater length by the Scottish philosophers than by the continental ones. Gay's conclusion that the remarks of the *Philosophes* on slavery were confined to 'exclamations', and that these remarks were intended as ammunition against the established order, are by and large true of the European writers, with the exception of Raynal and the physiocrats. Again, as regards the formation of an anti-slavery movement on an organised basis, this was a phenomenon of the English-speaking world, at least outside the circles of dilettanti like the French Société des Amis des Noirs. In this English-speaking world, in Britain and her colonies, the greatest circulation went not to the continental writers, but to the British and American scholars who synthesised and elaborated on them. The influence of Montesquieu was incalculable, on slavery as on other topics, but as well as being transmitted directly it reached the colonies through the work of Blackstone and the Scots. Voltaire, again, attracted enormous attention in the English-speaking world, but his statements on slavery had none of the force of those on Montesquieu, or for that matter Hume. The maimed Negro in *Candide* had suffered from only one of the enormous complex of cruelties and abuses which constituted 'civilised' society. Rousseau, too, was regarded with something of a morbid

[40] *Elements of Moral Science*, II 155–6.

curiosity, but he wrote nothing on slavery which could not have been found in the pages of the popular moralists of the Scottish Enlightenment, and the size of his circulation in his own time is in any case problematic. As for the Encyclopedists, their debt to Edinburgh has already been noticed. A great deal was added to the Enlightenment argument on slavery after *Lettres Persanes* and *L'Esprit des Lois*; but the additions and elaborations to Montesquieu's thought came not from Paris but from Edinburgh. As for the continental philosophers other than the French, their comment on African slavery was even more peripheral, for the very reason that it had no fundamental effect on the countries from which they came. Even in the Spanish and Portuguese cases, there was only relatively minor pamphlet criticism of slavery, in the period from the 1760s onwards.[41] The impact of the continental Enlightenment on the early stages of the Atlantic anti-slavery movement was principally an indirect one.

This generalisation on anti-slavery opinion and the Enlightenment is not a flawless one. Two of the less prominent groups of the continental *philosophes* did have a great effect on the later French anti-slavery movement in France itself, though a more modest one on the attitude of Europe as a whole to slavery. The first of these were the physiocrats. Their insistence that society should be structured in accordance with fixed utilitarian economic laws implicitly and sometimes explicity worked to modernise slavery and the slave trade. Secondly, a sustained and influential attack on slavery was launched by the team of scholars who collaborated with the Abbé Raynal in producing his massive *Histoire des deux Indes.*

The thought of the physiocrats provoked a great deal of criticism, largely because of the mystical language in which its attack on the mercantilist world was shrouded. In fact it is only recently that their sophistication has been fully understood. Their assumptions on the existence of a structure of economic laws are modern, and there is a great power about their insistence on a *laissez-faire, laissez-aller* approach to government.[42] The

[41] The only two Portuguese examples from this period are M. R. Rocha, *Ethiope resgatado, empenhado, sustentado, corregido, instruido, e libertado* (Lisbon, 1758); 'Negro Slavery in Brazil' [*Nova e Curiosa Relação* (Lisbon, 1764)], trans. and ed. C. R. Boxer, in *Race*, v 3 (1964) 38–47.

[42] R. L. Meek, *The Economics of Physiocracy* (Cambridge, 1963) passim.

bitterness of enlightened sneers at the physiocrats should not obscure their effect on attitudes towards slavery. There is little on slavery in the writings of du Quesnay, the founder of the group. However, their general approach to the study of society had an effect on Adam Smith, whose indictment of the utility of slavery in *The Wealth of Nations*, in spite of his somewhat dubious praise of the physiocrats and his insistence that industry rather than land was the true basis of national wealth, was precisely theirs. Moreover, the later physiocrats themselves turned specifically to attack the squandering of resources and potential involved in colonial slavery. Their arguments on the inferior profitability of slave labour as compared with free, and the tendency of slavery to keep out the healthy yeoman immigrants the colonies required for lasting prosperity, had been anticipated by Benjamin Franklin in 1755, in a pamphlet entitled *Observations Concerning the Increase of Mankind*. These were among the points made by Victor de Mirabeau, father of the later and more famous revolutionary, in *L'Ami des Hommes* (1758), his enormous work on population and commerce. He also looked forward to nineteenth-century abolitionist writing with the argument that the way to end slavery was to demonstrate its unprofitability by exposing it to competition in a world economy based on free trade. This was an exposition more sophisticated than Franklin's, and more extensive than the asides later made by Smith in *The Wealth of Nations*. It became the basis of a series of propaganda articles on the utility of slavery later published in the physiocrats' economic journal, *Éphémérides du Citoyen*. Though these were little read outside France, they stated every line of the nineteenth-century utilitarian argument on slavery – its unprofitability, its bad effect on population growth, and its crushing of incentive among the free population.[43]

In its immediate impact outside France, the work of Raynal and his team was even more important than that of the physiocrats. This international influence was not simply a product of the enormous circulation of the *Histoire des deux Indes*, though it ran through numerous editions, fifteen in English from 1776 to 1804 alone, as compared with the same number for *The Wealth of Nations*, and seven for Gibbon's *Decline and Fall of the Roman Empire*. Raynal visited England in 1771, and he was also one of

[43] See Davis, *Problem of Slavery*, pp. 427–33.

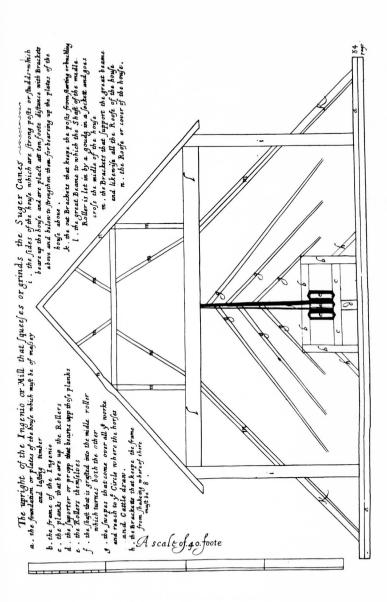

The upright of the Ingenio or Mill that squeeses or grinds the Suger Canes

a. the foundation or plates of the house which must be of massey and lasting timber
b. the frame of the Ingenio
c. the planks that beare up the Rollers
d. the supporter or propp that beares upp those planks
e. the Rollers themselves
f. the shaft that is grafted into the middle roller which turnes both the other
g. the swepes that come over all y worke and reach to y Cirile where the horses and Cattle draw.
h. the Brackets that keepe the frame from shaking whereof three myght be 8.

i. the sides of the house which are strong posts or studds which beare up the house and are placd att ten foote distance with Brackets above and below to strengthen them, for bearing up the plates of the house above.
k. the one Brackets that keepe the posts from starting or buckling
l. the great Beame to which the Shaft of the middle Roller is let in by a gould in a socket and goes cross the midle of the house
m. the Brackets that support the great beame and likewise all the Roofe of the house
n. the Roofe or cover of the house.

A scale of 40 foote

West Indian sugar mill in section

Gillray satirises the hypocrisy often imputed to anti-slavery idealists, in this case the Royal Family

Montesquieu, whose satire against enslavement was the most influential anti-slavery text of the Enlightenment

Francis Hutcheson, whose conception of an innate moral sense of benevolence completely changed the course of anti-slavery

Upon one of their Festivals when a great many of the Negro Musicians were gathered together, I desired Mr. *Baptiste*, the best Musician there to take the Words they sung and set them to Musick, which follows.

You must clap Hands when the Base is plaid, and cry, *Alla, Alla.*

Angola.

Koromanti.

Early European visitors to black slave societies, in this case Sir Hans Sloane in Jamaica, were often impressed by the unfamiliar structure of African music

A romantic Scottish conception of Haiti's black liberator, Toussaint l'Ouverture

Captain Hugh Crow, Master of the *Kitty's Amelia*, the last legal slaver to sail from England

William Wilberforce

Francis Barber, though not a slave, was a member of a substantial black community in eighteenth-century London

An atrocity picture from the memoirs of Theodore Canot, the maestro of all illegal slavers

The slavers' nightmare. Two of the slaves from the ship
Amistad, who managed to overpower the crew and sail
to New London. They were later liberated

A Cuban mill at the height of the island's sugar boom

Havana Harbour: the last major slaving entrepôt in the Atlantic world

'The Greek Slave' by Hiram Powers. An example of the increasingly romanticised Western vision of slavery.

Medallion of the *Amis des Noirs*

NE SUIS-JE PAS TON FRÈRE?

Anthony Benezet's numerous European correspondents.[44] Many other *philosophes* collaborated with Raynal on the project. The most important of these, fresh from his work on the newly published *Encyclopédie*, was Diderot. Again, however, the attack on slavery was incidental to larger problems. The most forcefully stated theme of the passages on slavery was that the Christianity which tolerated it must itself be modified. If there existed a religion 'which gave only a tacit sanction to such horrors', asked Raynal, 'ought not the ministers of it to be suffocated under the ruins of their altars?'[44a] By the time the *Histoire des deux Indes* appeared in 1770, the main lines of the Enlightenment position on slavery had been laid down. It was possible to draw on the sneers of Montesquieu, the utilitarianism of the physiocrats, and even de Jaucourt's Wallace-derived article in the *Encyclopédie*. Though it contained little in the way of original thought, Raynal's work may therefore be seen as summing up the Enlightenment's secular attack on slavery. His rejection of any rationalisation for slavery, in religion or nature, was complete – 'SAVAGE Europeans. . . . In order to repeople one part of the globe, which you have laid waste, you corrupt and depopulate another'[44b] – and he devoted a complete book to a consideration of the status of black people in Africa and the New World, and their right to freedom. Unlike most of the *philosophes*, but like later abolitionists, he set to work to find a solution to the problem of retaining an ordered society while getting a debased slave population out of its chains. The *Histoire des deux Indes* actually sets out an elaborate and not entirely impracticable scheme of gradual emancipation. Freedom could be given only to a tiny minority of mature slaves in the present generation. The moral condition of those who remained slaves would be improved by guaranteeing their family life, and their contentment (and output) improved by diversions like music and dancing. Educational programmes were to be

[44] D. D. Irvine, 'The Abbé Raynal and British Humanitarianism', *Journal of Modern History*, III (1931) 564–77; W. Sypher, *Guinea's Captive Kings: British Anti-Slavery Literature of the Eighteenth Century* (Chapel Hill, N.C., 1942) p. 96; Benezet to Raynal, 16 July 1781, in G. S. Brookes, *Friend Anthony Benezet* (Philadelphia, 1937) pp. 336–7.

[44a] G. T. F. Raynal, *A Philosophical and Political History of the Settlements and Trade of the Europeans in the East and West Indies*, trans. J. O. Justamond, 6 vols (Dublin, 1784) III 135.

[44b] Ibid., I 126–7.

begun at once to prepare the younger ones for life on their own. They would be freed at twenty – if they had reached a satisfactory level of responsibility, and if they had worked hard enough to be able to pay the costs of their maintenance during youth. Even at this point there was to be a five-year apprenticeship period, during which good conduct was to earn eventual freedom.[45] This kind of practical argument as to the problems which would ensue when slavery ended was to produce one of the great streams of pamphlet literature in the coming controversy over slavery.

The legalistic and 'rational' arguments of the Enlightenment did not emerge in isolation. They were partly produced by, and in turn reinforced, further important intellectual changes. Together these worked towards producing a more benevolent attitude towards the Negro, and indeed towards other apparently innocent objects of oppression. On the one hand, the obsessive concern of the *philosophes* and the eighteenth century in general with nature led to a concern and admiration for the natural man. It also brought a burning pity for those who, like the Negro and the Indian, had been abused and corrupted. This romantic conception of the black slave set him in sharp contrast to the vulgarity and decadence of the planter who oppressed him. On the other hand, the Christian structure of ethics which had for centuries rationalised slavery, just like the classical theories which Hutcheson had attacked, began to suffer from strains which led to a re-examination of the morality of slaveholding, and in extreme cases of hierarchy in general. The rational arguments of the Enlightenment, the benevolence brought about by emerging romanticism, and this new Christian egalitarianism, all closely interconnected, together represented a revolution in Western attitudes to slavery.

The conception of the natural man, uncorrupted by society, was by no means a new one. In the eighteenth century, however, it reached a new level of popularity. Moreover, the equation between natural man and the New World Indian was extended to include the African Negro, whether in his own country or in the grips of the American slavemaster. This stereotype of the black noble savage became the subject of a whole genre of literature, stretching from the various versions of Mrs Aphra Behn's *Oronooko*, through Samuel Johnson's *Rasselas*, up to de Tocque-

[45] Ibid., iv 118–23, 144–8; book xi passim.

ville's friend Gustave de Beaumont's *Marie*. In the essay and the novel, in poetry and on the stage, the polite classes of Europe were presented with the image of the suffering Negro who preserved his dignity and love of liberty amid the corruption of a world blighted by the selfishness of Westerners. His virtues not only threw the baseness of the slaveholder into relief, but also pointed by implication to the failure of Christianity to protect him from abuse. Certainly there was another side to the myth of the noble savage, for in spite of the eighteenth century's lip-service to simplicity, it could be pointed out by the most tactless commentator that primitive man lived in a state of squalor less dignified than the life of the coffee-house wit. Nevertheless, the emotions of pity and admiration stirred by the romantic presentation of the black bondsman certainly worked to reinforce the tendency to question the acceptance of slavery, however long established. The eighteenth century's worship of Reason did not exclude an intense emotionalism. The sentimental revulsion against slavery produced by romantic idealisation of the Negro may have been as powerful as the rationalistic argument in forming the abolitionist impulse. In the next century the simple message of pity, spelled out by Harriet Beecher Stowe in *Uncle Tom's Cabin*, was building on a stream of sensibility leading back to eighteenth-century romanticism.

The sentimental approach, indeed, was not absent from the writings of the most rational of the *philosophes*. Much more important in producing a romantic attitude to the liberty-loving slave was the world of popular fiction, drama and poetry. At the fountainhead of all such writing is Aphra Behn's *Oronooko*. It was published as early as 1688, and reached such popularity as to deluge the eighteenth century with new editions, dramatisations, operatic versions and, above all, imitations. Mrs Behn had herself visited Surinam, but there is little realism about her novel. Her interest was not in humanitarianism, but in holding the primitive virtues of her black hero up to admiration. What horrified her most of all was not slavery itself, but the disrespect for hierarchy implied in the enslavement of her prince *Oronooko*. Indeed, the same might be said of a great deal of anti-slavery writing, factual as well as fictional, but this did not make the revulsion against slavery any less real. The same legends can be picked out throughout the century, all showing the warmth of black love, the black hunger for liberty and the faithlessness of the European. It is significant that Dr Johnson's one venture into novel-writing, *Rasselas*, picked up this theme. In fiction, the tradition went far beyond the English-speaking world, to culminate in Kotzebue's *Die Negersklaven* (1796) and Herder's *Neger Idyllen* (1797). It is strangely absent from opera, or at least opera which reached any lasting popularity. Such African themes as emerged are Islamic rather than genuinely African, as in *Die Entführung*, where Osmin, though jolly, is in any case not the most noble of savages. *L'Africaine* was not produced until 1865, and Meyerbeer, who completed it the day before his death, seems to have suffered from considerable confusion as to the distinction between India, Africa and Turkey. In poetry, however, a long line of inaccurate and over-sentimental versifiers led into Chatterton's *African Eclogues*, into Cowper, and into the beauty of Blake's 'Little Black Boy'. The greatest of the English romantics were deeply concerned over slavery, particularly in the case of Southey. It is a measure of their deep interest in abolition that both the Wordsworths and the Coleridges considered Thomas Clarkson, the most dogged and unimaginative of abolitionists, one of their closest friends. The link is also there with the French. *Marie*, by de Tocqueville's travelling companion Gustave de Beaumont, is a major anti-slavery novel which expressly spells out the contradiction between black dignity and the corruption of the slave relationship. Romanticism and sympathy for the black slave went hand in hand.[46] In other circumstances the result might have been only a passing sentimental interest in the Negro, but in conjunction with the erosion of the philosophical and religious arguments for slavery, the outcome was revolutionary.

The pity for the slave produced by the romantic stereotype corresponded with changes in religious thought which were working in the same direction. It is tempting indeed to argue that it was the rise of the accompanying rationalist and sentimentalist threats to slavery which led to a rejection of its religious sanctions.

[46] Sypher, *Guinea's Captive Kings*, is by far the best survey of romantic writing on the Negro during this period. On the general romantic attitude to social change, see R. Harris, *Romanticism and the Social Order, 1780–1830* (London, 1969); A. M. Ellis, *Rebels and Conservatives: Dorothy and William Wordsworth and their Circle* (Bloomington, Ind., 1967).

The reality is considerably more complex. There is no doubt that the Christian churches sanctioned and even encouraged enslavement until the eighteenth century. Religion had been used to keep medieval slaves and serfs in their station, and it presented no major barrier to the emergence of Negro slavery in the Americas. Two centuries of polemic from Christians who distrust slavery have failed to prove that the Bible does anything other than sanction it. Augustine was only setting out an accepted Christian doctrine when, in *De Civitate Dei*, he exhorted bondsmen and the lowly in general to remain contented in their station since the reward for their humility would come after death. Yet this position implied certain contradictions which came to the fore after the Reformation, and which became more and more irreconcilable until, by the late eighteenth century, it was possible to launch a full-scale attack on slavery on Christian grounds.

This shift in attitudes implied an extraordinary intellectual volte-face. From the standpoint of the medieval church fathers, that slavery must be accepted as a necessary product of sin, later abolitionists reached the standpoint that it must be abolished outright as a major step in the battle *against* sin. The changes involved were complex, and they are discussed in detail in Davis's magnificent work on *The Problem of Slavery in Western Culture.* In brief, the flaw in the Augustinian assumption that slavery was the natural product of original sin is that the rigid hierarchy which it implied was at odds with two separate egalitarian assumptions of Christian thought. The first was that all mankind stand equal before God; the second that all mankind become equal in the incorporeal life beyond the grave. This tension was worsened with the Reformation, when the Protestant insistence on the equality of all believers stood even more starkly opposed to the assumption that man's sin had led to his slavery, in spite of the hierarchical assumptions which arose from the Calvinist delineation of an elect of God. In fact the conception of an elect, of a chosen people, in the end worked to speed up the dissolution of the Christian compromise on slavery. In the Protestant Americas the failure of the elects, however defined, to produce a satisfactorily godly society led to a casting around for explanations. Long accustomed to think of slavery as a product of sin, and indeed to see sin as a form of metaphorical enslavement, these New World Christians were psychologically prepared to see their endorsement of slavery as the root of the corruption they saw around them – as visible proof that Antichrist was in their midst. The result was that they turned on slavery as the linchpin of the whole system of sin which was preventing the realisation of Christ's kingdom on earth. The steps by which this level of consciousness was reached were many, but the theory put forward by Davis is by far the most convincing explanation of the emergence of a Christian testimony against slavery.

This development came earliest, and was most striking, among those sects whose insistence on the removal of intermediaries between man and God strengthened their belief in the equality of all believers, and thus further exposed the contradiction in the medieval compromise. At the same time they considered themselves as the groups foremost in the progress towards godliness, so that the whole fate of society in the battle with Antichrist depended on their purging their fellows from the sin of slaveholding. First there came the early Quaker pamphleteers, whose concern over the problem of general societal sin was often so great that their abolitionist writing scarcely mentioned the reality of slavery. Secondly, there were the various groups affected by the eighteenth-century revivals, by the Great Awakening in America and the Methodist movement in Britain. This is not to suggest a crude theory that the emotional religion of the revivals produced guilt feelings, or that the simple message of a Wesley or a Whitefield led to new benevolence towards the Christian's oppressed fellow-creatures. Both these responses may have been present peripherally, but the revivals also produced an intense feeling of urgency in combating the progress of sin. The symbols of sin, of the presence of Antichrist, were various, and different Christians might carry on the cosmic battle in different ways. For many, because of the obvious contradiction between slavery and the equality of God's children, and because of the long-accepted – though now reversed – equation between slavery and sin, the slaveholder became Antichrist's agent, the one with the number of the Beast on his forehead. This was not a class response. It was the outcome of a Western tradition which could equally well affect a little West Jersey Quaker, a Methodist craftsman from the North Country or an Anglican gentleman from Oxford. All in all, the final exposure of the Christian contradiction in the harsh light of the revivals opened the way to a revulsion against slavery and ultimately the construction of an anti-slavery movement.

By the late eighteenth century, then, slavery and the slave trade were in any case becoming less profitable in substantial areas of the world. Yet they now had enough institutional momentum to have carried on quite happily even in hard times. The tragedy for the West Indian planter, and the good fortune for his slave, was that the weakness in the system coincided with an overwhelming religious and intellectual onslaught. Even then, the plantocracy could probably have withstood the arguments of a group of rationally-minded *philosophes*, or the emotions of a number of sentimental novelists, or the denunciations of the godly. What it could not hold up against was the interaction between all three. All rooted in Western traditions of long standing, yet vitalised by the dramatic intellectual changes of the eighteenth century, their interaction produced a potentially devastating indictment of slavery. As a result, slavery and the slave trade were to fall in the areas where they were already weakened. At the same time, the ideas which had toppled them gained enough momentum to be able to go on, in the nineteenth century, to attack slavery even in areas where it was still viable as an economic system.

6 The Eighteenth-Century Triumphs: Slave-Trade Abolition and Northern Emancipation

THE weakening of the vested interest in slavery, at least in some quarters, and the erosion of its accepted philosophical and religious underpinning, brought the emergence of a genuine Atlantic anti-slavery movement. It was at this time that the first true abolitionists appeared, men who saw the attack on slavery and the slave trade as a priority over other good causes, and who developed a lifelong dedication to the service of the Negro. In the American case the central figure among them was Anthony Benezet, the Quaker schoolteacher from Philadelphia. In the British it was Granville Sharp, an eccentric London ordnance clerk in reasonably modest circumstances. In France it is more difficult to pick out a man who dominates the first stirring of a widespread anti-slavery sentiment, but the equivalent would probably be the revolutionary politician Jean-Pierre Brissot de Warville, or the Abbé Grégoire. Each of these individuals was instrumental, directly or indirectly, in forming a society intended to promote and organise agitation against the slave trade or slavery. The Philadelphia Society was founded in 1775. It became the centre of efforts to encourage the setting-up of similar societies in other American towns. In Britain it was not until 1787 that a small group of Quakers joined with Sharp to form the Committee for the Abolition of the Slave Trade. In France, Brissot and a number of other prominent French reformers organised the Société des Amis des Noirs in 1788.

The formation of all these bodies came late, considering the length of time during which individual polemicists had been presenting a critique of slavery to an unreceptive world. Yet their demands were radical, however modest they may seem compared with the cry for immediate emancipation which so dominated the heyday of the nineteenth-century movement. Their success, too, was spectacular, not only in scale, but also in its peaceableness, and the speed with which it came about. In the short twenty-five years from the gentle beginning of anti-slavery organisation in 1775, the American societies completed emancipation in several Northern states and set the others well on the way to it, as well as extorting a commitment from the Constitutional Convention of 1788 to abolish the slave trade in twenty years. The English abolitionists, by 1807, had begun experiments in West African colonisation at Sierra Leone, had got rid of the British slave trade, and were prepared to start persuading other nations to follow their example. The success of the French abolitionists is more difficult to gauge, because of their being swallowed up in the cataclysm of the Revolution of 1789. The immediate pledge of the revolutionary government to end slavery and the slave trade was never fulfilled. Owing to the success of later pro-slavery lobbyists in playing on horror at Toussaint l'Ouverture's revolution in Haiti, French colonial slavery ended only with a new revolution in 1848, and it was never restored by Louis-Napoleon. However, France came out of the Napoleonic wars and the Congress of Vienna having pledged that the carrying of slaves by her nationals would be stopped. Quite apart from their importance in fostering the abolitionist opinion on which the nineteenth-century movement was to feed, the concrete achievement of these three groups of eighteenth-century reformers, in a short space of time, was enormous.

Part of the reason for this success was a weakening of the opposition, intellectual and political. Another was the ironic success of anti-slavery's earliest pamphleteers, men who had had little success in their own time, in influencing the generation which followed them. This is not to say that their writing itself caused the growth of an anti-slavery movement. The abolitionists of the 1770s or 1780s, already predisposed against slavery by the new intellectual assumptions of their time, could seize on the ideas of past polemicists as part of a respectable tradition in which they could place themselves. The Sewalls and Sandifords had had little response from their own contemporaries. Until the period after the Seven Years War, almost all the white men and women who gave any thought to the subject at all had assumed that slavery and the slave trade were acceptable institutions, and that they were moreover in the national interest. Cruelty they were not concerned with. Liberty was a concept which was not intended to apply to all classes. Equality was an abstraction, and an undesirable one at that. It was when these assumptions had been changed, or at least modified, that the early pamphleteers found an audience eager to accept and elaborate on their arguments. Their writing pioneered many of the ideas which provided the small change of anti-slavery propaganda right through to the nineteenth century.

The earliest printed work which argued against British colonial slavery as an institution, as opposed to arguing for good treatment and evangelisation of the slaves, was the Germantown Protest, produced by a small group of Pennsylvania Quakers of Swiss and Dutch descent in 1688. This document progressed from their Monthly Meeting up to the Philadelphia Yearly Meeting. It drew the obvious distinction between holding fellow-beings in slavery, the love of liberty and the Golden Rule, but it had no impact outside the Society of Friends, and even within it it represented a small and premature revulsion against slavery. It was never printed or circulated publicly.[1] The first published Quaker protest was actually written by the lapsed Scottish Friend George Keith, in 1693, just after he had been disowned by the Philadelphia Yearly Meeting and founded the group of seceders who pointedly called themselves the Christian Quakers. Keith spent the later part of his life as a missionary for the Anglican Society for the Propagation of the Gospel, lecturing throughout the mainland colonies as the chief opponent of the Friends. Yet he too was concerned with the inconsistency between slaveholding and the Golden Rule. Again, as a modern commentator points out, his *Exhortation and Caution* was the first work to argue that, since slaves were taken in war, owning them was out of step with the Quaker testimony in favour of peace.[2] In the late seventeenth

[1] The Germantown Protest is printed in *Pennsylvania Magazine of History and Biography*, IV (1880) 28–30.

[2] T. E. Drake, *Quakers and Slavery in America* (New Haven, 1950) pp. 14–15. Keith's pamphlet was *An Exhortation and Caution to Friends Concerning Buying or Keeping of Negroes* (New York, 1693), reprinted in

century only a tiny minority even among the Friends were prepared to argue that the buying and holding of slaves was sinful.
However, the early move of some of them to this standpoint is
significant of the genuine egalitarianism of their religion, and of
their intense concern for the barriers to the creation of Christ's
kingdom raised by sinfulness among their own numbers – perhaps
also of a genuine economic modernity which would eventually
make slavery seem archaic. These protests look forward to the
central role the Quakers were later to play as propagandists and
organisers of the anti-slavery movement, on both sides of the
Atlantic.

Although the importance of the first printed non-Quaker protest against slavery, Judge Samuel Sewall's *The Selling of Joseph*,
has been exaggerated, it is a most interesting piece. Sewall was
English-born, but had taken a Harvard degree and taught there
briefly before becoming one of Boston's most prominent jurists
and public figures. Although they were still numbered in hundreds when *The Selling of Joseph* was written in 1701, the blacks
in the city had increased steadily throughout Sewall's lifetime. It
is likely that he, like many another later 'anti-slavery' pamphleteer, was as much concerned with the dangers of a large and
discontented servile population as with the morality of enslavement. 'The Numerousness of Slaves at this day in the Province,'
he began, 'and the Uneasiness of them under their Slavery, both
put many upon thinking whether the Foundation of it be firmly
and well laid; so as to sustain the Vast Weight that is built upon
it'. He went on to argue, in strikingly modern terms, that slavery
was excluded both by natural law and by Scripture:

> It is most certain that all Men, as they are the Sons of *Adam*
> are Coheirs; and have equal Right unto Liberty, and all other
> outward Comforts of Life. . . . Now although the Title given
> by the last ADAM, doth infinitely better Mens Estates, respect-
> ing GOD and themselves; and grants them a most beneficial
> and inviolable Lease under the Broad Seal of Heaven, who
> were before only Tenants at Will: Yet through the Indulgence

Pennsylvania Magazine of History and Biography, XIII (1889) 265–70. For
the early history of the Quaker critique, see *A Brief Statement of the Rise
and Progress of the Testimony of the Religious Society of Friends, against
Slavery and the Slave Trade* (Philadelphia, 1843); S. B. Weeks, *Southern
Quakers and Slavery* (Baltimore, 1896).

of GOD to our First Parents after the Fall, the outward Estate of all and every of their Children, remains the same, as to one another. So that Originally, and Naturally, there is no such thing as Slavery.[3]

It would be a mistake to make too much of *The Selling of Joseph*. Sewall's writing of the pamphlet was produced by a particular controversy with John Saffin, a fellow-merchant and judge whose slave had come to Sewall for protection against his master. Again, although Sewall's manuscript diary contains a number of references to slaves and Negroes, they hardly show a consistent body of ideas on slavery, and he did not carry on a public fight against enslavement except in this one pamphlet and in republishing a short journalistic piece from a London periodical entitled *The Athenian Oracle*.[4] Yet Sewall has an important place in the history of anti-slavery, for he was the first member of the colonial ruling class to turn publicly against slavery – in spite of the problem of reconciling his egalitarianism with assumptions on hierarchy which provided all too effective a rationalisation for enslavement. Yet he was near to being a minority of one in the Boston of 1700. The fact that he was not dismissed out of hand as a crank is a symptom of the colony's concern over the growing numbers of heathen immigrants at a critical time in its history, and a tribute to Sewall's own very great respectability.

Early anti-slavery writers with less social prestige than Sewall were either ignored or, when they persisted in their extraordinary viewpoint, ostracised. With the exception of the Welsh clergyman Morgan Godwyn, whose real interest in Negroes and Indians was a missionary's one, and Sewall himself, the early anti-slavery pamphleteers were Quakers. This in itself deterred most of them from a sustained attack on slavery, owing to the Society of Friends' formidable machinery for silencing debate on subjects likely to endanger its unity. The most important of this handful of pamphlets was written by the author of whom we know least: *The American Defence of the Christian Golden Rule*, by John

---

[3] S. Sewall, *The Selling of Joseph: A Memorial*, ed. S. Kaplan (Northampton, Mass., 1969) pp. 7–8.

[4] Kaplan's introduction to *The Selling of Joseph*, pp. 27–63, exaggerates the strength and consistency of his anti-slavery testimony. A more balanced assessment is D. B. Davis, *The Problem of Slavery in Western Culture* (Ithaca, N.Y., 1966) pp. 341–8.

Hepburn, who appears to have been a solid but obscure New Jersey Friend.[5] His name is Scottish, and he significantly states that his native land was 'the *Island of Great Britain*' rather than England, so that he may have been one of the group of Northern Quakers, like Barclay and Keith, with West Jersey interests. As important as his own rather cramped writing were the pieces Hepburn had reprinted with the pamphlet. One was the extract from *The Athenian Oracle* which Sewall had already republished. The other was a pamphlet, or part of one, which had been written in 1713, and perhaps never published, entitled *Arguments against Making Slaves of Men*. These writings Hepburn introduced to his readers with the dark hint that most anti-slavery writings 'are destroyed by *Negro-Masters*, [so] that the Reader will find them almost as scarce to be found as the *Phenix Egg*'.[6] Davis has correctly pointed out the importance of the pieces Hepburn reprinted in looking forward to later arguments as to the cruelty and irrationalism of slavery. However, this should not obscure the very real modernity of Hepburn's own ideas. He too was appalled by the gap between Christian precept and the ills of slavery, by the immorality the system fostered, by the use of the Old Testament to support it and by the obscene cruelties of the 'Negro-Masters'. But he also had the sensitivity to seek out the more subtle oppressions of the man-chattel. He pointed in general to the indignity of being a subordinate caste – a caste who are forced to sleep outdoors though the masters allow their best dogs 'to lie in the bed with themselves', a caste whose oppressors give them names like '*Toby, Mando, Mingo, Jack, Hector*, and *Hagar*, and such like Names they give to their *Dogs* and *Horses*'. Few other abolitionist pamphleteers, even in the mid-nineteenth century, saw the significance of this tyranny of name-giving. It was also Hepburn who remarked, like Jefferson, on the social danger that the bad example of cruel and tyrannical slavemasters would corrupt others. Again, like later writers, he

[5] J. Hepburn, *The American Defence of the Christian Golden Rule, or an Essay to Prove the Unlawfulness of Making Slaves of Men, by him who Loves the Freedom of the Souls and Bodies of All Men* (n.p., 1715), reprinted in facsimile in *Proceedings of the American Antiquarian Society* (1927) pp. 113–40.

[6] Ibid., Preface [p. iii]. The only complete copy of Hepburn's pamphlet is in the British Museum, and only it includes the whole *Athenian Oracle* section. Hepburn also reprinted items on subjects other than slavery.

took the position that the cruelty of slavery played into the hands of Turks and other infidels by giving them the opportunity of claiming that Christianity was responsible for it.[7] There is a much greater originality about Hepburn's ideas than about Sewall's, and his thought was not substantially elaborated upon for at least fifty years. Even the structure of his pamphlet included a dialogue between a 'Negro-Master' and a 'Christian' – a contrast of deep significance – in which the rationalisations for slavery were systematically refuted. This device was not new, but it was also used with great success by polemicists in the nineteenth century.

It was in another direction, however, that *The American Defence* was most revolutionary. It presented slavery not just as an ill in itself, but as the vehicle for the acting-out of the cosmic conflict between good and evil, between Christ and Antichrist. The implication of Hepburn's fellow-Quakers in slavery was only the symbol of an elaborate network of sin and backsliding through which their holy experiment was about to be overthrown. Slaveholding is not always the focus of the pamphlet, since it was by no means their only fault. They were guilty, for instance, of compromising to pay taxes for warlike purposes, and of gathering money to

> keep their Wives idle (*Jezebel-like*) to *paint their Faces*, and *Puff*, and *powder their Hair*, and to bring up their Sons and Daughters in *Idleness* and *Wantonness*, and in all manner of *Pride* and *Prodigality*, in *decking* and *adorning* their Carkases with pufft and powdered Hair, with *Ruffles* and *Top-knots*, *Ribbands* and *Lace*, and *Gay Cloathing* and what not.[8]

A great deal must be made of this aspect of Hepburn's work. His obsession with the moral declension of his fellows illustrates the way in which slavery became a vehicle for fears of the snares of the world. The Quaker abolitionists shared with later abolitionists from the evangelical Protestant churches the fear that the entire structure of society was being subverted by slavery. To a less spectacular extent, the same fears emerge from the writing of two other obscure Quaker writers of the early eighteenth century. William Burling, a merchant from Flushing, Long Island, appealed against slavery to Flushing Monthly Meeting in 1718, and a fragment of his argument is embedded in the writings of

[7] Ibid., pp. 4–9.   [8] Ibid., p. 4.

the more eccentric Quaker prophet Benjamin Lay. Fifteen years later Elihu Coleman, a Nantucket carpenter, published his *Testimony against that Antichristian Practice of Making Slaves of Men*. Like Burling, however, he either lost interest in slavery or proved susceptible to pressure from his Monthly Meeting, for nothing was heard of him thereafter as an agitator against slavery.[9]

None of these early polemicists spent a great part of his life agitating against slavery. Their testimony was a single act, not a credo to which they were to devote their lives. In this sense, the first true abolitionists were two eccentric, and more radical, American Friends, William Sandiford and Benjamin Lay. The *Journal* of John Woolman shows how consistent this gentle prophet was in his opposition to slavery.[10] However, slavery was not a single idea to him, and he did not attack it as being an all-encompassing evil which would bring down all other sin with it at its destruction. Both Lay and Sandiford did do this, seeing their constant preaching against slavery as the means of eradicating *all* sin from society. To this extent they look forward to the thought of nineteenth-century abolitionists like William Lloyd Garrison, with their millennial vision of a post-emancipation world, in which the burden of sin which slavery had deposited on the earth would be lifted. It was with this interpretation that the commitment to attacking slavery became so intense. The temptation to move on to dealing with other social abuses, even more obvious ones, became less. To Lay, Sandiford and their successors in this tradition, abolition became the focal point for *all* social and religious reform. Both were tortured by the consciousness of slavery as the universal sin upon which Antichrist had taken his stand. Both were obsessed with the single issue to the point of eccentricity. Theirs was a commitment much closer in intensity to that of a Benezet or a Clarkson, a Buxton or a Garrison, than to the short-lived interest of a Burling or even a Sewall.

Sandiford was the more orthodox of these two men, a middling Philadelphia shopkeeper, born in England in 1693 and actually

[9] Drake, *Quakers and Slavery*, pp. 36–9. The full title of Coleman's pamphlet was *A Testimony against that Antichristian Practice of Making Slaves of Men. Wherein it is Shewed to be Contrary to the Dispensation of the Law and Time of the Gospel, and Very Opposite both to Grace and Nature* (n.p., 1733).

[10] J. Woolman, *The Journal and Letters*, ed. A. M. Gummere (New York, 1922) pp. 173, 180, 194, 215, 233.

a Quaker convert.[11] Doubtless he was horrified by the cruelty and indignity of slavery, but the intensity of his loathing for it was linked with a deeper concern over the extent to which it was marring the fair face of the Quaker commonwealth. Slavery was the negation of the Christian message, the Beast embodied. Yet Sandiford saw it accepted, and its fruits enjoyed, by those who claimed to be the purest of Christ's children. He wrote with the urgency of one convinced of the imminent triumph of Antichrist. Conservative leaders of the Philadelphia Yearly Meeting were less alarmed, or perhaps less skilled in deciphering the number of the Beast on the slavemonger's forehead. Sandiford's appeals brought no action. In desperation he decided to publish on a controversial topic without the approval of Meeting. The result was his (long) *Brief Examination of the Practice of the Times*, which not only attacked slaveholding but also the Friends' implication in it. He was promptly disowned, ostracised by the Quaker community and boycotted in business. Though he tried to defend his position with a second edition entitled *The Mystery of Iniquity*, he was forced to leave Philadelphia. He died in the country nearby in 1733, broken by the strain of constant controversy and his tortured consciousness of responsibility for the sin of slaveholding.

One of the few men who remained in touch with Sandiford in his exile was Benjamin Lay, a birthright Quaker born in Colchester in England. An eccentric hunchback, Lay had been restless from his youth onwards. He had spent some time as a sailor in the Levant trade, and by the time he moved to Philadelphia in 1731 had already been disowned once for his extreme views on the divine prompting of preaching. He had some experience in Barbados, where he seems to have lived for two separate periods, once around 1718 and once just before his move to Philadelphia. He did not give his testimony against slavery in

[11] The following information on Sandiford and Lay is taken from R. Vaux, *Memoirs of the Lives of Benjamin Lay and Ralph Sandiford: Two of the Earliest of the Public Advocates of the Emancipation of the Enslaved Africans* (Philadelphia, 1815), and from their published works. See also Drake, *Quakers and Slavery*, pp. 39–47; Davis, *Problem of Slavery*, pp. 320–6; C. B. Rowntree, 'Benjamin Lay', *Journal of the Friends Historical Society*, xxxiii (1936) 3–13; S. V. James, *A People among Peoples: Quaker Benevolence in Eighteenth Century America* (Cambridge, Mass., 1963) pp. 124–7.

Barbados, but in Philadalphia, where he found to his despair that the various sins associated with it were corrupting even the Quakers. Although a penchant for personal eccentricity and public disturbances was nothing new for Lay, it was here that he came into his own with a series of disturbances designed to dramatise the horrors of slavery. As a general testimony, he abstained from the use of slave-grown produce or products which depended on the abuse of animals, living in a cave rather than a man-made edifice in the country outside Philadelphia. This involved the use of strange home-made linen clothes similar to those worn by John Woolman. Although he never 'went naked for a sign', as did some of the earlier Quakers, he did come to Meeting to deliver his denunciations of slaveholding Friends in the meekness of sackcloth. More dramatically, he would stand outside Meeting, barefoot in the snow, to draw attention to the poor slaves who spent the whole winter in that condition. His finest demonstration came at Burlington Monthly Meeting, in Jersey, where he began by rising in good order to address the assembled Friends on slavery. He then dramatised its anti-pacifist nature by throwing open his sombre cloak to hold up a naked sword and reveal his little body clothed in full military uniform. Next he symbolised slavery's negation of religion by piercing his Bible with the sword. Finally, since the Bible had been hollowed out and contained a bladder of red juice, the deaths caused by slavery were drama- tised when the sword-thrust produced a spray of Negro 'blood'. Such extravagant conduct would have led to disownment even if the Society of Friends had not been embarrassed by the difficulty of maintaining unity over slavery. He was not only disowned, but publicly denounced by his Meeting in 1738. By this time, indeed, his eccentricity had begun to verge on insanity. The feverish writing of his garbled book *All Slave-Keepers that Keep the Innocent in Bondage, Apostates* is the best indication of his paranoia, but it also reveals a sense of an imminent crisis in society. It is hopelessly disorganised, a long series of digressions on the various evils which in Lay's mind were associated with slaveholding, the great fundament of the system of sin. Lay also had a clear sense of having been victimised by the Philadelphia Quakers, as part of a conspiracy to prevent the unmasking of the Beast which was corrupting them. But this should not obscure the centrality of his standpoint in the history of the anti-slavery movement. The conception that slavery was dangerous to the well-being not of the immoral but of the moral, that it was thus opposed to their construction of a godly society, was what gave urgency to the appeals of a great many abolitionists, both in the eighteenth and nineteenth centuries. In the consciousness that slavery was the hub of the whole structure of sin against which it was the Christian's duty to fight, both Lay and Sandiford look to the future. Lay demonstrated a conception of the universality of sin very similar to Garrison's when he denounced ministers involved in slaveholding as 'a sort of Devils, that Preach more to Hell than they do to Heaven, and so they will do forever, as long as they are suffered to reign in the worst, and Mother of all Sins, Slave-keeping'.[12]

Lay did not die until 1759. By then the tide of opinion had turned, at least among Quakers, and successful attempts were being made to prevent Friends from holding slaves. In the earlier part of the century, he and other abolitionist pamphleteers were little heeded, and they were few and far between. Predominantly Quaker and predominantly American though they were, they enshrined ideas and assumptions fundamental to later abolitionist literature. But they do not represent a widespread revulsion against slavery, or anything approaching a movement.[13]

By the 1760s the situation was quite different. Among the Friends, other men and women had picked up the germ of the ideas used by the first eccentric pioneers. The questioning of the morality of holding slaves for life was a quiet one, with controversy kept within the circles of Friends. In 1759, however, the Philadelphia Yearly Meeting began to disown any member involved in buying or selling slaves. Similar movements meanwhile began in other American Meetings. Putting pressure on members for trading in slaves was only a short step away from disciplining them for abusing them, finally just for owning them.[14] Outside the Society, too, attitudes to slavery and the slave trade were being modified. In the American context, this is not to go back

---

[12] B. Lay, *All Slave-Keepers that Keep the Innocent in Bondage Apostates Pretending to Lay Claim to the Pure Holy Christian Religion ...* (Philadelphia, 1737) p. 106, quoted in M. S. Locke, *Anti-Slavery in America, 1619–1808* (Cambridge, Mass., 1901) p. 26.

[13] Cf. Locke, *Anti-Slavery in America*, p. 1.

[14] Drake, *Quakers and Slavery*, pp. 48–67.

to the theory that equality bred equality, and that the drive for freedom from the British produced an accompanying drive for black freedom. The emergence of the Enlightenment critique and the growing tension between Christian egalitarianism and Christian hierarchy had removed much of the underpinning of slavery by the end of the Seven Years War. The religious and secular reactions against slavery are not separate; in the colonies, as in Britain, the literate evangelical Christians influenced by the thought of Wesley or the Great Awakening were also well read in the moralistic writings of the Enlightenment. An important element in opposition to slavery was simple human sympathy for the slave, whose obvious sufferings made him a splendid object both for Christian compassion and for the benevolent sensibility pleaded for by Shaftesbury and Hutcheson. Moreover, black population had risen rapidly in the mainland colonies throughout the eighteenth century. Where blacks had accounted for only a little over a tenth of the population in 1700, in 1760 there were an estimated total of 325,806, that is, slightly more than one black for every five whites. The result was growing fear of the very real possibility of servile insurrection, of the sort expressed by Judge Sewall in *The Selling of Joseph*. The theory of a close connection between the rise of colonial opposition to the slave trade and security fears can easily be overstated.[15] However, this connection is there even in the North, where the danger posed by hostile foreigners and heathens must have made slave-trading and slavery seem economic luxuries in areas where chattel labour was not economically essential. There had been a great deal of alarm at the numerousness of the black population throughout the Northern colonies since the New York revolt of 1741, perhaps the most alarming – and most viciously repressed – of all North America's slave revolts.[16] Once the initial enthusiasm for butchering the ringleaders had worn off, the legacy, at least among those not economically committed to slavery, was the fear that such horrifying events might recur if steps were not taken to prevent

[15] As in W. E. B. DuBois, *The Suppression of the African Slave Trade to the United States of America, 1638–1870* (1896; reprinted New York, 1969) p. 15. Population figures from *Historical Statistics of the United States*, p. 756.

[16] See D. Horsmanden, *The New York Conspiracy, or a History of the Negro Plot*, ed. T. J. Davis (Boston, 1971).

the importation of further blacks. This anxiety unquestionably made it easier for abolitionists to find an audience on both sides of the Atlantic. It was not only the Friends who were affected. Attitudes to slavery had not changed and did not change overnight, but where an abolitionist commitment had seemed madness in the early part of the century, there were now various ways in which it was at least defensible.

For this reason, Anthony Benezet's campaign received a significant favourable response in the colonies. In spite of this success, and a personal gentleness sharply contrasted to the personalities of earlier and later abolitionists, he was not an orthodox man.[17] He had been born in Saint-Quentin, in Normandy, in 1713, immediately before his Huguenot parents fled to Rotterdam. He was actually brought up in London, although it seems unlikely that he became a Quaker until after moving to Philadelphia in 1731. He married an American, failed in business and worked as a printer. He finally found a post more suited to his personality teaching a class of poor children at the Friends' English School, later the William Penn Charter School, in Philadelphia. Next Benezet taught in the little girls' school set up by the Yearly Meeting. His teaching career was very much interrupted by weak health, but in 1782, at the age of sixty-nine, he became master of the Negro School in Chestnut Street, which he himself had induced the Friends to set up twelve years before. He left this school his modest fortune at his death in 1784.

Benezet's interests in reform were by no means limited to the cause of abolition. As a working schoolmaster he was concerned with removing the harshness of discipline from the classroom, and worked without the use of corporal punishments during his own career. His biographer remarks that he accepted temperance principles, through 'acquiring a love of tea early in life'.[18] But he also attracted attention in eighteenth-century Philadalphia through his work in looking after the French 'Acadian' refugees from the north, and British refugees from the Indian wars on the frontier. In no cause, however, was he as active as the anti-slavery one, and it was here that this gentle Quaker dominie reached international status. His influence on attitudes to slavery in the

[17] The only modern biography of Benezet is G. S. Brookes, *Friend Anthony Benezet* (Philadelphia, 1937).
[18] Ibid., p. 150.

colonies was great enough. He was deeply respected in Philadelphia, at this time the American centre of forward-looking reform ideas. He would have contributed a great deal to the Negro's future welfare if his only convert to abolition had been his friend Dr Benjamin Rush. Even more striking was his circle of acquaintances overseas. He took great pains to circulate his pamphlets in England, and at least two were translated into French and one into German, though the latter was probably aimed at the Moravian communities near Philadelphia rather than at Europe.[19] He in turn kept up on foreign abolitionist literature, as the lengthy quotations from European authors in his pamphlets amply prove. He seems to have had the distinction of passing on the first volume of Raynal's *Histoire des deux Indes* to his friend John Woolman.[20] At the same time, with his Quakerly love of letter-writing, he kept up an extensive correspondence with British abolitionists, particularly Granville Sharp, whom he helped in his preparation for the Somerset case, which was to end the legality of slavery in England. The relationship between these two men is fundamental to the history of the Atlantic anti-slavery movement. Each was the pioneer in launching an organised attack on slavery in his own country. Much of the similarity in developments on the two sides of the Atlantic leads back to their exchange of the pamphlets they and their colleagues had produced, and to the long correspondence between them.[21]

Benezet's first pamphlet against slavery, *A Short Account of that Part of Africa, Inhabited by the Negroes*, which stressed the connection between African 'barbarism' and the depredations

[19] *A Short Account of that Part of Africa, Inhabited by the Negroes, etc.* (Philadelphia, 1762) was published in German in 1763. A French edition of his *Caution to Great Britain and her Colonies, in a Short Representation of the Calamitous State of the Enslaved Negroes in the British Dominions* (Philadelphia, 1766) appeared in 1767. His book, *Some Historical Account of Guinea* (Philadelphia, 1771), was also translated into French, but not until 1788. The publishing history of these works is carefully treated in D. B. Davis, 'New Sidelights on Early Anti-Slavery Radicalism', *William and Mary Quarterly*, 3rd ser., xxviii (1971) 591 n.

[20] Gummere (ed.), *Journal . . . of John Woolman*, p. 15.

[21] P. Hoare, *Memoirs of Granville Sharp, Esq., Composed from his own Manuscripts, and Other Authentic Documents in the Possession of his Family and of the African Institution*, 2nd ed., 2 vols (London, 1828) 1 121–2.

of slave-traders, did not appear until 1762. By this time, however, he had gained a lot of experience in his struggle to have
slavery discountenanced within the Society of Friends. He had
composed an Epistle to the Philadelphia Yearly Meeting as early
as 1754, and gone indefatigably round its members lobbying
them to support those Friends who finally secured the decision
that trading in slaves should be grounds for disownment. It was
during this early period of his agitation for the slave that Benezet
began his collaboration and close friendship with John Woolman.
The principal role in winning the Yearly Meeting over to its
1758 standpoint was played by Woolman, and Benezet's letter
writing was built very much on his widely circulated pamphlet
of 1754, *Some Considerations on the Keeping of Negroes*.[22] But it
was Benezet who extended the campaign Woolman had begun
outside the Society of Friends. The audience he aimed at in his
pamphlets, and whom he later tried to organise, were those who
had the power, collectively or as individuals, to end the institution
of slavery – that is literate society as a whole, not just the
Christian commonwealth of Quakers. It is in this sense that his
publication of *A Short Account of that Part of Africa, Inhabited
by the Negroes* may be seen as the beginning of general as
opposed to denominational anti-slavery agitation.

In this and his future writing, Benezet brought a new argument to bear on the problem of slavery. Instead of attacking it by
relying purely on the dictates of natural law or of religion, he
brought empirical evidence from Africa into the equation. By
citing all the eyewitness accounts of the West African coast to
which he had access, he was able to show to his satisfaction that
what depravity and degradation appeared there was the product
of slave-trader influence; that the Negro in his natural state was
a human being of dignity and ability; that the corruption of such
men was an added sin on the slaveholders' conscience; and that
the enslavement of men equal in endowments to their captors
was in any case irrational. This train of argument was to become
a stock one for later abolitionists, who would insist with Benezet
that:

[22] J. Woolman, *Some Considerations on the Keeping of Negroes, Recommended to the Professors of Christianity of Every Denomination* (Philadelphia, 1754), reprinted in Gummere (ed.), *Journal . . . of John Woolman*,
pp. 334–47.

Negroes are generally sensible, humane, and sociable, and that their Capacity is as good, and as capable of Improvement, as that of the White People: That their Country, though unfriendly to the Europeans, yet appears peculiarly agreeable, and well adapted to the Nature of the *Blacks*, and so fruitful, as to furnish its Inhabitants plentifully with the Necessaries of Life, with much less Labour than is necessary in our more Northern Countries.[23]

This insistence on the economic potential was similar to that of later groups who helped to colonise parts of West Africa, but it is more important that Benezet's demonstration of black potential gave a new argument to the abolitionists. His grasp of travel accounts shows strikingly how far such books were available to colonists interested in Africa and in the origins of their slaves. In the *Short Account*, he quoted among others the books of Brue, Bosman, Adanson, William Smith, Barbot and Francis Moore – the majority of writers on West Africa then available in English. He was even able to turn the accounts of those unsympathetic to the Negro to good use. For instance, he laid the greed of the African, so often criticised, at the door of European traders, who had 'stirred up and strengthened the earthly Principle of Craft and Covetousness in the poor Africans', instead of preaching the Gospel.[24] His sources were even more impressive in *Some Historical Account of Guinea*, the longer work he published in 1771. It was reprinted in London both in French and English in 1788. It was 'in this precious book' that Thomas Clarkson said he had found almost all he wanted when he was preparing for his Cambridge prize essay, the work which brought him fully into the anti-slavery movement.[25]

In spite of the importance of Benezet's use of African evidence, it should not be supposed that this was his only line of attack on slavery. In all his writing, he pointed repeatedly to its being at odds with the Golden Rule. For a supposedly uneducated provincial Quaker, he also cited a surprising number of Enlightenment writers. In *A Short Account of that Part of Africa,*

[23] *Short Account*, p. 8.   [24] Ibid., p. 16.
[25] T. Clarkson, *The History of the Rise, Progress, and Accomplishment of the Abolition of the African Slave-Trade, by the British Parliament,* 2 vols (London, 1808) I 207–8.

Inhabited by the Negroes, he quoted extensively not only from Montesquieu, who appears in almost every colonial anti-slavery pamphlet, but from George 'Wallis', author of *A System of the Principles of the Law of Scotland.* As we have seen, this obscure work took the most advanced possible standpoint on the opposition between slavery and natural law. Montesquieu was again the key 'civilian' in *Some Historical Account of Guinea.*[26] Benezet was even prepared to argue that the abolition of slavery was in any case demanded by expediency. His *Caution to Great Britain,* published in 1766, graphically anticipated Jefferson in explaining the effect of slavery upon the morality of the colonies:

> It might be also shewn, that it destroys the bonds of natural affection and interest, whereby mankind in general are united; that it introduces idleness, discourages marriage, corrupts the youth, ruins and debauches morals, excites continual apprehensions of dangers, and frequent alarms, to which the Whites are necessarily exposed from so great an increase of a People, that, by their Bondage and Oppressions, become natural enemies, yet, at the same time, are filling the places and eating the bread of those who would be the Support and security of the Country.[27]

This was exactly the argument which had been used by Sewall, one bound to be effective on those who were untouched by moral arguments but lived surrounded by slaves. Most of this pamphlet, too, was given over to Benezet's usual themes of the contradiction between slavery and the Golden Rule, and the peace and plenty which would reign in Guinea without the presence of the Europeans. However, he began with a new argument brought out by current controversy, the contradiction between liberty from the power of the British, and liberty for the slave:

> At a time when the general rights and liberties of mankind, and the preservation of those valuable privileges transmitted to us from our ancestors, are become so much the subjects of universal consideration; can it be an inquiry indifferent to any, how many of those who distinguish themselves as the Advocates of Liberty, remain insensible and inattentive to the treatment

[26] *Short Account,* pp. 23–6; *Some Historical Account of Guinea,* 2nd ed. (London, 1788) pp. 62–71.

[27] *A Caution and a Warning,* 2nd ed. (London, 1784) p. 5.

of thousands and tens of thousands of our fellow men, who, from motives of avarice, and the inexorable decree of tyrant custom, are at this very time kept in the most deplorable state of Slavery, in many parts of the *British* Dominions?[28]

The abolitionist attack on the paradox of the republican slave-master had begun.

Benezet's writing thus included most of the major arguments which were used by the eighteenth-century abolitionists. The response to them was great enough for it to be possible, by the 1760s, to speak in terms of a genuine anti-slavery movement. Other colonial pamphleteers joined him in denouncing slavery and the slave trade. Several were Quakers and several from Philadelphia, but this kind of writing was by no means restricted to the Society of Friends or to Pennsylvania. Moreover, a rash of pamphlets explaining the natural inferiority of the African made it clear that the abolitionist sentiment of the 1760s, unlike earlier innocuous protests, was strong enough to provide a serious threat to those with vested interests in slavery.

The body of anti-slavery literature increased rapidly, although this does not mean that it was all pro-Negro. Most of it showed the fear of servile insurrection. This did not exclude the contradictory point that the Negroes were a gentle people corrupted by the Europeans. One pamphlet published in Boston in 1767, for instance, announced that Africans are 'a harmless people . . . and but for the interruption from white people might enjoy all the sweets of a rural life', but was not prevented from going on to describe the horrors of immorality and military insecurity caused by the presence of an alien slave population. The use of such arguments should not disguise the genuine radicalism of these pamphleteers. The same Boston writer of 1767 demanded whether 'any who are concerned in this black hellish business [could] pretend to the Character of Christians'. He also remarked, with considerable force, that if the end of the slave trade meant that 'many gentlemen of immense fortunes must be ruin'd, *let them, and beg.* 'Tis more honourable to seek a support by begging than by theft. . . .'[29] At the same time as this kind of argument was

---

[28] Ibid., p. 3.
[29] [A. Bennett], *Considerations on Slavery, in a Letter to a Friend* (Boston, 1767) pp. 5, 13–14, 11, 8.

being made in Boston, the first English attacks on slavery were filtering over to the colonies, and Benezet was finding new allies in Philadelphia itself. It has often been said, with a good deal of truth, that after the pacifist position of the Society of Friends forced its members to withdraw from the government of Pennsylvania, their energies were transferred into reform. This is borne out by the number of these allies who were Quakers, often with contacts both in England and the New World, like David Cooper, the author of *A Mite Cast into the Treasury; or, Observations on Slave-Keeping* (1772), or the immensely important William Dillwyn, who probably collaborated with Benezet in producing his *Brief Considerations on Slavery, and the Expediency of its Abolition* (1773).

Philadelphia's most important abolitionist after Benezet, however, was not a Quaker, though he was closely connected to the Friends and greatly admired their work and religious thought. This was Dr Benjamin Rush, one of the large group of Americans who had been trained in the Medical School at the University of Edinburgh. He had come home deeply influenced by the ideas of the Scottish Enlightenment. By the 1760s Rush was carrying on private practice, and also teaching the system of medicine he had learned from William Cullen at Edinburgh in the new college which was eventually to become the University of Pennsylvania. In later years, in spite of extraordinary medical misconceptions and a series of bitter controversies with other local men, he became Philadelphia's leading doctor, and one of its most influential citizens. He was a signer of the Declaration of Independence, and during the Revolutionary War followed a stormy course as head of the medical service of the Continental Army, incidentally crossing swords vigorously with George Washington in a series of incidents which led to his resignation. Like many abolitionists, he is not a specially attractive personality. He was often aggressive and unforgiving, and even the most sympathetic biographer could find little in the way of humour about his life. Yet he is a central figure in the history of reform in the Atlantic world. Aside from his work in education, and in organising the model Philadelphia Hospital, he was a pioneer of the American temperance movement. In the anti-slavery movement he is important both as polemicist and organiser, all the more so because of his international contacts, the most significant of whom was

Granville Sharp.[30] He first jumped into the slavery controversy with a callow essay published in 1773. It explained the debasement of the Negro slave with an environmentalist argument based on Montesquieu:

> Slavery is so foreign to the human mind, that the moral faculties as well as those of the understanding are debased, and rendered torpid by it. All the vices which are charged upon the Negroes in the southern colonies and the West Indies, such as Idleness, Treachery, Theft, and the like, are the genuine offspring of slavery, and serve as an argument to prove they were not intended for it.[31]

This pamphlet was immediately attacked anonymously by a Mr R. Nesbit, who observed that Rush's over-generalisation 'lays himself open to be refuted by every school boy'. He went on to argue, with absolute truth, that Scripture justified slavery.[32] Rush was provoked into defending his remarks with *A Vindication of the Address*. From this time on, although Rush published very little else on the slavery question, he devoted a great deal of his efforts in correspondence and personal contact to helping the Negro. He protected any slaves attempting to escape through Philadelphia to the best of his ability, and became a leader of the Philadelphia Abolition Society and later of the national anti-slavery movement. He was the chief white sponsor of the First African Church of Philadelphia.

[30] The most recent biography of Rush is D. Hawke, *Benjamin Rush, Revolutionary Gadfly* (New York, 1971). See also L. H. Butterfield (ed.), *Letters of Benjamin Rush*, 2 vols (Princeton, 1951); G. W. Corner (ed.), *The Autobiography of Benjamin Rush* (Princeton, 1948); L. H. Butterfield, 'The Reputation of Benjamin Rush', *Pennsylvania History*, XVII (1950) 3–20; D. J. D'Elia, 'The Republican Theology of Benjamin Rush', ibid., XXXIII (1966) 187–203; idem, 'Dr Benjamin Rush and the Negro', *Journal of the History of Ideas*, XXX (1970) 413–22. For the contact with Sharp, see J. Woods, 'The Correspondence of Benjamin Rush and Granville Sharp, 1773–1809', *Journal of American Studies*, I (1967) 1–38.

[31] B. Rush, *An Address to the Inhabitants of the British Settlements on the Slavery of the Negroes in America. To which is Added, a Vindication of the Address* (Philadelphia, 1773) p. 2.

[32] [R. Nesbit], *Slavery not Forbidden by Scripture, or a Defence of the West India Planters, from the Aspersions Thrown out against them, by the Author of a Pamphlet, Entitled, 'An Address to the Inhabitants of the British Empire, upon Slave-Keeping'* (Philadelphia, 1773) pp. iii, 4 ff.

The pro-slavery response to Rush's first abolitionist pamphlet leads on to the problem of the connection between the American Revolution and the rise of anti-slavery sentiment. It is often assumed that the first attacks on slavery came because the idea of liberty produced by the struggle with Britain logically had to be applied to the case of the African. Abolitionist propaganda did frequently point to the contradiction between the conception of republican liberty and the act of holding slaves. But the unpleasant fact is that this was no contradiction as long as the natural inferiority of the Negro was assumed. This was the answer to Samuel Johnson's question: 'How is it that we hear the loudest *yelps* for liberty among the drivers of negroes?'[33] The reason why it was not agonising for Jefferson the *philosophe*, Jefferson the humanitarian, to hold slaves was that unlike Rush he had not taken the step of accepting that black people had the degree of responsibility which would entitle them to take a place in society as free men. There is much in common between the ideological background of the Revolution and the ideological background of anti-slavery. Because the crucial question of the humanity of the Negro was as yet in a state of indecision, however, it is easy to imagine the Revolution's not having affected slavery, or the anti-slavery movement's having arisen if there had been no Revolution. It was a fine propaganda point that anti-slavery followed logically from liberty, but except for those whose religious and intellectual preconceptions on the Negro had already changed, the connection was meaningless. For this reason, Nesbit's pro-slavery response to Rush was not incongruous in its time – and indeed much comment on the Negro was much more damning than this, without necessarily being at odds with Enlightenment thought. The most crushing of such efforts, *Personal Slavery Established, by the Suffrages of Custom and Right Reason*, though it may have been a parody in some passages at least, expressed ideas quite acceptable to a large group of colonists. Woolman's *Considerations* is dismissed as 'the dull productions of a visionary enthusiast', and the opinions of Benezet's *Short Account* as 'idle and nugatory'. His *Caution* he thought 'merely theoretick', while he crushed all poor Rush's scriptural citations, with Enlightened zeal, under the comment

[33] J. Boswell, *Life of Johnson* (New York: Modern Library Edition, 1931) pp. 747–8.

that in any case 'the authority of scripture is now generally rejected by men of a liberal way of thinking'. Finally, he threatened Philadelphia merchants with the disruption of trade which would result from carrying on their agitation:

It is supposed that one hundred thousand slaves are yearly shipped in the African ports for the British West India islands. Of these perhaps twenty thousand die on the passage. Now when their death is not occasioned by any bad disorder, if there was a proper quantity of salt on board, the bodies might be cured in pickle or smoak; and the same method pursued with those that die on land, or are past labour. A considerable quantity of provisions might be thus procured that would furnish a tolerable succedaneum for *pork* and hams. I have never heard that this kind of meat is deemed unwholesome, but, on the contrary, that the Cannibals are a hardy robust race of people – the scheme is new, and might not be very eligible – I only mention it as a *dernier resort*, and which a very high degree of resentment only could ever incline them to have recourse to.[34]

Parody or not, the abolitionist William Dillwyn, whose copy is in the Franklin Collection at Yale, saw these arguments as being representative enough of the standard opposition position to underline the most 'vulnerable' passages furiously in red and blue pencil. If it is true that the ideological ferment of the revolutionary period produced an anti-slavery movement, it must be explained why it also produced a pro-slavery one. Abolitionism, in fact, represented an independent intellectual development which was connected only incidentally with the struggle against Britain.

In either case, as the body of anti-slavery literature grew, it became possible to organise for agitation. The result was the foundation of the Philadelphia Society in 1775. Its official title was the Society for the Relief of Free Negroes Illegally Held in Bondage. There were several reasons why Philadelphia should have been the city which formed the first anti-slavery society in

[34] *Personal Slavery Established, by the Suffrages of Custom and Right Reason: Being a Short Answer to the Gloomy and Visionary Reveries, of all the Fanatical and Enthusiastical Writers on the Subject* (Philadelphia, 1773) pp. 7, 8, 11, 26.

the world, some of which have already been explained. First there was the strong influence of the Quakers, with their humanitarian interests, their experience in handling anti-slavery ideas during the earlier controversy within their Society, and their close ties with Friends in other parts of the world. However, Philadelphia's advantage went beyond this. It was certainly the most cosmopolitan city in the British colonies of the late eighteenth century, much more so than New York.[35] Again, unlike Boston, it was at the centre of the rich farming areas of West Jersey, Delaware and Pennsylvania itself. In all three, slavery was widespread enough to be a major problem, but not so universal that it produced a vested interest who could crush attempts at abolition out of hand. Finally, there was the simple personal factor, accidental or not, that the city could be influenced by respected citizens who were the leading abolitionist writers in America.

The Philadelphia Society, however, was soon joined by others. In 1784 it was reorganised into the Pennsylvania Abolition Society, which also worked in the neighbouring state of New Jersey. It stated that it would work for 'the Abolition of Slavery [and] the Relief of Free Negroes', as well as the general improvement of the condition of the 'Colored Race'. Its president was Benjamin Franklin. The most important of the other American societies was the New York Manumission Society, founded in 1785, with John Jay as president. Societies were also organised in Maryland, Delaware and Connecticut, and in 1793 in New Jersey, the Northern state in which opposition to abolition was strongest. In the next year the New York Manumission Society organised a Convention of delegates from all abolition societies, with the intention of co-ordinating their efforts. It hoped to put pressure on Congress, largely through petitions, to use its power to regulate the slave trade. It was decided that the Convention should meet annually. This did not mean that any permanent office or organisation had come into existence, but at least the abolitionists had emerged as a pressure group in national politics, thirty-five years before the organisation of William Lloyd Garrison's American Anti-Slavery Society.[36]

[35] See C. Bridenbaugh and J. Bridenbaugh, *Rebels and Gentlemen: Philadelphia in the Age of Franklin*, 2nd ed. (New York, 1965).

[36] For an account of these organisations and their campaigns, see A. Zilversmit, *The First Emancipation: The Abolition of Slavery in the North*

The methods of agitation used by the abolition societies were varied, but a great deal of their attention was focused on the free black population, much of which was miserably poor. The general white assumption was that the squalor and crime which resulted from their condition was proof of black unfitness for freedom. The most practical approach to changing the assumptions which supported slavery was to 'elevate' free black people. Beyond this, the abolitionists spread as much propaganda as possible, largely through the medium of the pamphlet, but also through short articles in the colonial press. Some writers turned not to the direct argument over slavery, but to scientific writing designed to defend the capabilities of the Negro against his detractors. One such was Samuel Stanhope Smith of Princeton, whose work attacking Kames's and Hume's assumptions on Negro inferiority was brought out in an Edinburgh edition and was used by the Abbé Grégoire.[37] Apart from the scientific dimension, however, there is a certain sameness about the arguments used in abolitionist propaganda. Indeed, few new arguments appear in the debate on slavery from the 1760s until 1830. During the Confederation and the early years of the new nation, abolitionists were less concerned with elaborating their corpus of ideas than with pragmatic day-to-day work to turn opinion against slavery. The abolitionist societies attempted to dramatise the slavery issue by contesting the rights of masters in the courts whenever the opportunity arose, either because of shaky claims to ownership or because of particularly flagrant physical abuses. Unspectacular as it was, this kind of activity gave a number of men and women their freedom, and also produced splendid publicity. At the same time, changing opinion on slavery, perhaps partly due to abolitionist persuasion, led to extensive voluntary manumissions by individual masters, in both the North and the South. Finally, the abolitionist societies worked on raising petitions on slavery to go to

---

(Chicago, 1967). On Northern slavery, see L. J. Greene, *The Negro in Colonial New England* (New York, 1942); E. J. McManus, *A History of Negro Slavery in New York* (Syracuse, N.Y., 1966).

[37] S. S. Smith, *An Essay on the Causes of the Variety of Complexion and Figure in the Human Species. To which are Added Strictures on Lord Kaim's Discourse, on the Original Diversity of Mankind* (Philadelphia, 1787). This work was first delivered as a paper at the American Philosophical Society, in February 1787.

the various state legislatures. First they called for amelioration of conditions, next for gradual emancipation. By 1790 the individual societies were petitioning the national Congress to take control of the slave trade, although this function was taken over by the National Convention after 1794.

In the Northern colonies the success of these methods was astonishing. The slave trade was put under embargo by the Continental Congress as early as 1776, though this was done at least in part for security reasons. The Constitutional Convention of 1788 never fully came to grips with the contradiction between slavery and republicanism, perhaps because many of its members did not see such a contradiction. Their use of the three-fifths rule in working out state representation laid up a great deal of trouble for the future. However, it was agreed that the slave trade would come to an end in twenty years, that is in 1808. At state level, by the early nineteenth century, the abolitionists had managed to secure the abolition of slavery or the promise of abolition in seven of the original thirteen colonies. In those cases where the numbers of slaves involved were tiny, as in New Hampshire, slavery ended without legislation in the confusion of the Revolutionary War. In Massachusetts there was no true abolition law, and slavery ended during the early 1780s when the courts began to swing over to granting freedom to any slave who sued his master, on the grounds that the 1780 state constitution excluded it. In no case was there any legislation providing for immediate emancipation, which would have set all the slaves loose overnight as free men. Various schemes of gradual emancipation were enacted. Some were considerably more gradual than others. The first such law, for instance, the Pennsylvania Act of 1780, had no effect on those slaves already in bondage, though it stipulated that all those born thereafter were to serve as 'apprentices' until the age of twenty-eight, at which time they would be released. In 1784 similar Acts were secured both in Connecticut and Rhode Island. In New York and New Jersey, where vested interests in slavery were stronger and demands for compensation louder, the struggle was a longer one. In New York it was only after many years of lobbying that the legislature accepted a gradual Emancipation Act in 1799. This was similar in operation to the Pennsylvania law, except that it effectively allowed masters financial compensation for the loss of their slaves. In New Jersey the pro-slavery forces fought an even stiffer rearguard action. Gradual abolition was rejected there in the eighteenth century, but passed with relative ease in 1804.[38] The immediate effect of such legislation was imperceptible, and the next step for the abolitionists was to demand total emancipation in each state. In Connecticut this did not come until 1848, though the problem was by then academic. In Massachusetts it was unnecessary, and in Pennsylvania gradual emancipation reduced slaves to a handful before total abolition could be secured. In New York, where the numbers of men and women involved were greater, an 1817 law enacted universal emancipation for 1827. In New Jersey it was not until 1846 that a revised Act technically ended slavery. Many slaves remained as 'apprentices' and there were still eighteen New Jersey blacks classified as slaves at the 1860 census.

Long as this process now seems, the abolitionist achievement in the North was enormous. Apart from their contribution to later anti-slavery ideology, they had destroyed the slave status in their own region. The reason why this was possible was largely economic. Zilversmit's argument that slaves fetched good prices right up to the end, and that slavery as an institution was thought to be profitable, is accurate. However, this does not affect the fact that Northern slavery was not profitable, and never had been profitable, in the other sense that it was not necessary for the economic well-being of society as a whole. Since it was only important to individuals, it became vulnerable as soon as sentiment turned against it with the spread of anti-slavery ideology. In the Southern states there were also abolitionists in the eighteenth century; pamphlets attacking slavery and petitions demanding its abolition appeared there as in the North, and the border states of Maryland and Delaware had their own abolition societies. However, slavery was not a matter which concerned mere individuals, but one on which the whole economic system depended, quite apart from its importance in underpinning Southerners' conceptions of themselves as gentry. Without a weakening of these commitments to slavery, abolitionist ideology was a luxurious eccentricity, and could make little impression on the system in the South. In the North, slavery itself had always been a luxury. It collapsed as soon as its religious and intellectual supports were withdrawn.

[38] Zilversmit, *First Emancipation*, pp. 175–200.

The success of the British abolitionists was also connected with weaknesses in the opposition. Their history runs very much parallel to that of their American counterparts, though their campaign appears less radical because of their concentration on attacking the slave trade rather than slavery. Quakers are again much in evidence. The ideas in use were similar on the two sides of the Atlantic, both in terms of the sources on which the abolitionists drew, and the points which they made in their propaganda. This followed from the constant exchange of literature and correspondence between Britons and Americans – an exchange which was not interrupted by the Revolution – and from the fact that a number of important American abolitionists, most important among them Rush, Franklin and William Dillwyn, spent time in Britain. Another example in this context is the London house of the Quaker doctor John Fothergill, himself an important abolitionist, where American visitors almost automatically called and doubtless absorbed anti-slavery ideas.

There are fewer obvious pioneers of the anti-slavery idea in Britain than in America. There is an anti-slavery potential in the writing of Morgan Godwyn. At least one obscure pamphlet, published in 1760 and titled *Two Dialogues on the Man-Trade*, set out ideas on the natural law support for slavery as radical as anything which had been written in the colonies at the time.[39] However, it is now extraordinarily rare, and there are no contemporary references to it except in Benezet, so that its circulation and direct impact must have been small. The missionary attempts of the Society for the Propagation of the Gospel were aimed partly at the Negro; but the S.P.G.'s own attempts to demonstrate the ways of elevating slaves in the Codrington plantations in Barbados failed dismally. When brought to the test they flatly rejected the demand of Anthony Benezet that they should give a testimony against slavery. Granville Sharp, in fact, is the Anthony Benezet of England, but he was not preceded by other anti-slavery writers in the way in which Benezet was preceded by Sandiford and Sewall. Not even a Quaker, he did not have experience in the arguments over slavery which had kept both British and American Friends occupied in the 1750s. However, he was directly affected by his readings in the general work of the Enlightenment

[39] J. Philmore [pseud.], *Two Dialogues on the Man-Trade* (London, 1760), discussed by Davis, in *W.M.Q.*, 3rd ser., xxviii 592–4.

on sociology and politics, by extensive study of Scripture and English law, by the deep influence of evangelical religion, and perhaps most of all by a personal kindness which made the cruelty of slavery repugnant to him when it had little effect on less sensitive men.

Like most of the men who became leaders in the English anti-slavery movement, Sharp came from a relatively rich and distinguished background. Though his ancestors were provincials, Yorkshiremen, one of them had been Chancellor of England. His grandfather was Archbishop of York, and his father Archdeacon of Durham and Prebendary of Northumberland. Yet there is something extraordinarily humble about Sharp. At fifteen, in 1750, whether out of rebellion against his parents or simple eccentricity, he went to London to become apprentice to a Quaker draper, an extraordinary step for someone of his background. This did not exclude his later use of the contacts which he had been given by his upbringing among the princes of the Church of England. He educated himself to an astonishing level of competence in languages, dogmatics and jurisprudence, and yet was content to spend his life as a minor clerk in the Ordnance Department. After resigning in protest against the American war he was supported by his brothers. Throughout his life his main interest was not his work but the cause of the slave. This first attracted his attention because of the difficulties of the 15,000 slaves and free blacks then in England. Mainly concentrated in London, where they had been brought by masters returning from the colonies, those still slaves were visibly oppressed in the same way as their brothers in the West Indies. The condition of those who had become free was even more wretched, for few had managed to find any position in society which would prevent them from sinking into poverty and complete wretchedness.

Sharp later tried to solve the problem of the domestic black poor with his experiment in founding the colony of Sierra Leone, to which he hoped they could be shipped off. First, however, his attention was drawn to English slavery itself by an incident, which the wider public scarcely noticed, in which a slave named Jonathan Strong was abandoned by his master as worthless, brought back to health, and then reclaimed as a slave. After securing his release, Sharp turned to training himself in English law, in the hope of preventing such incidents in the future. Since his early writing was aimed at the specific problem of slavery within the United Kingdom, and at the hopeless confusion between villeinage and chattel slavery in English law, it lacks something of the universality of the writing of Benezet and the other Americans who had set out to prove that slavery was wrong in all places and under all circumstances. Again, Sharp's first and most important pamphlet, *A Representation of the Injustice and Dangerous Tendency of Tolerating Slavery in England* (1769), was written simply to expose the contradiction between the rights of Englishmen and the presence of slaves on English soil. Its conclusions did not have a direct impact on later pamphleteers, though it was not a great leap to go on to argue that if the common law was at odds with slavery in England, it was at odds with it in the English colonies. Yet this contradiction had already been exposed by Blackstone and others. The real importance of Sharp's lonely campaign was not in the ideas he used but in its dramatisation of English implication in slavery.

As in the colonies, attitudes towards slavery had changed significantly since the beginning of the century. In 1729 the Attorney-General Yorke and Solicitor-General Talbot, the two Law Officers of the Crown, when questioned as to whether slaves became free on coming to England, had given the opinion that they did not do so, whether or not they were baptised. There had been few protests at the time, and yet forty years later the incidents Sharp publicised after the Strong case received wide attention. His final success came with the Somerset case of 1772. James Somerset was a Virginian (not West Indian) Negro, who had escaped and been recaptured. His master was on the point of shipping him back to the colonies when Sharp discovered his plight and brought suit to have him released on the grounds that the state of slavery could not exist in England. After long delays which simply served to attract more publicity to the controversy, on 22 June 1772 Chief Justice Mansfield not only declared Somerset free, but confirmed once and for all that any slave, by the act of walking on the soil of England, became free. A few years later the same position was reached at Scots law in the James Knight case. The practical importance of these cases is not great, for they freed only a few thousand slaves, and had no direct effect on the situation in the colonies. They had no machinery for enforcement unless appeals were made by injured parties or their sponsors, not a difficult step for a careful master to prevent, and they left the whole allied structure of Scottish mining serfdom untouched. However, the decisions pointed to the way in which sympathy for the slave was growing, and the controversy they caused attracted attention to the more general problem of slavery. Sharp himself was not the only person who moved on to demanding an end to the slave trade and ultimately of slavery after the Somerset case had been won.

Organised activity against the slave trade did not begin in England until 1783. By then opinion had been turning against it in some areas for more than ten years. Again the change of attitudes was fostered by correspondence between those concerned over slavery on the two sides of the Atlantic. In fact Sharp had reprinted Benezet's *A Caution and a Warning*, incidentally without the author's consent, after coming across a copy in a London bookstall. An exchange of letters between them began when Benezet wrote to Sharp announcing that he had also reprinted an abridged version of *A Representation of the Injustice*. The fact that Sharp wrote condescendingly on the fly-leaf of his copy of one of Benezet's works 'that at present Mr B is obliged to earn his bread in the laborious office of a schoolmaster, and is also unhappily involved in the errors of Quakerism', did not make the relationship between the two men any less warm.[40] Benezet also influenced John Wesley, both personally while Wesley was in America, and through his writings. The Methodist leader's pamphlet *Thoughts upon Slavery* (1774) contained a number of passages in which this influence was clear. Indeed the contacts between English and colonial Friends deeply influenced the English anti-slavery movement as well as the colonial one. London Yearly Meeting had condemned the implication of Friends in the slave trade as early as 1727, and the correspondence through which it tried to turn the American Meetings against slavery also did much to familiarise English Friends with its abuses. In the 1780s they were to turn out from their own Society and become the main force behind the launching of a true movement against the slave trade. At the same time as the sympathies of Wesley and his followers, and the concern of the Friends, was preparing the way, secular influences were also changing attitudes to slavery.

[40] Hoare, *Memoirs of Granville Sharp*, I 48–137, 144–50.

In pure political terms, the outcome of the American Revolution opened the way to a successful attack on the slave trade. The West India lobby was left alone to stem the tide, without its natural allies, the well-organised planters from the mainland colonies.

In 1783 a small group of Quakers gathered in London to form a committee to work against the slave trade. Among them, incidentally, were some of the richest men in England – Samuel Hoare, William Dillwyn and John Lloyd. The efforts of the Friends, in the same year, produced the first petition to the British Parliament, which was subsequently published as a highly influential tract, *The Case of our Fellow-Creatures, the Oppressed Africans, Respectfully Recommended . . . by the People Called Quakers.* At the same time as the Quaker impulse was strengthening in this way, public attention was directed to the atrocities of the slave trade in a way bound to heighten the public revulsion against it, even in an age hardened to cruelty. The owners of the slave-ship *Zong*, out of Liverpool, in 1783 applied to their underwriters to claim compensation for the loss of 132 slaves who had to be thrown overboard late in the Middle Passage. A shortage of provisions, it was claimed, left this as the only way of saving the rest of the cargo. No one would have disputed the right of the owners to claim if these had been the facts, but at the subsequent enquiry it emerged that there had been no shortage of provisions at all. Sickness among slaves was not covered by insurance. Faced with an outbreak of dysentery which endangered his own and the owners' investment, the captain had hit on the bright idea of throwing all infected slaves overboard to preserve the rest, and then claiming insurance for losses at sea due to provision shortage. The *Zong*'s owners lost their case, but the effect on English opinion was unmistakable. It was immediately after this that the Quakers petitioned Parliament on the slave trade. Soon they found allies from other denominations. One was James Ramsay, an Anglican clergyman who had been a lifelong friend of James Beattie since their student days, and who returned from a long spell of service in St Kitts to publish his *Essay on the Treatment and Conversion of African Slaves in the British Sugar Colonies* (1784). Even more important, however, was the anti-slavery conversion of Thomas Clarkson, who devoted his life to gathering information to support the propaganda of the abolitionists. Clarkson was from a modest North Country background, with a solid mind for facts and a great share of the virtue of perseverance. Though dogged and somewhat humourless, he was not entirely immune to vanity: Dorothy Wordsworth records his coming over to Grasmere to show William and her what a fine figure he cut on a new horse. Yet intimate knowledge of Clarkson did not present his friend Thomas De Quincey from describing him as 'that son of thunder, that Titan, who was in fact the one great Atlas that bore up the Slave-Trade Abolition cause'.[41] He was not a first-rate mind – few abolitionists were – but his researches provided much of the raw material for propaganda against the slave trade until the victory of 1807. In 1785 he was in the final year of his B.A. at Cambridge. The subject for the annual Prize Essay in that year was announced as 'Anne liceat invitos in servitutem dare?' – 'Whether it is lawful to enslave men against their will?' The subject itself is an indication of the way in which interest was focusing among Anglicans. Clarkson spent a frenzied six weeks in preparing his paper. He relates that the turning-point in his research was finding a copy of Benezet's *Some Historical Account of Guinea*: 'In this precious book I found almost all I wanted'.[42] Actually, the resulting essay added nothing to existing anti-slavery ideas, although it won the prize. The brief controversy which followed its publication as *An Essay on the Slavery and Commerce of the Human Species, Particularly the African* (1786) was no different from many others in the history of the movement, and it was in any case easily demolished by West Indian replies. The real importance of the *Essay* is that his work on it drew Clarkson into the movement. After reading it at Cambridge he decided to begin full-time study of the anti-slavery issue. His subsequent painstaking fact-gathering not only uncovered atrocities against the Negro; it also revealed the difficulties of finding crews for the Guinea trade, and a massive mortality in sailors which completely disproved the mercantilist argument that the slave trade was the nursery of seamen. Naturally Clarkson's disclosures were resented in the port towns which he visited in his search for information. He guilelessly trotted

[41] Dorothy Wordsworth, *Journal*, ed. M. Moorman (London, 1971) pp. 99–100; T. De Quincey, *Recollections of the Lakes and the Lake Poets*, ed. D. Wright (London, 1970) p. 343.
[42] Clarkson, *History of the Abolition of the African Slave-Trade*, I 207.

round dockside taverns asking Guineamen for information which would condemn the slave trade. It is questionable whether he himself saw the humour of this situation. On one occasion he narrowly escaped being pushed off a pier in Liverpool, the nearest to a martyring of any English abolitionist.

As more and more non-Quakers developed a concern over the trade, it became inevitable that a society should be formed to co-ordinate political pressure on Parliament. In 1787 the old Quaker committee on abolition was reorganised with Granville Sharp and Thomas Clarkson as members. They aimed not at emancipation but at slave-trade abolition. This they intended to bring about through correspondence with contacts in other English cities, spreading of pamphlets, lobbying of politicians and endless petitions. Their main spokesman in the Commons, who would present their petitions, was the brilliant young member for Yorkshire, William Wilberforce.

It was when Wilberforce reached an understanding with the new Society for the Abolition of the Slave Trade that the true political battle was begun. Wilberforce had many advantages as a leader. He was a man of great personal charm and a brilliant orator. His evangelical frame of reference was appealing to the groups more likely to be won over to abolition. At the same time, his friendship with Pitt the Younger and his seat in Yorkshire, the most important county constituency in the unreformed House of Commons, gave him remarkable political prestige and power for a commoner still in his twenties. It was due to his influence with Pitt that a Select Committee of the Privy Council was called in 1788 to hear evidence on the conduct of the slave trade, its humanity, and its importance in the national economy.[43] Before this could be followed up, however, the whole movement was set back by Wilberforce's illness and long convalescence at Bath. Again, in the preliminary debate on the slave trade, much of the edge was taken off the abolitionists' attack by the passage of

[43] Its reports are a superb source of information for the trade, as are the many abolitionist abstracts of its evidence, the most common of which is *An Abstract of the Evidence Delivered before a Select Committee on the Slave Trade* (London, 1789). For the political history of the campaign, see F. J. Klingberg, *The Anti-Slavery Movement: A Study in English Humanitarianism* (New Haven, 1926); D. H. Porter, *The Abolition of the Slave Trade in England, 1784–1807* (Hamden, Conn., 1970); R. G. Anstey, *The Atlantic Slave Trade and British Abolition, 1760–1810* (London, 1975).

'Dolben's Bill', which regulated the number of slaves which could be carried per ton in the hope of mitigating trading conditions. By the time Wilberforce returned to the attack, enthusiasm in the provinces, on which the movement always depended heavily, had subsided, in spite of the revelations of the complete Privy Council Report, abstracts of which were vigorously circulated by the abolitionists. The first outburst of feeling against the slave trade was already subsiding when the dreadful events of 1789 turned attention across the Channel, and made it easy for the West Indians and the slavers to denounce any attempt to interfere with their vested interests as Jacobinical.

Indeed the eventual success of the abolitionists should not obscure the strength of the opposition they faced. The West India lobby, even in its declining years, had a great deal of political muscle. There is probably some truth in James Boswell's wistful and often quoted remark that the abolitionists would easily have been crushed at the outset if the fanatics involved had not seemed so insignificant.[44] The enormous difficulties of British West Indian agriculture – only a handful of Jamaican coffee-planters had enough credit to be able to buy slaves by 1807 – did not prevent many of them from being determined to preserve the trade in the hope of better times in the future. Moreover, the pro-slave-trade faction was able to produce a formidable body of anti-abolitionist literature, much of which was never replied to satisfactorily. Above all, they were able to make capital out of the confused assumption that the abolitionists, in attacking the slave trade, were intending also to attack slavery. But their arguments went beyond this. For instance, they were able to find a Liverpool ex-Jesuit, Raymund Harris, to compose a treatise demonstrating once and for all that Scripture and slavery were fully reconcilable.[45] Not all abolitionists were noted for charisma, and none for public humour. At the simplest level, it was easy to make *ad hominem* comments about the gloomy fanatics and dangerous visionaries, especially once the murk of suspicion was thickened by revolution across the Channel, controversy over radicalism and

---

[44] *Life of Johnson*, p. 749.

[45] R. Harris, *Scriptural Researches on the Licitness of the Slave Trade, Showing its Conformity with the Principles of Natural and Revealed Religion, Delineated in the Sacred Writings of the Word of God* (Liverpool, 1788).

sedition at home, and the fact that Britain was fighting for her life on the international scene. Men like Ramsay, with West India experience, could also be discredited, possibly with justice, by claiming that they themselves had mistreated their slaves while in the colonies.[46] It could be argued, too, that black slavery was essential since Europeans could not face the heat, 'added to which, the New Rum . . . debilitates them'. The Negroes were unfit for freedom, and if emancipated 'like those of Virginia, New York, etc., will die in the Streets, unprovided and unprotected; the Ground their wretched Bed, and the inclement sky their miserable Covering, no friendly Cott, Fuel, or Bannanah Walk to call their own'.[47] Even at this time, the idea that industrial enslavement was the basis of opposition to Negro bondage was crystallising: 'Does he [Pitt] think, that the Signature of Eight Hundred *ignorant, deluded*, People in a manufacturing Town, was done voluntarily?'[48]

Yet the telling points made by the West India polemicists could only postpone their defeat. Even in 1788 the strength of feeling opposed to them had become apparent. Pitt himself had not emerged to champion abolition, but an extraordinary coalition of radical and conservative orators – Charles James Fox and Edmund Burke side by side – had joined in the onslaught on the trade. In pure intellectual terms, though not at the level of grassroots opinion or Westminster voting instincts, the battle had already been won. The Abolition Bill introduced by Wilberforce in May 1789, immediately after the publication of the Privy Council Report, was shelved only on a technicality. Again, although support declined with the outbreak of the French Revolution and Clarkson's clumsy announcements in its support, a new Select Committee appointed in 1789 continued to gather evidence which could be heard and used by the abolitionists and their political allies. When Wilberforce tried to introduce his

[46] G. Francklyn, *Observations Occasioned by the Attempts Made in England to Effect the Abolition of the Slave Trade, etc.* (London, 1789) p. 2.

[47] *West India Trade and Islands: Commercial Reasons for the Non-Abolition of the Slave Trade in the West India Islands, etc.* (London, 1789) pp. 6, 17.

[48] [W. Innes], *The Slave Trade Indispensable: In Answer to the Speech of William Wilberforce, Esq., on the 13th of May, 1789* (London, 1790) p. 21.

Abolition Bill in 1791, he was defeated only by fifteen votes. In 1792 he tried again, backed by petitions from all over the country, especially the provinces. Although the result was an agreement in the Commons 'that the trade should be ended in four years', this had not been approved by the Lords when the whole issue was shelved, with the outbreak of the war with France, incidentally amid general horror at the uprising of the slaves in Saint-Domingue under Toussaint l'Ouverture. Wilberforce continued having his motion rejected each year until 1800, when he gave up in disgust until 1804. By that time the situation had again changed. The acquisition of substantial French sugar territory had lessened West India resistance by alarming the planters with the competition they would face if the labour supply from Africa were not interrupted. Again, Britain's international position was less alarming, horror of Jacobins had lessened, and Wilberforce had found new though unpredictable allies among the Irish members who had joined the House with the Union of 1801. His Abolition Bill was defeated only on a second reading in 1805. Eventual success came in 1807, but by then much of the work had already been done in an effort to protect the prostrated West Indians from the low sugar prices brought by general overproduction and the competition of foreign colonies. In the last stages, the abolitionists were able to present their demands for restriction of the traffic as national expediency, and the moral aspects of slaving were generally underplayed. In August 1805 the Pitt ministry issued an Order in Council prohibiting slave-trading to newly captured colonies. After Pitt's death, in 1806, the new Fox–Grenville–Addington 'Ministry of All the Talents' pushed through legislation to end the trade to foreign colonies as well as the captured ones. Yet what began as an attempt to protect the economy of the old West India possessions ended as total abolition of the trade. The Act of 1807 cleaned up the remnants. It was jockeyed through both Houses not through the ability of Wilberforce, but owing to the management of Grenville, by then Prime Minister. Though his importance has been missed by traditional historians of abolition, it was his commitment and personal political expertise which had the Abolition Bill made law.[49] 1 May 1807 was set as the last date on which a slave-ship could sail legally from a British port. The last one to do so was

[49] Porter, *Abolition of the Slave Trade in England*, pp. 125–43.

the *Kitty's Amelia*, Captain Hugh Crow, out of Bristol, which got her clearance papers in time and sailed on 27 July 1807.

There has been a great deal of scholarly debate over the reasons for this extraordinary success in overthrowing an institution which had so recently been considered vital to the nation. Until the publication of Eric Williams's *Capitalism and Slavery* in 1944, most historians accepted the self-image of the abolitionists. They assumed that their triumph over the slave trade represented a moral revolution among the common people, closely linked with the evangelical revival both within and outside the Church of England.[50] The most prominent of this school of historians was Sir Reginald Coupland of Oxford, who accepted the famous dictum of W. E. H. Lecky that 'the unweary, unostentatious, and glorious crusade of England against slavery [and the slave trade] may properly be regarded as among the three or four perfectly virtuous pages comprised in the history of nations'.[51] Williams jettisoned this assumption, and argued that the real cause of abolition was a change in the balance of power of economic pressure groups. Slavery and the slave trade had brought profits which were central to the rise of the industrial middle class. As society industrialised, however, its needs became different. Free trade was essential to find markets, and it was therefore of the essence to destroy the protectionist pressure group of whom the West India interest were chief allies. At the same time, many of the West Indians themselves turned against the slave trade because soil exhaustion in the older islands created intense fears of competition, over-production and declining prices which would result if newer islands, British or foreign, were able to get a supply of slaves. Apart from this weakening, however, Williams's main conclusion is that the West Indians were attacked not because they were distasteful as slaveholders, but because they were dangerous allies of those opposed to the creation of the economic conditions required by a modern industrialised state. The moral arguments of the abolitionists were thus

[50] As for instance in Clarkson, *History of the Abolition of the African Slave-Trade*, passim.

[51] R. Coupland, *The British Anti-Slavery Movement* (Oxford, 1933) p. 251. For other versions of this thesis, see C. M. McInnes, *England and Slavery* (London, 1934); Klingberg, *Anti-Slavery Movement*; G. R. Mellor, *British Imperial Trusteeship, 1783–1850* (London, 1951) pp. 31–80.

superficial, as indeed were the very issues of slavery and the slave trade.

Although it is quite true that economic change made slave-trade abolition possible, and that over-production was endemic in the islands, Williams's thesis now seems to require serious modification. It has been attacked by Anstey for its failure to show the relationship between economic forces and detailed political decisions on abolition.[52] Moreover, there are many scholars who do not admit his almost total rejection of the emergence of humanitarianism as a force in itself. Nor does Williams explain the fact that many of the Members of Parliament who eventually voted *for* abolition came from county constituencies with agrarian interests, which supposedly represented the most reactionary and protectionist elements in English society. The last blow to the thesis is that after emancipation the British abolitionists fought a desperate rearguard action *against* free trade in sugar, since this would give a new impetus to slavery in Cuba and Brazil.[53]

The history of the French anti-slavery movement in the eighteenth century, although it was cut short by the Revolution and the disaster of Saint-Domingue, also challenges Williams's assumption that abolitionists were primarily economic men. It has already been pointed out that the relationship between the West India trade and the growth of industrialism was even less marked in France than in Britain. The wares for the slave trade came primarily from Germany and the Netherlands, and profits, by and large, were not put into industrialisation. Certainly some French families did rise to prominence through the trade, but they appear to have ploughed their profits back into further ventures in Guinea and the West Indies rather than investing them in enterprises alien to the part of the economic world with which they had become familiar. In short, the French slave trade was largely a self-sufficient operation within the French economy,

[52] R. G. Anstey, 'Capitalism and Slavery: A Critique', *Economic History Review*, 2nd ser., XXI (1968) 307–20. Anstey has put forward an alternative hypothesis on the interaction between intellectual and political change in 'A Reinterpretation of the Abolition of the British Slave Trade, 1806–1807', *English Historical Review*, LXXXVII (1972) 304–32.

[53] C. Duncan Rice, ' "Humanity Sold for Sugar!": The British Abolitionist Response to Free Trade in Slave-Grown Sugar', *Historical Journal*, XIII (1970) 402–18.

little connected with the advance of industrialisation. Moreover, at the time when French sentiment against the trade was increasing, the country's economy was by no means mature enough for even its businessmen to call for free trade, which would have exposed them to ruinous competition with the English. As for the state of the opposition, it was not weakening but strengthening, since sugar cultivation was still booming in Martinique and Guadeloupe, and there was every reason to demand a stepping-up of the slave trade rather than its abolition to bring the virgin soils of Saint-Domingue under cultivation – at least until the cataclysm of its slave revolt. Although the tardiness of French industrialisation and the increasing vested interest in providing a slave labour force raised doubts as to whether the French abolitionists could have been successful even if events had not been interrupted by the Revolution, what is clear is that the French produced an anti-slavery movement completely outside the kind of economic environment which Williams insists was essential to the emergence of abolitionism in Britain.

The eighteenth-century movement in France has never been fully studied, although the pamphlet literature it produced was enormous.[54] The Société des Amis des Noirs was admittedly founded in 1788 after letters of advice had been dispatched to France by the London Abolition Committee, but it was the product of a growing revulsion against slavery in the articulate sectors of French society. Although some of its members, like Jean-Pierre Brissot himself, were men from a relatively modest background, a majority of the subscribers to the *Amis* were drawn from the ranks of the liberal aristocracy, the very elements to whom the *philosophes* had made their appeal. Men like Clavière, Lafayette or Rochefoucauld were hardly the lackeys of a nascent capitalism. Subscriptions were high, the society met only infrequently, and its success in raising grass-roots enthusiasm in the provinces was negligible. There was nothing here to compare with the magnificent organisation of the English abolitionists, whose propaganda and correspondence created contacts throughout the country. The French anti-slavery movement, in fact, was socially more substantial yet politically less effective than the British. The Société des Amis des Noirs did not attack slavery,

[54] A convenient selection has been reprinted as *The French Revolution and the Abolition of Slavery*, 12 vols (The Hague, 1968).

and as late as 1790 it was stating only that it would not end its efforts until 'la traite des noirs ne fut abolie et l'esclavage adoucie', though this was no more conservative than the position of its English counterpart at the same time.[55] In spite of France's relative economic backwardness, the message of the abolitionists became attractive as soon as the power of the monarchy was broken. One of the National Assembly's first acts was to denounce the slave trade. Although this was connected with the general flush of libertarian enthusiasm, and was in any case not enforced owing to the confusion of war-time and the outbreak in Haiti, it is an impressive indication of the strength of French sentiment opposed to the trade, upon which the *Amis des Noirs* actually failed to capitalise. Slave-trade abolition did not come until the end of the Napoleonic period, under strong British diplomatic pressure. But it is clear that changing philosophical and religious attitudes produced a widespread questioning of the French slave trade without stimulus from substantial economic change.[56]

The lesson here, in Britain and in America, was that the abolitionists could only succeed, as they did in England and the Northern English colonies, when the economic rationalisation for slavery or the slave trade had become weak. This is not to suggest that slaving and slaveholding survived only where they were economically essential. Like any institutions they acquired a momentum of their own, and they carried on even while they were effectively luxuries until seriously challenged. This challenge was not an economic one, for the abolitionist ideology emerged from a complex series of changes in European and American assumptions on hierarchy in society. Even then, where slavery or slave-trading was economically essential, it could defend itself against such change, as it did in the Southern states of the U.S.A., the French colonies and Latin America. Abolitionist success in the eighteenth century came only where the institutions then attacked were already weakening or where they had never really been necessary. It was only in the nineteenth century that abolitionist ideology and organisation gained its own

[55] *Adresse aux amis de l'humanité, par la Société des Amis des Noirs* (Paris, 1790) p. 1.

[56] E. D. Seeber, *Anti-Slavery Opinion in France during the Second Half of the Eighteenth Century* (Baltimore, 1937); G. Martin, *Histoire de l'esclavage dans les colonies françaises* (Paris, 1948) pp. 166–91.

momentum. Eventually it would be able to destroy slavery even in those areas where it was still perfectly viable as an economic system, as in the United States. The eighteenth century was a time when the abolitionists were able to establish their ideas and methods in trimming some of the surplus fat off the system of black slavery and the Atlantic slave trade.

7 The Nineteenth-Century Triumphs, from the Congress of Vienna to the Revolution of 1848

FEW European abolitionists had campaigned in earnest for the abolition of slavery in the eighteenth century. This is not to say that they did not envisage an end to slavery at some indeterminate point in the future, and indeed it was disapproval of slavery itself which was fundamental to the philosophical and religious works from which they drew their ideas. Future emancipationists, too, would build on eighteenth-century propaganda. Yet for various reasons most of them shrank in practical terms from the finality of extending their actions against the slave trade to the demand for an end to slavery. It could be argued that if the slave trade could be ended, masters would be forced to treat their slaves better. They would thus be prepared for the responsibilities of freedom. Many abolitionists, while they recoiled from the atrocities of the Middle Passage, were also appalled by the destruction of property rights which would be involved in freeing the slaves. Some, too, were horrified by the ferocity of the black population liberty had loosed on Haiti. For others, it seemed tactically wise to begin their work for the slave by suppressing the immediate horror of the slave-ships before going on to tackle the stronger vested interest in slavery. A small number were even concerned less with the unpleasantness of slavery in the New World than with the ravages of the trade on the Coast, and they attacked it from missionary motives as a first step towards the spread of civilisation and Christianity in Africa itself. For most, of course, such motives were mixed, but only a few saw the abolition of slavery itself as an immediate political objective. The success of the American abolitionists in setting emancipation on foot in the North, and indeed their setting this as a goal from the outset, was very much out of kilter with what their counterparts in other parts of the West did or tried to do. Their major achievement was the abolition of the English slave trade. This was somewhat hollow, since although English slavers disappeared, the volume of the trade as a whole actually increased in the decades after 1807.

The emphasis of the nineteenth century was a different one. The issue of the slave trade was certainly not dead. The British in particular, both abolitionists and government, spent most of their energy trying to suppress illicit slaving by force, or to persuade more sceptical nations that they should follow their example in outlawing the trade. Further intellectual and religious change, however, brought the conviction that it was no longer sufficient to tinker with the sin involved in slavery in this way. An immediate start had to be made in agitating for emancipation. The shift in assumptions on slavery was one which is most easily traced in Britain and the United States, but it had its effect throughout the Western world. This did not imply that abolitionists all demanded that slavery should be ended immediately, though some did. All sorts of schemes of gradual emancipation were proposed. But at least the minimal goal did now come to be freedom for the slaves rather than slave-trade abolition. The result was that by the 1880s black slavery had disappeared from all areas of the globe controlled by Westerners, at least in any form in which it was recognisable to them. Its destruction came at different speeds in different areas, according to its profitability and the degree to which it was entrenched in society. Future chapters of this work will discuss the struggle for emancipation in the countries where it was most difficult and most dramatic, in the United States, Cuba and Brazil. In other countries slavery succumbed more easily. In Latin America it was abolished first in the countries where it was relatively peripheral, just as the Northern states of the U.S.A. had preceded the South. By 1854 Venezuela's emancipation meant that slavery was now in the course of abolition in all the new Spanish American republics. The first sixty years of the century also saw emancipation in the Danish and Dutch West Indies, and in the English and French colonies. The commitment of these colonies to slavery as a social system was still great, but their relatively declining importance to their mother countries meant that it was possible for the abolitionists to succeed. This chapter traces the nineteenth-century attempts at the suppression of the slave trade, emancipation in the West India sugar colonies prior to about 1850, and finally the ending of slavery in the Spanish American republics.

As he brought his history of slave-trade abolition to a close, Thomas Clarkson assured his readers that Africa was 'now freed from the vicious and barbarous effect' of the slave trade.[1] In fact nothing of the sort had happened. As far as we know, English slavers dropped totally out of the trade, English cruisers had no difficulty in boarding and capturing ships of their own nationality, and after 1824 they were treated as pirates if caught. But even the Americans, who had banned slave-trading in the same month of the same year as Britain, and also treated it as piracy (at least on paper) after 1820, simply transferred their operations to the flags of other nations. Though the Danes had abolished their trade in 1802, and the Dutch in 1814, other countries were not directly affected by the legislation of the British Parliament. Actually they benefited greatly by being able to engross the share of the trade previously controlled by Liverpool; in 1790 about 25,000 slaves per annum were being carried in British bottoms to French, Spanish and Dutch possessions. Dale Porter has calculated that from October 1804 to October 1805 only 8,000 slaves were carried to Britain's old colonies and Trinidad. Three times as many, or three-quarters of the total British trade, went to foreign colonies or to the conquered possessions.[2] The foreign trade, together with an embarrassing trickle of men and women who continued to find their way from Africa into the hands of the British planters, were simply transferred to other flags. The Portuguese, Brazilians, Spanish and Americans were the most active in this respect. Even after their governments agreed to end slaving by treaty, they continued a thriving smuggled trade, usually under false flags and papers, in which conditions were

[1] T. Clarkson, *The History of the Rise, Progress, and Accomplishment of the Abolition of the African Slave-Trade by the British Parliament*, 2 vols (London, 1808) II 585–6.

[2] D. H. Porter, *The Abolition of the Slave Trade in England, 1784–1807* (Hamden, Conn., 1970) pp. 4–5, 134.

worse than ever before because high risks encouraged captains to pack their slave cargoes as tightly as possible. In the case of the Brazilian trade, the turning-point only came with Brazil's taking the domestic decision for abolition. The remaining slave trade to Cuba only ended once the outbreak of the American Civil War freed the United States government from having to pander to Southerners and made it possible for the Navy to co-operate energetically with the British in suppressing the illicit trade.[3] Suppression was a long and bitter process. Curtin's figures suggest that 1,898,400 slaves crossed the Atlantic from 1811 to 1870. Of these, 60·3 per cent went to Brazil, 31·9 per cent to Cuba and Puerto Rico, 5·1 per cent to the French West Indies and the remaining 2·7 per cent to the United States. At the same time, the continuance of the trade blighted all attempts to find an economic substitute for it in West Africa. A recent commentator has described the relationship between the legitimate and illicit slave trades as one of 'symbiosis'.[4] Peaceful traders not only refused to co-operate with British attempts at suppression, but on occasion took the opportunity of selling supplies to the slavers. The bills of exchange used in transactions on the Coast were common to both trades, and were circulated without scruple by European houses, including British ones. The opposition of African middlemen to ending the slave trade and moving on to an alternative commerce was almost total. Even as palm-oil production rose, cautious Slave Coast merchants kept the best of both worlds by using their slaves to gather oil while they waited for a buyer to take them to Cuba. The British, in fact, could not find allies against the slave trade among the Africans and legitimate traders who might have been expected to be its most enthusiastic enemies.

[3] On United States involvement, see W. E. B. DuBois, *The Suppression of the African Slave Trade to the United States of America, 1638–1870* (1896; reprinted New York, 1969); P. Duignan and C. Clenenden, *The United States and the African Slave Trade, 1619–1862* (Stanford, 1963) pp. 17–58; H. B. Soulsby, *The Right of Search and the Slave Trade in Anglo-American Relations* (Baltimore, 1933); W. S. Howard, *American Slavers and the Federal Law, 1837–1862* (Berkeley, 1963).

[4] G. E. Brooks, *Yankee Traders, Old Coasters, and African Middlemen: A History of American Legitimate Trade with West Africa in the Nineteenth Century* (Boston, 1970) p. 105. Figures from P. Curtin, *The Atlantic Slave Trade: A Census* (Madison, Wis., 1969) pp. 231–64.

The work of ending the slave trade, then, did not end with the bloodless triumphs of 1806 and 1807. A great deal of thought, both abolitionist and official, went into the problem of finding a way of forcing other nations to follow the British example. In effect, the recognised British policy emerged as the combination of two gambits. The first was to put diplomatic pressure on the other nations to enter into treaty commitments for the ending of the slave trade. The second was to keep as strong a British presence as possible in the waters off the west coast of Africa, to intercept slavers from the nations who had agreed to abandon the trade. In spite of occasional wavering, the suppression of the slave trade through these instrumentalities became a cardinal objective of Britain's international policy. Indeed, like the protection of India, it became a factor governing the official mind in the Foreign Office even at times when it would have been in the country's general interest to subordinate it to other goals.

As for the rank-and-file abolitionists, they were strong in Quaker influence and often doubtful about the morality of converting slavers from behind the barrels of long nines. Accordingly, they considered other approaches. The most radical, both in Britain and America, were arguing by the 1830s that the whole question of the slave trade was an enormous red herring, which diverted attention from the real issue of slavery in the New World. It would not be ended by sailing flamboyantly around in cruisers, which was in any case sinful, but by removing the demand for labour through an immediate emancipation in the Americas. A more conservative approach was to work through various agencies which would 'civilise' Africa, so that Christianity and peaceful commerce would stifle the slave trade at its origin. Various organisations of this sort were launched in London, starting with Granville Sharp's Sierra Leone Company. The most prominent example was Sir Thomas Fowell Buxton's African Civilization Society, but black American abolitionists like Martin Delany were still considering such schemes in 1859 and 1860. The wish to evangelise Africa and end the slave trade was also central to the hopes of the American Colonization Society, founded in 1817, though its missionary motives were missed by its opponents and have been underestimated by modern historians intent on exposing its tendency to uphold slavery in the United States. In a sense, however, what happened to the Atlantic slave trade had gone beyond the control of the abolitionists and into the hands of government officials. For the British at least, the main thrusts of the continuing offensive against the slave trade were diplomatic and moral.

The diplomatic tack was first tried by Castlereagh at the Congress of Vienna, and then continued by him and Canning at the subsequent Congresses until the Concert of Europe broke up. At the same time, and as an independent course of action thereafter, continual diplomatic representations were made at the various capitals of Europe. Success was mixed, and very slow. It was no difficult matter at the Congress of Vienna to persuade the Tsar, in his post-Napoleonic liberal enthusiasm, that Russia should give up a trade in which she had never been involved. With other nations there were greater complications. Although the Americans had themselves abolished the trade, at least in theory, it was impossible to make them grant British cruisers the right to search vessels flying the stars and stripes, which opened the way for every illicit slaver to sail unmolested under the American flag. It was only with the Civil War that bitter memories of the war of 1812 had faded enough to make a settlement of this problem possible. As for the Spanish and Portuguese, decrees outlawing the slave trade were unashamedly bought from them, and even then it was impossible to force them to agree to any form of mechanism whereby slavers could legally be seized by the West Africa Squadron, far less brought to punishment. Nevertheless, progress was made, although the diplomatic embargo on the slave trade was by no means complete when other factors made it possible to drive the last of the slave-ships off the Atlantic.

British diplomats had been working under great pressure to get guarantees of abolition at the Congress of Vienna: one historian concludes that the public 'seemed to be interested in the slave trade to the exclusion of almost everything else'.[5] The powers could only be made to unite on an innocuous general statement of enthusiasm for abolition, but at least Louis XVIII was persuaded to decree the end of the trade. Unfortunately this step

[5] F. J. Klingberg, *The Anti-Slavery Movement: A Study in English Humanitarianism* (New Haven, 1926) p. 151; B. Fladeland, 'Abolitionist Pressures on the Concert of Europe', *Journal of Modern History*, xxxviii (1966) 355–73.

was all but useless since the French took no steps to enforce it, and vigorously opposed any British interference with their shipping or vessels flying their flag, even if it was proven that they were carrying slaves. The French trade actually increased in the following years, and although a little French squadron was sent to the Coast after the revolution of 1830, it spent more time investigating British activities than patrolling to catch slavers, and no subsequent treaty ever gave the British a satisfactory right of search. This was the central difficulty in all attempts at suppression, for it meant that British officers of the West Africa Squadron could board suspected slavers, even those flying spurious colours, only at the risk of ruining their careers through getting their superiors into inextricable difficulties. The right of search was granted to the British in the Quintuple Treaty of 1841 with Russia, Austria and Prussia – France refused to ratify at the last moment – but none of these nations were slavers, though their flags had on occasion been used to prevent police interference. This treaty also dealt with the problem faced by the West Africa Squadron owing to the impossibility of condemning slave vessels in front of the international 'mixed commission' courts set up for the purpose unless they had actually had slaves on board at the time of capture. The 1841 treaty included an equipment clause ensuring that ships obviously fitted as slavers – for instance in loading more supplies than were needed for the crew, or carrying manacles – could be condemned. This did not apply to nations other than the signatories, but the combination of the right of search and the equipment provisions came to be the ideal towards which the British worked in their negotiations with the various slaving powers.

They had much less success with powers whose African interests were greater than those of the Prussians, Russians and Austrians. The Danes had abolished their slave trade before the British themselves, and the Dutch were persuaded to do so in 1814. The United States, however, never enforced their own laws against slaving until Lincoln's administration, and indeed blacks continued to be carried into the United States itself in unquantifiable volume. Worst of all, the United States government vigorously opposed all British pressure to be given the right of search, and all interference with ships flying their flag. The result was that even after the Brazilians had given up their own trade, and the Portuguese and Spanish had been forced out of it, slavers could still sail with impunity under the stars and stripes. Few officers of the West Africa Squadron could afford to board slavers flying the American flag and risk finding that their papers were in order – as they frequently were, since American capital and American-owned ships, in spite of the 1808 and 1820 legislation, remained heavily involved in the trade. By comparison, the Spanish and Portuguese, though slippery, were easy to control. Both made an enormous income out of British payments for abolitionist agreements which they had not the slightest intention of observing. In 1853 it was calculated that H.M. Government had paid £2,850,965 to Portugal and £1,134,179 to Spain in bribes and indemnities for 'outrages' on their shipping.[6] In 1817 both had agreed to abolish the slave trade, and grant the British the right of search, north of the Equator, and to the setting-up of Courts of Mixed Commission at Sierra Leone and Havana to try prizes taken by the cruisers. Partly owing to official venality, and partly owing to vagueness as to the proof required to condemn slave vessels satisfactorily, above all owing to the refusal of Spain and Portugal to use sanctions against nationals involved in the trade, those agreements had virtually no effect. It was only in 1835 that the Spanish flag became useless to the slavers, when Madrid was cajoled into signing a proper convention with effective right-of-search and equipment clauses. Portugal was only knocked out of the cruiser–slaver equation by Palmerstonian 'diplomacy'. In 1839 Palmerston took the crude but effective step of having the *British* Parliament authorise the Admiralty to capture any slaver under Portuguese colours as if it had been a British vessel. This worked, at least in making the flag of Portugal an ineffective umbrella for slaving, though Portuguese men, ships and capital remained deeply involved in the trade under Brazilian or United States papers. By the 1840s, too, vigorous initiatives had secured conventions with proper equipment clauses from all minor European nations and from the Latin American republics. The main remaining problem powers were Brazil and the United States. The so-called Aberdeen Act of 1845 put ships under Brazilian colours in the same category as Portuguese ones, but this did not prevent the implication of Brazil-

[6] C. Lloyd, *The Navy and the Slave Trade* (London, 1949) p. 45. The following account relies heavily on this work.

based merchants in the trade. Owing to changes in Brazil's internal politics, and British naval co-operation, the sailing of slavers from Brazilian ports was prevented after 1850. From then on the trade, principally to Cuba, was carried on under United States colours, often backed by United States capital. It only came to an end when the Civil War prompted the Americans to allow the efficient enforcement of the fifty-year-old laws of its own Congress. Though American units were withdrawn from the Coast for action against the Confederacy, the 1862 Treaty of Washington gave the Royal Navy the coveted right of search and provided for the trial of prizes captured under the American flag at Courts of Mixed Commission in New York, Sierra Leone and the Cape.[7] After the 1860s, with the Atlantic cleared, the British turned their attention to curbing the East African slave trade in the Indian Ocean and the Persian Gulf.

As a whole, however, the British diplomatic offensive against the slave trade never really succeeded. The Portuguese merchants living in São Paulo and other Brazilian slaving ports continued their operations after the Aberdeen Act, and they were curbed only because of a local nationalist revulsion against them. The long-overdue American commitment to suppression was a factor of Lincoln's political position, perhaps above all a sop to the embarrassingly strong anti-slavery sentiment in the Republican Party. The Royal Navy's attempts at suppression had so far failed because its ships were politically hamstrung. The West Africa Squadron was never given the full authority it needed to intercept illicit slavers without fear of causing international incidents which would ruin the careers of the officers involved. False flags, false papers, and the sheer speed of the beautifully designed slave-ships, many of them American-built, were bad enough obstacles in themselves. But they were insignificant compared with the problems created by the failure of British diplomacy to secure any satisfactory agreements against the trade

---

[7] L. Bethell, *The Abolition of the Brazilian Slave Trade: Britain, Brazil and the Slave Trade Question, 1807–1869* (Cambridge, 1970); Soulsby, *Right of Search and the Slave Trade*; Howard, *American Slavers and the Federal Law*. The diplomatic history of suppression to 1841 is summarised in J. Bandinel, *Some Account of the Trade in Slaves from Africa* (London, 1842) pp. 145–303, though the statistical information in this work should be used with caution.

under the United States flag. On the other hand, this failure did not come from want of trying. Indeed there were recurrent parliamentary complaints about interference with shipping and the cost of the Squadron. Yet the immense amount of Foreign Office effort is an impressive proof of the way in which Britain now represented an almost totally anti-slave-trade constituency, if not an anti-slavery one.

The story of the attempts at naval suppression is a fascinating one, although it may have been less interesting for the officers and men who had the misfortune to be posted to the West Africa Station. British slave-trade diplomacy aimed not only to secure effective and enforceable conventions to outlaw the trade, but also to have slavers tried in Courts of Mixed Commission instead of the politically corruptible courts of the nations under whose flags they had been jailed. Judges delegated by Britain, Spain, and eventually the United States, at one time or another sat on courts in Havana, Sierra Leone, St Helena, Rio, Surinam, Luanda and New York, with the power of condemning vessels from nations which accepted their jurisdiction to be sold, or in some cases broken up. The regular practice for cruisers which captured slave-ships with enough evidence to have them condemned was to put them in charge of a prize crew which would sail them into the nearest of the Courts of Mixed Commission. The crew would then be tried as pirates, and the owners tried indirectly by deciding whether or not their vessel should be confiscated. The latter was not an especially severe punishment, since in the heyday of the Brazilian and Cuban trade a slave-ship might pay off more than the capital invested in it in one or two voyages.

The great bulk of the work of patrolling the West African coast was undertaken by the Royal Navy. French presence there was on the Coast – a maximum of some twenty-three vessels in 1845 – but since they rejected R.N. jurisdiction over their ships and restricted themselves to looking for abuse of their own flag, this did not affect the balance of power between slave-ships and police vessels. Units of the U.S. Navy were regularly stationed on the Coast, in spite of its weakness as a fighting force, and a U.S. West Africa Squadron was formally in being from 1843 onwards. 'Old Bruin', Matthew Perry, was its first commander. But American effectiveness was much decreased by the effect of

Southern attitudes to slavery in weakening determination to suppress the slave trade, in lawyers, among officials in the Navy Department and among the officers of ships posted to Guinea – together with a refusal to compromise American concern over the right of search by interfering with ships of other nations.[8] The British themselves were always ill-equipped for their job, at least until the introduction of screw-driven warships in the 1850s made it possible for them to outsail anything the slave merchants could put in the water. The beginnings of the West Africa Squadron were modest indeed. Even without the problems of confused diplomatic rights, the few ships which the Navy could spare from its commitments in the North Sea, the Channel and the North Atlantic could have made little impression on the trade. In later years, as the British force on the Coast increased, and the diplomatic net tightened, the slavers were forced into using rakish Baltimore clippers, designed beautifully for speed, but at least until the end of the Napoleonic war the British force on the Coast was necessarily tiny. In 1808 the task of policing three thousand miles of coast was entrusted to a 32-gun frigate, the *Solebay*, and an 18-gun sloop, the *Derwent*. Although the number of ships on the station was normally six or seven in the 1820s, and later increased to a maximum of twenty-three, the whole operation was of less concern to the Navy than to the Foreign Office. The units sent by the Admiralty to West Africa were seldom its newest and never its most powerful. The same was true of the ships sent out by the lukewarm French and American governments. Frequently the British vessels were under the command of brilliant but very young men who had a great deal of energy but very little tact. The alternative was older men who had been overlooked for promotion, lacked the ability or influence to get a more glorious posting, and on the contrary had a great deal of tact and too little energy. Morale among men remained low. They not only had to contend with the usual discipline and conditions of the nineteenth-century Navy, but with appalling risks of tropical disease, unusually boring assignments, and the lack of opportunities for shore leave in salubrious conditions, at least

[8] R. Schnapper, *La Politique et le commerce dans le Golfe de Guinée, de 1838 à 1871* (Paris, 1961) pp. 73–86; A. R. Booth, 'The United States African Squadron, 1843–1861', in J. Butler (ed.), *Boston University Papers in African History*, vol. 1 (Boston, 1964) pp. 79–117.

until St Helena and Ascension were adopted as bases. Even without these disadvantages and without the weaknesses in the diplomatic position of the British, it would have been a near-insuperable task to seal off the long west coast of Africa, much of which is heavily indented. It offered an ideal refuge to slavers prepared to slip out at intervals between patrols. As it was, the slave trade went on increasing apace. In 1855 the Foreign Office estimated, with some exaggeration, that the average number of slaves annually being exported from West Africa was 135,000 – a 35 per cent increase over its estimate for the annual average of the eighteenth century. The West Africa Squadron was indeed capturing some slavers and liberating their cargoes, but the numbers of blacks involved were tiny – a matter of hundreds prior to 1820, and only 6,899 in 1835 itself. From 1810 to 1864 the Navy recaptured only 149,800 slaves.[9] The work of the West Africa Squadron was a gallant gesture against the slave trade, and an exceedingly costly one, on the part of the British. However, it had only a marginal effect on the flow of slaves from Africa to the Americas.

Prior to 1840, the most successful ships on the Squadron were actually two captured and converted ex-slavers, the *Fair Rosamond* and the *Black Joke*. Thereafter, however, British-built ships began to meet with more success. Much of this was due to relative success in extorting diplomatic guarantees from the powers most involved in the slave trade. The chance of catching slavers at sea was also increased with the introduction of fast Symonds brigs which could put up a better showing than previous clumsier craft. At the same time, the Squadron was reinforced by a group of energetic young officers, the most notable of whom was Captain Joseph Denman. They took to the policy of going ashore to sack barracoons in which slaves were stored. Denman's dramatic attack on the barracoons at Gallinas in 1840 caused controversy but was broadly speaking welcomed in Britain. It set off a rash of similar ventures by officers on other parts of the Coast. After a period of legal confusion in which the right of the Navy to behave in this way was at issue, Denman's actions were approved in 1848.[10] By this time, however, the possibility of crushing the trade through an energetic policy on the Coast, if it

[9] Lloyd, *Navy and the Slave Trade*, pp. 61, 275–6.
[10] Ibid., pp. 92–9.

had ever existed, had been removed by the Sugar Duties Act of 1846. This opened the British market to sugar from Cuba and Brazil, and raised the demand for slaves to such an extent that the trade became unstoppable at the African end until full American and Brazilian co-operation was gained.

Partly in response to the failure of the cruisers to make any impression on the slave trade, abolitionist thought turned to finding ways of removing its attraction for the Africans themselves. Indeed, substantial elements among the abolitionists had been doubtful about the use of the West Africa Squadron from the outset. A strong and nearly successful campaign for its withdrawal was mounted in 1840 by a group of ultra-free-traders led by Sir Joseph Hutt, who questioned the tax costs of the Squadron and its interference with the free operation of the laws of trade. They were supported by a group of abolitionists who insisted that only peaceful means should be used to end the slave trade.[11] By this time the most radical of the abolitionists had founded the British and Foreign Anti-Slavery Society, which still exists, aimed at the abolition of slavery throughout the world. For them the most logical way of ending the slave trade was to remove the demand for slaves. The flow of slaves from Africa would cease when there were no more slaveholders to buy them. At the same time, however, there was a renewal of interest in ending the trade by civilising Africa, removing its attractiveness by stimulating lucrative forms of peaceful commerce as an alternative. The result was the organisation of the African Civilization Society in 1840, and a flurry of interest in anti-slavery circles, both in Britain and America, in attempts to explore the Niger valley and the supposedly fertile hinterland of West Africa in general.

The idea of opening Africa to peaceful trade as a blow at the Atlantic slave trade was an old one. Anthony Benezet, as we have seen, made the assumption that one trade would drive out the other in his *Some Historical Account of Guinea.* Sharp's Sierra Leone scheme, the American Colonization Society and Buxton's African Civilization Society were all based on the idea that trade, Christianisation and liberation from the slave-traders would

[11] Ibid., pp. 104–14; H. Temperley, *British Anti-Slavery, 1833–1870* (London, 1972). The latter work is the most useful account of British anti-slavery activity after 1833.

proceed hand in hand. A priority in such plans was the spread of the Gospel and the conversion of heathens. The anti-slavery movement itself was much affected by the failure of slaveholders to Christianise their charges, and there is no reason to assume that the combined preoccupation with commerce and Christianity was insincere, in a fundamentally religious age. The very beauty of the various projects of African civilisation is that they satisfied the missionary-minded reformer that he was doing something immediate about the distressing problem of heathenism. At the same time, they worked to end the slave trade and further the British commercial expansion which he saw not only as being profitable – though that consideration was not absent – but as carrying with it the spread of the values of the Protestant Christian civilisation which he knew and approved. Thomas Fowell Buxton had had many predecessors, and others would try to follow his example after the failure of the African Civilization Society. Some abolitionists, especially in America, queried his wisdom in concentrating on Africa at the risk of diverting attention from the central problem of slavery itself, but few would have rejected his enthusiastic claim that

> It is impossible to spread education, scientific knowledge, and the civilizing influence of Christianity, without communicating that to the population, which will most materially contribute to the advance of commerce and agriculture; on the other hand, there is no better way of advancing the moral and physical condition of the people, than by the introduction of our skill, and the sagacious and successful employment of our capital amongst them.[12]

This double assumption was behind all British and American attempts to end the slave trade through activity on the African continent. It was fully accepted by Sharp, whose Sierra Leone Company not only appealed to its backers because of the benefits it would shed on Africa, but also because it provided a plan to rid London of the social problem caused by the hundreds of 'Black Poor'. These men and women had never been successfully re-settled after the Somerset case had given them or their parents

[12] T. F. Buxton, *The African Slave Trade and its Remedy*, 2nd ed. (London, 1840) pp. 521–2.

their liberty. Apart from their own obvious misery and the problem they proved for the Commissioners of the Poor, Sharp was
shrewd enough to realise that the presence of a group of free
blacks living in evident squalor was a fine advertisement for those
who argued that they were incapable of living in any condition
except slavery. Their numbers increased with the arrival of
several groups of blacks who had been liberated during the
American war, or brought to England by loyalist masters. In
1785 Sharp was instrumental in forming a Committee for Reliev-
ing the Black Poor. Sierra Leone was chosen as the place at which
a colony was to be founded, the committee was able to get
government approval for its scheme, and some 20 square miles of
land was purchased from King Tom in the Cape Mount area.
The Royal Navy provided three transports, convoyed by the
sloop *Nautilus*, and the first 500 settlers arrived in the little colony
in 1787. This first attempt at settlement was disastrous. The
settlers were an ill-assorted group – 440 black poor and some 60
white prostitutes. Even if they had been hand-picked for responsibility and endurance, they had no resistance to African diseases,
and they were decimated in a period of months. Many of those
who survived left the colony to work or trade on their own
account, and there is strong evidence that some turned to making
their fortunes from slave-trading. Once news of this disaster
filtered back to Britain, an attempt was made to rescue the colony
by putting it under the control of a regular commercial organisation, the St George's Bay Company. The town of Freetown was
founded in 1792, after Thomas Clarkson's brother, then a
lieutenant in the Royal Navy, brought over a shipload of 'Nova
Scotians', slaves of American loyalists who had been impounded
in Nova Scotia at the end of the War of Independence. This was
by no means the end of Sierra Leone's starving time. Freetown
was sacked by the French in 1794, and the settlers rebelled against
their English leaders in the same year. Indeed, they were constantly discontented to the point of revolt, even after the Scottish
abolitionist Zachary Macaulay became Governor in 1796. The
most serious disturbance in the colony's history came four years
later, and it was quelled only by the opportune arrival of a man-
of-war carrying the third wave of Sierra Leone's immigrants, a
group of Maroons from Jamaica who had been given the opportunity of coming to Africa at the conclusion of one of their spells

of warfare with the planter militia.[13] The real success of Sierra Leone, however, only came after 1807, when Freetown became the seat of a Prize Court, later a Court of Mixed Commission, and the main base for the ships on the West Africa Station. When loaded slavers were captured, 'liberated Africans' thus freed were given plots of land and minimal tools to begin cultivation in the colony. Many entered into peaceful trade on their own behalf. By the middle of the century the most successful formed an African bourgeoisie without a vested interest in the slave trade, content to live from peaceful commerce in the very way men like Sharp had imagined. Nineteenth-century Freetown, with its contacts between rescued slaves from almost every African culture, is a fascinating historical laboratory.[14] Modest though it was, it was also a centre to which the slave trade did not penetrate, and from which peaceful commerce, Christianity and European influence could hopefully radiate to the interior.

Sierra Leone was the most successful settlement of this sort, but it was not the only one. In the early part of the nineteenth century the British also tried to promote commerce and missionary activity in Africa, through the African Association and the African Institution, which were aimed at British commercial expansion but also to a great extent at eradicating the slave trade.[15] Other nations approached Africa in the same way. The French, for instance, attempted to resettle some of the Africans rescued from slavers condemned in their own courts at Libreville, in Gabon. Their numbers were few, and the Libreville colony was not planned on anything like the scale of Sierra Leone. But its foundation assumed in exactly the same way that a small group of free Negroes working from an area immune to the slave trade could spread Christianity and have enough commercial success to demonstrate the fallacies behind Africans' continuing slaving as their livelihood. The basic premise was that if legitimate trade was available, local rulers would be less tempted to sell their fellows into the hands of white slavers.

[13] P. Hoare, *Memoirs of Granville Sharp, Esq.*, 2nd ed., 2 vols (London, 1828) II 3 ff; C. Fyfe, *A History of Sierra Leone* (Oxford, 1962) pp. 13–104; P. Curtin, *The Image of Africa: British Ideas and Action, 1780–1850* (Madison, Wis., 1966) pp. 123–39.

[14] A. T. Porter, *Creoledom: A Study of the Development of Freetown Society* (Oxford, 1963).

[15] Curtin, *Image of Africa*, pp. 140–286.

Exactly the same premise was accepted by the American abolitionists who supported the American Colonization Society from 1817 onwards. In 1832 the leader of a more uncompromising group of abolitionists announced, among other things, that the A.C.S. seemed to have as 'their only anxiety and aim to outwit the vengeance of heaven', and asked why all tall men should not 'conspire to remove their more diminutive brethren, and all the corpulent to remove the lean and lank, and all the strong to remove the weak, and all the educated to remove the ignorant, and all the rich to remove the poor'.[16] The acceptance of this kind of nonsense by historians has led to the assumption that the Colonization Society as a whole was pro-slavery and anti-Negro, and also to a general failure to set it in its place as a legitimate agency through which one aspect of the benevolence of America's philanthropic community was channelled. In fact it was only one of a group of national societies which had emerged by the 1820s to institutionalise the good causes of interest to the churchgoing middle class.[17] All of them dealt with two preoccupations: to promote the spread of the Gospel among those, at home and abroad, who did not have access to it, and to promote the observance of the Gospel among those who did have access to it but had chosen to ignore its precepts. The American Colonization Society, with the Tract, Bible and Missionary societies, was an important agency in the former category. Garrison notwithstanding, it was certainly concerned with finding a long-term solution to the domestic problem of slavery, but it was equally driven by an impulse to evangelise Africa, with the best of intentions. Its agents in this task were to be black people who, however humble, had been exposed to American religion. It never occurred to them that liberated slaves were unlikely to have much enthusiasm for the religion which had endorsed their servitude, but given the comfortable world-picture of the nineteenth-century evangelical,

[16] W. L. Garrison, *Thoughts on African Colonization; or, an Impartial Exhibition of the Doctrines, Principles, and Purposes of the American Colonization Society, etc.* (Boston, 1832) pp. 103, 120.

[17] P. J. Staudenraus, *The African Colonization Movement, 1816–1865* (New York, 1961); C. S. Griffin, *Their Brothers' Keepers: Moral Stewardship in the United States, 1800–1865* (New Brunswick, N.J., 1960); S. I. Foster, *Errand of Mercy: The Evangelical United Front, 1790–1837* (New York, 1960); C. C. Cole, *The Social Ideas of the Northern Evangelists, 1826–1860* (New York, 1954).

there was no reason why it should have done. We should give credit to claims like the one made by the A.C.S. agent Ralph Gurley, that Liberia had been founded as a state which

> from the nature of its institutions, the development of its principles and resources, and the discipline of its circumstances must strengthen and elevate the intellect and moral character of its citizens; by example and endeavours plant and propagate a Christian civilization in Africa; suppress the slave trade; react powerfully upon America to promote emancipation by means disconnected from danger, demanded by general justice, and fraught with blessings never yet attained by it, to the liberated Africans and their race; thus showing by experiment and demonstrating in fact, how this race may cast off the entanglements of their thraldom, and self-respected, because deserving praise, stand in dignity and honour before the world.[18]

The colony of Liberia was founded with the same motives as Sierra Leone. It duly has its place as a practical centre from which the slave trade could be attacked. This potential was never realised. In the early stages of the colony's life the American Colonization Society officials were too weak to prevent slave-trading in the interior. Even after Liberia became an independent republic in 1847 its officials were corrupt enough to pay no attention to the slave trade, even if they had wished to do so. In any case, the new republic never had the capital or any staple product which could be the basis of the commerce the American Colonization Society had envisaged. But this should not obscure the way in which the Liberian experiment fits into the same category as those of Sharp in Sierra Leone or Buxton on the Niger. A final testament to the way in which Garrison's criticisms of colonisation were misplaced is the fact that by the late 1850s both Henry Highland Garnet and Martin Delany, two of the most radical of America's black leaders, were flirting with the idea of founding black American colonies in Africa. To a great extent their militancy on this issue was a product of American forces, but they too were preoccupied with spreading commerce and 'civilisation'

---

[18] R. R. Gurley, *Letter to the Hon. Henry Clay . . . and Sir Thomas Fowell Buxton . . . on the Colonization and Civilization of Africa* (London, 1841) p. 8.

in Africa.[19] By this time also, the hope was that slavery in the New World itself would be attacked through events in Africa, not merely by the ending of the slave trade, but through the cultivation of free-grown tropical crops which would eventually knock slave-grown American produce out of the market.

The plans of Martin Delany were enthusiastically supported by a group of the British abolitionists, who founded an African Aid Society, in support of his ventures, in 1860. Both Delany and his companion Robert Campbell visited England after their expedition to West Africa, lectured extensively there, and were generally well supported in attendance and funds, especially by men who had favoured Buxton's schemes for opening the Niger, and had not been disillusioned with its failure.[20] Indeed the tradition of interest in ending the slave trade through missionary and commercial activity was always stronger in Britain than in France or America. The Niger expedition of 1841, sponsored by Buxton's African Civilization Society, was only the most costly and best publicised in a series of British enterprises of this sort. Even in the late eighteenth century, apart from Sharp's Sierra Leone venture, the African Association had set itself to promoting African exploration, partly with the intention of gathering information on the possibilities of Guinea for commerce and evangelisation. It was founded in 1788, and was the principal sponsor of expeditions to Africa, all of which were seen as having a bearing on the slave trade, until it merged with the National Geographic Society in 1831.[21] After the Abolition Act of 1807 it was joined by the African Institution, a quasi-official British agency with a more direct concern with supplementing the efforts of the West Africa Squadron against the slave trade by civilising the hinterland. It announced proudly from the outset that its plan proposed 'to introduce the blessings of civilized society among a people sunk in ignorance and barbarism, and occupying no less than a fourth part of the habitable globe'.[22] The African Institution was

[19] M. R. Delany, *Official Report of the Niger Valley Exploring Party* (1860), reprinted in H. H. Bell (ed.), *Search for a Place: Black Separatism and Africa, 1860* (Ann Arbor, Mich., 1969) pp. 23–148; T. Draper, *The Rediscovery of Black Nationalism* (New York, 1970) pp. 14–43.

[20] Delany, *Official Report*, pp. 122–42.

[21] R. Hallett (ed.), *Records of the African Association, 1788–1831* (London, 1964).

[22] *Report of the Committee of the African Institution* (London, 1807) p. 9.

the major agency in its time for the spreading of information on the progress of trade and Christianity in Africa. Although it has not been studied fully by any modern historian, the revelations of its voluminous reports caused a great deal of abolitionist concern until events in the West Indies and the rise of the movement against colonial slavery diverted attention to the other side of the Atlantic. It was dissolved in 1826, three years after English abolitionists had formed the Society for the Mitigation and Gradual Abolition of Slavery to channel their West Indian efforts. After British West Indian slavery had been abolished, in 1833, and the apprenticeship which followed it ended in 1838, the direct drive against slavery was continued by the British and Foreign Anti-Slavery Society. It too was interested in the possibilities of ousting the slave trade from Africa with legitimate commerce, and the pages of its fortnightly paper, the *Anti-Slavery Reporter*, followed African developments closely. The main agency for carrying out the old plans for Africa, however, was not the B.F.A.S.S. but the short-lived African Civilization Society, founded by Sir Thomas Fowell Buxton in 1839.

On the face of it, the chances of success in the society's venture seemed great. The discoveries of Mungo Park, Clapperton and Lander had made it clear that the Niger did not find its outlet in a mysterious inland lake, or by connecting with the headwaters of the Nile, but through its multiple mouths in the Bight of Benin. As an enormously long waterway running from east to west, parallel to the Coast, it was hoped that the Niger could provide access to a chain of commercial and mission posts which would bisect the very heartland from which it was believed the slavers drew their main supplies. The Niger valley was known to be fertile, and there was nothing naïve in believing that the possibilities for displacing the traffic there were good. The African Civilization Society gained a great deal of publicity and support, including the patronage of Queen Victoria's new husband Prince Albert. The persuasive arguments of Buxton's *African Slave Trade and its Remedy* were accepted by most abolitionists, except for a small minority who insisted that the whole plan diverted attention from the Americas. An even tinier minority had doubts about the breach of pacifist principle involved in sending naval vessels along on the expedition.[23] Unfortunately, all

[23] (Boston) *Liberator*, 21 May 1841.

the armaments then at the disposal of the Royal Navy could not get the expedition across the most formidable of the Niger's defences – fever. Three iron paddle-steamers, the *Albert*, the *Wilberforce* and the *Soudan*, set out from the Oil Rivers in 1841. They managed to penetrate almost three hundred miles upstream before they were forced to return. By the time they struggled back to Lagos, almost everyone on board had been weakened by fever, and over a third of the European's involved – fifty-one – had died. The river was only to be opened after it became clear, on the 1854 Niger expedition, that malaria could be kept at bay by using Peruvian bark or quinine. In 1841, however, Buxton's whole plan ended in a fiasco. As the most radical abolitionists had insisted all along, it was not this kind of activity, nor all the men-of-war in the world, which would end the slave trade. Only the removal of the demand for slaves through the ending of American slavery would work. Yet the African ventures of other abolitionist groups should not be neglected, for they show dramatically the extent to which the ending of slavery and the slave trade were connected with the missionary impulse. This impulse was world-wide, and the long tradition of interest in civilising Africa points to abolitionist preoccupations which go far beyond the crude aims of changing European and American societies to fit the needs of a changing economic order.

Nevertheless, by the nineteenth century the main preoccupation of the abolitionists was with attacking slavery rather than the slave trade, at first within their own home countries, and latterly throughout the world. It was in this that the greatest nineteenth-century triumphs came, not in the inconclusive battle against the Atlantic slave trade. The most numerous and most active abolitionists were those of the English-speaking world, for it was in the context of the British and American democracies that the campaign to raise legislative support for emancipation generated most popular enthusiasm and most open controversy, for and against. Yet this period also saw quiet emancipations in the colonies of powers where the debate over slavery had been less open and less raucous – in those of Denmark and the Nether-lands, and in the Spanish American republics. In France, too, colonial slavery fell. The French had been exposed to three genera-tions of propaganda from a small but articulate anti-slavery movement, but emancipation came as an almost automatic side-product of the expulsion of the Bourbons and the change of regime after the revolution of 1848. The question of slavery had previously been raised with some frequency in the French Assembly, but emancipation was not preceded by a long legislative battle of the sort fought in Britain prior to 1833. The literature from the British debates on emancipation is much fuller than in any other country. With her great vested interest in slavery and her strong philanthropic pressure group, and with the unique stability of the Commons as a forum for debate, the course of the British fight for emancipation is not only a test case for the historian; it was also a test case for the Atlantic world of the nineteenth century.

The British attack on slavery did not begin immediately the Act for the Abolition of the Slave Trade had been secured.[24] This is not as illogical as it now seems. In the first place, for many of its supporters, even most of its leaders including Wilberforce, the campaign against the cruelty of the slave trade did not automatically imply a challenge to slavery, far less to the property interests of the West Indians. Moreover, the triumph of 1807 was followed, as with the end of many campaigns, by a space of apathy, based on the assumption that after so long a struggle the problem had been solved. It would have been very much of a luxury for a nation at war with the greater part of Europe to start experimenting with the social structure of possessions which were not only her most valuable but also strategically among her most important. Even after the end of the Napoleonic wars, the peace-time depression and its accompanying labour unrest diverted attention from the West Indians and at the same time discouraged any Jacobinical tampering with property.

Attention turned to the West Indies before any serious attempt had been made to organise the forces for the ending of slavery. It became clear at an early point that although British slavers had stopped operations, British planters were still glad to buy slaves smuggled by other nations whenever they could get them

[24] C. H. Wesley, 'The Neglected Period of Emancipation in Great Britain', *Journal of Negro History*, xvii (1932) 156–79. The emancipation campaign is studied in Klingberg, *Anti-Slavery Movement*; G. R. Mellor, *British Imperial Trusteeship, 1783–1850* (London, 1951) pp. 81–127; W. L. Mathieson, *British Slavery and its Abolition, 1823–1838* (London, 1926); W. L. Burn, *Emancipation and Apprenticeship in the British West Indies* (London, 1937).

and pay for them. The result was Wilberforce's Slave Registration Bill of 1815, which would have established that all slaves should be registered, and that all who could not be proven to have been in the islands prior to 1807 should automatically be free. This plan had been in operation in the Crown Colony of Trinidad since 1812. However, the Bill was defeated on the basis of a governmental compromise by which the colonial legislatures were invited to introduce registration mechanisms of their own. The real change in goals came as late as 1823. The period of concentrating on 'ameliorating' slavery rather than ending it was now over. A new phase of the English movement began. From now until 1830 the goal of the great majority of British abolitionists was gradual emancipation, although the situation became confused thereafter by the emergence of a group who wished to end slavery immediately. This change will be described below, but it was probably less important than the move to enthusiasm for gradual emancipation in 1823. This was an important year in the history of anti-slavery literature, for two veterans of the slave-trade controversy moved over to call for an end to colonial slavery itself. In 1822 Wilberforce had given up the leadership of the abolitionist pressure group in the House of Commons, where he had been succeeded by Sir Thomas Fowell Buxton. In the following year, however, he produced his *Appeal to the Religion, Justice and Humanity of the Inhabitants of the British Empire in Behalf of the Negro Slaves in the West Indies*. This confessed that the old hope that the planters would treat their slaves better if no new ones were available from Africa had been mistaken. It suggested a plan of gradual emancipation. Almost simultaneously, Thomas Clarkson, whose insistence that emancipation was not at issue had once been as strong as Wilberforce's, published his *Thoughts on the Mitigation and Gradual Abolition of Slavery in the British Dominions*, which took much the same standpoint. These pamphlets themselves influenced others, but at the same time they were symptomatic of increasing abolitionist disillusionment with the hope that the planters could be persuaded to treat slaves well enough to prepare them for eventual manumission. By now the first national British society specifically aimed at ending slavery had been founded. The Society for the Mitigation and Gradual Abolition of Slavery throughout the British Dominions first met on 23 January 1823. It was resolved by the first meeting that 'after a lapse of sixteen years they still have to deplore the almost undiminished prevalence of the very evils which it was the one great object of the Abolition [of 1807] to remedy'.[25] Its committee came from various backgrounds, with the inevitable sprinkling of Quakers and a small group of aristocratic names for decoration, but it was overwhelmingly evangelical – not necessarily Nonconformist. Its most active supporters were substantial businessmen or middling gentry. Like the pressure groups which had preceded it in agitating against the slave trade, it planned to raise as much support as possible in the provincial constituencies. This it would use as a lever in support of political initiatives at Westminster. Its views were also published by the circulation of a periodical edited by Zachary Macaulay. Indeed the abolitionist supporters brought to the struggle a degree of organisation, and a sophistication of propaganda, which had never before been seen in British politics. In 1824 they were provided with the first volume of the work which became their standard reference, James Stephen's *The Slavery of the British West India Colonies Delineated*.[26] It was written in a villainous style, was totally cantankerous, and presented a one-sided view of the treatment of blacks in the islands – yet it was a storehouse of information on the legal position of the slave. The second volume, published in 1830, progressed to listing the atrocities of the planters. Although Stephen was uncritical in gleaning his most horrifying incidents from the distant past and writing as if they were recurring daily in his own time, his book was drawn on again and again by other anti-slavery writers. It came to perform for the British abolitionists much the same function as a later work in America, Theodore Weld's *American Slavery as it Is*.[27]

In terms of practical politics, the Abolition Society quickly organised pressure groups in both Houses. They were supported from the outset by petitions from out of doors, many of them from the provinces, though the first came in 1823 from the Society

[25] *Report of the Committee of the Society for the Mitigation and Gradual Abolition of Slavery throughout the British Dominions* (London, 1824) p. 2.

[26] J. Stephen, *The Slavery of the British West India Colonies Delineated, as it Exists both in Law and Practice, and Compared with the Slavery of Other Countries, Antient and Modern*, 2 vols (London, 1824, 1830).

[27] [T. D. Weld], *American Slavery as it Is: Testimony of a Thousand Witnesses* (New York, 1839).

of Friends in London. In the Commons the abolitionists' spokesman was Sir Thomas Fowell Buxton, later supported by Zachary Macaulay and Dr Lushington. In the upper House the Abolition Society relied on Lord Suffield. One key political figure who was not accepted as an official abolitionist spokesman was Henry Brougham, probably because of his un-evangelical character. He was perhaps the most vociferous parliamentary abolitionist, but was somewhat indecorous in behaviour. To give one example, on one occasion he appeared roaring drunk at Musselburgh races, in full ceremonial dress as Lord Chancellor of England. This together with a marked Scottish accent, a cantankerous personality and a penchant for drinking extraordinary quantities of port while delivering his superb orations in the House, made him less than acceptable as an official mouthpiece. As for Buxton, he had all the qualities of an evangelical leader. A competent though not outstanding speaker, he was an enormously hard worker and good organiser, and had a large personal fortune made in brewing – his family had controlled Truman & Hanbury's, though he gave it up for temperance reasons. He was a strong evangelical within the Church of England, and a country gentleman, which gave him the contacts he needed in the political world at large, while his marriage to a Gurney had given him a good deal of influence in the richest Quaker circles.[28] He became M.P. for Weymouth in 1818, and he gained experience as a parliamentary philanthropist on the Select Committees on the penal code and the state of the jails before replacing Wilberforce as leader of the abolitionists. He brought his first motion on the gradual abolition of slavery before the House in May 1823. This was withdrawn when Canning proposed for the Liverpool government that the House should resolve its concern for adopting measures ameliorating the conditions of slaves in the West India colonies. Further to these resolutions, the government at once took steps to improve the situation of the slaves in the Crown Colonies, where it had direct control, through such measures as prohibiting the flogging of female slaves and setting limits on the punishment of males. At the same time Lord Bathurst, the Colonial Secretary, circularised the legislative colonies expressing the sense of the parliamentary resolutions on amelioration and strongly recommending that they

[28] *The Memoirs of Thomas Fowell Buxton, Bart.* (London: Everyman ed., 1905). There is no good modern biography.

adopt measures similar to those put into force in the Crown Colonies. Later he made additional recommendations: the abolition of the Sunday markets which involved the slaves in working for their living on the only day on which rest was available to them; recognition of slave marriage; a ban on the breaking-up of families by selling parents and children separately; requirement of punishment record-books; limited recognition of blacks as legal witnesses; and, as a testimony to British optimism on the freedmen's future as capitalists, the establishment of savings banks.

West Indian slavery might have survived for many decades longer than it did if the planters had lulled their opponents into apathy by accepting these recommendations quietly. As it was, there was a great deal of non-co-operation in putting them into force even in the Crown Colonies, while the island legislatures simply refused to act in the way the government required. The dramatisation of the slavery issue produced by this intransigence of the planters was all grist to the abolitionist mill. Apart from their defiance, and unrealistic comments on the second American revolution which would ensue if government attempts to interfere with slavery did not end, the series of incidents in the West Indies which followed the Bathurst circulars gave the abolitionists the very publicity they wanted and created a controversy which did not die down until the Emancipation Act was passed in 1833. The rage of the British public was roused by ill-treatment of missionaries in the islands, who seemed harmless and gentle churchmen from a European perspective but were doubtless thoroughly obnoxious to the planters. The most exciting of these incidents occurred in Demerara in 1824, immediately after the blacks there had revolted. This was a classic example of the planters' failing to credit their slaves with any political intelligence, of talking freely about the end of slavery in front of their own servants and putting their resulting discontent down to an abolitionist conspiracy. As a result of this airing of the debate over the slaves' position there were minor disturbances in most of the British islands in 1823 and 1824. The Demerara rising was only the most spectacular. The Demerara slaves certainly knew that an improvement in their condition was imminent, and in some cases believed that this improvement was to be actual emancipation. Whether or not they knew the specific recommendations of the Bathurst circulars, all were convinced in a perfectly loyalist way that concessions had been made to them by the king, but that these were being concealed and withheld by their own masters. Since they were, as usual, poorly armed, poorly organised, without horses or any base to retreat to, they were duly put down, and the ringleaders savagely punished. The fact that the blacks had revolted in this way would have been an excellent propaganda point for the West Indians if they had restricted their vengeance to their own slaves. As it was, they ruined their own British press by prosecuting a pastor, John Smith, whom they considered to have been implicated in the revolt. It is easy to see how the Demerara planters felt about Smith, for they had been sorely provoked by Nonconformist ministers lecturing them on their duties. Again, even if they had not considered religious institutions very much a luxury for slaves whom they saw as a strict labour investment analogous to machinery or livestock, they were only too well aware of the revolutionary implications which the slaves could draw from Christian belief. Smith was tried at a drumhead court martial for having fomented revolt among his black flock, and sentenced to death. It is likely that the sentence would never have been carried out, but unfortunately for the West India lobby's prestige Smith died of consumption in the filthy town jail at Georgetown. The anti-slavery group now had the martyr they needed. Smith came to play much the same role in British anti-slavery propaganda as the murdered newspaper editor Elijah P. Lovejoy in America. Moreover, Smith was not the only missionary molested, for the planters, with their characteristic assumption that blacks were incapable of kicking against the pricks on their own initiative, commonly blamed the outside agency of Methodist and Baptist missionaries for all disturbances among their slaves. Missionaries were harassed in most of the colonies, and their chapels burned. In each case, anti-slavery converts were made in the wave of British indignation on their behalf. There was a further crop of such incidents in the early 1830s, but those of 1823 and 1824 did a great deal to lay the groundwork of a national movement against slavery.

The remainder of the 1820s was spent in exchanges in Parliament, and between the Colonial Office and the island legislatures, on the enforcement of the various ameliorative recommendations made by Bathurst and his successors. The turning-point came in

1830. In that year a relatively small group of abolitionists moved beyond the old demands for gradual emancipation to a call for an immediate end to slavery. Sick of the long political process of haggling over detailed aspects of the slave's position *qua* slave, and his supposed preparation for freedom at some uncertain date in the future, they called for an immediate start to the practical business of freeing slaves. Behind the shift to immediatism lay a complex series of intellectual changes. The fundamental belief of eighteenth-century Christians in a slow and divinely regulated progress towards improved human institutions had made it possible to think in terms of lightening but tolerating slavery until such time as it could be abandoned without serious dislocation. By the late 1820s, however, the intense emotionalism of evangelical religion had brought a new impatience with all forms of truckling with evil. The result was a personally felt guilt for social abuses, and an increasingly strong insistence on the shaking-off of that guilt, and the immediate purification of the individual from sin. For many reformers, indeed, the struggle with slavery had very little to do with the Negro but was a symbol of their struggle with sin and their own sinfulness. In this light it was illogical to 'ameliorate' it or eradicate it gradually. If slavery was the ultimate sin, to continue any longer, on whatever grounds of security or expediency, was to compound it.[29] This position had been put forward as early as 1824 by an English Quakeress, Elizabeth Heyrick, in her *Immediate, not Gradual Emancipation.*[30] However, this pamphlet was little noticed at the time of its publication, though it was extensively quoted by later abolitionist writers. The work which changed the current of British anti-slavery thought did not come out until 1830. It was written by Andrew Thomson, a Presbyterian minister from Edinburgh who was already well known as a leader of the evangelical group within the Church of Scotland who eventually seceded in 1843 to form the Free Kirk. Thomson's pamphlet was the text of a speech given in front of the Edinburgh Abolition Society. The

[29] D. B. Davis, 'The Emergence of Immediatism in British and American Anti-Slavery Thought', *Mississippi Valley Historical Review*, XLIX (1962) 209–30.

[30] *Immediate, not Gradual Abolition; or, an Inquiry into the Shortest, Safest, and most Effectual Means of Getting Rid of West-Indian Slavery* (London, 1824).

Lord Provost of Edinburgh walked out in the middle in protest at its extremism, and indeed Thomson's standpoint was far in advance of most other abolitionists at the time. 'Slavery is a crime', he thundered, '. . . to engage in it is to contract guilt in the sight of heaven . . . being aware of this, we are bound to make no delay in hastening out of transgression, and putting an end to it, wherever it has obtained a footing in our dominions'.[31] Other abolitionists were also moving towards immediatism by this time, and Thomson's views had an extraordinarily wide circulation. The pamphlet went through many editions and became a standard work in British and American anti-slavery libraries. Though Thomson did not live to see West India emancipation, the great majority of abolitionists on both sides of the Atlantic make some reference to having been influenced by him.

In practical political terms, the shift to immediatism speeded up the whole organisational tempo of the anti-slavery movement. It also gave the West India defence an urgency which it had lacked when only symbols like Sunday markets or the use of the whip had been at issue. From 1830, too, Buxton had great difficulty in keeping his own supporters under control, and in getting them to agree to his proposing the kind of compromise legislation which would have any chance of getting through the Commons. It was out of disillusionment with his leadership and the slow progress of the Abolition Society that a small group of radical abolitionists in London formed the Agency Committee to campaign nationally for immediate abolition. Four of its five key members were Quakers: Emmanuel and Joseph Cooper, the Birmingham corn-merchant Joseph Sturge, and his father-in-law James Cropper, from Liverpool. The only really active non-Quaker on the committee was George Stephen.[32] The Agency Committee's simple intention was to publicise the whole issue of slavery as effectively as possible. To this end they appointed a group of eighteen agents who were instructed to go around the country, even in the smallest towns, lecturing on the position of the slaves in the West Indies, and denouncing the atrocities of

[31] A. Thomson, *Substance of the Speech Delivered at the Meeting of the Edinburgh Society for the Abolition of Slavery, on October 19, 1830* (Edinburgh, 1830).

[32] G. Stephen, *Anti-Slavery Recollections, in a Series of Letters to Mrs H. B. Stowe* (London, 1854).

their owners. These agents were in effect professional lecturers, and among them were two men of great importance in the later movement. One of them was an eccentric Scottish evangelical, Captain Charles Stuart, who had been cashiered from the Indian Army for refusing to fire on a group of sepoys, and who first interested the American abolitionist Theodore Weld in antislavery. The other was George Thompson, who later became one of William Lloyd Garrison's closest friends. Their power of dramatising the slavery issue was made all the greater since the West India Committee appointed a group of counter-agents to follow in the tracks of the Agency Committee lecturers contradicting their statements. In some cases agents from the two sides debated publicly with one another, and the attention attracted to the abolitionist cause was all the greater. The series of debates between Thompson and Peter Borthwick, the most successful of the West India agents, were published in various editions.[33] Their wide circulation gave the public an opportunity to see proslavery arguments refuted blow by blow. On each side it was of the essence not to allow opponents to speak in any area without opposition. At the lowest level, pro-slavery posters were countered in London by flocks of urchins hired by the Agency Committee to put abolitionist ones surreptitiously in their place. Even in totally equal debating conditions, however, all the tactical advantages were with Thompson and his colleagues, for few audiences would reject the abstract premise that enslavement was unjust. At the same time, the position of the planters became even more discreditable owing to their failure to understand that blustering on their part was only likely to help their opponents. Again because of their understanding that improvements in their position were under discussion, the slaves increased their resistance in most of the British West India islands. In 1831, as in 1823 and 1824, a wave of disturbances attracted more attention to slavery. The worst rising was in Jamaica, and once again, as in the Demerara case in 1824, the planters were frightened into taking vengeance not only on the blacks but also on the Nonconformist missionaries whom they blamed for their discontent. Throughout the West Indies they were abused, often physically, and in many

[33] e.g. G. Thompson, *Substance of a Speech Delivered in Manchester . . . being a Reply to Mr Borthwick's Statements on the Subject of British Colonial Slavery* (London, 1832).

cases had their little chapels burnt to the ground. Missionary Knibb, a Baptist pastor from Jamaica, became the Missionary Smith of 1831. Since the Jamaican planters had been foolish enough to allow him to escape to Britain, he was able to tour the country denouncing their anti-Christian behaviour, supported by a small group of persecuted missionaries who had been expelled from other islands.[34] Missionaries were very much hero-figures in the evangelical world of the 1820s and 1830s, and the effect of their revelations on public opinion, even in the Church of England, was electric.

Agitation in the provinces brought a flood of petitions to Westminster. There was also counter-pressure on Parliament, but the West Indians were never able to produce the spectacular volume of signatures gathered by the abolitionists, who also showed a great dramatic flair in presenting their petitions. They would carry vast rolls of signatures along the Strand to Westminster, with great processions of delegates from the provinces behind them. They would have them brought into the House for presentation by strong men who staggered under their weight. The furore over the first Reform Act of 1832 did not interrupt the growth of support for emancipation, and petitioning pressure was kept up when the first reformed House met. The abolitionists were greatly disappointed by the failure of the Speech from the Throne to mention slavery at all, though this may only have reflected William IV's personal distrust of abolition, for he had had experience in the West Indies and was convinced that the removal of slavery would reduce the blacks to anarchy. However, ministerial proposals were brought in by Lord Stanley later in the session, as sentiment built up out of doors. After a long series of debates the legislature enacted a compromise, but at least it ensured that slavery would cease to exist in the British dominions other than St Helena, Mauritius, Ceylon and India after 1 August 1833.

One of the ironies of 1833 was that although it was the pressure from the extremists of the Agency Committee which had roused public opinion enough to get an Emancipation Act passed at all,

[34] A typical performance was *Colonial Slavery: Defence of the Baptist Missionaries from the Charge of Inciting the Late Rebellion in Jamaica, in a Discussion between the Rev. Mr Knibb and Mr P. Borthwick* (London, 1833). On Knibb's life, see J. H. Hinton, *A Memoir of William Knibb, Missionary in Jamaica* (London, 1842).

the form of the legislation was a complete triumph for the old-fashioned gradualists of the Abolition Society. The American leader William Lloyd Garrison spoke for many of the more radical British abolitionists when he informed readers of the *Liberator* that the Act was 'a complete triumph of colonial chicanery over the philanthropy of the British people . . . not an example for us to imitate, but a precedent for us to shun'.[35] In the first place, the planters were granted a compensation of £20 million, much to the disgust of abolitionists who considered that holding slaves had been theft in the first place. Secondly, only slaves under six years of age were freed outright. Others were to serve an apprenticeship attached to their original masters for different lengths depending in whether they were predial (field) or non-predial – seven years for the former and five for the latter. This system survived for only four years before it became apparent that the planters were making no attempt to use apprenticeship as a preparation for freedom, and that the apprentices were being treated in exactly the same way as slaves.[36] This message was broadcast throughout Britain by the abolitionists, especially after a group led by Joseph Sturge toured the West Indies. Their own report of this tour was one of the most influential documents in convincing the Commons that the compromise of 1833 had been abused.[37] A completely new campaign was mounted, with the role of the Agency Committee now played by a new group called the Central Negro Emancipation Committee. They used the same methods – constant public meetings in the provinces, intensive propaganda and mass petitioning. Parliament passed an Apprenticeship Act in 1838, and the apprenticeship status ended on 1 August, exactly five years after the West India slaves had been technically emancipated.

The British fight against slavery was more intensive, more highly organised and generally more dramatic than that in other European countries. However, similar changes in opinion, and similar legislation, came in the first half of the nineteenth century in all those continental nations which had possessions where slavery was present but was not so fundamental to the well-being of the home economy that it could not be challenged. Only Spain,

[35] *Liberator*, 12 Oct. 1833.
[36] See Burn, *Emancipation and Apprenticeship in the West Indies*.
[37] J. Sturge and T. Harvey, *The West Indies in 1837* (London, 1837).

with her great vested interest in Cuba, and Portugal, which had lost her Brazilian empire but was in any case still deeply committed to the slave trade, were unaffected, at least at the level of political decisions, though Portugal did finally abolish slavery as early as 1836. Slavery was not abolished by the Dutch until 1863, though their possessions had dwindled to an extent where this has little meaning. It was ended in the Swedish West Indies in 1847, and in 1848, on 3 July, in the Danish possessions in the Virgin Islands. The number of slaves involved in these measures was small, but they indicate the extent to which a willingness to remove slavery where it was not essential was appearing throughout Europe.

However, the most important European emancipation legislation apart from the British was that of the French. The course of the French abolitionist movement had been changed by the revolution of 1789, but even more so by a second revolution in 1791 and the following years, in Saint-Domingue. Saint-Domingue, by then, was set to become the richest sugar island in the world, and the French planters had flooded its virgin soils with slaves, many of them newly imported from Africa. The ratio of white to black was low, slave conditions in this period of boom agriculture were appalling, and in the period of confusion which followed the French Revolution the slaves rose both against the French planters and the mulatto Creoles. Toussaint l'Ouverture was the master-mind behind the revolt, and after many years of bitter civil war, and struggles against French relief forces, his dream of an independent black Haiti was fulfilled.[38] This was one of the most significant events in the history of slavery in the Americas, for it brought numerically the largest emancipation of the eighteenth century, through violent action on the part of the slaves. A slave society in its prime had been dashed down, and it represented a token of hope for slaves, and a precedent of horror for masters throughout the hemisphere. Throughout the nineteenth century the success of Haiti helped stimulate slave revolts, and strengthen planter brutality in suppressing resistance. For

---

[38] C. L. R. James, *The Black Jacobins: Toussaint l'Ouverture and the San Domingo Revolution*, 2nd ed. (New York, 1963). On slavery in Saint-Domingue prior to the revolution, see G. M. Hall, *Social Control in Slave Plantation Societies: A Comparison of St Domingue and Cuba* (Baltimore, 1971).

France, however, Toussaint's revolt meant the loss of her richest slave colony. It discredited the Société des Amis des Noirs, who were widely thought to have been implicated in the rising, and at the same time gave colonial vested interests the opportunity to argue that meddling with slavery led to carnage. On the other hand, the position of the French planters was weakened, simply by virtue of the loss of their potential allies in Saint-Domingue.

The French fight for emancipation was a long one. The idealistic pronouncements of the early revolutionaries on slavery were quickly withdrawn by the First Consul, before they had ever gone into force. Martinique and Guadeloupe were still fertile and producing sugar richly when the majority of the British islands were approaching collapse. In spite of their temporary occupation, after their restoration at Vienna their stability was all the more important to France, given the backwardness of her industrialisation. It was also particularly difficult to meddle with anything involving property rights during the reigns of Louis XVIII and Charles X, even after the revolution of 1830. The anti-slavery tradition nevertheless continued. Many of the original *Amis des Noirs* and their supporters, including Brissot himself, died during the Revolution, or were exiled, but the society re-emerged in the late Napoleonic period. It continued its activities for another thirty-five years. Above all, anti-slavery was kept before the French reading public, even in the years of reaction immediately after the Revolution, by the Abbé Grégoire, editor of the *Constitutionnel*. He continued his learned and acerbic pamphleteering until his death in extreme age in 1831.[39] His place as leader of the French abolitionists was taken by a very young man, Victor Schoelcher, perhaps symbolically the son of a rich industrialist, a manufacturer of luxury porcelain from Alsace, which is reminiscent of the role of the provincial Josiah Wedgwood. Like Grégoire, Schoelcher – 'Schoelcher, brave jusqu'à la gloire', as Victor Hugo said of him – was a tireless propagandist and writer.[40] He also travelled extensively in search of information,

[39] See R. F. Necheles, *The Abbé Grégoire, 1787–1831: The Odyssey of an Egalitarian* (Westport, Conn., 1971). Grégoire's most influential work was probably *De la littérature des Nègres* (Paris, 1807), interestingly republished in a faulty translation (Brooklyn, N.Y., 1810).

[40] R. Tardon, *Le Combat de Schoelcher* (Paris, 1948). The African voyage is covered in D. Bouche, 'Un Voyage d'information bien dirigé:

and visited America in 1829 and the West Indies in 1840. It was after his Caribbean trip that he moved over to immediate abolition. He is the only major European abolitionist who actually went to West Africa in person. His most distinguished fellow-abolitionists were de Tocqueville, Lamartine, the distinguished economists Hippolyte Passy and Odilon Barrot, and the jurist Isambert. As in England, the position of the West Indians weakened as the century progressed. A *Société pour l'Abolition de l'Esclavage* was formed to attack them in 1834, with several economists including Barrot on its committee. Quickening industrialisation made sugar colonies less important to the economy. In any case, by the 1840s the thinning soils of France's little possessions were being pushed out of the world markets by the vigorous growths of Cuba and Brazil. The movement gained momentum after 1830, and it was made easier by a number of voluntary manumissions in Guadeloupe and Martinique – which, though they liberated a higher number of slaves than ever before, were not followed by the kind of cataclysm which pro-slavery die-hards had promised. Again, the more liberally chosen Assembly, and wider franchise under the new constitution, improved the chance of full political debate on slavery. As in the British parliamentary situation, publicity only made the pigheadedness of the planters clearer. As in Britain, too, there was an ameliorative phase in which departmental decrees of 1845 and 1846 insisted on regulations of punishment and minimum living and working conditions. With the revolution of 1848 the planters and their royalist associates were pushed out of political influence, and on 4 March, by executive decree, the provisional government ordered the setting-up of a commission, under Schoelcher, at the Ministry of Marine and the Colonies, to arrange the passage of legislation for immediate emancipation, 'sous le plus bref délai'. This was duly enacted in May, perhaps carried through on a wave of the same libertarian enthusiasm which had brought a paper emancipation in 1791. But the weakened planters no longer had the resilience to fight back, and in any case they were given compensation averaging about 50

Victor Schoelcher au Sénégal, Septembre 1847–Janvier 1848', *Conjonction*, no. 105 (1967). His most important work was *Des colonies françaises. Abolition immédiate de l'esclavage* (Paris, 1842).

francs per slave. The quarter of a million slaves in the French colonies were duly freed, immediately. There was no chance of their being brought back into bondage in the pseudo-liberalism of the Second Empire.[41]

The French colonial slaves were freed as an incidental to a revolution which occurred at a time when they had become a national luxury. In the same way, those in the Latin American republics were emancipated in the years after independence had been secured from Spain. Spanish America had a long tradition of concern over Indian slavery, but although the concepts used by Las Casas and his later followers influenced attitudes to slavery as a whole, few Spanish writers extended the attack to include black slaves until the nineteenth century. There were isolated individuals who questioned the justice of the system during the course of the Latin American Enlightenment. The Portuguese priest Manuel Rocha, writing in 1755, was one such. But the real Spanish American attack on slavery did not come until the early nineteenth century, and unlike the North American one it does not seem to have stemmed from local traditions. Instead it was inspired by works of the European Enlightenment which circulated in the colonies, and the example of foreign abolitionists and foreign liberalism in general. There is also a sneaking suspicion that during the Wars of Independence the nationalists made promises and concessions to blacks either to gain their support as auxiliary troops or to draw them away from the enemy – in spite of their moral outrage at the royalist commanders who endangered the whole fabric of white ascendancy by giving arms to black levies.[42] Most of the new republics freed their slaves gradually. The result was that there were still many

[41] G. Martin, *L'Abolition de l'esclavage* (Paris, 1948); idem, *Histoire de l'esclavage dans les colonies françaises* (Paris, 1948) pp. 280–92; A. Cochin, *L'Abolition de l'esclavage*, 2 vols (Paris, 1861) 1 1–92. There are short English accounts of the French abolition, rightly stressing black participation, in S. T. McLoy, *The Negro in France* (Lexington, Ky., 1961) pp. 124–44; idem, *The Negro in the French West Indies* (Lexington, Ky., 1966) pp. 141–59.

[42] J. V. Lombardi, *The Decline and Abolition of Negro Slavery in Venezuela, 1820–1854* (Westport, Conn., 1971) p. 40. The place of anti-slavery in the Spanish American revolutions is carefully examined in J. Lynch, *The Spanish American Revolutions, 1808–1826* (London, 1973) pp. 83–6, 154–6, 203–4, 223–4, 275–6, 288–9, 314–15.

slaves in Latin America outside Cuba and Brazil even by the 1850s, but in most countries emancipation legislation was at least initiated soon after the successful revolutions at the beginning of the century. This came in Mexico, Uruguay, Chile, Argentina and Bolivia in the 1820s, though it was delayed until the 1850s in Venezuela and in Peru. In the latter country and in Chile, mining slaves were still used extensively. Even in areas where slaves were in a tiny minority, vested interests surrendered to the abolitionists slowly and with deep reluctance. A recent study of Venezuela, for instance, finds that the small handful of slave-holders were able to hold out until the Act of 1854, partly because they were firmly entrenched in the ruling class. Moreover, even the most liberal Venezuelans were hampered by the dilemma between abstract disapproval of slavery and fear of ex-slaves. At independence, everyone was agreed that 'slavery was a nasty business and by right slaves should be free. But on the other hand, blacks subjected to slavery were an exceedingly nasty group whose inclusion in society was hardly advisable'.[43] This sad dualism was not confined to Venezuela, or for that matter to Latin America.[44] Nevertheless, by the beginning of the second half of the century the only parts of America in which slavery remained unshaken were Brazil, now an independent empire under the Braganza dynasty, Cuba, a colony of Spain, and the United States, a modern democracy. Its survival apparently had little to do with the polity of the country involved, but much to do with the requirements of the slaveholders and their physical ability to defend their own interests.

In fact the inroads made on slavery and the slave trade during the first half of the century should not be exaggerated. The abolition of the Brazilian slave trade in 1850 was an optimistic sign, but there could be no real suppression without the abolition of slavery or the co-operation of the United States, or both.

[43] Ibid., p. 47.

[44] Apart from Lombardi's study on Venezuela, there is no English work on slavery and emancipation in the Spanish American republics. J. A. Saco, *Historia de la esclavitud desde los tiempos más remotos hasta nuestras días*, 2nd ed., 6 vols (Havana, 1937–45) vols IV and V, is useful, but for the nineteenth century concentrates almost exclusively on Cuba to the exclusion of the republics. See also J. F. King, 'The Latin American Republics and the Suppression of the Slave Trade', *Hispanic American Historical Review*, XXIV (1944) 387–411.

Slavery had ended in the colonies of all important European powers except Spain, in the Northern states of the U.S.A., and in independent Latin America except Brazil. These achievements had been possible because of a relative weakening of the power of the slaveholding interest in each area. But even then there were cases where success had been possible only in the aftermath of a violent revolution, as in France and in the Spanish American republics. Haiti was the only place where slavery had been overthrown in its prime, and this had been achieved with endless bloodshed by the blacks themselves. So far, to repeat a metaphor, only the fat had been trimmed from slavery, and the real struggle, the onslaught on the bone and muscle, lay ahead. Yet the ideology of abolition had gained a momentum which made it possible to turn against slavery even where it was still highly profitable, and still well able to defend itself. The next steps were to attack slavery in Cuba, Brazil and the South. Here the triumph of the abolition idea came only in the second half of the century, at the cost of political upheaval or mass bloodshed. Slavery was not the only issue which produced the holocaust of the Civil War, but it was the main one. In Brazil, emancipation narrowly avoided causing a civil war, but helped bring the expulsion of the Braganzas and the institution of a dictatorship. In Cuba, the war of independence and the bloody Spanish–American war were linked closely with forces unleashed in the contest over slavery. If the early history of slavery had not proved it already, the period after 1860 brought out the full bitterness of Africa's curse on the New World.

8 Slavery as a Mature System in an Industrial World

AT the same time as the strength of anti-slavery sentiment was increasing in some parts of the world, slavery itself, as an economic system, was becoming more attractive in others. This was so in parts of the American South, which flourished on the soaring world demand for cotton; in Brazil, where the growing profitability of sugar and coffee cultivation gave slave agriculture a new lease of life; and in Cuba, where the opening of the island's rich, untouched soils made it possible to grow cane at low prices at a time of rapidly rising European consumption. In these areas, where the return on investment in slaves was high, and where masters were only too well aware of the boom–bust fluctuations in plantation prosperity, the drive for speedy profits made black slavery as brutal as it had ever been. In this century of benevolence, many more slaves than the relatively few who had been rescued by the philanthropists of Boston, Manchester and Paris still had no reasonable hope of getting out of bondage. Moreover, in spite of attempts which have been made by comparative-minded historians to prove the contrary, it made little difference to these black men and women which white culture had moulded the attitudes of their owners. The United States was an English-speaking Protestant democracy. Cuba was the colony of Catholic and absolutist Spain. Brazil, also Catholic, was a Portuguese-speaking constitutional monarchy. In each case, wherever the staple crop was being cultivated under pressure to get returns as fast as possible, slaves were kept working at a pace which reduced their active life to a period of several years. Spectacular atrocities and brutalities there certainly were, but these are much less significant than the collective toll of consistent overwork. Throughout the history of black slavery the condition of the slave was dictated by the demands of the world which absorbed his products. The balance between paternalism and brutality was a delicate one, but it had little to do with the culture or religion of the slaveholder. The kind of easy-going slave regime which has been described by men like Freyre for Brazil, or Ulrich B. Phillips for the United States, could survive only when plantations were established, returns were low, and the urgency of the planter drive towards profits had mellowed – owing to falling demand, weakening soil, or simple indolence – though the ownership of slaves could still be the basis of status and power to an extent which ensured that the planters' determination to preserve the system was as strong as ever. Yet the conditions of slavery were most atrocious when world demands made profits spectacular. Planters then took new land into cultivation and pressed to pay off initial capital debts and make maximum profits before the bottom fell out of the market or the source of riches disappeared. This was so from the sixteenth to the nineteenth century. It is the shared experience which links the Indian slaves who were decimated to produce silver for the Spaniards, and the blacks who were dragged to Cuba to provide the Western world with cheap sugar in the last decades of slavery.[1] In the nineteenth century, as a generalisation, the position of the slave changed for the worse in Cuba, and in much of the United States and Brazil.

Since the early nineteenth century many English and American authors, including the abolitionists themselves, have assumed that Brazilian slavery somehow took a much milder form than in other parts of the world. This tendency has recently been strengthened by the translation and popularity of the writings of the great Brazilian historian Gilberto Freyre.[2] The reality of nineteenth-century slavery in Brazil was quite at odds with the

[1] The relationship between economic change and slave conditions is suggested in M. Harris, *Patterns of Race in the Americas* (New York 1964); S. Mintz, 'Review of Stanley M. Elkins' *Slavery*', *American Anthropologist*, LXIII (1961) 579–87. Cultural and national determinants are stressed in F. Tannenbaum, *Slave and Citizen: The Negro in the Americas* (New York, 1946); S. Elkins, *Slavery: A Problem in American Institutional and Intellectual Life* (Chicago, 1959). The debate is reviewed in E. D. Genovese, 'Materialism and Idealism in the History of Negro Slavery in the Americas', *Journal of Social History*, 1 (1968) 371–94.

[2] G. Freyre, *The Masters and the Slaves: A Study in the Development of Brazilian Civilization*, trans. S. Putnam (New York, 1956). Cf. C. Vann Woodward, *American Counterpoint: Slavery and Racism in the North–South Dialogue* (Boston, 1971) pp. 47–77.

paternalistic picture Freyre presents. Yet there is something very attractive about his work. On a first reading of his superbly written *The Masters and the Slaves*, his *Casa grande e senzala*, it is difficult to reject his sweeping conclusions on the effect of the long Portuguese traditions of contact with darker races. Familiarity bred not contempt but indulgence, and he describes an exotic society of particoloured tropical sybarites. Its dominant theme was the constant copulation of the planters and their sons with their Indian, Negro and mulatto slave girls. Where his counterpart Ulrich B. Phillips found the central theme of Southern history in the physical control of slaves, Freyre found the stuff of Brazil's destiny in a saga of cross-racial fornication. This was produced not by the sensuality of the slaves, but by the 'lubricity' of the master-class. Miscegenation was so universal that a Jesuit, it is said, was once able to close his sermon with calling for an Ave Maria 'for the Bishop's woman, who is in labour'. The whole ethic of planting Brazil favoured indulgence:

> No Big House in the days of slavery wanted any effeminate sons or male virgins. In the folklore of our old sugar and coffee zones, whenever there is a reference to sexually pure youths, it is always in a tone of mockery, by way of holding the ladylike fellow up to ridicule. The one always approved was the lad who went with the girls at as early an age as possible. A 'raparigueiro', as we could say today. A woman-chaser. A ladies' man. A deflowerer of maidens. One who lost no time in taking Negro women that he might increase the herd and the parental capital.[3]

The Brazilian planters, in intimate contact with numerous offspring of varying hues, moulded a unique and relaxed patriarchal society in which the lot of the slave was the same as that of any other member of the family.

It is now clear that the hierarchical habits of slavery prevented rapid social mobility in Brazil after emancipation.[4] However, since she did not reap the same kind of bitter whirlwind of modern racial dislocation as the United States, there is an obvious attraction in accepting Freyre's conclusions as to the relative

[3] Freyre, *Masters and Slaves*, p. 395.
[4] F. Fernandes, *The Negro in Brazilian Society*, trans. J. D. Skiles, A. Brunel and A. Rothwell (New York, 1971).

peaceableness of Brazilian slavery. It is for this reason that comparative historians like the Columbia Latin-Americanist Frank Tannenbaum were uncritical of *The Masters and the Slaves*. One of his pupils, Stanley Elkins, has gone on to argue brilliantly that in both Brazil and Spanish America a benevolent religious and legal structure protected the slave from the capitalistic excesses of North America, and gave him goals which strengthened him psychologically.[5] In fact the reality of Brazil's slave system undercuts all these theories. Freyre's work is not a general study of Brazilian slavery, but extrapolates from conditions in the great sugar plantations of the north-east, at a time when demands for their crops had slackened and the brutal urgency of boom agriculture had temporarily disappeared. In the mining, coffee and sugar industries in their expansive phase, Freyre would have found conditions entirely different. Indeed, a detailed comparative study of Brazilian and North American slavery by Degler shows that their custom could be very much the same, in similar conditions, though their aftermath had been different owing to the separate status of the mulatto.[6] Moreover, such legal or religious sanctions as were intended to protect the slave were meaningless in the frontier coffee and mining areas where masters were most brutal and conditions were at their worst. Availability of manumission, protection of slave marriage and the position of the slave in the courts were if anything less favourable than in the United States, at least in practice. The master, in fact, *was* master on his own plantation, a fact which Freyre is the first to admit. The only validity in the argument for the mildness of Brazilian slavery lies in the impact of its boom–bust economy. This enabled masters to relax into relative paternalism during slack periods, but also made it advisable to rent their slaves out as *negros de ganho* as a response to recession.

The real history of Brazilian slavery, then, is far removed from Freyre's idyllic account. Brazil, like the Spanish colonies, had at first experimented with Indian labour, first through the 'barter' system and latterly through chattel slavery.[7] By the second half

[5] Elkins, *Slavery*, pp. 81–139.

[6] C. N. Degler, *Neither Black nor White: Slavery and Race Relations in Brazil and the United States* (New York, 1971).

[7] For references on the treatment of Indians in Brazil, see above, pp. 35–8.

of the sixteenth century, however, substantial numbers of blacks were being imported. Principally they were brought to Pernambuco and Bahia in the north where a growing sugar industry was stimulated by Dutch capital and often managed by Dutch factors. Sugar production expanded further during the brief Dutch occupation of north Brazil, and this area provided much of Europe's sugar until the Caribbean islands were put under cane later in the seventeenth century. Even after the Dutch were driven out, to pass on their expertise to the English in Barbados and elsewhere and thus indirectly undercut Portuguese sugars, the sugar economy continued to expand, though the most important eighteenth-century Brazilian export was gold, at first extracted from the south-central region, as the Marquis de Pombal bitterly complained, under the commercial aegis of London. However, slave labour was as fundamental to the Brazilian gold-mining industry as to sugar. At the same time, slavery was maintained and indeed expanded slowly on the easy-going old plantations of the Bahia and Pernambuco areas, where the amount of land available prevented complete stagnation.[8] It is of these, in their declining condition, that Freyre speaks so lyrically – not of the slavery of the early sugar boom, or of the nineteenth-century coffee industry which grew up in the great central and southern hinterland for which São Paulo and Rio rather than Bahia were the principal cities. A great spurt in the Brazilian demand for slaves began with the French revolutionary wars, when the destruction of Saint-Domingue and general dislocation in the Caribbean made it possible once again for Brazilian sugar to compete in the world market. The value of Brazil's sugar exports rose by ten times during the Napoleonic wars. This false prosperity was smashed when Cuban sugar production really got under way, but the real strengthening of the Brazilian slave system came with the expansion of coffee cultivation. Coffee had become the country's major crop by the 1830s, and it produced a slave regime as oppressive and brutal as any in Brazilian history.

[8] A. K. Manchester, *British Preeminence in Brazil: Its Rise and Decline* (Chapel Hill, N.Y., 1933) p. 40; C. R. Boxer, *The Dutch in Brazil, 1624–1654* (Oxford, 1957) pp. 112–58; N. Deerr, *A History of Sugar*, 2 vols (London, 1949) 1 102 ff; C. Furtado, *The Economic Growth of Brazil: A Survey from Colonial to Modern Times*, trans. R. W. de Aguiar and E. C. Drysdale (Berkeley, 1963) pp. 50–71.

This is not to say that seventeenth- and eighteenth-century slavery had not been brutal. There is plenty of evidence that, even at its most easy-going, it produced overwork and individual instances of sadism.[9] Even the gold area of Minas Gerais shows many such instances, though the system of mining gave the slaves some individual initiative and their proportion to the white population was less alarmingly high than in the north-east. In the nineteenth century, however, the demands of industrial Europe and North America for coffee and sugar brought a renewed severity to Brazilian plantation slavery. Apart from purely economic demands, the need for harsh discipline was strengthened by the sheer numbers of slaves brought into the country during this agricultural boom. The proportion of blacks in Brazil was always much higher than in the United States, and this became even more of a problem when the volume of the slave trade increased in the nineteenth century and the numbers of potentially dangerous raw Africans, *negros boçais*, in the black population rose. It was partly fear of this disproportion which led to abolition of the slave trade. But for the average Brazilian master the solution to such problems was simply to work his slaves hard enough to make sure they had no time for resistance, and to punish them savagely at the first sign of insubordination.

Slave population began to increase rapidly in the early part of the century. In 1798 there were 1,582,000 slaves to 1,010,000 whites; in 1818, 1,930,000 to 1,143,000.[10] During this twenty years, coffee was being hesitantly tried out in the upland areas in which adventurers attracted to the interior in the eighteenth-century gold rush had settled when the mining boom broke. As the Brazilian beans began to ease Dutch Javanese coffee out of the international market, and world consumption of coffee soared

[9] C. R. Boxer, *The Golden Age of Brazil, 1695–1750: Growing Pains of a Colonial Society* (1962; reprinted Berkeley, 1969) pp. 7–9, 138–40, 170–5; idem, *Race Relations in the Portuguese Colonial Empire, 1415–1825* (Oxford, 1963) pp. 101–14. The best modern work on Portuguese colonial slavery is allegedly M. Goulart, *Escravidão africana no Brasil* (São Paulo, 1950), which I have not had the opportunity of consulting owing to the perverse Brazilian practice of publishing scholarly books in tiny editions. See also A. de E. Taunay, *Subsidios para a história de tráfico Africano no Brasil* (São Paulo, 1941).

[10] A. M. P. Malheiro, *A escravidão no Brasil. Ensaio histórico-juridico-social*, 2 vols (São Paulo), 1944) II 26.

in the flourishing urban societies of Europe and North America, the demands of these planters for new African labour became insatiable. This was reflected in an alarming upward jump in imports of slaves. Brazil was by far the largest importer in the nineteenth century, and the most reliable statistics suggest that an annual average import of 39,500 for the years 1811 to 1820 rose to 50,600 for 1821 to 1830, fell back to 36,600 in the next decade, and rose again to 40,700 per year in the 1840s.[11] The great majority of these slaves were taken not to the older sugar area of Bahia, but to the thriving coffee metropolis of Rio de Janeiro, and to a lesser extent to São Paulo. At the same time, incidentally, their ethnic background was markedly different from that of the blacks of the United States, for they came not from Guinea but from Congo, Angola and the slaving entrepôts of East Africa. The positive side of this great movement of black humanity is that these great concentrations of black population and the high proportion of first-generation arrivals made possible the preservation of a polyglot but rich African heritage in music, religion, dance and language – much more so than in the United States. It is unthinkable, for instance, that any North American slaves could have used a complete African language, like the Nago patois used by the *negros de ganho* or hired slaves of Bahia.[12]

European and North American abolitionists were by and large too concerned with the problems of slavery among Protestants to notice the full misery of these unfortunate forced immigrants. Until recently the English-speaking historians who are their successors fell into the same trap. Their remarks on Latin America, when they made them, they confined to Cuba and the Spanish-speaking republics. Brazilian slavery, if considered at all, was

[11] P. Curtin, *The Atlantic Slave Trade: A Census* (Madison, Wis., 1969) p. 235. Curtin's estimate is based on the British Foreign Office's 1845 'Report of the Number of Slave Vessels Arriving in the Transatlantic States since 1814', *P.P.* (1845) XLIX (73) pp. 593–633, and Goulart, *Escravidão africana no Brasil*, p. 270. Cf. L. Bethell, *The Abolition of the Brazilian Slave Trade: Britain, Brazil and the Slave Trade Question, 1807–1869* (Cambridge, 1970) pp. 388–95.

[12] A. Ramos, *O Negro Brasileiro* (Rio de Janeiro, 1934) pp. 16–18 and passim; D. Pierson, *Negroes in Brazil: A Study of Race Contact at Bahia* (Chicago, 1942) pp. 71 ff. In general, see also R. Bastide, *African Civilizations in the New World*, trans. P. Green (New York, 1972). Much of the evidence in M. J. Herskovits, *The Myth of the Negro Past*, 2nd ed. (Boston, 1958) is based on deduction from the Brazilian and Caribbean cases.

vaguely assumed to be mild. To some extent this was due to the relative decency of the condition of the urban slaves in the port towns which were visited by those travellers who left non-Portuguese accounts behind them. The great English travel-writer Maria Graham, for instance, had to qualify her determination to denounce slavery: 'I love to collect . . . proofs of the evils of slavery – even here where it exists in a milder form than in most countries'. She was impressed by the enormous diversity of slave occupations. A third of the orchestra in the Rio opera house were black, although the singers, rather like American Football League quarterbacks today, were apparently all white.[13] Yet the inland story was a different one. The leaders of the Brazilian abolitionist movement which flourished from the 1860s onwards, like Joaquim Nabuco, were not so blind to the atrocious conditions of the slaves held by their countrymen. This was not a matter of the form of Luso-Brazilian slave law, but of the hard labour requirements of nineteenth-century businessmen who had to meet the demands for a quick return on their investments. Whatever the attractions of town life, especially for the *negros de ganho*, and however strong the paternalism of the large, established sugar plantations of Pernambuco and Bahia, the booming coffee areas of the nineteenth century were still true to the apophthegm around which Charles Boxer has crystallised his studies of the eighteenth – that Brazil was 'a Hell for Negroes, a purgatory for Whites, and a paradise for Mulattoes'.[14] The essence of the slave situation was not only the physical atrocities which Brazilian abolitionists dramatised, but chronic and soulless overwork which broke the average slave in a period of years, and indeed was intended to do so.

The old reply that masters would not treat their slaves badly because of their desire to protect their investments is irrelevant. If slaves were thought of simply as industrial plant, their owner had a choice of two strictly economic decisions. He could treat his slaves well, and prolong their working life at the cost of lowering his immediate return; or he could work them to death and replace them with the extra short-term profit their work gained. In a

[13] M. Graham, *Journal of a Voyage to Brazil, and Residence there, during Part of the Years 1821, 1822, 1823* (London, 1824) pp. 273, 197.

[14] J. A. Antonil, *Cultura e opulência do Brasil por suas drogas e minas* (Lisbon, 1711) liv. I, cap. 9, quoted in Boxer, *Golden Age of Brazil*, p. 1.

slave society which was in the grip of an industrial world, where the demands of mortgages had to be met, where the demand for staples was insatiable, and where there was no guarantee that soil or ore would hold out, or that boom conditions would continue, the policy of working slaves and other machinery out and then replacing them was often the more attractive. So it was in parts of Brazil, and this mentality was by no means confined to coffee cultivation. Its repercussions in terms of human suffering among the slave population have been traced by modern Brazilian historians in other sectors of Brazil's nineteenth-century economy – by Octavio Ianni for the mixed production of Curitiba, by Fernando Cardoso for the cattle and coffee country of Rio Grande do Sul, and by Emilia da Costa for the coffee plantations of São Paulo and Rio de Janeiro.[15] Whatever staple their masters were producing, the slaves of nineteenth-century Brazil were in exactly the same position as those in any slave economy at a comparable stage of economic development.

Doubtless there were areas of Brazil, and individual plantations, in which the slaves were treated in the easy-going way of which Gilberto Freyre writes, but in general their lives in the nineteenth century were squalid, cruel and perilous. This was often so even in the older activity of sugar-growing, for Brazilian sugar went into boom conditions not only after the collapse of the Haitian industry, but also after the lifting of the British sugar duties in 1846 opened a new and lucrative market to Latin American products. It must also be remembered how many of these slaves were Africans by birth, already debilitated and in a state of shock after their forced removal from the culture and surroundings which were familiar to them. Their sheer misery becomes clearer the more local studies of Brazilian slavery are produced. In one coffee-growing county in the Paraíba valley, for instance, the planters were omnipotent in their own bailiwicks, unrestricted by the pressures of law, religion and public opinion with which their counterparts in the cities had to contend.

[15] O. Ianni, *As metamorfoses do escravo* (São Paulo, 1962) pp. 28–79; F. H. Cardoso, *Capitalismo e escravidão no Brasil Meridional* (São Paulo, 1962); E. V. da Costa, *Da Senzala à Colônia* (São Paulo, 1966) pp. 227 ff. There is no full account of nineteenth-century Brazilian slavery in English, but see Degler, *Neither Black nor White*, pp. 25–92; P. A. Martin, 'Slavery and Abolition in Brazil', *Hispanic American Historical Review*, XIII (1933) 151–72.

Punishments were swift and brutal, if only as a matter of security for owners and masters surrounded by a hostile and volatile labour force. Even if the courts had been prepared to protect slaves who were flogged to death as an example to others, Brazilian law made no provision for slave complaints, and the likelihood of one *fazendeiro* testifying against his neighbours was negligible. Lesser offences also had their punishments, through the stocks or *tronco*, minor whippings, chaining, and beating on the hand with the *palmatorio*, a wooden instrument rather similar to the pandybat used in Jesuit schools, of which James Joyce complains so bitterly in *A Portrait of the Artist* and *Stephen Hero*. In turn, suicide and escape were as commonly used as pathetic means of resistance as in the United States. The working day could go on, at peak periods of plantation activity, from dawn to well after sunset, labour for men and women alike was carried on on an impersonal gang basis – which may have left the strongest with energy to spare, but pushed the weakest to their utmost. Food was monotonous though not always scarce, holidays few, living quarters filthy and medical care rudimentary. The conclusion of the historian of this *municipio* of Vassouras is that 'slaves were worked hard, and they were not expected to last'.[16]

Though many of the tasks involved in the mining industry were different, its conditions and its impact on the slave population were similar. In the possession of Yale University Library there survives the punishment book kept by the English manager of 'Gongo', a mine near Socorro in the Minas Gerais district up-country from Rio de Janeiro. This was one of a group of workings bought by English companies after 1825, when the heyday of Brazilian gold-mining was over.[17] It was probably much better regulated than most mining enterprises. Even the keeping of a punishment book was not typical of Brazilian slave management. The mine slaves were encouraged to work well by small allowances and gifts of money. Medals of various grades

[16] S. J. Stein, *Vassouras: A Brazilian Coffee County, 1850–1890*, 2nd ed. (New York, 1970) pp. 183, 132–95.

[17] J. F. Carrato, *Igreja, iluminismo e escolas mineiras coloniais. Notas sôbre da decedência mineira setecentista* (São Paulo, 1968) p. 254. The manuscript is catalogued as 'Slavery. Original manuscript of the punishments administered to slaves in a South American mine'.

were awarded for good conduct. Such a plan certainly bespeaks some intention of making conditions humane, probably based in the English origins of the overseer, but even here life was dismal and harsh. What is clear also is that it was a handful of slaves on whom the punishments were concentrated. Some had no punishments against their names, though the book covered eleven full years from 1836 to 1847. These were the individuals who fitted their lives, however unwillingly, between the parameters of the slave camp's life. Others were constantly in trouble, either for repeated minor acts of resistance, including theft and escape, or for trying to forget their misery and hardship in drink. One such was the most inappropriately named Felisberto, whose misdeeds took up a great deal of the overseer's attention from 1836 to 1841, when the entries against his name mysteriously stop. In July 1836 he spent eighteen hours in the *tronco* for having *restillo* in his house. His serious troubles begin on 13 January 1837, when his wife was drunk and absent from muster. When the *feitors* or overseers went to his house to look for her, they found 'some Restillo, 20 horse shoes, and a small bit of Gold. On hearing this he ran away into the Woods'. On the 16th he 'Came back to deliver himself up put into the Tronco & next day received 72 lashes & put an iron on his neck'. It was taken off two weeks later, but on 22 March he went back into the *tronco* for an unspecified offence. By 15 June, Felisberto was again being punished. He was 'Taken returning from Socorro with two bottles of Restillo put into the Tronco and next day recd 80 lashes; also strongly suspected of stealing a large piece of iron belonging to the steam engine'. In September, when Felisberto was off in Rio delivering the mine's output with the 'Gold Troop', it was discovered that the stamp-head of the steam engine had been sold there. On his return other stolen articles were found in his baggage, for which he received forty-four lashes and again had an iron put on his neck. After a few more small misdeeds he had a year of relatively good conduct, until his worst punishment came in June 1839, when he 'Recd Palmo (24) put into Tronco for 24 hours & recd 72 lashes for appropriating to his own use a found 1400 note, purchasing Restillo at Socorro, & consuming Co's oil in a Co's lamp at his house'. After this, although there were still minor offences, he was apparently cowed into conduct acceptable to *feitors* and managers until his death.

Other slaves were abused equally, often for somewhat pathetic attempts to break the routine of the camp – like Silvester, who was fined 'for wearing his best jacket on a working day', and later 'for wearing the Sunday clothes of another and impertinence'. He later graduated to more dangerous offences, and the book records cryptically that he was given sixty lashes for being engaged in 'the disturbance'. Gongo was apparently an exceedingly well-run plantation, under managers determined to treat their slaves with what they understood as humanity. Moreover, though Brazilian gold was important until the strikes in California, Alaska and South Africa later in the century, it was not in as much of a boom condition as coffee; yet the slaves were forced into a soulless and crushing routine of work, and brutalised by constant punishment and rigid discipline. There is very little here that is different from the position of Indian and Negro slaves in other areas where investment was high but returns were quick: for those engaged in sixteenth-century Spanish silver-mining, in seventeenth- and eighteenth-century English sugar-growing, in the nineteenth-century Cuban sugar industry or in the cotton cultivation of the Black Belt of the United States. What dictated slave conditions was not the culture of their owners, or the law of the country in which they worked, but the demands of the industry to which they were tied and the needs of the world market for their produce. The Freyreian interpretation is a piece of romanticism except in special cases. Indeed the second volume of Freyre's trilogy, *The Mansions and the Shanties*, itself points to the relatively bad conditions of the coffee-growing south, though these are presented as being an aberration outside the mainstream of developments in the author's beloved and patriarchal north-east.[18]

The only problem about discarding the picture of a benevolent plantation regime is that it removes one plausible explanation of the relative weakness of racial tensions in post-emancipation Brazil. These have not been by any means absent; they are much stronger on an *informal* level than Americans assume. Assumptions of white supremacy, rooted to a greater or lesser degree in the slave period, are still built into the power structure of modern Brazil. Florestan Fernandes, the leader of the Marxist São Paulo

[18] G. Freyre, *The Mansions and the Shanties: The Making of Modern Brazil*, trans. H. de Onís (New York, 1963) p. 131.

school of sociologists, summed this up when he wrote in the preface to the English edition of his major work that

> the class system absorbed and continues to absorb archaic social structures in the sphere of racial relations, structures which were necessary in the old social world of slave society. Contrary to what might be presumed, the market economy, free labour, and institutional modernisation did not eliminate these structures; consequently the whole range of adverse stereotypes regarding the slave or the freed slave continues in force, with explicit reference to the Negro . . . racial accommodation in the form of passive capitulation by the Negro or acceptance on his part of extreme social, economic, and educational inequality are signs of the persistence of predemocratic and undemocratic racial stratification, *whatever may be the patterns of decorum, tolerance, or affection involved in social contact between persons or groups of persons belonging to different racial categories.*[19]

Yet there is clearly a qualitative difference from the United States case, where the Brazilian social intermixture between the races, or at least between mulattoes and whites, would until recently have been unthinkable. Not only this, but the black and the mulatto are portrayed as admirable figures in the mainstream of Brazilian literature, which is certainly not the case in North America. These are the differences which have interested American historians like Carl Degler.[20] At the simplest level, of course, the demographic make-up of each society has had an impact: there are more men and women of African descent in Brazil than in the United States. Degler, however, makes two further points. The first is that North American slavery and racial categorisations are unique in classifying every human with *any* African blood as 'black'. Although this terminology has latterly been accepted and glorified by American militants, only a small proportion of Afro-Americans in the United States are black. More subtly, *Neither White nor Black* points to the special treatment Brazilian society has given the mulatto, who takes a place of equality or near-equality to the white since he is given credit for his Portuguese blood rather than being debited for his African

---

[19] Fernandes, *Negro in Brazilian Society*, pp. [x, xii–xiii].
[20] Degler, *Neither Black nor White*, pp. 25–92, 207–64.

blood. Although Degler never explains how this change of emphasis came about, it is presumably rooted in the very traditions of contact with dark races and long periods of paternalism of which Freyre writes so lyrically – as well as being linked with Brazil's much higher concentrations of Afro-Brazilian population. Though this does not mean that there is anything liberal in the attitudes of mulattoes *or* whites to men and women of pure African descent, whose status remains frozen at the bottom of the scale, it does go far towards explaining the relatively benign aftermath of Brazilian slavery. In another sense, it makes that slavery itself all the more horrifyingly harsh. At least in boom conditions, Brazilian slaveholders were prepared to treat mulatto men and women against whom they had relatively little prejudice in exactly the same way as their black slaves. Racial prejudice clearly formed much of the underpinning of slavery as a whole, but if Degler is right, slavery could also exist at its most brutal for those against whom such prejudice was minimal. This again suggests that the central pressures driving Brazilian and other masters to their worst excesses were economic. In either case, there is little left of Freyre's picture of the Brazilian plantation, or of the arguments that church and state in Portuguese America prevented the conditions which Protestant capitalists allowed in the United States.

In nineteenth-century Cuba, slavery also responded to world demands for the sugar which its virgin soils could produce more cheaply than any other part of the world. Slavery had not been centrally important in the early history of the island. Beef and hides had been its main staples up to the eighteenth century. What stimulated Cuba's first extensive sugar cultivation was the gap left in the world market by the collapse of production in Saint-Domingue after Toussaint l'Ouverture's revolution and the expulsion of the French. In the early nineteenth century Cuba became the new frontier of Caribbean sugar cultivation. Get-rich-quick planters flooded the island, sometimes bringing their slaves with them, but more often relying on buying *bozal* Negroes from the Portuguese and American slave-ships which began to converge on Havana. Indeed many of the planters who opened Cuba to sugar were French refugees from Saint-Domingue. Sugar cane had been planted as early as 1571, but none was exported until 1576. Even in the 1760s production was negligible. In 1800

Cuba produced 28,419 tons of sugar; in 1820, 43,119 tons; in 1870, 726,000 tons.[21] Cuba's frightful climate had little attraction except its opportunities for making money fast. Like the Brazilian coffee and mining areas, or the new settlements of the Cotton Belt in the American south-west, it came to have all the characteristics of a frontier area – with plenty of land, plenty of capital and plenty of profits for those who were prepared to take the risk that the sugar bubble would burst and leave them penniless. The slave population increased dramatically, for it had been small until the disaster of Saint-Domingue. At the same time, a stimulus to Cuban commerce, whether in tobacco, coffee, sugar or hides, was given by the Spanish change towards a free-trade policy which would benefit the colony in the last quarter of the eighteenth century. By the time of the royal census of 1792 there were 44,333 slaves – to 31,847 free blacks and 96,440 whites. After this came the deluge. The geographer Alexander von Humboldt, working from customs-house returns, calculated that 225,574 slaves were imported to Havana alone in the three decades from 1790 to 1820 – more than twice the number imported in the whole of the island's history prior to 1790.[22] After this the Cuban trade spurted upwards even more. Curtin's estimates of its volume in the nineteenth century suggest that a total of 550,000 slaves were landed in Cuba from 1811 to 1870. Of these, 79,900 were imported from 1811 to 1820, 112,500 from 1821–1830, 126,100 from 1831 to 1840. The figure dropped to 47,600 for the 1840s, but soared back to 123,300 from 1851 to 1860 under the impetus of British removal of the sugar duties. Even in the 1860s, 61,500 slaves arrived in Cuba. Sugar production rose in proportion. In 1830, exports from Havana were 7,868,881 arrobas or 70,258 tons. By 1850, however, the island was producing 223,145 tons, and by 1860, 447,000 tons. In 1870 it reached the startling annual output of 726,000 tons. In 1855, 83.78 per cent of the island's exports were made up of sugar or sugar products.[23] With importations

[21] Deerr, *History of Sugar*, 1 126–31.

[22] A. von Humboldt, *The Island of Cuba*, trans. J. S. Thrasher (New York, 1856) pp. 218–19, cited in A. F. Corwin, *Spain and the Abolition of Slavery in Cuba, 1817–1886* (Austin, Tex., 1967) pp. 16–17.

[23] Curtin, *Atlantic Slave Trade*, pp. 36–40, 234. Curtin's data are taken from various British government estimates, and H. S. Aimes, *A History of Slavery in Cuba, 1511–1868* (New York, 1907) p. 269, though he rejects Aimes's estimates for the period after 1820. Figures on sugar output are

proceeding as fast as this, Cuban masters obviously faced the same difficulties of discipline as those in Brazil. To the pressures towards overwork created by the state of the sugar market, the chronic nightmare of slave revolt added a new severity of discipline.

Cuba yet has to find a Gilberto Freyre to suggest that its nineteenth-century slavery was at any time idyllic. The closest approach is the near-poetic comparison of sugar and tobacco cultivation by the politician Fernando Ortiz, who hardly touches on the use of slavery in Cuban agriculture at all.[24] The implication of Tannenbaum's work was that, with the rest of Spanish America, the island, even in boom conditions, shared in a tradition of clerical interference and royal paternalism which protected the basic rights of the slave and prevented his undue physical abuse by his master. The net result was the recognition of the slave's 'moral personality', a recognition which facilitated his taking his place in free society after emancipation. More recently Herbert Klein has built on these assumptions with specific reference to the comparison between Catholic Cuba and Protestant Virginia. His study tries to show that even in the nineteenth century the Catholic church paid more attention to the religious needs of the slaves than the Anglican, and that Spanish law curbed excessive slave punishments, protected their marriage, gave them redress in the courts against undue abuse and generally recognised them as legal personalities in a manner quite foreign to the case of Virginia.[25] The weakness in this theory is that those cases of slaves who managed to gain legal protection against their masters do not imply that all or even a majority did so. In general, Klein accepts that because statute law stated an intention of circumscribing the power of the master over the slave, this law was uniformly enforced through the colonial courts.

In the Caribbean itself, slavery was moulded by stronger forces than the letter of the law. By the nineteenth century, Cuba was considered the 'Pearl of the Antilles' because it produced a great

taken from Ramiro Guerra y Sánchez, *Azúcar y población en las Antillas,* rev. ed. (Havana, 1970) pp. 225–8, and F. W. Knight, *Slave Society in Cuba during the Nineteenth Century* (Madison, Wis., 1970) p. 45 n.

[24] F. D. Ortiz, *Cuban Counterpoint: Tobacco and Sugar,* trans. H. de Onís (1947; reprinted New York, 1970).

[25] H. S. Klein, *Slavery in the Americas: A Comparative Study of Virginia and Cuba* (Chicago, 1967) pp. 40–192.

deal of money for Spain. It would have been absurd for the authorities in Madrid to allow a squeamish enforcement of their own law to interfere with the process by which slaves were whipped into producing sugar and revenue. In fact it is hard to see what royal civil servants could do to modify the conduct of masters on their own plantations. This would have involved attacking men who were habitually their closest friends. Even if they *had* succeeded in giving a basic protection to slave marriage, or protecting the slave from being murdered or maimed by his owner, no Spanish jurist ever seriously thought of dealing with the problem of overwork. It was this which had the greatest tendency to brutalise the slaves, weaken their health and lead to their premature death, especially in sugar production, where harvest time meant working around the clock. Nineteenth-century visitors to Cuban plantations commented almost to a man on the shattering labour of feeding the *ingenios* at cropping time. If every beneficent law on the Spanish statute books had been fully operative – and they were not – they would have left this principal danger untouched. It was as a result of back-breaking work and miserable standards of subsistence that the Cuban slave population failed to maintain itself, not because of individual atrocities by planters, or because of the courts' recognition or otherwise of the slave's personality. Even the institution of *coartación*, by which custom entitled slaves to buy their own freedom at a price agreed with the master, left these hardships largely unaffected. Though *coartación* certainly held out hopes for slaves, removed the fear of fluctuations in the price at which they might expect to buy their freedom, and produced a much higher manumission rate than in most American slave societies, it did not affect the treatment of those still in bondage, or the prospects of those for whom accumulation was impossible.[25a] As for the church, its powers of persuasion were largely moral. Its position that slavery was acceptable, but that abuse of the slave and neglect of his spiritual needs was not, was essentially similar to that of many Protestant clergymen in the United States; and if any kind of moral points system is to be used to compare Catholic and Protestant clergy, it should be remembered how many of the British and American abolitionists were ministers.

[25a] H. S. Aimes, '*Coartación*: A Spanish Institution for the Advancement of Slaves into Freedmen', *Yale Review*, XVII (1909) 412–31.

In the nineteenth century, Cuban sugar production was as much a part of the world economy as American cotton-growing. It was 'capitalistic' in its needs, and it was geared in exactly the same way to making the maximum profit as fast as possible. It seems naïve to assume that when Cuban priests denounced ill-treatment of slaves, they had much effect on the hard-bitten planter frontiersmen whose primary goal was to extract a fortune from the Cuban wilderness, regardless of the suffering caused to anyone else, not even to themselves, but least of all to their slaves. As the geographer von Humboldt remarked: 'The civilisation of a nation seldom extends to a great number of individuals; and does not reach those, who in the plantations are in immediate contact with blacks'. Added to this problem of enforcement of the law, the 1842 code which responded to the needs of the sugar boom was as savage, apart from the recognition of *coartación*, as anything produced in the United States.[26]

Klein, then, has not succeeded in his attempt to delineate a slave society relatively much more beneficent than those of the United States. Such avenues as Spanish law and religion left open for the development of the personality of the slave and freedman in Cuba, though they were doubtless significant in other areas of the economy and for city bondsmen, did little to help the men and women in thrall to the sugar industry. The great value of his study is the extent to which it shows the diversity of Cuban slavery. It contains a mass of information on the forced labour of Indians and on the free black and mulatto population, though it exaggerates the extent to which the latter were absent from Virginia. Again, Klein stresses the extent to which the Cuban economy remained diversified even at the peak of the sugar boom. Only approximately a quarter of the slave population – a little under 70,000 – worked on sugar plantations, though another eighth were involved in the similarly expansive tobacco industry, and yet others in coffee-growing. Nevertheless, this was the element which gives the lie to the whole theory of the cultural moulding of slavery. In boom conditions, as the more recent work

[26] A. von Humboldt, *Personal Narrative of Travels to the Equinoctial Regions of America, during the Years 1799–1804*, 3 vols (London, 1853) III 282–3. See also Knight, *Slave Society in Cuba*, pp. 121–36; G. M. Hall, *Social Control in Slave Plantation Societies: A Comparison of St Domingue and Cuba* (Baltimore, 1971) pp. 43–51, 102–12.

of Franklin Knight shows, they were savagely treated, and it was they whom the great rise in the Cuban slave trade was intended to replace after they were worn out.[27] In the expansive phase of the Cuban sugar industry, the position and treatment of its slaves were not different from those of boom periods of the development of other parts of the Americas, even in a strictly legal sense, as the terms of the 1842 slave code suggest. It is a mistake to reject the testimony of abolitionists who commented on Cuban conditions, on the assumption that they were writing propaganda and therefore cannot be trusted. As a general rule of thumb, abolitionist reporters did not bother to record the instances of kindness they saw but did not want to see in the slave system. But however lurid their language became, they seldom fabricated instances of cruelty and general poor treatment. In the Cuban case they did not have to. Bitter descriptions of slave conditions were given by visiting English abolitionists like R. R. Madden, or David Turnbull, who was British Consul in Havana over a period of years. Many travellers fell into the trap of generalising from the condition of slaves they saw in the very city environment where Spanish law and Catholic religion were most likely to protect them. This was not so of Madden, whose conclusion was that no other part of the Americas had slave conditions 'so desperately wretched' as those he saw on the plantations of inland Cuba.[28] The prolific writings of the Spanish and Cuban abolitionists, who were also propagandists, but had reached their conclusions from much longer observation of Cuban life, have the same telling information about the appalling living conditions, chronic overwork, physical abuse and mortality of the Cuban slaves. At the same time, they pointed indignantly at the failure of the law or the church to protect them.[29] In the diversified areas of Cuban agriculture, on the other hand, slavery sometimes attained a relaxed paternalism which differentiated it from the capitalistic plantation slavery of North America, and encouraged large-scale manumission long before emancipation; but exactly the same

[27] Klein, *Slavery in the Americas*, pp. 128–64, 194–253. Cf. Knight, *Slave Society in Cuba*, pp. 59–120.

[28] D. Turnbull, *Travels in the West: Cuba, with Notices of Porto Rico and the Slave Trade* (London, 1840) p. 48; R. R. Madden, *The Island of Cuba* (London, 1849).

[29] Corwin, *Spain and the Abolition of Slavery in Cuba*, pp. 165–6.

happened in Virginia in the late eighteenth century, and in any case this improvement in slave conditions in older areas of the Cuban economy did not affect the iron discipline of the opening sugar plantations which they adjoined. On these the lot of the slave was a short and hopeless life of unending hardship, with little protection from the whim of his master or Europe's inexorable demands for sugar, at law or anywhere else.

This picture, not essentially different from that of the more profitable sectors of the slave economy of Brazil or the United States, has also been made clearer by modern research. A recent American study concludes:

> . . . comparative studies [of slavery] should be concerned less with concurrent time spans and metropolitan institutional differences than with equivalent stages of economic and social growth . . . sugar and slavery have had a familiar historical association from Cyprus in the middle of the fifteenth century to Cuba in the middle of the nineteenth century.[30]

The life of the Cuban slaves can be seen not only as being typical for the labour force during the sugar revolution which came to Brazil, Louisiana and most of the West Indies, but of the point of economic development where production was rapidly being put under way for staples which could be produced by unskilled gang labour and for which world demand was feverish. On the large Cuban plantations, working hours were endless, punishments vicious. Diet and medical care were frills on the planter's investment which he frequently skimped. The plantation was a closed industrial unit in which the possibility of outside interference in the relations between master and slave was negligible. Knight's detailed study of Cuban slavery in the nineteenth century makes this abundantly clear. It also shows, as does Klein, that after the 1860s the strength of the vested interest in slavery weakened owing to the dislocation of the Ten Years War from 1868 to 1878, competition from beet sugar, increased use of machinery and a gradual diversification of agriculture, even in the old-fashioned Eastern Department. It became less attractive to have a totally slave labour force, even on the largest holdings.[31] It was this change which eventually made emancipation possible,

[30] Knight, *Slave Society in Cuba*, p. 194.
[31] Ibid., pp. 154–78; Klein, *Slavery in the Americas*, pp. 256–8.

and even then the transition to a free society was a stormy one. In its heyday, however, in the 1830s, 1840s and 1850s, the Cuban slave interest was unchallengeable. As in Brazil, the irony was that at the very time that slaves were being emancipated in other parts of the Caribbean, perhaps even partly because of this, Cuban slavery was becoming more unshakeable than ever before.

The routine of the Cuban sugar plantation was very similar to that of plantations of the sugar frontier at any other time in the history of cane cultivation. The sugar revolution put a group of *nouveaux riches* planters in the place of the old Cuban and Spanish-born ruling class, who might conceivably have been more paternalistic in their attitude to dependants. The physical structure, agricultural methods and day-to-day tasks on the plantations were similar to those on a Jamaican plantation like Worthy Park. A major difference, however, was that in the last decades of Cuban slavery masters increasingly used steam engines instead of animal or water power to drive their machinery. The engines, incidentally, were usually built in abolitionist Scotland or England, and maintained by Scots or American engineers. As the planters struggled to maximise production, the result for the field slaves at harvest time was hell. Work went on around the clock, since crushing machinery did not become exhausted and, unlike livestock, had no need to rest. Those who survived the shattering work of cutting and clearing cane, the Otaheite variety of which could grow 15 feet high in the fertile Cuban soils, had every chance of being maimed during the hot and exhausting night hours they spent feeding the crushers and fuelling and filling the boilers at the plantation *ingenio*. It is also a mistake to see the harvest period as being short. On large plantations, where the maturing of different sections of the crop was staggered, the machinery of the *ingenio* could keep churning on from February to May. At the planting time of the year, in the rainy season from July to October, the field slaves were kept busy hoeing for new canes, and thereafter weeding and manuring saplings and the ratoons of second- and third-year canes. Above all, any spare time was used for clearing jungle for new cultivation. There was no time of the year when working hours were short. The various Catholic holidays were seldom observed if they interfered with the labour needs of the plantation. The working life of slaves was short, death from accident and above all overwork common.

Since the overwhelming need was for muscle, the proportion of females to males was low, and the possibility of even a rudimentary family life non-existent. In Cuba's miserable climate, with its hot, wet summers, slaves weakened by bad diet and living in wretchedly unhygienic quarters were prey to all manner of tropical diseases. The net result was that Cuba's slave population, unlike that of the United States, fell drastically in the nineteenth century. Annual loss has been estimated at 4 per cent, though other guesses are higher.[33]

Indeed it was partly because of this failure of the slaves to keep up their own numbers, let alone reproduce, that the demand of Cuban planters for *bozal* blacks, with all the dangers to security they presented, was so insistent. In fact the great problem for scholars who extol the humanity of Latin American slavery is that they do not explain why it was nineteenth-century Cubans and Brazilians, not the Protestants of the United States, who looked after their slaves so badly that all natural increase stopped. If cultural factors did dictate slave conditions at all, it seems to have been Protestant and not Catholic masters who were mellowed by them. The slaves of nineteenth-century Catholic Cuba became ciphers in an economic struggle to squeeze the highest possible return from investments in the sugar industry. Paternalism may have played some part in the diversified areas of Cuban agriculture, on small plantations and, above all, in the complex urban slave structure. Yet the overwhelming majority of slaves worked in country areas: in 1846, it has been estimated, 207,583 out of 252,534.[34] Paternalism had no place in the rat-race of the large-scale producers and their backers to get their share of the prices that Europe and the United States would pay for the island's sugar.

Though cotton is the key to nineteenth-century American slavery, the Louisiana sugar industry went through a similar phase to Cuba. The collapse of British and French West Indian sugar-growing owing to soil exhaustion and emancipation gave it the chance it needed to supply the United States domestic market.

[33] Knight, *Slave Society in Cuba*, pp. 69–75, 82.
[34] C. A. Page, 'Development of Organized Labour in Cuba', unpublished Ph.D. dissertation (University of California at Los Angeles, 1952), cited in P. Foner, *A History of Cuba and its Relations with the United States*, 2 vols (New York, 1962) 1 189.

It had 36,000 slaves in 1830, and 244,895 twenty years later. In the same period its production of sugar leapt from 27,288 tons to 255,441 tons in 1853.[35] For the slaves, this meant the same kind of transition from paternalism to industrial-minded brutality which they had seen in Cuba. From being a state with relatively humane slave relations, except in the murderous conditions of the rice plantations, Louisiana gained a reputation which made it the most terrifying of all the various hells of the deep South to which blacks from the older slave economies of the tidewater states could be sold. There are few slave narratives from Lousiana, for the simple reason that so few slaves managed to escape from there to the North. One example, however, is the story of Solomon Northup, who was actually a free black from New York, but who was kidnapped and sold south to the Gulf. Unfortunately, although he had some experiences in being hired out to sugar-planters at the peak cane-cutting time of the year, and although his narrative is one of the most important sources of its kind, Northup was employed principally in the cotton and lumber industries.[36] Yet the hardship of the sugar slaves during the long weeks of harvest time was probably worse than in any other sector of the North American slave system, with slaves at harvest time habitually working sixteen or eighteen hours a day.[37] Perhaps the main reason why the American slave population increased during the nineteenth century, with only insignificant importations, was that so small a proportion of it was involved in cane cultivation.

The principal staple of nineteenth-century American slavery was not of course sugar but cotton. If the only vested interest in slavery in the United States had been the relatively small Louisiana sugar industry, which was only a fraction of that of Cuba, there is little doubt that slavery would have been abolished much sooner than it was, without the cataclysm of the Civil War. There are many indications that the hold of slavery, and its perceived economic importance, were weakening in the confederation and early national periods. The abolitionist sentiment which

[35] Deerr, *History of Sugar*, I 248.

[36] S. Northup, *Twelve Years a Slave*, ed. S. Eakin and J. Logsdon (Baton Rouge, La., 1968).

[27] Cf. F. L. Olmsted, *The Cotton Kingdom*, ed. A. M. Schlesinger (New York, 1953) pp. 249–57.

accompanied a decline in the economic viability of slavery in the Northern colonies was not entirely without effect in the South. Abolitionist societies were founded in the border states of Delaware and Maryland, and correspondence opened with men throughout the Southern colonies who were sympathetic to the ending of slavery. The serious doubts of a Virginian like Thomas Jefferson, though they were prompted more by the effects of slavery on whites than on blacks, were symptomatic of an intellectual concern over slavery which had its effects, however rudimentary, throughout the new nation.[38] Much more significant was the rise in the number of voluntary manumissions by masters who were coming to have serious doubts about slavery's being acceptable. Sometimes these stemmed from new moral scruples. Sometimes, perhaps more often, changing economic conditions made it seem that persevering with the upkeep of slaves was to throw good money after bad into a hopeless investment. Relative to the size of a slave population, most slaves were freed in this way in Maryland and Delaware, but they also made major inroads into the slave population in Virginia and North Carolina. It was upon manumissions and self-purchases allowed during the late eighteenth and early nineteenth centuries that the large and sometimes prosperous free communities of these two states were built.[39] These were tidewater states whose exhausted tobacco soils had left them without a major export staple and with large numbers of surplus slaves whose discipline was lax, appetites great and output slight. Only a shift to diversified agriculture and new prospects for selling spare slaves to states where they were needed could revive enthusiasm for slavery in these conditions.[40] As it was, the early part of the century saw the publication of a substantial number of abolitionist pamphlets written by Southerners, and in Virginia the growth of powerful political support for

[38] *Notes on the State of Virginia, Query* XVIII. On Jefferson's attitudes to slavery, see W. W. Freehling, 'The Founding Fathers and Slavery', *American Historical Review*, LXXVII (1972) 81–93; D. B. Davis, *Was Thomas Jefferson an Authentic Enemy of Slavery?* (Oxford, 1970). Cf. R. McColley, *Slavery and Jeffersonian Virginia* (Urbana, Ill., 1964) pp. 114–62.

[39] L. P. Jackson, *Free Negro Labour and Property Holding in Virginia, 1830–1860* (1942; reprinted New York, 1969); J. H. Franklin, *The Free Negro in North Carolina, 1790–1860* (Chapel Hill, N.C., 1943).

[40] A. O. Craven, *Soil Exhaustion as a Factor in the Agricultural History of Virginia and Maryland, 1606–1860* (Urbana, Ill., 1926) pp. 72–161.

emancipation. This culminated in the famous legislative debates of 1830, in which proposals for gradual abolition were narrowly defeated.

The fact that this near-successful attempt to rid Virginia of slavery was never renewed has been put down to various causes. Most commonly it is argued that Virginia turned back to its support for slavery either out of horror at the extremist statements of immediate abolition which were made in the North, through the *Liberator*, after 1830. Alternatively, it is often alleged that sheer terror at the great insurrection of Nat Turner in the following year brought a hardening of the slave system, to prevent further insurrections. A highly sophisticated study has recently suggested, too, that Virginian slavery lost flexibility in the late eighteenth century. The number of dangerous acculturated slaves, capable of resisting the system successfully, was now large enough for them to be a real threat to security. This transition was dramatically signalised by the attempt of an élite group of slaves to overturn Virginia society in Gabriel's insurrection of 1800.[41] Actually, Virginian anti-slavery would have reached its highwater mark by 1830, and the state later turned back to an acceptance of slavery, even if no one had ever heard of Gabriel, Garrison or Turner. Anti-slavery ideology had no chance of making peaceful headway among those who still had vested interests in slavery. By 1830 these interests had begun to gain strength owing to developments much further south. By that time, slavery had been given a new lease of life by the beginning of a vast cotton boom which opened great tracts of land to slave agriculture. It stimulated a demand for products which only Virginia and the other older tidewater states were able to supply. In this way the system of slavery was strengthened not only in the new cotton lands themselves, but on old soil too exhausted to cultivate tropical produce by the old wasteful methods. With the help of more scientific agricultural practices, advocated by pioneer agronomists like Edmund Ruffin, Virginia and her neighbours were not only able to sell their surplus slaves south, but to use the remaining ones to grow what food supplies the new cotton areas did not produce for themselves.[42]

[41] G. W. Mullin, *Flight and Rebellion: Slave Resistance in Eighteenth Century Virginia* (New York, 1972).

[42] A. O. Craven, *Edmund Ruffin, Southerner* (Baton Rouge, La., 1966)

What made this great revolution in Southern history possible was the introduction of the cotton gin. Prior to Eli Whitney's invention, cotton production in North America had been very much a minor affair, restricted to a narrow belt of coastal estates and the Sea Islands of South Carolina. The reason for this limitation was that in the eighteenth century no machinery was available to card and remove the seed from varieties of 'short staple' cotton, in which fibres were short, brittle and easily broken. Since these varieties were the only ones which would grow inland, only the coastal areas which could raise 'long staple' cotton could provide the textile industry with a commercially viable strain. Output naturally remained small. Manufacturers could not weave cloths in quantities economical enough to compete seriously with wool or with lighter fabrics from the Far East. Whitney, who had been born in Massachusetts and was a member of the Yale class of 1792, brought out the first model of his gin the year after his graduation, while living on a Savannah plantation owned by the Rhode Island revolutionary hero Nathaniel Greene. It was symbolic that Savannah was the site of this invention, for it speeded intensive cultivation of short-staple cotton right across the vast belt of land stretching from the South Carolina coast, through Georgia, to Alabama, Mississippi, Louisiana, Texas and Arkansas. In 1791 the United States produced 0·4 per cent of world cotton – 2 million lb. out of 469 million. By 1860 it was growing 1,650 million out of a world output of 2,500 million lb., or 66 per cent of the total. For the same years, British exports of manufactured cotton were 28,706,675 lb. and 1,390,939,000 lb. The expansion also had an effect on American industry. Total consumption of raw cotton by United States manufactories rose from 146 million lb. to 297 million lb. in the ten years between 1840 and 1849.[43] The volume of cotton goods exported by the United States – and this was a fraction of output – moved up

pp. 49–72; L. C. Gray, *History of Agriculture in the Southern United States to 1860*, 2 vols (Washington, 1933) II 908–36.

[43] These figures are taken from the tables in S. Bruchey (ed.), *Cotton and the Growth of the American Economy, 1790–1860* (New York, 1967) pp. 7–40, a useful anthology of primary sources. See also Gray, *History of Agriculture in the Southern United States*, II 691–720, 888–907. On Whitney, see C. M. Green, *Eli Whitney and the Birth of American Technology* (Boston, 1956).

from $1 million in 1830 to $11 million thirty years later.[44] Southern yields could hardly expand fast enough to meet the demands of the mills in Manchester and Massachusetts.

There was only one factor which prevented every inch of Black Belt soil being under cotton at the same time. This was the exhaustion produced by reckless cultivation aimed at quick profits, to the exclusion of preserving the land's fertility. Indeed it was this very soil exhaustion which drove the cotton frontier forward so quickly. Doubtless there were many estates, even in the Black Belt, where the evangelical sense of responsibility was great enough for planters to make every endeavour to treat their 'people' with a proper sense of Christian stewardship. But the world demand for cotton made it inevitable that most planters should farm and drive their slaves as if there was to be no to-morrow for either of them, with much the same kind of boom mentality which was appearing in Cuban and Brazilian agriculture during the same period. The boom never completely broke, though it collapsed temporarily during minor slumps and in areas where the soil finally failed. There was no serious competitor for American cotton until Egypt and India entered the world market on a major scale after the Civil War. As far as the slaves were concerned, this made it unlikely that they would ever benefit from the kind of paternalism which had emerged in tidewater plantations after the decline of the tobacco industry, or Brazilian sugar culture in its lean years. It is clear that the best-run plantations showed a concern for the family, physical, and religious welfare of slaves, but owners who allowed this to encroach on the slaves' work-load were either flirting with economic disaster or refusing to interfere with the working arrangements made by their overseers. Even when soil became too thin to make constant pressing for higher returns profitable they always faced the danger of being sold south to liquidate some of the planter's original investment, or simply having the master gather his whole operation and move it lock, stock and barrel to the rich, unexploited soils of the frontier. At the same time, however, the dangers of a rapidly moving frontier were counterbalanced by the regard for slave life produced by the absence of a foreign slave trade able to provide manpower to replace blacks who were worked to the

[44] *Historical Statistics of the United States,* p. 547.

point of becoming valueless. However many slaves could be bred
and sold from the Upper South to the cotton frontier, they were
never enough to allow total profligacy of slave life. The surmises
of militant black historians to the contrary, the smuggled trade
from Africa and the Caribbean after 1808 was never more than
a trickle – if only because its difficulties and risks would have
pushed the price of such slaves up to an unacceptable level.
Curtin's estimate is a total of only 50,000, and even this may be
on the high side.[45] It is reasonable to see the absence of ready
outside sources of labour as something of a restraining factor on
masters and managers, at one level in their physical brutality, but
more important in their work demands and standards of accommodation and maintenance. North American blacks, alone among
the slave populations of the New World, managed to maintain
their numbers even in this brutal period of expansion. The total
slave population of the United States increased from 1,191,362
in 1810 to almost 4 million in 1860 – 1,982,625 male and
1,971,135 female.[46] This healthy balance between the sexes, indeed, must be one of the main reasons for the increase in population over the period. The family life of blacks in the United
States, also, was always more stable than in other American slave
societies, perhaps because of the Protestant stress on the family
as the basic unit of civilised society. Yet it is likely that the increase
was caused principally by a rapid birth rate in the older breeding
states. There are no indications that blacks were flourishing on
the cotton frontier, where conditions were not different, except
in so far as the needs of cotton cultivation made them so, from
those in any other boom period of American slave agriculture.
Again such law as protected the slave had little power to interfere
with plantation management, although in the Black Belt as in
Latin America it is possible to find isolated cases of excessively
brutal masters who were brought to the courts, just as it is possible to find many masters who were uncharacteristically humane.
The gang-labour demands of the plantation produced a disproportion between men and women, though not so striking
a one as in, say, Cuba. Again, specially brutal masters committed individual acts of cruelty. But they were much less of a
danger than the crushing physical hardship of a labour system

[45] Curtin, *Atlantic Slave Trade*, p. 234.
[46] *Historical Statistics of the United States*, p. 9.

which was tied not only to the whims of the planter or the overseer, but to the impersonal needs of the world economy.

The opening of the Cotton Belt was nothing less than a complete revolution in Southern history. Its significance has not
always been understood, and it is because of this that so many
attempts to generalise about the history of slavery in the United
States are invalid. There is a whole school of twentieth-century
apologists for slavery, just as there was a whole school of pro-
slavery pamphleteers in the last century. They present what
appears on the surface to be sound evidence that slaves in the
South were treated with responsibility by masters who were
basically benevolent. At the very least, so the argument runs, the
slaves were in a better situation than many of the proletariat in
the nineteenth century's growing industrial cities. This standpoint is taken in a great body of pro-slavery pamphlet literature,
and it was fundamental to the arguments of most of the South's
greatest propagandists and statesmen, particularly John C.
Calhoun and George Fitzhugh of South Carolina.[47] Abolitionists,
who fundamentally misunderstood the structure of the Southern
economy, were only able to counter this kind of argument by
pointing to individual Southern atrocities which they claimed
could not have occurred in an industrial society. Alternatively,
they insisted, with much more success, that good or bad treatment
was a slavocratic red herring. The real damage done by slavery
could not be measured in the slave's physical hardship, but only
in the spiritual cost of removing the God-given free will which
was the basis of the nature of all men, black or white, as rational
and perfectible beings.[48] What they did not do was expose the
fallacy of over-generalisation about Southern slavery, for the
logic of their own position that all slavery was equally bad prevented them from attacking the positive good assumption that all
slavery was equally benevolent. The working planter was only
too well aware that there were many slaveries and many Souths,

[47] R. Hofstadter, 'John C. Calhoun: The Marx of the Master Class', in
The American Political Tradition and the Men who Made it (London,
1962) pp. 67–91; E. D. Genovese, *The World the Slaveholders Made* (New
York, 1969) pp. 118–244; G. Fitzhugh, *Cannibals All! or, Slaves without
Masters*, ed. C. Vann Woodward (Cambridge, Mass., 1960); W. S. Jenkins,
Pro-Slavery Thought in the Old South (Chapel Hill, N.C., 1935).

[48] Samples of the abolitionist argument are collected in W. H. Pease
and J. H. Pease (eds), *The Anti-Slavery Argument* (New York, 1965).

or at least if he was not he was unlikely to survive very long in the market-place. Occasional sophisticated commentators shared this awareness.[49] In the world of polemics, however, slavery was presented, whether in defence or attack, as a monolithic system with characteristics common to its working throughout the South.

A number of the earlier historians of Southern slavery made exactly the same mistake. From their work there has grown a series of myths about the civilisation and benevolence of American planters. Indeed, there is some truth in these myths as long as they are applied to restricted areas of the South; but as general conclusions they are wildly inaccurate. The corollary of planter benevolence, also, was black inferiority. Most of the 'plantation school' of Southern historians worked on the assumption that the Negro was only fitted for a subordinate position in American society, and that the plantation was the ideal vehicle for his civilisation. The most prominent and most sophisticated of this group was Ulrich Bonnell Phillips, who broods over the historiography of slavery in North America in much the same way as Gilberto Freyre, a man of similar views, has dominated debate on Brazil. Yet it is unfair to blame Phillips for work done by men who thought along the same lines as he, but were considerably more naïve. One such was Phillips's predecessor Thomas Nelson Page, who once announced in a Chautauqua reader that he was far from denying

> that the social life of the Old South had its faults. . . . But its virtues far outweighed them; its graces were never equalled. For all its faults, it was, I believe, the purest, sweetest life ever lived. . . . It has passed from the earth, but it has left its. benignant influence behind it to sweeten and sustain its children. The ivory palaces have been destroyed, but myrrh, aloes, and cassia still breathe amid their dismantled ruins.[50]

Much the same tradition has been carried on in more recent works on the eighteenth-century like those of Thomas Jefferson Wertenbaker.[51] But it is unfair to judge Phillips by the distasteful-

[49] e.g. Olmsted, *The Cotton Kingdom*, passim.

[50] T. N. Page, *The Old South: Essays Social and Political* (New York, 1919) pp. 184–5.

[51] T. J. Wertenbaker, *The Old South: The Founding of American Civilization* (New York, 1942). Cf. C. Bridenbaugh, *Myths and Realities: Societies of the Colonial South* (1952; reprinted New York, 1970).

ness of some of his views or the greater weaknesses of many who share them. Phillips is possibly the greatest Americanist of this century, and at least until the last decade certainly the greatest historian of the South. The sheer bulk of his research on plantation management and day-to-day life in the South has never been equalled. His output of writing during a life devoted to history was enormous, and he has added more to our knowledge of the plantation than any other single scholar. Not all the conclusions which he drew from this knowledge are the accurate ones, but this need not disguise the sheer achievement of his research.[52]

No one now takes the assumptions of Phillips and his followers on black inferiority seriously, but some of his other conclusions are also open to doubt. He was only too well aware of the difference in conditions from one part of the South to another, but he did not allow this to prevent him from over-generalising on two scores. First, he deduced that the attitude of planters to slaves was largely benevolent, and that the plantation unit was therefore the most effective vehicle for assimilating them to the norms of American society. Secondly, he deduced that plantation agriculture, even in cotton, was unprofitable, largely owing to soil exhaustion and the incompetence of the slaves as a labour force. The first point is easy enough to refute, for it is as easy to find examples of plantations where slaves were treated badly as to find examples of plantations of the sort he generalised from where their lot was relatively easy. This was the point made in the earliest major attack on the plantation legend that Phillips buttressed, which pointed out that the plantations from which he had taken most of his details were large and well-run ones – the completeness of their records itself suggested this. Moreover, they

[52] For Phillips's writings, see D. Potter, 'A Bibliography of the Printed Works of Ulrich Bonnell Phillips', *Georgia Historical Quarterly*, xviii (1934). His best-known books, the culmination of his writing career, now republished with excellent introductions attempting to rehabilitate him, are *American Negro Slavery* (1918), ed. E. D. Genovese (Baton Rouge, La., 1966); *Life and Labor in the Old South* (1929), ed. C. Vann Woodward (Boston, 1964). See also E. D. Genovese, 'Race and Class in Southern History: An Appraisal of the Work of Ulrich Bonnell Phillips', *Agricultural History*, xli (1967) 345–58, reprinted in Genovese, *In Red and Black: Marxian Explorations in Southern and Afro-American History* (New York, 1971) pp. 276–98; A. Winkler, 'Ulrich Bonnell Phillips: A Reappraisal', *South Atlantic Quarterly*, lxxi (1972) 234–45.

were not in the brutal early stage of opening cotton or sugar cultivation.[53] Many historians have broken lances with Phillips on this issue, but the fact remains that it is not so much his findings as his attempts to generalise from them which are at fault. It is certainly true that there were areas of the South in which hours were shorter and tasks lighter than on the cotton frontier; where the ratio between the sexes was more balanced, diet better, manumissions more frequent and discipline more lax. Phillips is not warping evidence in writing about such plantations, but he is writing about parts of Georgia and South Carolina in the lull after the boom had passed them by, when the frontier of the staple they cultivated, cotton or indigo, had moved on. As neighbourhoods became more fully settled, the alarming imbalance between blacks and whites slackened, more leisurely conditions brought more slaves into domestic service, and the improving standards of decency in a more settled society brought sanctions of public opinion against the kind of glaringly brutal treatment of slaves which would have gone unnoticed on the cotton frontier. This is not to say that slavery was ever an easy condition, or that the slaves were happy with their situation in the way that the plantation idyll suggests they were. But it is of the essence that Phillips, and indeed many of his critics, have underestimated the difference in the slave's life and life-expectancy created by different stages in the economic development of the plantation. It is no reply to Phillips, or to anyone else, to announce that all slavery was equally bad. The slaves who so frequently ran away whenever they heard the slightest rumour that they were to be sold south were only too well aware of this.

On the question of profitability, Phillips's problem was again one of over-generalisation, and again he has been attacked by other historians who have over-generalised equally wildly in the other direction. The idea that slave agriculture was a losing concern which was kept alive only by the difficulty of getting rid of it was seriously attacked in 1958 by two econometric historians who argued that cash return on investment was a meaningless concept. They suggested that total increase in the value of resources, including reproduction of slaves and appreciation of land, should be taken into account. On this level, the return on

[53] R. Hofstadter, 'Ulrich B. Phillips and the Plantation Legend', *Journal of Negro History*, xxix (1944) 109–24.

plantation agriculture was as good as, if not better than, profits on other nineteenth-century activities, even railroading.[54] The debate on this article still continues. Genovese has also defended Phillips on the grounds that the Conrad and Meier study under-estimates the cost of maintenance and medical care of slaves, and above all the depreciation of livestock and equipment by their handling.[55] Certainly the constant examples of planters falling on hard times are persuasive. They seldom complained of hard-ship in newly settled areas, but they constantly faced disaster whenever cotton prices fell owing to over-production or recession in Europe. This was true even of a relatively recently opened state like Mississippi in the late 1830s and 1840s.[56]

Genovese's sophisticated Marxism leads to the much more startling point that it did not matter whether slaveholding was profitable or not. Obviously it was profitable, even in recession conditions, to take new land under cultivation. The high return on newly cleared land had moved the cotton frontier to the Brazos river in Texas by the time of the Civil War. But slavery lost none of its strength even in areas where the conditions of cultivation had changed and the profits had fled. At this point, planters clung to slavery neither from benevolence nor from blind habit, but because ownership of slaves and the ideology which went with it was the basis of their power as a ruling class.[57] To reject it out of expediency or anything else would have destroyed their whole scale of values and the civilisation which they genuinely saw as the richest in the world. It would also, or so they thought, have been to resign their power over the poor whites and Southern yeomen who accepted their political and social leadership. In a world of changing values they genuinely

[54] A. H. Conrad and J. R. Meier, 'The Economics of Slavery in the Ante-Bellum South', *Journal of Political Economy*, LXVI (1958) 95–130, reprinted in Conrad and Meier, *The Economics of Slavery and Other Econometric Studies* (Chicago, 1964).

[55] E. D. Genovese, *The Political Economy of Slavery: Studies in the Economy and Society of the Slave South* (New York, 1964) pp. 275–9. Literature on the profitability problem is surveyed in H. D. Woodman, 'The Profitability of Slavery: A Historical Perennial', *Journal of Southern History*, XXIX 303–25.

[56] C. S. Sydnor, *Slavery in Mississippi* (1933; reprinted Baton Rouge, La., 1966) pp. 181–202.

[57] Genovese, *Political Economy of Slavery*, pp. 13–39; idem, *The World the Slaveholders Made*, pp. 118–244.

felt embattled, genuinely felt that a general crisis threatened the system on which their position as an élite depended. Profitable or no, slavery would not have died out in the foreseeable future. Under violent criticism from the North, it was possible for the South to lurch into the Civil War with complete confidence in its righteousness, irrespective of the cash returns which its peculiar institution was bringing in.

No slave had much of an interest in increasing his master's wealth. Yet all of them were deeply affected by his success or otherwise in making profits. As in Brazil and Cuba, different forms of slave society appeared in different conditions. In all three cases, slavery was never a total system. All, including the United States, had substantial free black populations. The plantation was nowhere universal, and all three had groups of whites or, in the Latin American case, mulatto or mestizo yeomen who either carried on staple production on a small scale, or more frequently farmed mixed subsistence crops. The diversity of Southern society as a whole, and of the black experience in particular, was quite missed by Phillips, who refused to use the written slave narratives which made this clear. It is not true that the slave was emasculated by the absence of any roles he could fill or examples to which he could aspire other than those set by the master. On the one hand, there was the refuge of life in the quarters, with its rich black heritage in religion, in dance and in song, often distinctly tinged with opposition to the master. The veiled hints of the spiritual about the escape from Egypt, the 'poor John' stories glorifying the underdog who always outwits his superiors in strength and power, and the whole egalitarian imagery of black religion all had the same implications.[58] Beyond this, too, however monstrous his life, the plantation slave could always see men and women of his own race doing work different from his own. It is only recently that the size and responsibility of the free black communities in the South has been understood. Large plantations put slave labourers in a wide range of employ-ments, many of which involved high skills, while the non-plantation aspects of the Southern economy used substantial

[58] See L. Jones, *Blues People* (New York, 1963) pp. 1–59; Herskovits, *Myth of the Negro Past;* M. M. Fisher, *Negro Slave Songs in the United States* (Ithaca, N.Y., 1953); L. Hughes and A. Bontemps (eds), *The Book of Negro Folklore* (New York, 1958).

numbers of slave labourers in industrial or commercial occupations.[59] Slave society also had its own internal status system, based on age, religious lore, musical skill or simple personal leadership qualities. There was no need for the slave to develop as a weak imitation of his master, for the complexity of the system presented him with a wide range of men and women from his own race on whom his personality could be modelled.[60] Different plantations had different characteristics, whatever their staple, at different stages of economic development. These also deeply influenced the lot of the slave. They might appear at different points in linear time, or in different areas, but they might also exist side by side. In the United States the newly opened plantations on the advancing cotton frontier were the ones geared most ruthlessly to the frantic cotton production which had the worst effect in brutalisation and physical hardships among the slaves. As the frontier went on its way and agriculture became more settled, there was a relative improvement in conditions, with more care for slave lives which could not be replaced on falling profit margins. In the older tidewater states, in spite of the enormous toll in human suffering levied by selling slaves south, concern for slave welfare was greatest, and discipline and work-loads most lax. As in Latin America, however, it was not slave law or the white man's culture but the progress of an economic system which dictated the situation in which the slave found himself.

One thing which is absolutely clear is that even the mildest form of slavery was less attractive to the slave population than freedom. In spite of slavery's enormous burden in physical suffering, the old abolitionists were perfectly right in saying that the worst aspect of the system was the indignity of losing the

[59] R. S. Starobin, *Industrial Slavery in the Old South* (New York, 1970). A useful account of slave society as a whole is K. M. Stampp, *The Peculiar Institution: Slavery in the Ante-Bellum South* (New York, 1956), although some of my personal conclusions, for instance on the slave's responses to his condition are different from Stampp's. Since the completion of this manuscript, most work on the slave's life in the nineteenth-century South has been replaced by J. Blassingame, *The Slave Community: Plantation Life in the Ante-Bellum South* (New York, 1972). Unlike many other studies, this relies primarily on sources left behind by the slaves themselves.

[60] Cf. Elkins, *Slavery*, pp. 81–139. Papers for and against Elkins's views on the roles available to the black slave are collected in A. J. Lane (ed.), *The Debate over 'Slavery': Stanley Elkins and his Critics* (Urbana, Ill., 1971).

power to make free decisions. Even in areas where slave conditions were apparently at their mildest, the slave was always open
to becoming the victim of his individual master's brutality. But it
was not this so much as the assumption of his soullessness, the
affront to his pride in constantly having his being revolve
around the character of another, which most often provoked the
slave into resistance, covert or otherwise. This is borne out in the
United States at least, by the fact that it was in areas where
the system was mildest and physical coercion least, that is in the
border and tidewater areas, that there occurred the great majority
of North American acts of rebellion.[61] In either case, the process
of resistance went on throughout the slave systems of the
Americas, although this resistance was not often as spectacular
as some romantic writers suggest. It is not true even for the
United States that the slave was so cowed by the agony of the
Middle Passage that his will to resist the demands of his master
was broken.[62] However, too much should not be made of the
number of organised revolts in slave society, either in the Catholic
or Protestant Americas. The fear of revolt was always present for
the masters, to the point of neurosis. Yet the slaves had a perfect
grasp of the art of the possible, and were unlikely to rise as a
group when the chances of success were negligible, and the
penalty of failure inevitable death. Most of the slave 'revolts' in
the nineteenth-century United States, even the famous ones of
Denmark Vesey and Gabriel Prosser, were conspiracies which
were detected before they broke out. Again, there were plantation
risings which arose spontaneously when the slave's ability to
restrain himself from violence finally broke. But the three major
organised rebellions in America were the insurrections of Gabriel
Prosser in Virginia in 1800, Denmark Vesey's revolt in South
Carolina in 1822, and the Nat Turner insurrection which flared
up in Virginia in 1831. More serious, though less well known, are
the New Orleans rising of 1811, and the earlier South Carolina
one of 1739. Given the overwhelming power of the masters,
planned violent revolution was surprisingly seldom considered as
a serious response to the situation.[63]

[61] M. de B. Kilson, 'Towards Freedom: An Analysis of Slave Revolts in
the United States', *Phylon*, xxv (1964) 175–87.

[62] Cf. Elkins, *Slavery*, pp. 81–139.

[63] Cf. H. Aptheker, *American Negro Slave Revolts* (New York, 1943).

In Latin America the situation was somewhat different. Slave revolts there certainly were, notably the Jamaican ones of the eighteenth century and the Bahian town risings of the early nineteenth century, but only the Santo Domingo one was permanently successful. Many were again the kind of unorganised spontaneous outbreaks which occurred on single or adjoining plantations when the slaves were finally pushed beyond the breaking-point. Thriving colonies of escapees managed to maintain their independence in most Latin American countries – the small slave colonies of the Great Dismal Swamp dramatised in Harriet Beecher Stowe's novel *Dred* are the Northern equivalent. However, even the great seventeenth-century Brazilian republic of Palmares, and the other *quilombos* of escaped slaves which organised themselves at other points in Brazilian history, were prepared to be peaceful if left alone. They were concerned more with maintaining their independence than working to overthrow the slave society they had left. The same was true of the *cimmarones* in Cuba and the Maroons in Jamaica, as well as their equivalents in the French possessions.[64] Indeed it would have been surprising if the picture had been any different. Faced with enormously superior armaments and organisation, there was little incentive to fight a revolution just to get killed.

The day-to-day expression of slave resistance, throughout the Americas but particularly in the United States, was less spectacular than open revolt, and at the same time ultimately more

---

On Turner, see idem, *Nat Turner's Slave Rebellion* (New York, 1966). This is the rebellion on which William Styron's *Confessions of Nat Turner* is based; Arna Bontemps's *Black Thunder* is based on Gabriel Prosser's rising. Two useful reprints of conspiracy trials are J. O. Killens (ed.), *The Trial Record of Denmark Vesey* (Boston, 1971); T. J. Davis (ed.), *The New York Conspiracy; or, a History of the Negro Plot* (Boston, 1971). A fine recent survey of slave resistance in Virginia is Mullin, *Flight and Rebellion*.

[64] Degler, *Neither Black nor White*, pp. 47–52; Hall, *Social Control in Slave Plantation Societies*, pp. 52–7; H. O. Patterson, *The Sociology of Slavery: An Analysis of the Origin, Development and Structure of Negro Slave Society in Jamaica* (London, 1967) pp. 266–83. An excellent anthology, not available until this book was complete, is R. Price (ed.), *Maroon Societies, Rebel Slave Communities in the Americas* (New York, 1973).

successful. Apart from personal violence against whites, which was constantly feared by masters in all parts of the Americas, the most spectacular individual protest against the system was escape – sometimes undertaken spontaneously, but often after long and careful planning. In Latin America the result was the creation of fugitive settlements like the Brazilian *quilombos* or the groups of *cimarrones* in Cuba, which were incidentally organised in many cases along the lines of African state structures. In the United States case, though such settlements existed in embryo, the road to escape was northwards, except for a handful of slaves from the deep South who managed to get across the border to Mexico. Annoyance at escapes is a perennial theme in Southern papers, and though the most modern studies present the numbers of slaves who successfully got to the North as a fraction of the slave population, it also demonstrates the extraordinary initiative of the men and women who took the risks of flight – as does the great body of printed narratives left behind by escapees.[65] Other ways of resistance were open to those who shrank from the horrifying risks of escape. Work could be slowed by role-playing along the Sambo lines which made it possible to avert the anger of the master yet step outside his discipline system. At the same time, the master's equipment could be broken, the roots of his crops damaged, his livestock injured, his provisions stolen. Malingering was a constant complaint among masters, and it was behaviour of this sort, really covert aggression, which made slavemasters from the Plate to the Chesapeake, who quite missed the real significance of such behaviour, agree on the incompetence, stupidity and dishonesty of the African race. Suicide, abortion and child murder were more grim aspects of the same response. At times the slaves could also act in a docile manner, and it would be a mistake to miss the bonds of genuine human friendship and trust which occasionally grew up between masters and slaves even amid the horror of the system. These covert protests need not even be seen as genuine reasoned responses to the slave system, in the way which Stampp portrays them, but at least

[65] L. Gara, *The Liberty Line: The Legend of the Underground Railroad* (Lexington, Ky., 1967). The most famous of the narratives is F. Douglass, *Narrative of the Life of ... an American Slave* (Boston, 1845). A useful modern collection, with the lives of Bibb, Brown, and Northup, is G. Osofsky (ed.), *Puttin' on Ole Massa* (New York, 1969). The slave narratives are exhaustively analysed in Blassingame, *The Slave Community*.

there were very many slaves who would take every opportunity of revenging themselves against the master whenever it offered, and the possibility of the façade of obedience breaking down was probably present in every slave in the Americas.[66]

The real measure of the slave's success in bearing up under slavery was his consistent refusal to assimilate to the culture of his master. His sheer *survival* under the system was a more real triumph than physical resistance. His own culture, the area of his life which the slaveholder could not touch, was used as a means of strengthening his personality and enriching his life, and of expressing his hatred of the system in which he was forced to live. The life of the quarters was a source of mystery and often alarm to the masters in North and South America. As much as slavery and colour themselves, it is the common bond between blacks in all parts of the hemisphere. It was also the common horror of the master class. It was only their inability to interfere with black culture which made it possible, at least where slavery was in its expansive phase, for the slave to retain his self-respect and will to live. Slave religion, with its legacy of an African pantheon, created a world completely separate from the formalism of the master's church, whether as an adjunct to the ceremonies of Christianity or a complete series of forms in itself. The practice of magic and medical lore created a hierarchy within the community to which the slave himself could aspire. Story-telling could be used as an analogue for the triumph of cunning slaves, the weak animals, over the masters, the strong ones. Brer Rabbit is Tortoise of Nigerian and Brazilian fable. John, the slave who always outwits his master, is the Uncle João of the Portuguese plantations. The ritual of dance could be incorporated into the adapted form of the master's religion or it could create a separate bonding process of its own, a form of release from the tedium and despair of the plantation. Music, too, survived, and song could be the resting-place for hidden allusions to coming liberation, to hatred of the plantations or to the idiosyncrasies of the whites.[67]

[66] Stampp, *The Peculiar Institution*, pp. 34–85. Cf. G. Fredrickson and C. Lasch, 'Resistance to Slavery', *Civil War History*, XIII (1967) 315–29; E. D. Genovese, 'Rebelliousness and Docility in the Negro Slave: A Critique of the Elkins Thesis', ibid., pp. 293–314; Blassingame, *The Slave Community*, pp. 123–216.

[67] The best introduction to New World African survivals is Bastide, *African Civilizations in the New World*.

The blacks survived. Yet their suffering was great, in spite of the abolitionists' successes and the prevalence of anti-slavery ideas in the nineteenth century. Indeed there were areas where slavery developed structures which were as rigid and as brutal as ever before. As the demands of the new industrial Europe and America for tropical staples rose, and the possibility of making fortunes on new land became more attractive, slavery again entered an expansive phase which spelt disaster for the slave population – which meant endless work, a paring of their standards of subsistence and a general disregard for their lives. The profits which came from their sufferings and the vested interests they built up strengthened the slaveholders in Brazil, Cuba and the United States in a world fundamentally hostile to them. At the same time, the ideological momentum of the abolitionists gathered strength. If W. E. B. DuBois was right in saying that the problem of the twentieth century was the colour line, the problem of the nineteenth, at least in the Americas, would be the liberty line.

9 Radical Abolitionists in the United States, 1830–1861

THE exact motives behind anti-slavery agitation are as difficult to pinpoint in North America as in Britain. The abolitionist impulse, confused and half-conscious as it was, is strikingly similar on the two sides of the Atlantic. Economic distrust of an outmoded agrarian system, evangelical enthusiasm for the oppressed, and 'rationalistic' doubt over the justification for slavery constantly interacted, perhaps strengthened above all by simple pity for the slave. In both countries abolitionist propaganda was brilliant, and abolitionist leadership able and well organised. The methods of the British and American movements were also similar. The pamphlet, the petition and the pulpit were their three main vehicles for agitation. But anti-slavery ideas were passed on at almost every level of the nineteenth-century media, in the newspapers, in the monthly and quarterly reviews, in ballads, broadsheets and poetry, in gift 'annuals' and in the novel. Yet the problems of British and American abolitionists were not exactly the same. The task of the latter was considerably less easy. The vested interest in an aggressive slave system was much greater than anything the declining West India lobby had had to support it. Not only this, but English and Scottish reformers could work with a Parliament which accepted no doubts as to its right of legislating for the West Indians – just as the later Brazilian and Spanish abolitionists, whatever their other difficulties, could at least appeal to an authority competent to deal with slaveholding among its subjects. Only in the United States did they have to work through a federal structure which left real constitutional doubt over government's right to interfere with slavery in the individual states of the South.[1]

[1] H. Temperley, 'The British and American Abolitionists Compared', in M. B. Duberman (ed.), *The Anti-Slavery Vanguard* (Princeton, 1964) pp. 343–61.

Perhaps because of the frustration caused by these difficulties, the history of American anti-slavery is more violent, and also more exciting, than the relatively docile campaign of the British. Ironically, it was often the fear of British interference in the affairs of the republic which drove pro-slavery mobs to attack abolitionist lecturers. For instance, when the American leader William Lloyd Garrison was almost lynched in Boston, in 1835, no one was primarily interested in hurting this obnoxious but apparently harmless newspaper editor. In fact the Boston mob, largely Irish-Americans, gathered in the hope of catching George Thompson, who was then in the country as an abolitionist missionary. It was only when they found that Thompson had escaped that they seized on the project of tarring and feathering Garrison as a sort of consolation.[2] Nevertheless, throughout the history of the American movement there were countless violent confrontations between abolitionists and their opponents. The long series of anti-abolitionist riots indicates the pervasiveness of pro-slavery or at least anti-Negro sentiment throughout the North, particularly in the mid-1830s.[3] Boston had its great riot at the time of Thompson's visit; in New York the premises of the anti-slavery brothers Tappan had been attacked in the previous year; in Philadelphia the abolitionist-controlled Pennsylvania Hall was burned to the ground by pro-slavery rioters in 1838. Violent responses to abolitionism were not confined to Eastern cities or to the mid-1830s. The evangelical leader Theodore Weld came to accept attempts to lynch him as part of the everyday business of converting the small upstate New York townships where he lectured. The worst example of mob action came in 1837 when Elijah P. Lovejoy, a prominent anti-slavery editor,

[2] C. Duncan Rice, 'The Anti-Slavery Mission of George Thompson to the United States', *Journal of American Studies*, II (1968) 13–36.

[3] L. L. Richards, '*Gentlemen of Property and Standing': Anti-Abolition Mobs in Jacksonian America* (New York, 1970) pp. 3–19 and passim; L. A. Ratner, *Powder Keg: Northern Opposition to the Anti-Slavery Movement, 1831–1840* (New York, 1968). On the psychology behind the apparent abolitionist desire to court violence, see S. S. Tomkins, 'The Psychology of Commitment: The Constructive Role of Violence and Suffering for the Individual and for his Society', in Duberman (ed.), *The Anti-Slavery Vanguard*, pp. 270–98; H. L. Wolf, *On Freedom's Altar: The Martyr Complex in the Abolition Movement* (Madison, Wis., 1952); E. Wigham, *The Anti-Slavery Cause in America and its Martyrs* (London, 1863).

was murdered at Alton, Illinois, while trying to defend his presses from a mob determined to push them into the Mississippi river. Violent behaviour was not confined to the pro-slavery camp. Lovejoy had defended his printing apparatus by force, and nothing could be more violent than John Brown's raid on Harpers Ferry, which drew surprisingly little criticism even in pacifist anti-slavery circles. Though the disputed Kansas–Nebraska Territory was overrun with Southern thugs determined to entrench slavery there, they were met by groups of Northern settlers prepared to use their rifles, sent out from the liberal East as 'Beecher's Bibles', to keep the territory free. The Fugitive Slave Law re-enacted in the Compromise of 1850 sanctioned the forced return of escaped slaves to the South. It is often forgotten that the abolitionists used force to hamper the law, as in the rendition of Anthony Burns from Boston, where a U.S. deputy was killed in the riot, and no court could be persuaded to convict his murderers. All this has pushed historians into a characteristically American double standard on the violence of the anti-slavery years – into an assumption that violence was distasteful when used to defend slavery, but excusable when used to attack it. There is much the same ambivalence in the modern formula which, on the campus or on the international scene, defines violence as fascist brutality or revolutionary zeal according to circumstances. At least when faced with its dilemma over slavery, American society, as a whole and not only on the conservative side, responded with violence. 1861 was by no means the first year in which differences over the status of the Negro led to bloodshed. The violent confrontation of the Civil War is less of an aberration than has been supposed; it was a logical outcome of a tradition in which disagreements led not to compromise but to armed conflict.

The violent aspects of American anti-slavery history link with two controversies over the abolitionists. Several historians have argued that the irresponsible extremism of the abolitionists was what produced a nation emotionally polarised on the question of slavery, to an extent which made a violent solution the only one, and led America into the unprecedented disaster of the Civil War.[4]

[4] Among others, D. L. Dumond, *Anti-Slavery Origins of the Civil War* (Ann Arbor, Mich., 1939); A. O. Craven, *The Repressible Conflict, 1830–1861* (Baton Rouge, La., 1939).

A more recent, and highly sophisticated, study further suggests that at least one group of the abolitionists maximised their demands through the simple concentration on slaveholding as a sin, with the intention of dramatising the issue in a way which constitutes a definite radical strategy – aimed not only at eradicating slavery but at the total restructuring of a fundamentally corrupt society. The fact that so many abolitionists used extra-legal methods in the 1850s certainly seems to be a measure of their discontent with the institutional structures of a society which tolerated slaveholding.[5] Some may also have provoked violence deliberately as a way of dramatising the slave's position and the extent to which it was eroding the basic freedoms of the whole American population. Certainly at least one editor thought that this was their intention as early as 1835.[6] William Lloyd Garrison himself, however strong his pacifism, eventually realised not only that the conflict between pro- and anti-slavery forces was proceeding on a continuum which meant that a solution was inevitable, but also that this solution might well be violent. Twenty-five years to the day after the Thompson riot, he wrote to an ally in Philadelphia that

> The conflict between free institutions and slave institutions is seen and acknowledged to be irrepressible – not of men's doing but of God's ordering – and it is deepening in intensity daily . . . all this is a sign that the end is rapidly approaching. Peaceably or by a bloody process, the oppressed will eventually obtain their freedom, and nothing can prevent it. Trusting that it may be achieved without the shedding of blood. . . .[7]

Probably the truth is that a 'radical strategy' did exist in abolitionist circles, but that it only appealed to a very small minority of the Americans convinced that slavery must be ended.

---

[5] A. Kraditor, *Means and Ends in American Abolitionism: Garrison and his Critics on Strategy and Tactics, 1830–1844* (New York, 1969); J. H. Pease and W. H. Pease, 'Confrontation and Abolition in the 1850s', *Journal of American History*, LVIII (1972) 923–37. A major recent contribution to the intellectual history of mid-nineteenth-century abolitionism is L. Perry, *Radical Abolitionism: Anarchy and the Government of God in Anti-Slavery Thought* (Ithaca, N.Y., 1973).

[6] Extract from *Boston Recorder*, n.d., in *Liberator*, 31 Oct 1835.

[7] Garrison to C. M. McKim, 21 Oct 1860, Garrison Papers, Boston Public Library.

Even extra-legal action could be used by men and women convinced that the channels of political communication had broken down, without this meaning that their concern went beyond the slavery issue or that they saw need for any restructuring of society beyond emancipation. As for the old Southernophile accusation that the extremism of the abolitionists caused the Civil War, this too may be true in the limited sense that a series of historical accidents gave the public of the South the mistaken impression not only that all Northerners were abolitionists, which to their shame they were not, but that all Northerners were extremist abolitionists 'of the Garrison stamp', which was even less true. However, since Southern editors insisted on predicating the attitudes of the North as a whole on the columns of Garrison's sensational though little-read *Liberator*, the South understood Northern attitudes as those of the very extremists who *did* have a 'radical strategy'. With such men there could be no compromise, given the cultural rooting of Southern society in slaveholding. At the same time, the South's fears of the North – and indeed the North's fears of the South – were intensified by the haunting images of conspiracies to subvert the entire fabric of society. Abolitionist conspiracy and slave-power conspiracy fantasies alike compounded sensitivity to the threat posed by the other section's culture and political aims. For the South, the result was over-violent reaction to an abolitionism which most of the North in reality found highly distasteful; growing distrust of the South's aggrieved counter-accusations in the North; secession; war.[8]

The reality of Northern opinion was much less of a threat to the South. The great majority of Northerners were in favour of slavery and distrustful of blacks, or at best apathetic to both, until the logic of the controversy pushed them into forming anti-Southern and to some extent anti-slavery (seldom pro-Negro) views. If a date must be chosen for this change, it probably comes soon after the re-enactment of the Fugitive Slave Law in the Compromise of 1850. Until then few Americans were

[8] The Southern ruling class's cultural and societal stake in slavery, even in areas where it was not profitable economically, is explained in E. D. Genovese, *The Political Economy of Slavery: Studies in the Economy and Society of the Slave South* (New York, 1964) pp. 3–39; idem, *The World the Slaveholders Made* (New York, 1969) pp. 118–244. On the crucial problem of conspiracy assumptions, the central essay is D. B. Davis, *The Slave Power Conspiracy and the Paranoid Style* (Baton Rouge, La., 1970).

abolitionists, and far, far fewer 'Garrisonians'. Unfortunately, it was not only the ante-bellum South which fell into the trap of assuming that all the country north of the Mason–Dixon line was a hotbed of radical anti-family, anti-Union, anti-war, anti-liquor abolitionists. Until recently most American historians, who also assumed that William Lloyd Garrison had been the nation's moral leader on the slave question from his arrival on the scene in 1830 onwards, have made the same mistake.

Garrison is less important than most writers on slavery have assumed him to be. On the other hand, to express it tortuously, it is immensely important that his contemporaries, especially in the South, thought he was important. To historians, his work has been given disproportionate significance partly because of this latter consideration, but also because of a further mistaken assumption. No one has ever successfully got rid of the idea that the 'real' American anti-slavery movement only began in 1830 or 1831. This impression was first created just after the war because of the absence of any abolitionists who had been active in the movement for more than thirty-five years, and who were neither dead nor too senile to write. Moreover, since the abolitionists of longest standing could claim to have been right longest, the older they were in the 1860s the more credit their writing gained. Since the oldest men writing immediately after the war had joined the movement during its short Garrisonian phase, the earliest and best-accepted histories of anti-slavery enshrined two unfortunate inaccuracies in America's consciousness of its abolitionist past. The first was that the *first* true abolitionists had been the Garrisonians, and the second that the *only* true abolitionists had been the Garrisonians. These assumptions were central to the first two short histories of anti-slavery, written by the Unitarian minister Samuel J. May and Oliver Johnson.[9] Indeed the error that real 'uncompromising' action began with Garrison had already been accepted in the great journalistic history of the war by a much younger man, Horace Greeley, first editor of the *New York Tribune.*[10]

Garrison himself wrote no real history of the movement. It is a

[9] S. J. May, *Some Recollections of our Anti-Slavery Conflict* (Boston, 1869); O. Johnson, *William Lloyd Garrison and his Times* (Boston, 1879).

[10] H. Greeley, *The Great American Conflict*, 2 vols (Hartford, Conn., 1870) I 115–16, 122.

great pity that he did not. In the mellowing years when he considered his work done and began to forget the vendettas of the past, he merged with his background enough to become a sort of nice Boston antiquarian who might have produced a considerably more accurate account of the abolitionist years than the historians who have either accepted his acerbic editorials and pamphlets at their face value, or reacted violently against them. However, Garrison's sons did produce a massive four-volume *Life* of their father.[11] It is probably the greatest single collection of printed sources on the extremist abolitionists, though now much underestimated. Its authors sometimes showed extraordinary flashes of insight. For instance, they fully realised that their father had seen the last great movement in which Christian morality had been the basis of propaganda. 'No one now aiming to effect a great moral revolution', they wrote in 1885, 'would consider it indispensable to yoke the churches to his scheme, or to prove its legitimacy by chapter and verse from either Testament'.[12] However, the Garrisons' biases have done more harm to the accurate writing of the history of the abolitionist movement than those of all other authors put together. They were not immune to producing the awful hagiography which characterises so much nineteenth-century biography. They also inherited their father's hatreds, and assumed that everyone with whom he disagreed was an anti-abolitionist. Since he disagreed with almost everyone, at one time or another, this left very few reformers whose anti-slavery credentials could be accepted. Again, the fact that they dealt primarily with the movement where Garrison was concerned in it, that is in the East, meant that they tended to miss the significance of black abolitionists who were more prominent in the West. Worst of all, however, their readers are left to assume that their father had launched the anti-slavery movement with his first issue of the Boston *Liberator*, on 1 January 1831.[13]

[11] W. P. Garrison *et al.*, *William Lloyd Garrison, 1805–1879: The Story of his Life Told by his Children*, 4 vols (Boston, 1885). The fiercest attack on Garrison, directly and by implication, is G. H. Barnes, *The Anti-Slavery Impulse, 1830–1844* (1933; reprinted New York, 1964). Cf. W. Merrill, *Against Wind and Tide: William Lloyd Garrison* (Cambridge, Mass., 1964); J. Thomas, *The Liberator: William Lloyd Garrison* (Boston, 1964). A needlessly cantankerous review of both books is L. Filler, 'Garrison Again, and Again: A Review Article', *Civil War History*, XI (1965) 69–75.

[12] *Garrison . . . Life*, I xiii.   [13] Ibid., pp. 219–76.

It is now sixty years since a scholarly book fully demonstrated the extent of American anti-slavery activity prior to 1831. The work of the local anti-slavery societies which continued agitation against slavery, of the Colonization Society itself, and of great individual abolitionists like Benjamin Lundy, went on actively throughout the early part of the century, even in the 1820s.[14] One of the main points of the present book is the depth of the historical roots of Western doubts over black slavery. Yet the great shadow which this sprightly little man with bald pate and shining glasses has cast on the later movement has ensured that the 'neglected period' remains pretty well neglected. There are several reasons for this, the most obvious of which is that although Garrison did not begin or even revive the movement against slavery, he did make it a great deal more extreme, and generally accelerate the pace of agitation. The South had been quite sufficiently intransigent towards the North long before Garrison came on the scene; one pamphleteer, somewhat confusedly, accused the far from radical Colonization Society of 'a murderous attempt to rid the soil of America from the pollution of African industry'.[15] However, Garrison entered the ranks at a time when the successive Denmark Vesey and Nat Turner insurrections had made the South increasingly nervous of all open criticism of its peculiar institution. Added to this, there may be a great deal of truth in Miss Kraditor's theory that Garrison was the first abolitionist who was a genuine revolutionary, using a preconceived strategy to destroy a society essentially at odds with his own millennial views.[16]

Like most revolutionaries, he came from a conservative background. His birthplace was the little Massachusetts fishing village of Newburyport, his mother a working woman who sought solace for the break-up of her marriage to a sailor in the orthodox

[14] A. D. Adams, *The Neglected Period of Anti-Slavery in America, 1808–1831* (Cambridge, Mass., 1908). See also P. J. Staudenraus, *The African Colonization Movement, 1816–1865* (New York, 1961); M. L. Dillon, *Benjamin Lundy and the Struggle for Negro Freedom* (Urbana, Ill., 1966).

[15] W. B. Seabrook, *A Concise View of the Critical Situation, and Future Prospects of the Slaveholding States, in Relation to their Colored Population* (Charleston, S.C., 1825) p. 5.

[16] Kraditor, *Means and Ends in American Abolitionism*, pp. 8–9 and passim.

Baptist church and solid Federalist social morality. It is not much of a surprise to find that one Garrison brother became an incurable alcoholic and the other a rather vindictive saint. The latter quickly developed a strong political consciousness during his apprenticeship as a printer – a trade which probably produced more abolitionist activists, in both Britain and America, than any other. After moving into journalism, in Boston, Garrison met the eccentric abolitionist Benjamin Lundy, who had done so much for the movement in the so-called 'neglected period'. From this point his abolitionism became more fervent, and by the end of 1829 he was actually working with Lundy in Baltimore, on his little *Genius of Universal Emancipation.* Already enthusiastic in attacking individuals rather than the impersonal *institution* of slavery, Garrison soon managed to have himself jailed in Baltimore for refusing to pay libel damages awarded against him. Apart from corresponding feverishly from prison with any newspaper editors who would pay the postage on his letters, he managed to dramatise his situation as much as possible in the pamphlet *A Brief Sketch of the Trial of William Lloyd Garrison.*[17] His greatest good fortune was that he attracted the attention of the New York merchant Arthur Tappan, who paid his fines, and doubtless encouraged him to make a permanent career of anti-slavery. Convinced of the bankruptcy if not direct malice of the Colonization Society, and devoted to 'immediate' emancipation, Garrison had now moved far beyond his predecessors. He took the gamble of launching the *Liberator* in Boston virtually without funds, and almost lacking in subscribers except among the city's articulate free black community.[18]

The story of Garrison's early anti-slavery career has often been told. But anti-slavery was meanwhile accelerating and consolidating in other areas and under the leadership of other men. In fact the American movement was never confined to New England, although the flamboyance of such abolitionists as Wendell Phillips, James Russell Lowell, Maria Weston Chapman, Lydia

[17] *A Brief Sketch of the Trial of William Lloyd Garrison, for an Alleged Libel on Francis Todd, of Newburyport, Massachusetts,* 2nd ed. (Boston, 1834).

[18] For Garrison's life to 1831, see Garrison *et al., Garrison ... Life,* 1 1–218; Merrill, *Against Wind and Tide,* pp. 1–55; Thomas, *The Liberator,* pp. 1–128.

Maria Child, Henry Clarke Wright, John Anderson Collins, Nathaniel Peabody Rogers, and Garrison himself, often creates the illusion that it was. Recognisably 'regional' brands of anti-slavery sentiment also developed in three other areas: Pennsylvania, New York City, and the agricultural section of newly opened land stretching from upstate New York through Ohio and Illinois. Perhaps a fifth section might be defined as Upper Canada, or Ontario, where abolitionist ideas were formed by Western cities like Cincinnati, after the pressure of 'slave-catchers' on escaped blacks stimulated a series of educational settlements of a more or less Utopian stamp north of the border.[19] Colonisationist activity also continued throughout the North and in some parts of the border South, largely because of its connection with the strength of interest in American missions to Africa. Even in the three years between the launching of the *Liberator* and the formation of the national American Anti-Slavery Society in the winter of 1833–4, however, Garrison's vigorous campaign against the Colonization Society was being supported by a small coterie of New York businessmen and landowners headed by the brothers Arthur and Louis Tappan, and including Gerrit Smith and William Jay. Arthur Tappan's support for Simeon Jocelyn's abortive black manual-labour college in New Haven, and the help he gave to Prudence Crandall in her fruitless struggle to continue integrated female education in Canterbury, Connecticut, both failed. However, they reveal the extent to which the New York abolitionist impulse was strengthening at the same time as the early *Liberator*s were more stridently proclaiming the anti-slavery millennium in Boston. Tappan and his friends also supported as many local state societies as possible, and early in 1833 launched the *Emancipator*, also an immediatist newspaper but one which approached the opposition considerably more tactfully than its Boston counterpart.[20]

It is certainly a point in Garrison's favour that whereas he abandoned the Colonization Society because of its failure to

[19] W. H. Pease and J. H. Pease, *Black Utopias: Negro Communal Experiments in America* (Madison, Wis., 1963); R. Winks, *The Blacks in Canada: A History* (New Haven, 1971) pp. 142–271.

[20] L. Tappan, *Life of Arthur Tappan* (New York, 1870) p. 175; B. Wyatt-Brown, *Lewis Tappan and the Evangelical War against Slavery* (Cleveland, 1969) pp. 87–91.

abolish slavery, Tappan did so because he surreptitiously discovered that it had allowed rum-runners to land 'FOURTEEN HUNDRED BARRELS of the liquid poison in Liberia', no doubt to the great pleasure of the black émigrés whose welfare he had at heart.[21] More seriously, the publication of Garrison's *Thoughts on African Colonization* represented one of the genuine turning-points in the history of American anti-slavery.[22] This fat pamphlet's circulation – it went through innumerable editions – indicated the extent of American discontent with the abolitionist promises of the Colonization Society, and the way in which the demand for a speedy solution to the problem of slavery was growing in the North. In another direction, the mass of information which Garrison had collected on black responses to colonisation projects for the first time demonstrated the intensity of free Negro suspicion of the society.[23] The black American community had already developed enough consciousness of its Americanism to have little interest in returning to a strange and 'uncivilised' continent which had become alien over the passage of the generations. Garrison's *Thoughts*, indeed, is one of the most interesting documents produced during the course of the movement. Nevertheless, it may have had less influence in turning the sedate reformers from whom anti-slavery drew its recruits away from colonisation than the later *Inquiry into the Character and Tendency of the American Colonization Society* published by the aristocratic William Jay.[24] With all the prestige of one of New York's great revolutionary names, Jay's declaration of support for the immediatists was one of their great early triumphs.

The development of the American movement in the early 1830s is a good example of the regional factor in American history. In Britain, later abolitionism was to be bedevilled by rivalries between the provinces, especially Scotland, and London. In the United States there were not only rivalries between Boston

[21] Ibid., p. 103.
[22] W. L. Garrison, *Thoughts on African Colonization; or, an Impartial Exhibition of the Doctrines, Principles, and Purposes of the American Colonization Society. Together with the Resolutions, Addresses, and Remonstrances of the Free People of Color* (Boston, 1832).
[23] Ibid., part II, separate pagination, pp. 1–76.
[24] W. Jay, *An Inquiry into the Character and Tendency of the American Colonization Society and American Anti-Slavery Societies* (New York, 1835).

and New York, though this was probably the strongest line of tension, but also between Philadalphia and the other two cities, and between East and West. While Tappan and Garrison were raising support in New York and Boston, the long-standing Quaker movement was reorganising itself in Philadelphia under the inspiration of Isaac T. Hopper, a Friend who had been born in West Jersey and later became a highly successful Pennsylvania businessman.[25] Until the Civil War, indeed, Philadelphia anti-slavery was dominated by the Society of Friends, just as it had been since the days of Benezet and Dillwyn. It is of the greatest importance, however, that the city's most important abolitionist Quakers were not 'orthodox' but 'Hicksite', members of the American section of the Friends who had seceded from the Society in 1817 in an attempt to get back to the primitive purity of the religious testimony given by Fox and Woolman. Hopper himself was a Hicksite, and he is an important figure in the national American movement. The same was true of Philadelphia's three aggressive female leaders, Lucretia Mott, Abby Kimber and Sarah Pugh. A recent study has shown that the Hicksite movement represented a reaction of rural Friends, or those who had failed to come to terms with modern large-scale business, against the conservative and by now commercially successful leadership of the Society.[26] The question of *who* the abolitionists were, and what background they came from, is bewilderingly complex because of the extent to which the situation varied from city to city, and indeed from point to point in time, but the predominance of disaffected Hicksites in the Philadelphia movement may usefully be compared with the leadership in other cities – for instance New York, where it has been suggested that the leading abolitionists were provincial businessmen like Tappan unable to come to terms with the city's old mercantile aristocracy; or Boston, where there is a strong element of aristocrats like Wendell Phillips and Edmund Quincy. These have been seen as expressing their contempt for the increasingly *nouveau riche* and distressingly powerful men who were taking their place as social

[25] See L. M. Child, *Isaac T. Hopper: A True Life* (Boston and Cleveland, 1853).

[26] R. W. Doherty, *The Hicksite Separation: A Sociological Analysis of Religious Schism in Early Nineteenth Century America* (New Brunswick, N.J., 1967).

leaders by becoming active in abolitionism and other radical reforms.[27] The variety of apparent abolitionist motives is so great that it is tempting to return to the belief that the real reasons for the rise of the movement were intellectual and religious – that the anti-slavery idea had an appeal of its own which told in groups whose backgrounds and aspirations were widely divergent but who shared the world-picture of their American generation. This fits in with a recent study of the abolitionists of New York State, which suggests that they were generally men and women of comfortable wealth, deeply religious, and somewhat higher in status than their parents. They did not turn to anti-slavery as a mechanism for 'tension-reduction' in a situation of frustration: 'these leaders suffered no more or different frustration than that which human beings tend to experience, and were therefore, in their militant behaviour, simply responding normally to a challenge to their particular vision of America'.[28] In short, the abolitionist commitment arose not because of anxiety or neurosis, but because careful thought, whether on a religious, political or economic level, showed slavery to be undesirable. These various interpretations are not mutually exclusive, but the last seems to come closer than any other to dealing with the complexity of American anti-slavery.

In either case, the Philadelphia movement developed along distinctive lines of its own. Its abolitionists welcomed the co-operation of black leaders in the early 1830s, at a time when white reformers in other Northern cities were paying little attention to their importance or even existence. Pennsylvania's most influential black abolitionist was James Forten, who owned a sailmaker's business large enough for him to keep a private

[27] Wyatt-Brown, *Lewis Tappan*, p. 61; D. Donald, *Lincoln Reconsidered: Essays on the Civil War Era*, 2nd ed. (New York, 1961). Cf. R. Skotheim, 'A Note on Historical Method: David Donald's "Towards a Reconsideration of Abolitionists"', *Journal of Southern History*, xxv (1959) 356–65.

[28] G. Sorin, *The New York Abolitionists: A Case Study of Political Radicalism* (Westport, Conn., 1971) pp. 119, 18. Another approach is to stress the disparity of the abolitionists, and the difficulty of generalising their background and motives. This is brilliantly done in J. H. Pease and W. H. Pease, *Bound with them in Chains: A Biographical History of the Anti-Slavery Movement* (Westport, Conn., 1972), which has been published since the completion of this manuscript.

carriage and country house, and to have his children tutored privately instead of facing the rough and tumble of getting an education in the public schools. Throughout the 'neglected period' Forten had been leading a campaign to improve the condition of Philadelphia's free blacks, and to have the legislature testify against slavery *outside* the state.[29] The whole tone of the Philadelphia movement after 1830 was uncompromising. Although the city later came to be a key way-station on the Underground Railroad, U.G.R. work never became more than a supplement to the call for immediate eradication of slavery. This call was made in as radical tones by someone like Lucretia Mott, or the younger Philadelphia leader Charles Miller McKim, as it ever was by Garrison himself, although Pennsylvania's douce Quakerly atmosphere prevented the wholesale attacks on the churches and the Union made in the 1840s by New England extremists like Henry Wright or Nathaniel Rogers.

The fourth area in which the anti-slavery movement gained strength after 1830 was the belt of newly settled land stretching from upstate New York across to Illinois. As in Britain, the evangelical impulse is central to all areas of the American crusade against slavery, but this is nowhere more so than in the small and unstable communities of the 'burned-over district', of New York and the frontier West generally. In future years the Midwestern states, and also the new Western territories, lent their support to the fight against the South on free-soil rather than abolitionist grounds, that is to ensure that the Negro should be kept out of the North as a labour competitor and general racial threat.[30] Lincoln himself, in 1860 and thereafter, sought and gained much more support from this quarter than on the grounds of religious or other pity for the slave. Yet Lincoln, who was nothing if not a Westerner, must have remembered the enthusiasms at the camp-meetings of his boyhood. From 1827 onwards, the Northern frontier was swept by a religious revival which gave a release for the tensions created by the loneliness of wilderness life – and also

[29] There is a short sketch of Forten in the *Dictionary of American Biography*, vi 536–7.

[30] V. J. Voegeli, *Free but not Equal: The Midwest and the Negro during the Civil War* (Chicago, 1967); E. Berwanger, *The Frontier against Slavery: Western Anti-Negro Prejudice and the Slavery Extension Controversy* (Urbana, Ill., 1967).

enshrined some of the egalitarianism of the rapidly moving society from which it came.[31] The catharsis of conversion not only involved the removal of personal sin, but also created a responsibility for immediate purging of evil from all other humans and from society at large. The great revival thus created a massive outward urge into good works of all kinds. Some of these were cranky in the extreme, some merely distressingly puritanical. A great deal of learned attention has been given to the comical aspects of the revivalist camp-meetings and the benevolent campaigns which followed them;[32] but there is no doubt that the revivals created an excruciating awareness of personal guilt and responsibility for the sins of society at large. Since one of the most obvious sins of society at large was slaveholding, the anti-slavery movement was the first to benefit from the great revival. Moreover, given the existing consciousness of the inconsistency of slavery and accepted religious belief, the revivals' urgent thrust towards purification from guilt brought the demand for immediate rather than gradual emancipation. This did not mean that the immediatists had the slightest intention of setting the entire slave population free overnight, but they did act under an overwhelming compulsion to institute concrete measures which would be the first steps towards such an emancipation.[33] It is no accident that there was an element of the camp-meeting in every abolitionist lecture-hall, a tradition which perhaps continues in the civil rights and pacifist rallies of our own time. Charles Grandison Finney, who 'began' the great revival in 1825, though he wrote and said very little on slavery directly, is one of the most important

[31] W. R. Cross, '*The Burned-over District*': *The Social and Intellectual History of Enthusiastic Religion in Western New York, 1800–1850* (Ithaca, N.Y., 1950) passim.

[32] Ibid., pp. 29, 158, 211 ff.; G. Seldes, *The Stammering Century: Minor Movements, Cults, Manias, Fads, Sects and Religious Excitements in Nineteenth Century America* (1928; reprinted New York, 1965). Cf. the more constructive view of A. F. Tyler, *Freedom's Ferment: Phases of American Social History from the Colonial Period to the Civil War* (1944; reprinted New York, 1962); T. L. Smith, *Revivalism and Social Reform: American Protestantism on the Eve of the Civil War* (1957; reprinted New York, 1965).

[33] See D. B. Davis, 'The Emergence of Immediatism in British and American Anti-Slavery Thought', *Mississippi Valley Historical Review*, XLIX (1962) 227 ff.

figures in the American anti-slavery movement. Few abolitionists were unaffected, directly or indirectly, by Finney's work.

Finney's call for an assault on the empire of sin was translated into abolitionist terms by a young student, a Westerner, named Theodore Weld. Weld had a relatively brief career – he retired from the gruelling work of campaigning in 1841 – but he was responsible for moulding the raw material provided by Finney into a peculiarly Western branch of the movement. He then co-operated with Tappan to launch a national anti-slavery society which formed the basis of a unified if somewhat disparate crusade throughout the country. Although deeply influenced by Finney, Weld was personally converted by a British evangelist, Captain Charles Stuart, the eccentric Scot born in the West Indies. He retained his military title, and insisted on wearing a kilt even in America, a practice which takes considerable gall even in our own more enlightened time. Stuart later became an Agency Committee lecturer. Even before West India emancipation, certainly before Garrison, he was attacking the American Colonization Society for its gradualist views at a time when few British abolitionists knew of its existence, let alone its defects.[34] After this he divided his time between Britain and America. He worked in support of Garrison until his Scotsman's horror at the latter's cavalier attempts to improve the position of women and destroy the Sabbath led him to dismiss the Garrisonians as 'rhapsodists'.[35] Stuart ended his life in a disgruntled retirement in Ontario, but in 1825 he was principal of Utica High School. It was there that he met Weld, adopted him as a protégé and sponsored his education at the new Oneida College. For a brief period Stuart himself became one of Finney's 'Holy Band' of evangelists, and Weld remained closely under his influence, being bombarded with pamphlets on the increasingly fevered slavery controversy on the other side of the Atlantic.[36] It has been argued

[34] C. Stuart, *Liberia: or, the American Colonization Scheme Exposed: A Full and Authentic Report of a Lecture Delivered ... in the Rev. Mr Anderson's Chapel, Glasgow, 13th April, 1833* (Glasgow, 1833).

[35] Stuart to Wardlaw, 8 Feb 1841, printed circular in Gerrison Papers, Boston Public Library.

[36] Stuart to Weld, 16 Nov 1825, 19 May 1828, 30 Apr 1829, ? June 1831, 30 Apr 1832, in G. H. Barnes (ed.), *Letters of Theodore Dwight Weld, Angelina Grimke Weld, and Sarah Grimke, 1822–1844*, 2 vols (New York, 1934) I 6, 19–20, 25, 48–9, 74.

that, owing to Stuart's influence, Weld transmitted British anti-slavery ideas to Americans.[37] In 1831 Arthur Tappan, now converted by Finney and the head of a great complex of philanthropic associations in New York City, gave funds to form a new Western college, Lane Theological Seminary, at Cincinnati. Weld enrolled to improve his qualifications as an evangelist. The greatest American churchman of the time, Lyman Beecher, became president at Tappan's invitation. Unfortunately Beecher was at this time devoted to reuniting colonisationists and abolitionists, and after his attempt to prevent the organisation of an immediatist society on the campus, Weld led the majority of the student body to secede and form the independent Oberlin Seminary. Weld himself, James G. Birney and Elizur Wright were only three of the many 'Lane rebels' who later became prominent abolitionist leaders. Oberlin itself continued to spread anti-slavery principles until the war. Weld's great work, however, was to link the great force of the growing Western movement to the national society being organised under the inspiration, financial and otherwise, of the Tappan brothers of New York.

The national American Anti-Slavery Society, which first met in 1833, was very much a joint effort between the four regions in which abolitionist sentiment was strengthening. Isaac Hopper had by now moved his business to New York, but the society was formed at a Convention held in Philadelphia, at the suggestion of two of his old allies, Evan Lewis and Abram L. Pennock. Lucretia Mott was one of the three women present. The call to the Convention was drawn up by the New York leaders and signed by Elizur Wright, a Western-educated clergyman who was to be salaried secretary of the new Society once its permanent organisation was set up. The meetings of the Convention were chaired by Beriah Green, president of Oneida College in the centre of the 'burned-over district'. Garrison headed the committee which drew up its 'declaration of sentiments'. His colleagues were two other New Englanders, Samuel J. May and the Quaker poet John Greenleaf Whittier.

The effect of the British movement on the organisation of the American Anti-Slavery Society was incalculable. When the Philadelphia Convention met, it had received the startling and encouraging news that Britain had abolished Negro slavery in

[37] Barnes, *Anti-Slavery Impulse*, p. 33.

her West India possessions. Garrison himself had just returned from a visit to Britain, during which he had walked behind Wilberforce's coffin and followed the progress of the Emancipation Bill through Parliament. Organisationally, Garrison at least had always expected to use the same methods as the British. He had begun his famous *Thoughts* by demanding that Americans should found a national society,

> the object of which shall be, to quicken and consolidate the moral influence of the nation, so that Congress and the State Legislatures may be burdened with petitions for the removal of the evil – to scatter tracts, like rain-drops, over the land, on the subject of slavery – to employ active and intelligent agents to plead the cause incessantly, and to form auxiliary societies.[38]

In the early months of 1834 the new society's headquarters was set up, with a small permanent staff in New York, part of whose duties was to edit the society's own newspaper, the *Emancipator*. Following the British model, as Garrison had suggested, the campaign to form a chain of provincial 'auxiliaries' dependent on the national society began. However, the vast staff of 'agents' or 'lecturers' whom the society eventually put into the field went far beyond anything the London Agency Committee had envisaged. Their leader was Weld himself, who accepted the society's invitation to organise its lecturing staff early in 1834. Most of them had been educated in the new Western theological colleges rather than the sedate colleges of the East. For several years, from 1834 to 1837, the 'Seventy' were the real heroes of the movement, stumping for anti-slavery from village to village of the rural North, working at a gruelling pace, and constantly facing the threat of riots from Southern sympathisers, and from those who saw the abolitionist critique as a threat to their own position in local society.[39] Weld was not the only lecturer who came to see physical abuse as part of the meagre return for his work. It is now easy to peddle scholastic sneers at the American abolitionists, at their combination of self-righteousness with blindness to the dangers of sectional conflict. The blue-chip godliness of a Tappan, the vanity of a Garrison and the patrician rage of a Phillips are distasteful in varying degrees. But it is very

[38] *Thoughts on African Colonization*, p. iii.
[39] See Richards, *Gentlemen of Property and Standing*, pp. 20–46.

difficult to feel anything but admiration for the courage, self-sacrifice and sheer athletic endurance of Weld's 'Seventy'. The work of these lecturers in getting anti-slavery down to grass-roots in the country areas of New England, New York and the West was as important as the impact of abolitionist editors and pamphleteers on relatively sophisticated urban audiences. The rural North never came to love the Negro, but it did eventually come to hate the South. Much of the moral underpinning of this attitude came from the British-style lecturing by American Anti-Slavery Society agents from 1834 onwards.

After 1830, then, anti-slavery feeling strengthened in these four regions of the North to an extent where it was possible to form a viable national anti-slavery society. The quickening of momentum was caused by factors felt throughout the whole nation. The impact of revivalism was not as dramatic everywhere as in upstate New York, but it was felt in all the American churches and throughout the North. In general it produced a great upsurge in the felt responsibility for good works. The institutional result was the organisation of the great complex of national benevolent societies, among which was the American Anti-Slavery Society.[40] Again, though it must be repeated that Garrison built on a long anti-slavery tradition, and that he was by no means the only or the most respected leader in abolitionist circles, his incomparable gifts as a propagandist meant that his writings attracted attention to the slavery issue throughout the country. The fact that the *Liberator*'s readership was small and largely confined to Boston's black community was of little importance, owing to the nineteenth-century practice of copying editorials and articles from one paper into another. Since Garrison's dramatic productions were likely to be good press in papers of all shades of opinion, extracts from the *Liberator* had far more than their share of the compliment of reprinting. Part of the tragedy was that Southern newspaper readers gained the mistaken impression that all abolitionists were Garrisonian, and that the *Liberator* was expressing the general Northern attitude to the South. In the North, Garrison's practice of portraying

[40] See C. S. Griffin, *Their Brothers' Keepers: Moral Stewardship in the United States, 1800–1865* (New Brunswick, N.J., 1960); C. I. Foster, *An Errand of Mercy: The Evangelical United Front, 1790–1837* (Chapel Hill, N.C., 1960).

slaveholding as a crime gave a new urgency to abolitionism in a generation whose revivalist modes of thought strengthened their sense of responsibility for launching an immediate attack on the evils around them. The movement must also have gained strength because evangelical interest in slavery turned men with the stature to become national leaders towards abolitionism. It is difficult to imagine the great expansion of the 1830s unaided by the dynamism of Weld or the long purse of Arthur Tappan.

In purely sectional terms, there is also a central truth behind the Marxist interpretation of the movement. By 1830 the rapid maturing of Northern business made a labour system based on black slavery increasingly archaic, especially since the opening of the Erie Canal in 1827 brought large areas of what had been the isolated rural West into contact with the capitalistic world of the North as a whole. While Northern distrust of the South was growing, the South itself had become even more nervous over its perennial security problem since the Denmark Vesey and Nat Turner insurrections. Its growing bitterness towards Northern agitators strengthened the suspicion that it was hopelessly at odds with the modern free world, and in turn reinforced the very pro-slavery position the abolitionists meant to discountenance. Finally, there is no doubt that American abolitionists were encouraged by the apparent success of the British emancipation. Garrison was appalled by the idea of giving compensation to the West Indians – 'not an example for us to imitate, but a precedent for us to shun'[41] – but as far as propaganda went, it was important that British emancipation had not produced another Santo Domingo. Northern black communities were particularly heartened by the British news. With other abolitionists they continued to hold 1 August anniversary celebrations right up to the war years. In fact the impression of British success lasted even longer than this. As late as 1914 Marcus Garvey arranged that his Universal Negro Improvement Association should be launched in America on 1 August.[42]

Nevertheless, the success of the new national society formed in 1833 was short-lived. By 1840 it was ineffective and hopelessly divided. The movement had entered a new phase, and indeed it shows quite different characteristics in each of the three decades

[41] *Liberator*, 12 Oct 1833.
[42] E. D. Cronon, *Black Moses* (Madison, Wis., 1955) p. 16.

from 1830 to 1860. The 1830s, as we have seen, were dominated by the growing extremism of the movement, the organisation of the national anti-slavery society and the spreading of anti-slavery ideas through increasingly radical newspapers and the lecturing activities of Weld's 'Seventy'. In the closing years of the decade there came a new development with the struggle to have anti-slavery petitions accepted by Congress. After 1840, however, the disintegration of the American Anti-Slavery Society meant that abolitionist propagandising fell back into the hands of local societies, which frequently spent as much time arguing against one another as against the South. Since the Liberty Party ran James Birney as its presidential candidate in 1840, and some form of abolitionist candidate went to a national electorate in every presidential election from then until the war, the 1840s may be seen as a decade when the movement came to be concerned with politics rather than the simple spreading of propaganda. After the Compromise of 1850, however, the absence of further ground for negotiation between North and South, and the excitement caused by attempts to enforce the Fugitive Slave Law by dragging escaped slaves back from Northern states, created a much sharper degree of political polarisation. By 1860 even the party system had become sectional; Lincoln effectively fought as the Northern (though not necessarily anti-slavery) candidate of the Republican Party against Breckenridge as the Southern (and indubitably pro-slavery) nominee of the Democrats. *Very* roughly, the 1830s may be seen as the decade of propagandising, the 1840s as the decade of political campaigning and the 1850s as the decade of polarisation. However, although it may seem that Clio was expressly considering the needs of the hard-pressed undergraduate in arranging such neat chronological divisions, it should be remembered that this one is not watertight. For instance some abolitionists, notably Garrison himself, eschewed all political action throughout the period, and relied on moral persuasion, which in any case continued of necessity as an adjunct to political action. Although polarisation becomes most marked after 1850, it had begun long before then. Without trying to trace it back to the landing of the first 'negars' in 1619, the arguments in the inflammatory pamphlets published after the debates on the Missouri Compromise and the Denmark Vesey conspiracy in Charleston have an eerie similarity to the Southern 'positive good' theories of the 1850s.[43] Political action continued in the 1850s, too, although abolitionists had largely given up hope of having an independent party of their own, and the anti-slavery issue was taken up by the Free Soil and Republican parties.

Again, it should be remembered that although these three decades have distinctive characteristics, certain trends continue throughout them. The most important was the gradual but tragic erosion of understanding between North and South. At each incident where the sections found themselves at odds, from the Missouri debates of 1820 to the firing on Fort Sumter, their exchange of abuse became more violent, their self-justification more dogged, and their openness to argument less. Without the gift of seeing, Americans developed a curiously even bitterness towards sectional controversies of quite different importance. Excitement was as great over minor incidents like the imprisonment and death of the abolitionist Charles Torrey or the visit of the British reformer George Thompson as it was over crises we now consider major like the petition war of 1838 or the Compromise of 1850. Again, extremism bred extremism: Garrison's attitude to the South was no more representative of his section than Bully Brooks of South Carolina, who almost caned Charles Sumner to death, was of his – but in each case the easy assumption was either that *all* Northerners were fanatics, or that *all* Southerners were barbarians. The result, reinforced by the ever-present fantasies of conspiracy, was to drive each section's moderates further into the camp of the extremists. Extreme accusations produced even more extreme counter-accusations. Propagandists North and South gradually found themselves taking standpoints which would have been unthinkable in the 1820s, and which would never have been listened to in an atmosphere less charged with hysteria and mutual misunderstanding. One of the reasons why no one has ever reached any satisfactory conclusion on the origins of the Civil War is the ghastly fascination of the continuum of growing alienation between the sections.[44] Perhaps the

[43] e.g. [E. C. Holland], *Refutation of Calumnies Circulated against the Southern and Western States, Respecting the Institution and Existence of Slavery among them* (Charleston, S.C., 1822).

[44] Interpretations of the origins of the war are usefully summarised in T. J. Pressly, *Americans Interpret their Civil War*, 2nd ed. (New York, 1962).

reason for this is that there is another continuity over those years. The institution of slavery itself still flourished, now so grotesquely at odds with the times, and yet still so much the basis of Southern society, that it excluded compromise and could be purged only through violence.

The extremism of the abolitionists was increased by frustration over the limited number of ways in which they could carry on their work. Pro-slavery violence was enough of a problem in the North. In the South, the perfectly understandable neurosis over slave revolts meant that preaching abolition there was suicidal. Martyr complex or not, few abolitionists brought themselves to try the experiment. The most active Southern resistance to slavery always came from within, among the slaves themselves. They hardly needed to be told about their grievances by the 'abolitionist missionaries' whose largely imagined presence gave the South so many unnecessary nightmares.[45] Abolitionists also had to face the fact that national political action was largely closed to them. Even if the constitution had not made it doubtful whether the Federal government had any right to interfere with slavery in the states, no Whig or Democrat politician in his senses was willing to lose important Southern support to gratify a handful of abolitionist agitators. It is significant that the few who did so were men whose principal constituency was an anti-slavery one. The only exception was John Quincy Adams, who had after all been President already, so that there was little else the political structure could give him. Though he regarded abolitionists with contempt, he was at least concerned over their right to a hearing.[46] It was he who became the spokesman of the abolitionists in the late 1830s, when they set about dramatising the slavery issue by flooding Congress with petitions against the internal slave trade, and against slavery in the District of Columbia, where the government had unchallengeable jurisdiction. The abolitionist assumption that Southerners would absorb anti-slavery ideas by reading such petitions was at best shaky. Their effect in the South was to stimulate more enthusiastic defences of slavery. However, the years of

[45] H. Aptheker, *American Negro Slave Revolts* (New York, 1943); K. M. Stampp, *The Peculiar Institution: Slavery in the Ante-Bellum South* (New York, 1956) pp. 86–140.

[46] S. F. Bemis, *John Quincy Adams and the Union* (New York, 1956) pp. 326 ff.

the petition war, from 1836 to 1844, represent the transition from the simple concern over spreading propaganda to the beginnings of political action. It was not until 1844 that Adams succeeded in removing the 'gag rule' imposed in 1836 by Southern politicians to prevent the reading of anti-slavery petitions. In 1840 this became a standing rule of the House. Adams spent eight years struggling to subvert it. Sometimes he disguised anti-slavery petitions as pleas against the annexation of Texas. He ridiculed the rule by trying to present petitions *in favour* of slavery, presented demands that the Union be dissolved, or that Washington be moved to the more libertarian atmosphere of the North. The issue was kept before an infuriated House until it finally gave up the right to exclude petitions on slavery – by which time abolitionist attention had moved elsewhere. Nevertheless, the period of the petition struggle was a formative one for the movement. It leads into the formation of the Liberty Party, more especially since frustration with the slowness of this indirect political device may have speeded the decision to found a political party specifically devoted to attacking slavery. In other directions, however, impatience with Adams's dogged fight may have created a revulsion against all forms of political action. It is no accident that by the time the gag rule was repealed, although the Tappan brothers were firmly backing the new Liberty Party, Weld had completely retired from anti-slavery work, while Garrison was calling on his followers to avoid all implication in politics and to demand withdrawal from a corrupt Union. The frustration which drove the Garrisonians in this direction also led to the disintegration of the American Anti-Slavery Society, which was splitting into a series of warring factions during the first few years of Adams's campaign in the House.

It was at the very point when the petitioning campaign had attracted national attention to the political problem of slavery that unity among the abolitionists broke down. One of the problems of trying to harness the evangelical impulse to good works was in deciding which reforms were priorities, which legitimate and which not. Ralph Waldo Emerson, who was well placed to be aware of this, once wrote of his colleagues in the philanthropic world that

They defied each other, like a congress of kings, each of whom had a realm to rule, and a way of his own that made concert unprofitable. What a fertility of projects for the salvation of the world! One apostle thought all men should go to farming; and another, that no man should buy or sell; that the use of money was the cardinal evil; another, that the mischief was in our diet, that we eat and drink damnation. These made un-leavened bread, and were foes to the death, to fermentation. It was in vain urged by the housewife, that God made yeast, as well as dough, and loves fermentation just as dearly as he loves vegetation: that fermentation develops the saccharine element in the grain, and makes it more palatable and more digestible. No; they wish the pure wheat, and will die but it shall not ferment. Stop, dear nature, these incessant advances of thine; let us scotch these ever-rolling wheels! Others attacked the system of agriculture, the use of animal manures in farm-ing; and the tyranny of man over brute nature; those abuses polluted his food. The ox must be taken from the plough, and the horse from the cart, the hundred acres of the farm must be spaded, and the man must walk wherever boats and loco-motives will not carry him. Even the insect world was to be defended, – that had been too long neglected, and a society for the protection of ground-worms, slugs, and mosquitos was to be incorporated without delay. With these appeared the adepts of homoeopathy, of hydropathy, of mesmerism, of phrenology, and their wonderful theories of the Christian miracles! Others assailed particular vocations, as that of the lawyer, that of the merchant, of the manufacturer, of the clergyman, of the scholar. Others attacked the institution of marriage, as the fountain of social evils. Others devoted themselves to the worrying of churches and meetings for public worship; and the fertile forms of anti-nomianism among the elder puritans, seemed to have their match in the plenty of the new harvest of reform.[47]

By association, this range of eccentric ambitions brought the more responsible proposal to abolish slavery into a disrepute which it might have avoided if it had been treated as a single issue on its own merits. In a generation of universal reformers, few abolition-ists were without an interest in some other philanthropic

[47] R. W. Emerson, 'New England Reformers' (1844), in *Essays, First and Second Series* (London: Everyman ed., 1906) pp. 338–9.

movement, eccentric or otherwise. Some were prepared to subordinate these concerns to the tactical needs of the fight against slavery. Others were not. Broadly speaking, the problem which broke up the American anti-slavery societies at the end of the 1830s was whether abolition was a single issue divorced from all others, or whether it was only one of a series of good causes which should be championed universally, in defiance of all tactical considerations. On the one hand, there were conservative reformers who were not prepared to work with colleagues whose esoteric commitments prejudiced the success of the fight against slavery. On the other, behind William Lloyd Garrison, were a group of radicals whose millennial vision increased the urgency of promoting reform on all fronts. The danger of frightening the public away from anti-slavery by an anti-everythingarian attitude became irrelevant. The great tragedy of the division was that it could not prevent the conservative element from being associated with lunatic-fringe rivals whose excesses made abolition seem terrifying. To large sections of the public, especially in the South, even the most reasoned proposals of the abolitionists emerged as anarchical fantasies, which had to be opposed at all costs, even at the risk of violence.

Although the national American Anti-Slavery Society did not divide formally until 1840, strains had developed in the local movements several years before this. Some committed abolitionists had long been intermittently doubtful of the tactical wisdom even of Garrison's abrasive generalisations about slaveholders. In 1831 Arthur Tappan, for instance, had complained that Garrison would do better if he had 'more argument and less invective'.[48] The strain of invective became even more alarming to 'orthodox' abolitionists as the widening reform interests of Garrison and his Boston group led them into savage attacks on the Sabbath, on the ministry as a whole and on the subjection of women. The clear public reaction which resulted, and which affected all abolitionists whether they shared Garrison's catholicity of reform or not, produced serious efforts to rid the movement of the embarrassment of its association with him.[49] By 1838 the *Liberator* was concentrating less and less on the single issue of abolition, and

[48] Tappan to Garrison, 12 Oct 1831, typescript copy, Garrison Papers, Boston Public Library.

[49] Barnes, *Anti-Slavery Impulse*, pp. 92–4, 153–5.

the reaction against him among the rank-and-file abolitionists who had to answer for his views strengthened both in Massachusetts and in the nation as a whole. Apart from the tactical problems of having anti-slavery saddled with highly unpopular 'extraneous issues', some of Garrison's attitudes had revolutionary implications distasteful to reformers who had no wish to alter the established order around them beyond softening some of its abuses. The most frightening of all was Garrison's enthusiasm for 'nonresistance', an extreme form of pacifism which challenged the whole institutional basis of society by disavowing any authority based on the ultimate sanction of force, direct or indirect.[50] After he became president of the New England Non-Resistance Society, many supporters who were sincerely committed to working for emancipation were put in an impossible position. For the slaves' sake and their own, they had to explain away a man who was generally supposed to be their leader, but who was preaching anarchy directly through nonresistance, and indirectly through attacking the Sabbath, the church and the subordination of women. All three were fundamental to society as the nineteenth century knew it, though the radicals had a positive and coherent vision of societal change which their critics almost always missed. Quite understandably, they set about trying to discredit Garrison. The result was to split the movement down the middle throughout the United States, and indeed in England and Scotland as well.

At the national level, the attempt at disassociation from Garrison and his ideas was unsuccessful. After managing to prevent the exclusion of women from the annual meeting of the American Anti-Slavery Society in 1839, the Garrisonian group, who were undoubtedly a tiny minority in the nation at large, managed to rout their opponents in the following year. The general secretary of the radical Massachusetts Society, John Anderson Collins, chartered the steamer *Rhode Island* to ferry sympathetic voters from Boston to the annual meeting in New York. The result was an incongruous situation where the annual covention of a national society was taken over by several hundred rank-and-file female members on an outing from Essex

[50] See P. Brock, *Radical Pacifists in Antebellum America* (Princeton, 1968) pp. 77–169. The structure of radical anti-slavery thought is brilliantly analysed in Perry, *Radical Abolitionism*.

County in Massachusetts. They dutifully voted out the old committee backed by Lewis Tappan and replaced it with a new Garrisonian one, complete with women members. The conservatives, who lacked Garrison's obvious willingness to harm the whole movement through a distasteful public controversy, then withdrew gracefully but bitterly to form their own American and Foreign Anti-Slavery Society. The issues which had divided the two groups seem complex, though Garrison's supporters were stronger in New England than in other areas. Broadly speaking, too, the conservatives were attached to the traditional churches, while many of the Garrisonians had rejected the trammels of denominationalism. At its simplest, however, the division was a difference of opinion on tactics, between those who were unconcerned with the realities of working reform politics, and the single-issue abolitionists who saw any enthusiasm tending to bring anti-slavery into disrepute as bad in itself. The recent suggestion that Garrison's extension of his reform demands was a radical strategy which worked may be accurate, but his standpoint on *slavery* was not substantially different from the single-issue abolitionists with whom he differed.[51] Unfortunately, for contemporaries, the most important thing about Garrison was not his position on slavery. His insistence on championing 'extraneous issues' which were revolting to nineteenth-century Americans not only split the movement, but antagonised potential supporters, played into the hands of the South by discrediting *all* those opposed to slavery as immoral visionaries, and generally slowed the emergence of a solid Northern abolition camp. Though the leaders of the American and Foreign Anti-Slavery Society confined their other interests to reforms acceptable to the middle-class public, they were never able to get rid of the taint of fanaticism which Garrison had left them. Most of them eventually moved over to support for the Liberty Party, and involvement in the various political ventures which culminated in the Republican Party. Abolitionists as individuals tried to continue their work as opinion-formers, but it was in the political world and in the churches that the principal anti-slavery events took place after 1840.

The organisation of the Liberty Party was principally the work

---

[51] Cf. Kraditor, *Means and Ends in American Abolitionism.*

of reformers from New York State and the West, rather than New England or Philadelphia. Its direct political strength was tiny, but by upsetting the balance between the existing parties it radically changed the course of American history. It made the attempt to break into the existing party structure, in the face of constant Garrisonian denunciations of 'cabals', 'conspiracies' and 'corruption'. The new party was founded at a Convention in Albany in 1840, nominating the ex-slaveholder and abolitionist lecturer James Gillespie Birney for President and a respected Philadelphia Quaker, Thomas Earle, for Vice-President. The party had substantial support from wealthier abolitionists like the New York landowner Gerrit Smith, but it had no success in organising the kind of grass-roots support which would have been essential to make a serious impression on the major parties. In fact, Birney sailed for Britain immediately after his nomination. Ironically, the Liberty Party caused most excitement among extremist abolitionists who were determined to denounce it. In the event, William Henry Harrison and John Tyler, the running-mate who was soon to succeed him as President, romped home against Van Buren and the discredited Democrats. During Tyler's term in the White House, distrust of slavery – perhaps also of the Negro – increased in the North. The country as a whole was also seized with enthusiasm for expansion towards the south-west, an issue closely connected with the question of slavery owing to the effect of the acquisition of new territory on the political balance between slave and free states.[52] By 1844 the Democratic Party was running James K. Polk on a platform demanding expansion to the north against the British in Oregon and to the south-west against the Mexicans. Much of the pressure for an advance against Mexico came from the South, which saw that new land could be used for slave agriculture. Indirectly the Liberal Party itself contributed to the victory of Polk and the expansionists in the 1844 election. A little encouraged by evidence of growing support throughout the North, Birney again ran as presidential candidate. Unfortunately he was only too successful. The 15,000-odd votes his party picked up in the delicately balanced New York State was enough to lose its electoral votes for the Whigs.

[52] F. Merk, *Manifest Destiny and Mission in American History* (1963; reprinted New York, 1966) pp. 24–88.

The opposite result would have defeated Polk, but as it was he was put into the White House. The sequel was the hysteria leading up to the Mexican war, and the acquisition of the great swathe of territory which eventually became the states of Nevada, California, Arizona, Utah and New Mexico, with parts of Colorado and Wyoming. At the same time, Mexico was forced to give up its claims to the Republic of Texas, which had been prematurely admitted to the Union in 1845. The major political controversy of the future was whether new territories admitted to the Union were to be slave or free. Ironically, it was the first venture of the abolitionists into politics which had led indirectly to these enormous annexations. In future political activity the abolitionists were to find themselves working in alliance with forces who had little concern over the welfare of the slave but every commitment to preventing the expansion of slavery and of Southern power into the territories.

As political excitement flared over the war and slavery expansion, American opinion continued to polarise in response to incident after incident dramatising the brutality of the slaveholders and the defencelessness of the slave. Some of these involved white abolitionists. Like the visit of George Thompson and the shooting of Elijah P. Lovejoy, they went to point up the tendency of slavery to endanger the liberty and even the life not only of the Negro but of any white who sympathised with him.[53] This was, for instance, the effect of the incarceration of the Massachusetts abolitionist Charles Torrey in a Maryland prison in 1842. In spite of Garrison's sneers at his conservatism and love of the church establishment, he had spent the years prior to his imprisonment helping blacks to escape from the border states. His death after two years in jail was well publicised and attracted a great deal of sympathy. An even more dramatic incident was the punishment of a Florida seaman, Captain Jonathan Walker, for running slaves from South Carolina to the Bahamas and freedom. His hand was branded with 'S.S.', the initials for 'slave-stealer', and he was briefly imprisoned. Small blocks of 'Walker's Hand', with the initials prominently displayed, were used extensively in abolitionist propaganda and periodicals, though Walker's

[53] R. B. Nye, *Fettered Freedom: Civil Liberties and the Slavery Controversy, 1830–1860* (East Lansing, Mich., 1949); Wolf, *On Freedom's Altar.*

sympathy for anti-slavery must be very much open to doubt.[54] Each case compounded Northern horror at what was taken as representative of the South as a whole, and Southern resentment of increasingly vehement abolitionist denunciations. At the same time they maintained anxiety over the very interference with the slave population which had led to the incidents in the first place – all the more so because of the stress laid on previous bloody slave revolts in Southern propaganda, and the increased publicity given to slave escapes throughout the nation.

Even in the North, the most important opinion-formers on slavery were often the slaves and ex-slaves themselves. One of the biases in most works written on the movement against slavery has been the failure to credit the work done by the free black communities of the North and by fugitives from the South.[55] Much of this was done within the black communities themselves. By and large, black abolitionism was relatively conservative, dedicated to publicising the atrocities of slavery, working for its overthrow by political means, but rejecting the unpopular radical enthusiasms of the Garrisonians. These were a luxury which men and women struggling to find a place in a fundamentally hostile society could not afford. The *Appeal* of David Walker, the Boston old clothes dealer, which so horrified the South with its call for violent revolution among the slaves, would also have been discountenanced by most free blacks.[56] However, much black anti-slavery activity was entirely independent from the white movement, perhaps partly because many of its members did not entirely welcome co-operation from black colleagues. The black Convention movement which emerged in 1825, and continued sporadically until the 1850s, was aimed as much at furthering the interests of the free black communities in the North as at attacking slavery. However, it did act as a forum for the airing of black opinions on slavery, as well as being an early vehicle for black nationalist

[54] See *The Trial and Imprisonment of Jonathan Walker* (Boston, 1845).

[55] Black abolitionists, like the huge and crucially important membership of the women's anti-slavery societies, have not been given their due even in recent monographs on the movement. See B. Quarles, *Black Abolitionists* (New York, 1969); Kraditor, *Means and Ends in American Abolitionism*, pp. 39–47; G. W. Lerner, *The Grimke Sisters from South Carolina* (New York, 1967).

[56] David Walker, *Appeal . . . to the Colored Citizens of the World* (Boston, 1829).

ideas. Many black abolitionists gained extensive experience in the Conventions before approaching a national audience, and indeed the Convention proceedings themselves attracted attention outside the black communities. They dramatised the vast potential among black people which was being crushed by the slave system. At the same time, the revelation of the poor treatment of Negroes in the North increased white guilt over their own shared responsibility for the system of slavery on which this repression ultimately rested.

Yet the most important black abolitionists did not confine their activities to the Convention movement, for it was essentially concerned less with overthrowing slavery than with the problems and aims of free blacks. The black abolitionists were many of them themselves escaped slaves. A minority had been born free in the North, but shared the perception that one of the proofs of the prejudice which surrounded their race was the system of slavery. In the 1830s the tendency was for them to work with white abolitionists, who were glad to patronise them as living proofs of the talents obliterated by slavery, but reluctant to undermine their own position too much by accepting blacks as leaders or even equals. The result was that in the 1840s and 1850s black abolitionists were moving away from co-operation with the white anti-slavery movement. Partly this was due to an unwillingness to be involved in the undignified squabbling of white leaders, who often seemed to spend more time talking to each other than to the country at large. It was more directly tied to the domineering way in which they refused to allow full scope for black abilities on the lecture platform whenever these seemed likely to gain too large a share of public attention. Many went on to operate as individuals, touring the country alone and lecturing and writing against the slave system. Others turned to the heroic work of helping fellow-blacks escape from the border states, or to manning the Vigilance Committees which protected the fugitives during their journey through the North to the Canadian border. In some cases, by the 1850s, it was possible to form organisations which were at least black-led and in some cases wholly black in membership.

The breach between the black and white movements was never complete, and indeed most black leaders followed a pragmatic course of co-operating with white anti-slavery societies, working as individual lecturers, or leading their own organisations as the occasion offered. Yet they were clearly more independent in the 1840s and 1850s than in the 1830s. At a time when white abolitionists were either discredited from their excesses, or absorbed in politics, it was black abolitionists who took over the initiative of the movement and continued the work of dramatising the horror of slavery. The real focus of the North–South struggle was now a political one, but the backdrop to the political stage was provided by an American opinion which was being eased into an anti-slavery position by the work of these brilliant black propagandists. Indeed the drama of their lives might itself have been enough to catch the public imagination. There is an element of romance about all escape stories, and this was all the more so in evangelical circles which frowned on novel-reading and where an exciting story was doubly welcome. At the same time, the stories of the ex-slaves had a great deal of potential for moral improvement. The flight of the slave came to take on the tones, and provide an analogue for, the direct confrontation between good and evil. Again, nothing provided a finer example of Victorian self-help than the thrift and industry of the Negro who struggled virtuously to clothe and educate himself in spite of the blows of prejudice and the demoralisation of his own or his parents' years as slaves. Finally, the lives of the escaped slaves must subconsciously have filled much the same need as pornography did for those ungodly enough to read it. The black abolitionists could give first-hand accounts of attacks on the chastity of female slaves, and the unbridled violence of their masters. The fascination of their audiences for these horrors may have been only a way of sublimating their own appetites for the same kind of licence, but it was none the less real. Even if they had not had a restraint, sincerity and grace often lacking in their white colleagues, it was the black abolitionists who had the greatest wherewithal to rouse American interest over slavery.

Few of these men and women have had their proper due in histories of anti-slavery. Partly this is due to the old assumption that a black leader in a white society is an anomaly, partly also to the turning of attention to political activity over slavery at the very time when black abolitionism was at its most important. To underestimate the black abolitionists, however, is to miss the shifting of opinion on slavery which made political activity itself possible. Frederick Douglass was only one of many ex-slaves whose narratives became common reading and whose names became household words.[57] Although he now seems to stand out in his generation, other men and women had equally exciting escapes from slavery. A number, too, approached him if they were not his peers in power of intellect and oratory. Nevertheless, Douglass had all the attributes which made the arguments of the ex-slaves compelling. He had been born as a slave on the Eastern Shore of Maryland, around 1818, of a union between a slave mother and a white man. He was able to relate that one of his earliest memories was the sadistic beating of one of his aunts, a particularly beautiful woman, by their master. Various masters had frequently and severely punished him during his servitude, but he had still struggled to learn to read and write, and even to get a smattering of political knowledge. He had had opportunities denied to most, in the sense that he eventually became a hired slave, bound out to various masters. It was this which made his eventual escape possible. Yet his story was one of the triumph of determination and self-discipline in almost impossible conditions. In his *Narrative* he left the details of his escape from Maryland in 1838 to conjecture, to shield those who had been involved with him, but he had already been thwarted in one attempt, and his perseverance was in itself heroic. Douglass was a most remarkable man by any standards, entirely self-taught but one of the greatest orators and propagandists of his time. But the elements which went to make up his appeal to mid-nineteenth-century America were shared by many other brilliant escapees and freemen who joined in the abolitionist movement.

Douglass himself had first been befriended by a fellow-black, David Ruggles of New York, who was one of the city's most active workers in the efforts to help escapees from slavery. He was married by another, the Revd James W. C. Pennington, one of the leading black clergymen of the ante-bellum years. Pennington was active not only in the Convention movement, the Negro churches and the New York Vigilance Committee, but also in freelance abolitionist lecturing. This carried him all over the

---

[57] *Narrative of the Life of Frederick Douglass, an American Slave* (Boston, 1845). See also F. Douglass, *My Bondage and my Freedom* (New York, 1855); idem, *Life and Times* (Hartford, Conn., 1884); L. Foner, *Life and Writings of Frederick Douglass*, 4 vols (New York, 1950); B. Quarles, *Frederick Douglass* (1948; reprinted New York, 1968).

States, and also on two separate trips to meet enthusiastic anti-slavery audiences in Britain. On a different level, the work of the U.G.R. was publicised, and some of its financial needs met, by the appeals of one of its most heroic conductresses, Sojourner Truth. Another black leader with immense appeal to white audiences, especially in the 1850s, was Josiah Henson, who had some influence over Harriet Beecher Stowe in writing *Uncle Tom* and later claimed to be the 'original' of Uncle Tom. He had escaped from the border state of Kentucky as a young man, and like Sojourner Truth he made several trips back to the South to help other slaves to safety. His most important work, however, was in trying to organise the agricultural community of escaped slaves and other free blacks in Wilberforce Colony at Dresden, Ontario. Partly because of the association with Mrs Stowe, partly because of Henson's real though unlettered personal dignity, the various editions of *Uncle Tom's Story* became best-sellers. Other fugitives caught the imagination of the Northern and European public with the sheer excitement of their escape. Henry 'Box' Brown had made the long journey from Richmond to Phila-delphia nailed up inside a packing-case – which, in spite of the express instructions written on the lid, had been loaded upside-down, with Brown correspondingly out of alignment. There was also a great deal of public sympathy for the personable mulatto couple William and Ellen Crafts, who eventually settled in England after escaping as an ailing young planter (Ellen), travel-ling north for his health, attended by his body-servant (William). Their plan later became part of the fictional adventures of two of the characters in *Clotel*, a novel by the black writer and abolition-ist William Wells Brown. Yet it would be a mistake to assume that these black men and women made their appeal solely through the romance of their past. Men like Henson, 'Box' Brown and William Craft were uneducated, and relied for their appeal on this romance and the sincerity of their message. Others had developed an elegance and force of expression which would have made its mark irrespective of their race or background. This was true of Douglass above all, but there were many other black spokesmen, born free and slave, who had worked endlessly to build up the formal literary and rhetorical skills needed to make them master propagandists. David Ruggles, a leader of the Convention movement and the New York Vigilance Committee and co-founder of the American Anti-Slavery Society, was one such, and the younger New Yorker, James McCune Smith, another. Smith had returned from doing his medical degree at Glasgow University to practise in his home town, where he lent his calm but highly articulate support to any effort which he thought would combine the best interests of the local black community with the fight against slavery. Smith is hardly mentioned in any standard history of the anti-slavery movement, and yet he probably had a better mind than any other black leader of his time, including Douglass. The efforts of other men of the same sort have been greatly underestimated: for instance, the Revd Robert Purvis, a Philadelphian who had taken his degree at Amherst, and who greatly influenced his British and American audiences against the American Colonization Society long before Garrison had dreamt of attacking it; or Charles Remond, who with his sister Sarah devoted his life to lecturing to white audiences against slavery, and incidentally spoke extensively to British audiences on the need for land reform in India.

Even those black leaders who are relatively well known, like William Wells Brown, Henry Highland Garnet and Samuel Ringgold Ward, have not been given their due in modern studies for their success in dramatising the evils of slavery in the North.[58] Even less attention has been paid to the most radical of all ante-bellum black leaders, Dr Martin Delany. Delany had read medicine at Harvard, and had become impatient with the slowness of orthodox abolitionist methods after working for some time under the aegis of Frederick Douglass. He then managed to break through the distrust of things African bred in the free black communities by the activities of the American Colonization Society.

[58] The best modern introductions are Quarles, *Black Abolitionists;* L. Litwak, *North of Slavery: The Negro in the Free States, 1790–1860* (Chicago, 1961); C. H. Wesley, *Neglected History* (Washington, 1969) pp. 56–85; Pease and Pease, *Bound with them in Chains*, pp. 140–90. Modern biographies of these men are slowly being produced, but they are still best studied through their own autobiographies, most of which were published in several editions, and many of which have now been reprinted. Good examples are W. Crafts and E. Crafts, *Running a Thousand Miles for Freedom* (London, 1851); S. R. Ward, *Autobiography of a Fugitive Negro* (London, 1855); J. W. C. Pennington, *The Fugitive Blacksmith*, 3rd ed. (London, 1850); *The Life of Josiah Henson, Formerly a Slave* (London, 1851); *Narrative of William Wells Brown, a Fugitive Slave* (Boston, 1848).

He called for a reassertion of black cultural identity against the American mainstream, and the establishment of wholly black colonies in West Africa. His *The Condition, Elevation, Emigration and Destiny of the Colored People of the United States* was little read, but he was able to win a substantial section of the Convention movement over to his side, and travelled in Nigeria in search of a suitable site for a colony before his attention, like that of other blacks, was diverted by the new hopes for a solution to slavery raised by the Civil War.[59] Indeed they were right in assuming that Northern opinion had turned further against slavery by this time. However, an essential element is left out of the historical equation if the words and writings of black people themselves and their effect on this shift are missed.

Changes in attitudes to slavery were not confined to the North. At the same time as escaped slaves and free blacks were continuing the work of whipping up opinion against slavery, the South was hardening in its determination to protect its special social institutions from all outside interference. There is probably some grain of truth in the old argument that this new intransigence was provoked by what appeared to be the increasingly fanatical position of the North. It is now realised that the South was tied to maintaining its slave system not only by a profit motive, real or imagined, but also by a complex series of psychological and social associations which made slavery the cornerstone of the ruling class's ascendancy. To abandon slavery, for Southern leadership, would have been to abdicate power not only over the black population, but also over non-slaveholding whites and the South as a whole. Northern attacks on slavery would have been bad enough, but they came at a time when the white South was suffering increasing anxiety over world disapproval of slavery, probable future unavailability of land into which plantation agriculture could expand, and relative decline in its political power as balanced against the rest of the nation.[60] At the same time, in crude profit terms, slavery in the expanding areas of the

[59] T. Draper, *The Rediscovery of Black Nationalism* (New York, 1970) pp. 21–37; F. R. Rollin, *Life and Public Services of Martin R. Delany* (Boston, 1868); M. R. Delany, *Official Report of the Niger Valley Exploring Party* (1860), reprinted in H. H. Bell (ed.), *Search for a Place: Black Separatism and Africa, 1860* (Ann Arbor, Mich., 1969) pp. 27–148.

[60] Genovese, *Political Economy of Slavery*, pp. 13–39.

cotton South was now making a great deal of money and likely to make a great deal more – a very different situation from the revolutionary period, when profitable slave agriculture had seemed to be on the way out. When criticised sharply over tolerating slavery, given this unique combination of profit motive, vested interest in the social system as a whole and acute anxiety, the South was bound to lash out in its own defence. Yet the corollaries do not apply. It is not true that if there had been no abolitionists, the South would not have so lashed out, further polarisation of opinion would have been avoided and there would have been no Civil War.[61] Apart from the fact that this would have left the black population enslaved, the fanaticism of the South was principally bred by its own anxieties. In fact the equation can be set the other way round. In many ways it was the sheer obstinacy of the South in refusing to admit any wrong in slavery, especially as expressed through its clergymen, which pushed large sections of the North into taking the extreme position that slavery should be ended at whatever cost. This is not to refer to the emergence of a 'positive good' school of pro-slavery literature, for this was a development which came later, but to the refusal of Southern clergymen to make responsible criticisms of slavery. Their justification of this position, though scripturally correct, gave the appearance of an attempt to suppress the whole message of Christianity. In intensely evangelical Northern circles it was easy to leap to the further conclusion that the South was anti-Christian, that slavery was what had made it so, and that it should therefore be opposed. The result was the complete division of church institutions along a line between those prepared to remain silent on slavery and those determined to attack it. These church institutions would otherwise have been, and hitherto had been, the most important unifying force among the American middle and upper classes, probably even more so than the Federal government.

Indeed, this failure of consensus in clerical circles is the most important and at the same time the most neglected of the many steps which opened the way to the Civil War. The ambiguity of the Christian message on slavery has already been explained, but the fact remains that by the end of the Jacksonian period world

[61] Cf. Dumond, *Anti-Slavery Origins of the Civil War.*

Protestant opinion had moved to the position that this ambiguity should be interpreted in favour of the slave and against his master. By and large the Southern clergy, in spite of an intense internationalism of church ties which has often been missed, preferred to set themselves at odds with their colleagues in other areas of the world than with their own country's ruling class. The result was to wreck unity in the American churches, which at the time were the only platforms for expressing a reasoned liberal opinion on slavery.

In fact slavery had been a matter for dissension in the British and American churches since the colonial period – and indeed for the European churches since the early sixteenth century, as we have seen. What made the issue so disruptive in the nineteenth century was partly the greatly increased number of Christians with scruples over slavery, but more immediately the urgency of concern produced by the early nineteenth-century revivals, which made it distasteful to continue co-operation with those who appeared to be compromising with sin. At the same time, sharpening sectional distrust was making national church unity an even more volatile issue around which rivalries on other counts could crystallise. In fact most of the American churches were divided into separate Northern and Southern wings, or were far gone towards such a division, by the 1840s. Though complex, the disastrous division of the Presbyterian church into Old and New Schools in 1837 fell along sectional lines and undoubtedly implied differing attitudes to the slavery issue. Years later, Harriet Beecher Stowe satirised the clergy of both churches as being prepared to reunify now that the Northerners, too, had cast aside their responsibilities over slavery.[62] In the 1840s the Methodists were rent by the same kind of division, first by the secession of the small but radical Wesleyan Methodist Connection in 1843. Later they split into two completely separate organisations, the Methodist Episcopal Church North and the Methodist Episcopal

[62] H. B. Stowe, *Dred: A Tale of the Great Dismal Swamp* (London, 1856) pp. 375–97. See C. B. Staiger, 'Abolitionism and the Presbyterian Schism of 1837–1838', *Mississippi Valley Historical Review*, xxxvi (1949) 413–14. Clerical divisions are summarised in S. Ahlstrom, *A Religious History of the American People* (New Haven, 1972) pp. 657–69, and fully studied in H. Shelton Smith, *In His Maker's Image, But ... Racism in Southern Religion, 1780–1910* (Durham, N.C., 1972) pp. 23–207.

Church South.[63] The Baptists suffered a similar schism in 1845, so that the only major Protestant denomination left united was the Congregationalists, whose situation was simplified by a membership confined largely to the North. The Quakers also managed to avoid open discussion over slavery, except in Indiana, where the Yearly Meeting divided vociferously in 1843, not over slavery versus anti-slavery, but over the way in which the Society's testimony against slavery could most effectively be expressed.[64] By this time the Friends, like the Congregationalists, were largely confined to the Northern states, where they had moved partly out of genuine discomfort at their association with slavery. The Roman church, too, owing to the combination of its hierarchical nature and the modest compromise position it took on slavery, managed to prevent the wide range of opinions among its members from leading to serious disunity.[65] Yet the 1840s saw slavery destroy those Protestant church institutions which stretched across the sections.

This division was all the more serious since it was accompanied by similar developments in the interdenominational societies which provided another area of contact between churchmen from the slave South and the free North. The national missionary societies – the American Bible Society, the American Board of Commissioners for Foreign Missions, the Tract Society and the Home Missionary Society – were severely weakened in the course of the 1840s, essentially through disagreement over the kind of Christian literature they were to distribute and the places in which it was to be distributed. Southern clergymen were under enormous pressure from their congregations not to sanction the circulation of tracts or the preaching of sermons among the slave population if they made clear the potentially revolutionary nature of Christianity. By and large they succumbed to this pressure or moved north rather than fighting in their own communities for the evangelisation of their slaves. Northern ministers, especially

[63] D. G. Mathews, *Slavery and Methodism: A Chapter in American Morality, 1780–1845* (Princeton, 1965) pp. 212–82.

[64] W. Edgerton, *A History of the Separation in the Indiana Yearly Meetings of Friends, which Took Place in the Winter of 1842 and 1843, on the Anti-Slavery Question* (Cincinnati, 1856); T. E. Drake, *Quakers and Slavery in America* (New Haven, 1950) pp. 133–66.

[65] M. H. Rice, *American Catholic Opinion in the Slavery Controversy* (New York, 1944) p. 158 and passim.

the Congregationalists, who were active in the missionary societies but had no colleagues to embarrass in the South, saw no barrier to pressing for freedom to educate and evangelise slaves without planter supervision, or indeed to calling for exclusion from communion in their mission churches of all who were implicated with slavery.[66] To take one example, the result in the case of the American Board of Commissioners for Foreign Missions was a bitter dispute lasting from 1846 to 1848, the eventual victory of the Southern ministers and their sympathisers, and the withdrawal of a great proportion of the Board's Northern supporters. These in turn swung over to supporting strictly Northern and anti-slavery organisations, like the denominational Baptist Free Missionary Society, or the interdenominational American Missionary Association. It emphasised its distrust of the slavocracy by refusing to elide egalitarian passages from its publications, or to admit slaveholders to communion, even in foreign mission stations where slavery was an 'organic' part of society. The position of the Southern clergy in the nineteenth century was not an easy one. Yet it is arguable that this collapse of unity was due to their refusal to bring their attitudes to slavery up to the same level as those of enlightened churchmen throughout the Protestant world, not to any unreasonableness in the suggestions of the Northern evangelists, at least within the traditional churches and missionary societies. In either case, in a country with only the frailest of true national structures, the results were disastrous. At a time when the churches were undoubtedly the most important of all opinion-forming bodies, the intransigence of the Southern clergy not only made a reasoned compromise on abolition impossible, but drove the pulpits in the two sections towards opposite poles. This is quite different from saying that abolitionist extremism broke down American institutions, and this whole aspect should be balanced against the argument that it was this same extremism which drew the South to secession. The destruction of these precious church institutions, mainly owing to the Southern refusal to grasp nineteenth-century realities, left the country with no agency which would or indeed could mediate between the sections over slavery. The only pos-

[66] C. C. Cole, *The Social Ideas of the Northern Evangelists, 1826–1860* (New York, 1954) pp. 96–131; J. R. Bodo, *The Protestant Clergy and Public Issues, 1812–1848* (Princeton, 1954) pp. 138–51.

sible one left was the Federal government. By definition, its existence was bound to become counter-productive as soon as slavery became the main issue in politics, the main political parties became sectional, and elections were fought, at least in appearance, on the issue of abolition. This is exactly what happened by the end of the 1840s.

Slavery became America's most pressing political issue against a backdrop of division in the churches and general polarisation in national opinion. This polarisation was not only the result of the irresponsibly radical position taken by the Northern abolitionists. For one thing, by no means all of them were irresponsibly radical, and it is equally important that the American voter was faced not only with the rhetoric of abolition, but with the 'positive good' propaganda of Southern pro-slavery writers. Though a logical product of the needs of the Southern ruling class, they were as totally wrong-headed and quite as much behind the mainstream of nineteenth-century thought as Garrison and his followers were ahead of it. Both groups were equally dangerous, and both had equal effect in perverting the opinion of the opposite section against them until it was impossible to mount any reasoned campaign against slavery in either section, let alone in the nation as a whole.

It is easy to underestimate the pro-slavery literature published in the decades before the Civil War, both in quality and sheer volume. This built on a substantial tradition of support for slavery, which goes back to Sepúlveda and beyond in Europe, and at least to John Saffin's replies to Judge Sewall's *Selling of Joseph* in the colonies. By the mid-nineteenth century, however, the pro-slavery argument took on a new tone. It had traditionally been based on two theories. The first was the classical assumption that slavery was justified by the 'natural' inferiority of the lowest classes in society. The second was the Christian assumption that heathens could legitimately be enslaved, and that it was for their good to be converted and brought under the civilising influence of Christendom. Both assumptions had their effect on nineteenth-century thought, but they were supplemented in the case of the unfortunate Negro's servitude by 'scientific' attempts to prove his 'biological' inferiority. There evolved the corresponding argument that slavery was appropriate and indeed advantageous for blacks, but at the same time the only social system upon which a true civilisation could flower. The 'positive good' theorists were able to claim that while industrial society based on free labour was sinking into corruption and weakness, the plantation South, with its patriarchate of a Protestant American master class and a black slave labour force, was evolving into a modern reproduction of classical Greece. An attack on the inequities of Northern society and the oppression of its labouring or mud-sill class was implied or stated in the writings and speeches of a host of Southern propagandists like J. H. Hammond, George Fitzhugh or, to a lesser extent, the great South Carolinian statesman John C. Calhoun. In book-length works, but also in newspaper articles, pamphlets and political orations, the South was bombarded with material on the hopeless abuses of the capitalist system and its contrast with the benevolent stewardship of the plantation. For Southerners, the effect was to rationalise any doubts they may have had about slavery, and to strengthen their determination to resist any attempts to interfere with it. There were even more unfortunate results in the North. The circulation of 'positive good' literature, largely through sensationalist quotations printed in Northern newspapers, naturally produced resentment at their denigration of the free labour system. But they also had a quality of aggression about them, and expressed a distrust of the whole middle-class free-enterprise structure, which gave some colour to abolitionist warnings of the danger that the slave power would eventually pull it down. What gave the abolitionists enough credibility to pull a substantial number of otherwise dubious Northerners over to their side was not the merit of their own utterances. It was the reaction to the utter condemnation of the whole Northern social system in the South's 'positive good' propaganda. The 'scientific' attempts to set out a conclusive proof of Negro inferiority were much less important in the North, since few Americans of either section held much of a brief for black equality. Yet they too were immensely important in rein-forcing Southern assumptions on the dangers of tampering with the slave status. The work of scientists like Dr Eliphalet Nott of New Orleans, or J. Van Evrie of New York, which 'demon-strated' the lack of intellectual abilities of all black people and set out conclusive anthropological 'proofs' of the Negro's close relationship to the apes, was enthusiastically received in the South. It would be resurrected near the end of the century as part of the racist literature which reinforced Southern clamping down on the black population during the populist period. Before the Civil War it had incalculable effects in justifying and hardening support for the slavery of beings who could now be seen as sub-human – certainly far more so than any response to the demands of abolitionist writers north of the Mason–Dixon line.[67] Polarisation of American opinion before the Civil War owed something to the more extreme abolitionists, whose harangues did a great deal for their egos but very little to help the slave. But their colleagues as other villains of the piece were the extremist pro-slavery writers and, paradoxically, the apparently moderate clergymen from both sections.

What is certain, in either case, is that the division of American opinion along sectional lines continued to sharpen in the 1840s and 1850s. The collapse of the existing party structure during the debates on slavery was simply a reflection of this division. At the same time, the conflicts of politics themselves created controversy which worked to widen the division, until a party election was finally fought along sectional lines. This development had been started with the emergence of an anti-slavery third party in 1840, and it continued with the subsequent campaigns of the Liberty Party and its successors. The disaster of its splitting the New York vote and putting James K. Polk in the White House in 1844 has already been noted. By 1848 the Liberty Party had weakened, yet slavery was ironically all the more of an issue owing to the problem of what to do with the territory acquired at the end of the Mexican war. The Liberty Party found itself in the extraordinary position of endorsing ex-President Martin Van Buren, the candidate of a new 'Union' Party, with Charles Francis Adams. Van Buren actually gained some 10 per cent of the vote cast in the election, but unlike 1844 the 'abolitionist' candidate drew votes not only from the minority concerned with ending slavery, but also from the growing number of Northerners who

[67] W. S. Jenkins, *Pro-Slavery Thought in the Old South* (Chapel Hill, N.C., 1935); W. Stephen, *The Leopard's Spots: Scientific Attitudes toward Race in America, 1815–1859* (Chicago, 1960); R. Hofstadter, 'John C. Calhoun: The Marx of the Master Class', in *The American Political Tradition and the Men who Made it* (London, 1962) pp. 67–91; G. Fitzhugh, *Cannibals All! or, Slaves without Masters*, ed. C. Vann Woodward (Cambridge, Mass., 1960); H. Wish, *George Fitzhugh, Propagandist of the Old South* (Baton Rouge, La., 1943).

were both anti-Southern and anti-black. They were determined to keep slaves and indeed black people out of their own communities and off the vast lands about to be opened to settlement. The 'free soil' vote was primarily an anti-Negro vote. It was in the 1848 election that it first became important, although blacks had been consistently and sometimes brutally discriminated against in the North throughout the ante-bellum decades. The true anti-slavery political movement, as a party organisation in itself, was now dead. The future lay with the free-soilers who eventually gravitated towards the Republican Party. Especially strong in the young Midwestern states, often strangely yoked to abolitionist voters, and indeed using an anti-slavery rhetoric which disguised their principal aim of keeping the Negro, slave or free, at arm's length, the free-soilers became the rank and file of the political attack on the South. At the same time, the out-of-doors activities of the abolitionists, especially black ones, were continuing to inflame Northern sympathy for the slave population. It was the combination between this sympathy and the total lack of sympathy of the free-soilers which created a solid anti-Southern political bloc immediately before the Civil War. Their intentions were not necessarily to abolish slavery, but their rhetoric was an abolitionist one, their loyalties sectional and their shared distrust of the South and its allies profound.[68] This was a situation where the two sections, entirely different in social and political organisation, were pitted against one another. The Negro was the vehicle around whom the division crystallised, but the irony was that on both sides there was an unholy alliance between those who hated him and those who believed they loved him.

The full extent of anti-Southern feeling, which had a long history going back to the Missouri Compromise, again became clear in the bitter debates over the Mexican cessions which resulted in the Compromise of 1850. It is questionable whether a failure to reach a compromise would have had a worse effect in increasing distrust between the sections than the unsatisfactory terms of the 'Omnibus Bill' which sealed it. In fact the whole slavery issue had now become so volatile that it may have been

[68] These developments are discussed in E. Foner, *Free Soil, Free Labor, Free Men: The Ideology of the Republican Party before the Civil War* (New York, 1970), though Foner's interpretation differs from the one presented here.

impossible to work out any *modus vivendi* between slave and free sections. It was agreed that California should be a free state, but the decision to allow the Utah and Nebraska territories to settle their attitudes to slavery by popular vote, when sufficiently populous, created a good deal of nervousness for the future. The banning of slavery and the slave trade in Washington and the District of Columbia was satisfactory to abolitionists, but nothing worked more to inflame feelings than the confirmation and reinforcement of the Fugitive Slave Law. For the next few years anti-Southern feeling was kept alive in Northern communities by attempts to drag fugitive blacks back to slavery. Few of these attempts were successful – the Sims case and the rendition of Anthony Burns in Boston being notable exceptions. However, each incident caused great popular excitement, and fleshed out the abolitionist warnings that the slaveocracy would doom freedom not only where slavery was tolerated but in the nation as a whole. It was at this time that the anti-slavery movement gained the vocal support of brilliant orators like Henry Ward Beecher, George Barrell Cheever, Thomas Wentworth Higginson and Theodore Parker himself.[69] Meanwhile, public romanticisation of the Negro increased, partly owing to the simple pathos of Mrs Stowe's *Uncle Tom's Cabin* and its cadre of imitators, but equally to the growing stream of fugitive slave narratives turned out by black writers, whose plight was all the more real in the light of the Fugitive Slave Law's atrocities. As for the South, its fears of a Northern conspiracy to overthrow its institutions became more pressing in the light of non-co-operation in returning runaways. Although the Fugitive Slave Law and the incidents arising from it probably did more to make the gulf between North and South complete in the 1850s, other controversies worked in the same direction, towards fostering the mutual paranoia which made the Civil War possible.[70] All these controversies had slavery as their central issue. The caning of the anti-slavery Senator

[69] Pease and Pease, in *J.A.H.*, LVIII 923–37; T. G. Edelstein, *Strange Enthusiasm: A Life of Thomas Wentworth Higginson* (New Haven, 1968) pp. 100 ff. On the Compromise, see H. Hamilton, *Prologue to Conflict: The Crisis and Compromise of 1850* (Lexington, Ky., 1964).

[70] The 1850s are conveniently covered in L. Filler, *The Crusade against Slavery, 1830–1860* (New York, 1960) pp. 192–280, and at much vaster length in A. Nevins, *The Ordeal of the Union*, 2 vols (New York, 1947); idem, *The Emergence of Lincoln*, 2 vols (New York, 1950).

Charles Sumner by 'Bully' Brooks of South Carolina satisfied the North that the abolitionists had been right in arguing that slaveowning bred unbridled violence. The battles of 'Bleeding Kansas', over the future Kansas–Nebraska Territory, made it clear to each section that the other was determined to extend its way of life throughout the nation. The Dred Scott decision, in which the Supreme Court judged that a slave's travels on free Northern soil had not given him his freedom, convinced the North that the South now had a judicial loophole to extend slavery (and, even worse, Negroes) throughout the Union. Finally, John Brown's raid on Harpers Ferry convinced the South that its extremists had been right all along. The North had now signified its determination to promote the ultimate horror of servile rebellion. Each of these incidents took its toll in distrust against the background of the chain of fugitive slave cases, and the increasing output of extremist literature in both sections. Anti-abolitionist and pro-slavery groups in the South, anti-slavery and anti-black groups in the North, were now united in their common hostility towards the opposite section. The Union was in a precarious state when Lincoln went to the polls as leader of the Republicans in 1860. The party had done relatively well in 1856, but in 1860 it was faced with a majority of the Democratic Party which confessedly represented Southern interests. It never pledged anything more than the intention of keeping slavery in the South. Although much of the Republican Party's support was free-soil rather than anti-slavery, Lincoln's victory was seen as a guarantee of a Federal attack on the peculiar institution. The result was secession and war.

In spite of this disaster, a minority of Northerners were in favour of abolition in 1861. The Emancipation Proclamation only came in 1863, and then largely as a war measure. The determination of the majority of Northern voters was to keep blacks in the South. But though it was this and not true anti-slavery feeling which led to the war, it was the great presence of slavery, the uncompromisable institution, which had brought the nation to ruins. It is true that the abolitionists and the extreme propagandists of the South had created the charged situation where a peaceful solution was out of the question. But given the moral imperatives of the nineteenth century, the extremists were themselves the children of slavery. There are countless theories on the origins of the Civil War, but all come back to the fact that slavery itself created the conditions which led to sectional rivalry, to sectional extremism and sectional war. Itself conceived in centuries of violence and fear, American slavery ended fittingly in the short, bloody years of the Civil War.

10 The Final Phases

In the retrospect of the nineteenth century, the importance of the American Civil War seems gigantic, so much so that it is easy to see it as the agency which ended black slavery. There is some truth in this. The war saw the emancipation of the slaves in North America, the freeing of the Union government from Southern influence enabled it to give the naval co-operation which doomed the Atlantic slave trade, and the abolition in the United States had great effects in Latin America. The critical importance of the American controversy and conflict is that after great publicity they left Brazil and Cuba in an isolated position where they were more prone to tampering with slavery. On the other hand, the slaves freed in 1863 were only a proportion of those still in bondage in the Americas, and did not even include all those in the States. The ending of the Atlantic slave trade had no effect on the vast Arab-dominated trade of East Africa. Lincoln's Emancipation Proclamation technically ended slavery in the United States, but even then it gave no guarantees that black people would not in fact be retained in slavery. If Churchill had taken it upon himself in 1943 to announce full civil rights for all German Jews, he would have been doing the same kind of thing as Lincoln in 1863. Even once victory actually put the Emancipation Proclamation into force, many anti-slavery leaders found themselves moving on, in the reconstruction period, to the educational and other work needed to enable the slaves to take their place in free society.

On a world scale, the grand design of universal emancipation was only half realised. The British abolitionists collected funds and gave moral support to the American work in reconstruction, but also retained their concern for slaves and ex-slaves in other areas which had now become more important. While the Civil War itself was in progress, they were lobbying against the officials responsible for ruthlessly repressing the ex-slaves involved in the

Governor Eyre rising in Jamaica. Later they turned their attention to the horrors of the East African slave trade, and campaigned for a strong British presence to combat it, eventually succeeding in bringing about the protectorate over Zanzibar, the greatest slaving entrepôt of the Indian Ocean. Indeed their concern over slavery went on right into the twentieth century, when a minority of them continued agitation against various forms of survivals from slavery – in Islam, among the 'blackbirds' in the Pacific, in Abyssinia and in China. There was strong British pressure to force international action on slavery through the League of Nations, and indeed the British and Foreign Anti-Slavery Society, now amalgamated with the Aborigines' Rights Protection Society, is still in being at the present day. With an estimated million slaves in the contemporary world – over a third of the number in the United States in 1860 – the society still continues its work, without attracting significant interest in liberal circles. As for Latin America, the real fight against slavery had hardly begun in the early 1860s. The slave trade to Brazil had effectively ended. Slavery was extirpated from all countries except Cuba and Brazil, but in these two it continued to flourish. It was partly under the stimulus of interest in North American emancipation that true anti-slavery movements emerged in Brazil and Spain – in much the same way as the British Emancipation Act of 1833 had once had its effect on the United States. Yet the Brazilian and Spanish abolitionists were not successful for another twenty years, so that it was really only by the 1880s that it could be said that the slave systems of the Americas had been dismantled. In Cuba, the result of emancipation was the speeding-up of the tempo of resistance to Spain which led to the Spanish–American war of 1898. In Brazil, slavery brought the Braganza dynasty down with it and converted the empire to a republic. Throughout the Americas, indeed, slavery still leaves its legacy in ignorance, poverty and tortured race relations. Neither the Emancipation Proclamation nor the surrender at Appamattox ended the monster slavery's lease of life.

Even in the United States, the war itself did not bring freedom. At its outbreak, few Northerners had been in favour of an abolition of slavery at all, let alone an immediate one. If Lincoln's administration had had any plans of ending slavery as opposed to checking it, it would have been far in advance of public opinion, quite apart from the problem of keeping the border states within the Union. Lincoln spoke for most of the nation in 1862 when he wrote to Greeley that

> My paramount object in this struggle *is* to save the Union and is *not* either to save or to destroy slavery. If I could save the Union without freeing *any* slave, I would do it; if I could save it by freeing *all* the slaves, I would do it; and if I could do it by freeing some and leaving others alone, I would also do that.[1]

In fact the war saw an intensification of public hostility to the Negro. This was epitomised by a series of attacks on black people and black property throughout the North. The culmination was the savage New York Draft Riots of 1863. These were caused by an attempt to use black strike-breakers, and to continue what was popularly considered the fight for the liberty of their brethren in the South by drafting the strikers lock, stock and barrel into the Union Army. There followed two nights of looting, burning and rioting against New York's black population, only a tiny majority of whom had been involved as blackleg labourers. This was only the most extreme expression of violent race prejudice which was quite independent of competition for jobs. Most of the Northern states retained their existing legislation discriminating against blacks, which looked forward to the Southern 'Jim Crow' laws of the later part of the century. In the most extreme cases, those of the Midwestern and far Western states, the war gave an opportunity to strengthen discriminatory laws which in some areas specifically banned black citizens from remaining overnight in that locality.[2] At the outset of the war, the abolitionists still faced as much of a problem in changing the heart of their neighbours as that of the South. Because of a combination of fear that the war would bring blacks, refugee or liberated, flooding to the North, and resentment at Lincoln's party having broken the country to pieces for the sake of barbarous aliens, anti-black feeling actually increased in most Northern communities in the first months after Fort Sumter.

[1] Lincoln to Greeley, 22 Aug 1862, in R. P. Baisler (ed.), *The Collected Works of Abraham Lincoln*, 9 vols (New Brunswick, N.J., 1953) v 388–9.

[2] V. J. Voegeli, *Free but not Equal: The Midwest and the Negro during the Civil War* (Chicago, 1967); E. Berwanger, *The Frontier against Slavery: Western Anti-Negro Prejudice and the Slavery Extension Controversy* (Urbana, Ill., 1967).

The change in public attitudes was brought about partly by the vagaries of the war itself. Sentiment towards the slaveowner, though not necessarily the slave, also changed, among the public and within the administration. Lincoln's personal wish by 1862 was for a compensated and gradual emancipation, not for an unconditional abolition of the sort which most abolitionists had been demanding since the 1830s. Even worse, he tried to persuade any black leaders who would listen to him that their best plan was colonisation in some area of Latin America which he hoped the State Department could secure for the purpose.[3] It was not until the end of the war that he was willing to take the political risk of emancipating the bondsmen of loyal slaveholders in the border states. The position of those slaves in territory already occupied by the Union troops remained similarly anomalous. However, by September 1862, after the Confederate defeat at Antietam, it was possible to issue a preliminary Emancipation Proclamation which stated that all slaves held in states still in a state of rebelliousness on 1 January 1863 should be freed. Even when 1 January and the final Emancipation Proclamation came, the freedom given by the President was incomplete. The slaves of the Confederacy remained without the power to take their freedom, even supposing they all heard of it. Lincoln's sensitivity to the political importance of the border states left the slavery of something not far short of a million black people untouched. Though it opened the way to later and more concrete legislation, the Emancipation Proclamation was a military measure which left the problem of slavery unsolved. It is doubtful whether it would have been tolerated by Congress if it had tried to do anything more. As for the abolitionists, apart from the most unperceptive, among whom William Lloyd Garrison was numbered, their response was one of disappointment and scorn. Their triumph did not come until the Constitutional Amendments passed to enfranchise blacks at the end of the war.[4]

The effect on the slaves, or at least on those who heard of the

[3] 'Address on Colonization to a Deputation of Negroes', 14 Aug 1862, in *Collected Works*, v 370–5.

[4] J. H. Franklin, *The Emancipation Proclamation* (New York, 1963) surveys the background to the document and its significance. On the abolitionist response, see J. M. McPherson, *The Struggle for Equality: Abolitionists and the Negro in the Civil War and Reconstruction* (Princeton, 1964) pp. 52–133.

Proclamation, was to increase their discontent. The general slow-ing down of work which had gone on since the beginning of the war continued, and the incidence of escape probably increased. Yet these were differences only of degree. In spite of the obvious slackening of discipline due to the departure of able-bodied white Southerners for the front, slaves in the Confederacy were still living in the middle of an armed camp. The patterns of covert resistance were the same, but punishments still savage enough to ensure that they would not generally become overt. The constant white fear of insurrection, made all the greater by horror at the Proclamation, the slaves' gradually intensifying non-co-operation, and their escape towards Union lines, were in the long run more effective than violent resistance in slowly sap-ping the power and morale of the Confederacy.[5] The reaction of the slaves to the Emancipation Proclamation was not such as to have immediate effect in destroying the South, but its nature leaves no doubt as to black understanding of the issues at stake in the conflict. The 'happy darky' legend notwithstanding, the main goal of the vast majority of the South's slaves was to leave the slave status. They were fully aware, perhaps with a shade of optimism, that the victory of the North would bring this result. It was for this reason, again contrary to the legend, that these slaves co-operated with the Union troops whenever possible, and escaped to the Union lines whenever they could do so without taking risks which made the attempt preposterous. The Emancipa-tion Proclamation itself affected these problems but little, except perhaps in the sense that it worsened the slaveholders' constant concern over the problems of maintaining discipline and a reasonable work output among a fundamentally hostile slave population.

Freedom only took on a reality with the end of the war, and it was on having this announced to them that 'Old colored folks . . . that was on sticks, throwed them sticks away and shouted'.[6] The slaves were now told of their emancipation. The coercive

[5] B. Wiley, *Southern Negroes, 1861–1865* (New Haven, 1938) pp. 63–84; V. L. Wharton, *The Negro in Mississippi, 1865–1890* (New York, 1965) pp. 14–22. Documents on the black response to the war in general are collected in J. M. McPherson, *The Negro's Civil War* (New York, 1965).

[6] Interview with ex-slave, quoted in B. A. Botkin, *Lay my Burden Down: A Folk History of Slavery* (Chicago, 1945) p. 226.

power of their old masters was at least technically removed. Their response varied from plantation to plantation, perhaps partly according to the relative severity of their regime. Although the plantation legend would have us believe that the ex-slaves wished nothing more than to stay with their own white people after 1865, and some doubtless did so, the compulsion for the vast majority of freedmen was to emphasise their freedom through the simple physical act of movement or, significantly, through contracting or formalising the marriages for which the old regime had given them no security. On a few plantations it may have been the case that 'pretty nigh every nigger sot tight till he died of the old sets',[7] but for many the end of the war meant the break of old ties. Yet this in itself did not mean a complete freedom. Many slaves who had left their plantations because 'they was so happy they had no sense'[8] found themselves inexorably drawn back by the hopelessness of finding a living and the simple lack of anywhere else to go. Until the passing of the Fourteenth Amendment in 1868 and the Fifteenth two years later, blacks in the South lacked the civil rights needed to protect themselves from their masters. They were also without the land or other means of subsistence which could preserve them from becoming thralled to the plantation again as wage labourers. The proposals of the radical Republicans, the political heirs of the abolitionists, much as they have been abused by Southernophile historians, were a reasonable response to these difficulties. They were solidly supported by abolitionist constituencies whose interest in giving blacks the means to protect themselves was perfectly genuine. More naïve were their hopes of doing so overnight, and it was the waning of their enthusiasm in the latter half of the 1870s which allowed the South to regain control of its affairs and push the Negro back to a status close to peonage. There is a great unfairness about the accusations of vindictiveness and banditry which are often levelled at men like William Pitt Fessenden of Maine, Thaddeus Stevens of Vermont, or Charles Sumner of Massachusetts. Their plan of reconstruction was exactly what blacks in the South needed, exactly the prescription for the continuing malaise of oppression that slavery left behind in all postemancipation plantation societies. The only tragedy was that it was not followed through fully. Thus the Fourteenth Amendment

[7] Ibid., p. 234.   [8] Ibid., p. 228.

guaranteed the civil rights essential to negate ante-bellum legislation aimed not at slaves but at the black population. The
Fifteenth specifically made the vote a universal right.[9] The
enthusiasm and responsibility with which the freedmen set about
participating in politics makes it clear that this legislation was not
mistimed.[10] The only thing required to make the ending of slavery
a permanent reality was the continuance of Northern support.

   In either case, whatever the national excitement of the events
of the reconstruction, its real drama was played in the South by
the ex-slaves and the successors of the abolitionists. It is simply
not true that the freedmen became supine as soon as they had
received their liberty, or that the abolitionists washed their hands
of the situation on the day of the Emancipation Proclamation. As
soon as slaves were liberated by the advancing Union Army,
Northern philanthropists formed associations to rehabilitate,
evangelise and educate them. A Freedmen's Relief Association
had been founded in New York City at the beginning of 1862,
closely followed by the Western Freedmen's Aid Association of
Cincinnati. From this point onwards, Freedmen's Aid Societies
and Associations proliferated throughout America and in Britain,
with the strongest in old abolitionist strongholds like Philadelphia
and Boston. At the same time, Lewis Tappan's anti-slavery
American Missionary Association turned its energies almost
wholly to teaching and preaching to the ex-slaves throughout the
areas opened by the Northern troops. Apart from providing much
of the political muscle behind the radical Republican group in
Congress, the ex-abolitionists also embarked on practical and
unpleasant work for the good of the freedmen, at least as they
conceived it. It is easy to sneer at the secondary army of Yankee

[9] The best introductions to the vast literature on reconstruction are K.
M. Stampp, *The Era of Reconstruction: America after the Civil War,
1865–1877* (London, 1965); P. Brock, *An American Crisis: Congress and
Reconstruction, 1865–1867* (London, 1963); K. M. Stampp and L. Litwak
(eds), *Reconstruction: An Anthology of Revisionist Writings* (Baton Rouge,
La., 1969). See also B. Weisberger, 'The Dark and Bloody Ground of
Reconstruction Historiography', *Journal of Southern History*, xxv (1959)
427–47.
[10] Participation of blacks in political reconstruction is discussed in
Wharton, *The Negro in Mississippi*, pp. 157–80; J. Williamson, *After
Slavery: The Negro in South Carolina during Reconstruction, 1861–1877*
(Chapel Hill, N.C., 1965) pp. 363–417; O. E. Uya, *From Slavery to Public
Service: Robert Smalls, 1839–1915* (New York, 1971).

schoolmarms (and schoolmasters) who flooded into the South in the wake of the Union troops, but in many ways their dogged efforts to help the freedmen were the finest hour of the abolitionists.[11] The need of their charges for land and money was doubtless greater than their need for Christianity. But their enthusiasm for attending the classes of the missionaries, whose 'schoolchildren' were often in their sixties, shows the extent to which the slaves themselves saw education as the key to their escape from the servile status. At first the Northern exiles came as missionaries of one or other of the benevolent societies concerned with freedmen's aid, later as agents of the Freedmen's Aid Bureau set up as a Federal organisation in 1865 under General Otis O. Howard. They had to struggle with ignorance and impiety among blacks, but also against Northern soldiers and bureaucrats whose priority was to keep the ex-slaves working, and whose sympathies were often much more with the Southern ruling class than with the huge and unruly people they had liberated. At the same time, the evangelists also had to fight, often without success, against their own prejudices towards a black population which was degraded beyond their worst nightmares about the South.

Starting on the South Carolina Sea Islands in 1862, and following the troops on their advance into the South, they struggled on to guide the ex-slaves towards the morality and world-picture of Northern evangelicals. The attempt to efface black culture in this way may have been short-sighted, and the presence of so huge a captive audience ripe for conversion was a nineteenth-century Protestant dream come true, yet these men and women were spreading a faith which for them would unquestionably benefit their charges. Their long campaign was essentially a selfless one. It furthered the humane aims of the anti-slavery movement – not only to free the slaves, but to enable them to take their place in the larger liberal society which the nineteenth-century reformers were working to create. Most would have agreed with the black missionary Charlotte Forten, when she prayed in her diary, at the beginning of her experiences in the Sea Islands, for her 'Dear children! Born in slavery, but free at last! May God preserve to you all the blessings of freedom, and

[11] McPherson, *Struggle for Equality*, pp. 154–77, 386–416; W. L. Rose, *Rehearsal for Reconstruction: The Port Royal Experiment* (1964; reprinted New York, 1967).

may you be in every possible way fitted to enjoy them.'[12] As for Freedmen's Bureau itself, it too attempted fairly conscientiously to carry out the wishes of a Northern public which at this late stage had become abolitionist if not pro-slave. Yet it swung with public opinion, and in response to administration pressure. Where it had worked well in the early stages of its life to care for the freedmen's economic wants, not all its officials were prepared to resist co-operating with the planter class in the communities where they were posted. In the final accounting, General Howard shrank from standing up to presidential pressure against the distribution of land to the freedmen. The promise of 'forty acres and a mule' was never carried out.[13] Without the means of economic independence, the only thing which protected Southern blacks was the continued concern of the North, and the continued presence of Union troops in the conquered territory. With these conditions gone, they were left at the mercy of their old owners.

The reconstruction era came to an end with President Harrison's executive order to withdraw troops from the South in 1877. By this time Northern vindictiveness and humanitarianism had alike waned, and there was nothing electorally dangerous about the administration's decision. Even among the evangelists, a majority had returned north. A changing public opinion reduced the funds at their disposal, and many were themselves disillusioned at the sheer scale of the problem, and perhaps by the unpromising material offered, as far as they were concerned, by the black population. With slavery technically abolished, the temptation was to assume that the crusade had been victorious, whenever the immediate warmth of feeling towards the freedmen wore off. As men and women who had been missionaries in the field just after the war became older, it was natural for them to move back to more settled employment in the North, where enthusiasm was no longer great enough to produce recruits to take their place. America's anti-slavery impulse was not dead. It resurfaced at the turn of the century in the form of the partially anti-imperialist movement to protect the coloured populations of the territory annexed during the Spanish–American war, including Cuba and

---

[12] R. A. Billington (ed.), *The Journal of Charlotte L. Forten*, 2nd ed. (New York, 1961) p. 146.

[13] W. S. McFeely, *Yankee Stepfather: General O. O. Howard and the Freedmen* (New Haven, 1969).

Puerto Rico. Indeed, in social, intellectual and in some cases family terms, the white sponsors of the N.A.A.C.P. were lineally descended from the old soldiers of the abolition campaigns. In 1877, however – perhaps earlier – concern over other races temporarily waned, at a time when slavery had by no means been eradicated from the world. Indeed it was about to be replaced by other forms of oppression in a lily-white South determined to undo the interrupted work of reconstruction. The aftermath of American emancipation has been described at such length here because it is so fine an example of the problems which remained even in societies which had formally abolished black slavery. Race relations in a plural society are difficult enough even in the best of conditions, and slavery in the United States and elsewhere in the Americas left a legacy of aggravated bitterness which made them all but insoluble.[14] Emancipation did nothing to avert the Jim Crow future, nor indeed to avert the closely related injustice of class oppression or the central blight of poverty. American philanthropy was unable to step far enough outside the beliefs of the nineteenth-century middle class to present any long-term solutions to these problems. Even if it had been, it would have had absolutely no support from an American public whose concern for the Southern black had never been more than transitory.

The British movement took considerably longer to wind down. This was not because it was any more alive than the American one to the economic reorganisation required to deal with the problems left in the wake of emancipation, but because its intense internationalism made it more sensitive to the survival of slavery outside its own dominions. The triumphs of the Emancipation and Apprenticeship Acts of 1833 and 1838 slowed anti-slavery activity but by no means ended it. British abolitionists were now organised into the British and Foreign Anti-Slavery Society, which was internationalistic in aim, although it also used its periodical, the *Anti-Slavery Reporter*, to report and publicise any areas in which it felt the West India planters were abusing their ex-slaves. It was also concerned with Latin America and with

---

[14] W. Kloosterboer, *Involuntary Labour since the Abolition of Slavery* (Leyden, 1960). See also C. Vann Woodward, *American Counterpoint: Slavery and Racism in the North–South Dialogue* (Boston, 1971) pp. 234–60.

correspondence with abolitionists in other European countries which still maintained slave colonies in the West Indies and elsewhere. Above all, however, the *Reporter* and British abolitionists as a whole were interested in the United States, a Protestant sister-country with which they had substantial cultural and institutional ties, particularly through the churches. When the American movement divided in 1840, the British went through exactly the same painful process. The B.F.A.S.S. became 'new organisation' or Tappanite, while a number of provincial societies, principally those in Glasgow, Edinburgh and Dublin, remained firm in their support of Garrison, notwithstanding his alarming heresies. Throughout the 1840s and 1850s, without any outlet for political activity, the British anti-slavery societies lost relatively much less support than their American equivalents. They welcomed American guests and sponsored visits to America, gathered funds to use for the Northern campaign, and spread publicity about the wickedness of the South throughout Britain and Europe.[15] *Uncle Tom's Cabin* sold a million copies in Britain alone. With the outbreak of the war, though the B.F.A.S.S. still soldiered on, the more radical abolitionists formed themselves into a Union Emancipation Society to co-ordinate activities in support of the North, which they assumed had gone into battle to end slavery. Subsequently, British abolitionists joined in the Freedmen's Aid movement, and formed a chain of societies throughout the country to transmit funds and moral support in aid of the educational and missionary work in the liberated South.[16] Not only was this work continuing an anti-slavery tradition, but, as one English investigator reported, it went far 'to soften the hostile feeling which was engendered towards England during the war'.[17] Whether this was so in the South may

[15] H. Temperley, *British Anti-Slavery, 1833–1870* (London, 1972) passim; F. Thistlethwaite, *America and the Atlantic Community: Anglo-American Aspects, 1790–1850* (1959; reprinted New York, 1963) pp. 103–133. See also the forthcoming monograph by the present author, and B. Fladeland, *Men & Brothers: Anglo-American Antislavery Cooperation* (Urbana, Ill., 1972) pp. 221–381.

[16] C. Bolt, *The Anti-Slavery Movement and Reconstruction: A Study in Anglo-American Co-operation, 1833–1877* (London, 1969) pp. 26–170. This work concentrates on the period after 1861.

[17] *The Industry of the Freedmen in America* (n.p., n.d. [London, 1867]) p. 21.

be questioned, for the most significant result of British aid to the abolitionists was to saddle them with the nativist accusation of being in league with foreign powers, and increase the Southern paranoia of conspiracies which did so much to produce a war situation. These activities may be seen either as compulsive internationalism or as compulsive meddling in other people's affairs. In either case the British doggedly continued them, until the American abolitionist impulse itself began to run into the sand in the early 1870s, and the American institutions through which they worked became either apathetic or defunct.

This in itself did not dampen British interest in slavery as a world problem. However, since the abolitionists lacked any means of bringing serious pressure to bear on Latin American slaveholders, apart from sympathising with those who were beginning to attack them, they turned increasingly back to dealing with the problems of slavery within the Empire, which had concerned them intermittently since 1838.[18] In time their interest merged imperceptibly with the movement to evangelise and protect the subject races of Africa during the period of the New Imperialism. One of the major problems which took their attention came ironically during the American Civil War, thus giving Southern propagandists ample scope to sneer at the inconsistency between British support for a Northern victory and their tolerating atrocities against the black population in Jamaica. The Governor Eyre controversy, in fact, saw much the same division of forces as the old abolitionist campaigns, with a Liberal free-trade lobby battering at a Tory group determined to protect Governor Eyre from punishment for his part in executing eighteen Negroes summarily after their rising against his rule.[19] At the same time, humanitarian sentiment in favour of the Negroes was complicated by distrust of the planters' constant demands for new labour, and the shrewd suspicion that their various schemes to bring manpower to the Caribbean by 'emigration' were thinly disguised plans to resurrect the slave trade. Such schemes had been tried at various points since the shipowner McGregor

[18] See G. R. Mellor, *British Imperial Trusteeship, 1783–1850* (London, 1951) pp. 181–426; Temperley, *British Anti-Slavery*.

[19] B. Semmel, *Democracy versus Empire: The Jamaica Riots of 1860 and the Governor Eyre Controversy* (1962; reprinted New York, 1969); C. Bolt, *Victorian Attitudes to Race* (London, 1971) pp. 75–108.

Laird's 'toll-free bridge' of 1840, aimed at bringing labourers from Africa itself. At other times the planters had tried 'coolies' from Singapore; had made intensive efforts, with government support, to recruit black recaptives in Sierra Leone; and had constantly tried to reshuffle what black workers were at their disposal from island to island as the need arose. Finally, they had made somewhat inconclusive experiments with Madeiran labour. With only a few exceptions, notably Glasgow abolitionists with an interest in promoting shipping from Africa to the West Indies, the British anti-slavery lobby had strenuously opposed such plans, through petitioning Parliament and presenting ponderous memorials to ministers involved. The burden of their argument was that the recruitment of labourers, especially among illiterate East Indian coolies, was anything but voluntary; that their conditions of work were not understood; that the imbalance between the sexes made perversion inevitable; that work conditions were if anything worse than in slavery; that the chance of the contract labourer ever returning from the Caribbean was negligible; and that, in short, the West Indians remained unregenerate, and were attempting to build a new slavery and slave trade. The *Reporter* for the 1840s and 1850s is full of articles on their unchanged character, and indeed there was little sign that the West Indians, genuinely in desperate difficulties with their labour force, had developed any enthusiasm for using free black labour.[20] It is also fair to say that there was a good deal of truth in their complaints that the free black population refused to work for them; the opposite situation would have been much more surprising. Emancipation had been followed by economic disaster in British sugar-growing, although this was not the fault of the ex-slaves but of soil exhaustion, Cuban competition and, as the *Reporter* was quick to point out, the incompetence of the planters. By the late 1840s the pro-slavery position had strengthened, and a flood of articles in the London reviews, particularly *Frazer's*, were declaiming against the hopelessness of attempting to farm sugar with free black labour. The most prominent pro-slavery propagandist was Thomas Carlyle, whose famous essay on *The Nigger Question*, which was published in *Frazer's* in 1849, denounced the Quashees of the West Indies who were 'sitting

[20] *Anti-Slavery Reporter*, 29 Jan, 11 Mar 1840, 8 Aug 1841, 25 Jan, 18 Oct 1843, 1 Mar 1847, 1 May 1848.

yonder with their beautiful muzzles up to the ears in pumpkins, imbibing sweet pulps and juices; the grinder and incisor both ready for ever new work ... while the sugar crops rot round them uncut, because labour cannot be hired, so cheap are the pumpkins'.[21] The pro-slavery lobby in Britain was composed of planters and ex-planters, high Tories and a sprinkling of Liberals disillusioned with the complete economic failure of benevolent efforts at emancipation and at the suppression of the Atlantic slave trade. It lined up in defence of Governor Eyre in its old position of hostility to the philanthropic middle class. The debate had many of the characteristics of the old campaign on slavery; the rhetoric used by Eyre's critics was exactly that of the abolitionists, and his defenders used much the same arguments as those who had justified the trial of Missionary Smith in 1823. There is an extraordinary sense of *déjà vu* about the whole Governor Eyre controversy, and both its form and content point to the continuing vitality of British preoccupation with slavery and its aftermath in the colonies. Their absorbing interest in events in America, and even their enthusiasm for helping the blacks freed in the maelstrom of the Civil War, did not mean that the British abolitionists had lost their concern for the problems of race posed in their own possessions.

This British concern continued until the later part of the century, when it re-emerged in a rather more distasteful form as the 'white man's burden' sentiment of the New Imperialism. The principal issue which inspired abolitionist zeal in the 1870s was the continuance of slavery and the slave trade in East Africa, both in the hinterland and from the coast to the Persian Gulf and the markets of Islam. This involved a complex network of slave-trading routes, much of which had been in existence since the Middle Ages. Since the sixteenth century the Portuguese had further complicated the structure of the Coast trade by carrying slaves across the Atlantic from their East African bases, principally to Brazil. This trade was still thriving in the nineteenth century, and a good deal of the energy of the British Navy was devoted to attempting its suppression as well as that of West

[21] T. Carlyle, *Occasional Discourse on the Nigger Question* (London, 1853), reprinted in *Critical and Miscellaneous Essays*, 7 vols (London, 1872) VII 79 ff.

Africa.[22] But the Portuguese trade was only superimposed on a more ancient structure. Forms of slavery were structured into many traditional East African societies, and Arab traders had been siphoning off as many slaves as were available from the nations of the hinterland since the eleventh and twelfth centuries. Their caravans travelled from the interior down the river valleys to the coast, with a mortality which was greater than anything in the history of the West African trade. From the city-states of the coast, from Pemba, Kilwa and Zanzibar, they forwarded their slaves to the vast markets of Asia Minor, some to become eunuchs, a few to become concubines, but the vast majority of the survivors to become menials doing the most degraded tasks in Islamic households.[23] Attempts to estimate the volume of this trade are largely guesswork, but it is clear that it was a great element in founding the wealth of the East African Islamic city-states, that it continued right down to the late nineteenth century, and that it had as much impact on the structure of East African society as the Portuguese trade, if not more.

The efforts of the Royal Navy to curb Portuguese slaving, and its occasional interferences with Arab slave dhows, did not focus British interest on East Africa until the ending of the Guinea trade. The real awakening of concern came as a side-product of the explorer mania of the 1860s, most particularly through the revelations in the widely read accounts of Livingstone's journeys. Indeed, explorers' reports of the brutality and suffering in the slave caravans they met were always a prime source of information to feed philanthropic interest in East Africa. Even the unemotional Frederick Lugard carefully noted the barbarity of the slavers in his diaries. His anti-slavery attitude was not atypical of many of the early imperial soldiers and administrators. 'Truth is', he noted after destroying an Arab slave caravan in Uganda, that

[22] C. Lloyd, *The Navy and the Slave Trade* (London, 1949) pp. 187–274. A short introduction to the East African trade is D. Alpers, *The East African Slave Trade* (Nairobi, 1967).

[23] Blacks in Islamic society are discussed in B. Lewis, *Race and Color in Islam* (New York, 1971). On the pre-Portuguese trade, see G. S. P. Freeman-Grenville, 'The Coast, 1498–1840', in R. Oliver and G. Mathew (eds), *History of East Africa*, vol. 1 (Oxford, 1963) pp. 148–58; R. Coupland, *East Africa and its Invaders, from the Earliest Times to the Death of Seyyid Said in 1856* (Oxford, 1936) pp. 17–20, 30–6 and passim.

I did not feel absolutely sure that my action would be approved, but those who employ me must take me as they find me on the Slavery question, on which I have always laid an emphasis. Regarding personal pay or prospects I have not fought, but I *have* strongly declined to be tied or my mouth shut on any question connected with slavery.[24]

However, what finally collated the findings on the eastern slavers and set them before the anti-slavery public was the work of Joseph Cooper who, as a very young man, had been one of the leading lights of the Agency Committee. The East African situation, partly owing to the efforts of the Marseille firm of Victor Régis et Cie. to recruit 'contract' labour in Madagascar for use in other colonies, had already stirred some interest among French liberals who saw Régis's schemes as a veiled resurrection of the slave trade. This had led to interest in the general problem of East African slavery, which had been specifically attacked immediately after the disaster of the Franco–Prussian war by a liberal professor, Étienne-Félix Berlioux. This work Cooper translated and edited in 1872 as *The Slave Trade in Africa in 1872*. Three years later he brought out a much more widely read work of his own, *The Lost Continent*.[25] This relied to some extent on Berlioux, and drew heavily on explorers' travel accounts, principally those of Dr Livingstone, who was by this time a British national hero. It made it absolutely clear that, quite apart from the Portuguese, the Arab slave trade from East Africa was still continuing on a prodigious scale; and that when the Royal Navy did capture slaving dhows, they were finding conditions of overcrowding, starvation and disease infinitely worse than anything they had seen on the Atlantic. The entrepôt of this vicious trade was Zanzibar, which had been made into the major port of East Africa in the first half of the century, by the great Sultan Seyyid Said of Oman. He had used it as a funnel through which he could distribute the coast's wealth in slaves, ivory and cloves to Islam.

An abolitionist outcry followed the publicity given to these discoveries. Propaganda was handled by the old British and Foreign Anti-Slavery Society, and by the Aborigines' Rights

[24] F. Lugard, *Diaries*, ed. M. Perham and M. Bull, 4 vols (London, 1959–63) 1 257–60.

[25] J. Cooper, *The Lost Continent, or Slavery and the Slave Trade in East Africa in 1875* (London, 1875).

Protection Society, along much the same lines as the old campaign against the West Indians. Since it proved quite impossible to make any serious impression on the trade by treaty or naval patrolling, this campaign did not end until the protectorate over Zanzibar was declared in 1890. The lobbying and petitioning of those whose primary interest was in the slave trade was later a major factor in strengthening the political case for the annexation of Uganda, and the acceptance of the Zanzibari protectorate itself.[26] The campaigns for these annexations made major use of the claim that they would curb the slave trade and facilitate the continuance of mission activity. There were certainly economic and strategic factors behind Britain's scramble into East Africa, but they worked in conjunction with a humanitarian wish to end the slave trade and spread the only kind of civilisation the Victorian philanthropist understood. This sentiment should not be underestimated, and it is grotesquely wrong to see it as a deliberate cover for a sinister self-interested imperialism. It was the logical outgrowth of a century-old tradition of humanitarianism, certainly complementing an economic world-picture of a certain type, but with religious and ideological roots which gave it a momentum independent of incidental economic interest. The protectorate over Zanzibar is the point at which the anti-slavery movement and the imperialist one finally meet. Within the limits set by their imperfect perception of the structure of African society, it spelt success for the abolitionists. Slavery, or at least permanent relationships of bondage, were only eradicated from the British possessions in forms recognisable to Whitehall. However, one justification of the abolitionist demand for British expansion was that it did succeed in ending the Zanzibari slave trade. This trade was not carried out by Europeans, but it equalled the Atlantic slave trade both in volume and brutality, and showed no signs of being stopped by any other means. It is hard to see how this can be set against the British in the history of their adventures in Africa.

While the last vestiges of the Atlantic slave trade were disappearing, while the North Americans were facing the problems

[26] R. Coupland, *The Exploitation of East Africa, 1856–1890: The Slave Trade and the Scramble* (London, 1939); J. Flint, 'The Wider Background to Partition and Colonial Occupation', in Oliver and Mathew (eds), *History of East Africa*, I 353–8.

of building a post-emancipation society and the campaign against
the East African slave trade was mounting, Cuba and Brazil
were also approaching the point where they would abandon their
slave systems. In numerical terms, the emancipation of these
last groups of Latin American slaves was of equal importance to
those of the British, French and Dutch possessions in the Caribbean, or the United States. Yet the political campaigns against
them were shorter than elsewhere, largely because the preconditions for the success of the abolitionists had already been set
by their colleagues in other countries which had ended slavery.
In retrospect there seems to be a certain inevitability about Latin
American emancipation, an impression that by the 1860s the tide
of Atlantic history had turned against black slavery. Yet successful emancipation was by no means a foregone conclusion. Even
in areas where slaves had been in a tiny minority, for instance in
Venezuela or in the Northern states of the U.S.A., the anti-slavery
fight had been a hard and long one. In Cuba and Brazil the
vested interests whom the abolitionists faced were enormously
strong, in some ways stronger than they had ever been. Brazil was
not only still using slave labour extensively in the sugar and
mining industries, but had invested heavily in coffee production.[27]
In spite of the beginnings of competition from Indonesian cane
sugar and European beet, Cuba produced 447,000 tons of sugar
in 1860, 620,000 in 1865 and 749,000 tons in 1868.[28] Much of
this was produced by slave labour, quite apart from the involvement of slaves in coffee cultivation and domestic service. In
neither country was slavery a dying institution at the time when
its abolitionist movement began to present it with a serious threat.
These were not situations where the economic unviability of
slavery made emancipation possible, although it was seriously
threatened by the cutting-off of the supply of new slaves from
the other side of the Atlantic. Both Spanish and Brazilian liberals
were greatly affected by the Emancipation Proclamation in the
United States. They were also aware of the incongruity of
accepting a slave system when they were trying to drag their

[27] C. Furtado, *The Economic Growth of Brazil* (Berkeley, 1963) pp.
119–26.
[28] N. Deerr, *A History of Sugar*, 2 vols (London, 1949) I 129–31. Figures
are from R. Guerra y Sanchez, *Azúcar y población en las Antillas* (Havana,
1970) p. 227.

countries into a modern world which had universally discountenanced it. Others turned to opposing slavery for frankly racist reasons – because of fear of the servile population, or because of the belief that black stupidity stood in the way of technological progress. As in the United States, slavery ended in the prime of its life, because the idea of emancipation had gained enough momentum to triumph, irrespective of the damage it might do to vested interests.

Although Cuban and Brazilian emancipation came quickly once the third major slave power, the American South, had fallen, this should not obscure the extent to which anti-slavery ideas had been developing in Latin America since the beginning of the nineteenth century and before. We have already seen how much attention was paid to Indian slavery in Spanish and Portuguese clerical circles in the sixteenth century. Although this did little to save the Indian, it gathered a body of literature on the institution of slavery and its injustice. This and subsequent debates in the church, or the ministering to their black and red flocks in the New World, seldom led to actual interference with the master's power over his slave. It was only with very occasional exceptions, like the Portuguese cleric Fernando Oliveira, whose *Art of Sea Warfare* in 1553 denounced the enslaving of heathens, that they specifically included blacks as well as Indians in their denunciation of slavery. But they did keep alive concepts of the slave's right to religious institutions, protection of his family relationships and redress against brutal physical treatment. The practical effect of such churchly standpoints was probably slight, but their importance as an intellectual legacy to later abolitionists was great. Yet the main thrust of the Spanish and Portuguese reaction against slavery, when it began in the eighteenth and early nineteenth century, was secular and not religious. In spite of imperial proscription of the dangerous writings of the European Enlightenment, they circulated clandestinely throughout Spanish and Portuguese America, in Havana, in Bahia, in São Paulo and in the other colonial cities. Raynal's *Histoire des deux Indes*, for instance, in spite of its great bulk, was if anything better known in the Spanish colonies than in the English ones. Such works had their influence over the slavery question, just as they had in Europe. They were slightly supplemented by polemical pamphlets written in Spanish and Portuguese by men concerned over their nation's involvement in slaveholding in much the same way as English- and French-speaking abolitionists. There is not much such writing, but one example is the 1758 pamphlet by a Bahian priest, Manuel Ribeiro Rocha, *The Ethiopian Ransomed, Indentured, Sustained, Corrected, Instructed and Liberated*.[29] This denounced brutal treatment of slaves, touched on the immorality of slave-trading and proposed what was in effect a scheme of long-term gradual emancipation. Slaves arriving in Brazil were to be apprenticed to masters rather than becoming their permanent chattels. They were to be given their freedom after the master had given them enough knowledge of Christianity and civilised life to make this possible. Similar ideas were being put forward in the Spanish colonies in the eighteenth century, but never in enough volume to form a genuine Latin tradition of anti-slavery. Latin America's revolutionary generation drew its hostility to slavery partly from their church's concern over enslavement, partly from the French Enlightenment and partly from the example of much-admired European abolitionists. The result of this combination of influences, though it was by no means an immediate one, was the ending of slavery in the Spanish American republics. Reinforced by their example, and by the success of the British, French, Dutch and Danish abolitionists, the same forces had their effect in the later nineteenth century in independent Brazil, in colonial Cuba and in Spain itself.

Brazil became an independent empire in 1825, under Dom Pedro I of the House of Braganza. As we have seen, this was the very time when the slave trade was still thriving and slavery was taking an even firmer hold on the Brazilian economy. At the same time, however, the abolitionist conceptions of the Enlightenment remained alive, and the close ties with Britain after independence brought the empire into contact with a country anxious to have others follow its example, and prestigious at least in some sectors of Brazilian society because of its constitutional monarchy and

[29] M. R. Rocha, *Ethiope resgatado, empenhado, sustentado, corregido, instruido, e libertado* (Lisbon, 1758). I have not seen this work, and my summary of it is based on C. R. Boxer, *The Portuguese Seaborne Empire, 1415–1825* (New York, 1969) p. 264. See also 'Negro Slavery in Brazil' [*Nova e Curiosa Relacão* (Lisbon, 1764)], trans. and ed. C. R. Boxer, in *Race*, v 3 (1964) 38–47, and, on the general impact of the Enlightenment, A. P. Whitaker (ed.), *Latin America and the Enlightenment* (New York, 1942).

reputation for liberalism. Brazil's own adoption of a constitutional monarchy opened channels through which the abolitionists could press their ideas. In spite of the gigantic strength of the slave system, in fact, anti-slavery ideas were at work in Brazil from independence onwards.[30] This is not to say that the country's enthusiasm for constitutionalism in 1825 led its sugar- and coffee-planters, its mining magnates or its slave-traders to apply concepts of liberty and equality to their slaves. Most had too much confidence in their own right to rule to see the contradiction between securing liberty for one race and withholding it from others. It has frequently been pointed out that there was no true pro-slavery argument of the North American sort in Brazil. This does not imply lack of faith in the institution. To the very last it was simply assumed that slaves were part of the established fabric of Brazilian society, and that their ownership by church, by state and by individuals was perfectly natural. Moreover, the national interest in slave investments was colossal. Figures compiled in 1817 and 1818, just before independence, show that a total population of 3,817,000 included 1,930,000 black slaves to 1,143,000 whites, the balance being made up of non-savage Indians and free blacks.[31] It is true that even at this time the enormous number of slaves presented a serious security threat, and also that many were used in domestic, craft and urban occupations where free labourers would have done just as well. But the investment in men and women in these activities was just as great as in any other, and the returns from hiring them out as *negros de ganho*, which gave almost as much flexibility as a free labour market, were great. Here too, at least as long as slave prices remained high, slaves were a centrally important source of collateral for negotiating loans. Even if they had been quite unviable as a work-force, it was attractive to retain them because of the capital leverage they provided in this way. In either case, the need for mining and plantation labour was still desperate, so much so that the first half of the imperial period was the heyday

---

[30] A. M. P. Malheiro, *A escravidão no Brasil. Ensaio histórico-jurídico-social*, 2 vols (São Paulo, 1944) part III, chap. ii.

[31] Figures from P. da Silva, *Historia da fundadacão do Imperio Brasileiro* (Rio de Janeiro, 1964–8) IV 261, quoted in P. A. Martin, 'Slavery and Abolition in Brazil', *Hispanic American Historical Review*, XIII (1933) 153.

of the Brazilian slave trade. Curtin's figures estimate that 1,145,400 *negros boçais* were brought to Brazil between 1811 and 1870, out of an American total of 1,898,400. The corresponding figure for Cuba was 550,000. Of the Brazilian imports, 875,300 arrived between 1821 and 1850.[32] Such enormous purchases were not made by men who had doubts about the profitability of slavery – or indeed by men who saw the abolitionists as a serious threat to their investments. What is astonishing is not that abolition took so long to gain, but that it was gained at all.

This demand for labour in itself explains the long Brazilian delay in co-operating fully with the British in suppressing the slave trade. Given the unwillingness of successive Brazilian governments to take any concrete steps in this direction, the slave-trading interests seemed impregnable. There were only two flaws in their position. The first was the depth of British commitment to ending the trade, a commitment which could lead Whitehall into international gestures apparently quite at odds with the larger interests of the Empire. The second flaw was the fact that most of the major businessmen involved in the trade were peninsular Portuguese, and that their capital came from (and profits returned to) Lisbon or New York. In 1845 Lord Aberdeen's government set about sweeping the Brazilian flag off the seas by the same method as Palmerston had used for Portugal. The so-called Aberdeen Act authorised British cruisers to treat Brazilian slavers in exactly the same way as if they were flying the British flag, and provided for their condemnation in Vice-Admiralty courts instead of in the accepted Courts of Mixed Commission. When even this did not work, British cruisers set about seizing vessels fitted out for the trade in Brazilian territorial waters. In spite of great public and governmental indignation against this Anglo-Saxon high-handedness, a situation which could only lead to a breach of relations with Britain, Brazil's major commercial ally, was out of the question. At this juncture, Rio was able to capitalise on nativist hatred for the largely Portuguese slave-traders. It was clear that the benefits of the trade went into their hands, and that they were also in a somewhat precarious relationship with the very *fazendeiros* who were their customers. They sold them their slaves at what seemed extortion-

[32] P. Curtin, *The Atlantic Slave Trade: A Census* (Madison, Wis., 1969) p. 234.

ate prices, and also exploited them a second time through the mortgages they gave out from the capital made on the Atlantic. It also seems that planter demand had been temporarily blunted by a glut in slaves caused by the feverish importations of the previous decades. Liberals unconnected with the slave system, too, could readily be persuaded that if there was anything rotten in the state of Denmark (and its business), it was the Portuguese. On 4 September 1850 Eusebio de Queiroz, the Brazilian Minister of Justice, submitted an Abolition Bill satisfactory to the British, with equipment clauses and a provision that convicted slavers should be tried summarily for piracy before non-jury Admiralty courts. This worked. From 1851 to 1860, after the floods of African arrivals in the previous decades, an estimated total of 3,300 new slaves were brought to Brazil.[33]

The abolition of the trade had two important effects on the bigger issue of slavery itself. In the first instance, it deprived the great *fazendeiros* of the Portuguese trading magnates who, their mutual distrust notwithstanding, would have been their natural allies in the defence against the abolitionists. In the long run, too, the discussion over the slave trade prompted discussion over slavery. Brazil had joined the other civilised nations in ending her commitment in the slave trade, and once the issue of slavery was brought fully out into the open, it would be more difficult to rationalise the refusal to follow their further example over slavery. Queiroz's slave-trade abolition Bill had knocked most of the logical props from under the pro-slavery case. Yet discussion did not move on to slavery overnight, and there was a surprising apathy towards the whole question during the 1850s and much of the early 1860s. Brazilian slave agriculture continued to boom, with labour demands in expanding sectors helped out by inter-provincial slave-trading – much of it along the coast in conditions as bad as the Middle Passage – and by an increasing trickle of European immigration.[34] What reopened the debate was the American Civil War. Emancipation in the United States removed the one nation admirable in Brazilian eyes – or at least in liberal

[33] Ibid. On the struggle for abolition of the slave trade, see L. Bethell, *The Abolition of the Brazilian Slave Trade: Britain, Brazil and the Slave Trade Question, 1807–1869* (Cambridge, 1970); Martin, in *H.A.H.R.*, XIII 152–96.

[34] Bethel, *Abolition of the Brazilian Slave Trade*, pp. 376–8.

Brazilian eyes – which was hanging on to slavery. This, together with recurrent petitioning of the government by British and French abolitionists, many of them intellectuals of world reputation, increased what one historian has described as Brazil's 'sense of moral isolation'. Dom Pedro II, the highly able emperor, was acutely aware of this. He was firmly convinced, after extensive reading of Brazilian and foreign literature, of the need for abolition. Like the leaders of the Spanish American revolutions, the Brazilian government were also prompted to make abolitionist gestures by the catalyst of war. During the bitter Paraguayan war of 1865 to 1870 they set about attracting black recruits by promising freedom to all slaves – and their wives – who would enlist in the army. Titles of nobility were granted to all slave-holders who released their men for the same purpose. Once the Brazilians won the war, in fact, the slave population of Paraguay was freed by military decree.[35]

By this time the debate over slavery had been fairly raised in Brazilian politics, on the initiative of the emperor himself, who recommended turning legislative attention to emancipation in his Speech from the Throne in 1867. As in all Latin American countries, those with great vested interests in slavery were disproportionately well represented in the most influential circles of government and society. They reacted to this anarchical royal suggestion with absolute horror. Even in liberal circles, which felt the force of foreign example, there was no support for immediate emancipation; indeed, such a plan could only seem visionary, with so large a slave population containing such an alarmingly high proportion of first-generation African arrivals. Yet support for a gradual Abolition Bill quickly mounted, principally in liberal circles, but also among a small but significant sector of the conservative party. The leader of the latter group was the greatest statesman of nineteenth-century Brazil, José Maria da Silva Paranhos, the Viscount Rio Branco. In the hopeless disarray of the liberals, principally over the slavery question, he was called upon to form a conservative government in 1871. Almost single-handed, he then set about dragging Brazil into the ranks of the

[35] Martin, in *H.A.H.R.*, XIII 172–4. The following account relies heavily on this work. Emancipation is set in the context of changing economic conditions in E. V. da Costa, *Da senzala à colônia* (São Paulo, 1966) pp. 331–467 passim.

nineteenth-century nations. Foremost among his plans for modernisation was the gradual abolition of slavery. Even this, in 1871, was not supported by any organised movement of anti-slavery societies who could bring pressure to bear on legislators from out of doors. Public opinion against slavery there certainly was, but it had not been organised for quasi-political action as in the British, French and American cases. In the legislature, too, Rio Branco was opposed by many members of his own party, and by some of the official opposition as well. It was only after five months of savage debate, in September 1871, that he was able to get his Abolition Bill accepted. This was the purely political triumph of a man who equated abolition with modernity, a triumph quite different from the bloody outcome of the United States debates, or the long extra-parliamentary campaigns of other countries. The only flaw in Rio Branco's work was that his law postponed emancipation so long as to be unsatisfactory to any Brazilians with a serious abolitionist commitment. Only minor categories of slaves were freed outright – for instance, those who could save or borrow enough to buy themselves from their masters, on the lines of the Spanish *coartación* system, or those whose masters died intestate. More important, a *ventre livre* provision, backed by an elaborate slave registration scheme to prevent fraud, stipulated that all children born of slave mothers were henceforward to be free. However, until the age of eight they were to remain under the care of their master, who was then to have the choice of handing them over to the state for an indemnity of 600 milreis, or retaining them as *ingenuos* or apprentices, effectively still slaves, until they were twenty-one.[36] Assuming thorough enforcement, the Rio Branco Law ensured that slavery would end some day, but beyond that it had only a peripheral effect on most of those already in bondage.

The second phase of the Brazilian campaign was therefore devoted to substituting an immediate emancipation measure for Rio Branco's legislation. It was during this period that a true anti-slavery movement emerged in Brazil, furthered by genuine abolitionist societies and with regular channels of propaganda. Its major political spokesman was Joaquim Nabuco de Araujo.

[36] Martin, in *H.A.H.R.*, XIII 176–80. The details of Rio Branco's work are available in B. do Rio Branco, *O Visconde do Rio Branco*, ed. R. de Mendanca (Rio de Janeiro, n.d.) pp. 175–280.

In background, character and role, he was a man similar to a Wilberforce or a Wendell Phillips. From an ancient Pernambuco family, he had good birth, good looks and a good voice as advantages to begin with. Added to these, his talents make him not only the greatest of the Brazilian abolitionists, but one of the most important figures thrown up by any of the movements against black slavery. There were still a little over $1\frac{1}{2}$ million slaves in Brazil when Nabuco first took his seat in the Chamber of Deputies in 1878, though their numbers were beginning to decline in this period of uncertainty. Two years later, after Nabuco had made his position clear in the political arena, serious out-of-doors organisation began with the founding of a national society devoted to replacing the Rio Branco Law. With Nabuco as president, the *Sociedade Brasileira contra a Escravidão* was founded, with a constitution demanding immediate and unconditional abolition. Immediatist propaganda at once stepped up, in the entire Brazilian press, through lecturing, pamphleteering and political speechifying. Thanks to the Rio Branco triumph of 1871, however, it was no longer at issue whether slavery should be kept. Indeed, it was already weakening economically, and at least some of the slaveowning opposition was quickly moving towards the use of a more diversified labour force. The debate had moved on to a bitter contest between the gradualist and immediatist positions. The conservative opposition produced virtually no genuinely pro-slavery propaganda. Even Nabuco's most famous polemic, *O abolicionismo*, wasted little time attacking slavery itself. Instead it concentrated on exposing the fallacies of the Rio Branco Law and gradualism in general, and denouncing the way in which the continuance of slavery was blighting the whole tone of the nation's life.[37] To this extent the battle had been won since 1871, but the abolitionists continued to flood the country with immediatist propaganda. Much of this work, incidentally, was done by black leaders like the great orator José de Patrocinio. Blacks were even more prominent here than in the campaigns in the United States, and they were certainly treated more fairly as

[37] J. Nabuco, *O abolicionismo* (Rio de Janeiro, 1883), reprinted in *Obras completas*, 14 vols (São Paulo, 1949) VII 1–221. See also C. Nabuco, *The Life of Joaquim Nabuco*, trans. and ed. R. Hilton (Stanford, 1950). The absence of genuine pro-slavery literature is stressed by C. N. Degler, *Neither Black nor White: Slavery and Race Relations in Brazil and the United States* (New York, 1971) pp. 84–8.

equal allies. By 1883 their work had been successful enough to allow the amalgamation of all the Brazilian abolition societies and their auxiliaries, as the *Confederação Abolicionista.*

From this time the Brazilian campaign took on even more of the characteristics of the North American one. The organisational relationship between the different societies was similar, their propaganda methods the same, and the Brazilians also laid great stress on their correspondence with overseas sympathisers. The whole Brazilian movement is also tinged with sectional rivalries, which are almost as important in Brazilian history as in the United States. In São Paulo, world demand for coffee meant that slave agriculture, though its slave population was declining, and new forms of labour being tried, was still expansive. In the north, however, foreign competition had reduced the sugar and cotton industries to an extent which made slavery seem a thing of the past – although Martin points to the irony that here it was the tropical north which became apathetic over slavery, and the temperate south which remained wedded to it. This was not simply a conflict between slave and free societies, between two classes and two conceptions of civilisation, but one between two areas with differing historical and cultural traditions, and strong regional loyalties. The similarity is completed by the rudiments of a Brazilian underground railroad, running slaves from the Paulista coffee plantations to the provinces in the far north where slavery was more marginal and all the blacks had already been freed. Where the parallel breaks down is in the eventual triumph over slavery. With gradual emancipation already accepted with moderately good grace, even in planter circles, total abolition was secured politically without the holocaust which the mere suggestion of ending slavery had brought about in the United States. By 1884, in fact, many of the great planters, even in São Paulo, were aware that further resistance was hopeless. They began to contemplate promoting the European immigration which later was so important to Brazil. Some voluntarily manumitted their slaves. Others found they had no way of preventing workers who had heard of their coming freedom from walking off the plantations *en masse.* In 1887 Brazil had only three-quarters of a million slaves, where there had been a million and a half in 1873, fourteen years before. The back of planter resistance had been broken by 1888, when the Regent Isabella, Isabel a Redemptora, recommended total abolition without compensation. A few days later the government, again ironically a conservative one, secured passage of one of the shortest pieces of legislation in the history of democratic governments:

Article 1. Slavery is declared extinct in Brazil.
Article 2. All contrary dispositions are revoked.

This triumph had been secured through established constitutional channels, fully debated at each step in the Senate and Chamber of Deputies. The monarchy itself, particularly in the person of the somewhat headstrong Regent Isabella, had been one of the most active allies of the abolitionists – a very different standpoint from that of William IV at a comparable point in British history. After the 1888 Act the slaves took up their new lives amid great popular enthusiasm but with little disorder. What lay ahead of them, or many of them, was a form of peonage only debatably more desirable than their previous lot, but at least the ending of the slave status had come without violence. As an epitaph on Brazilian slavery, we may quote the black abolitionist José Patrocinio's description of Nabuco, as he was received by the people after the passage of the abolition law:

Joaquim Nabuco came to the window, and the people applauded him with the enthusiasm that only fidelity to principles can inspire. He was the victor. His hair was plastered with perspiration and petals. . . . After a long pause, he became himself again. Then he saw the people, with their heads uncovered as if before an idol, and he led a bravo to the imperial princess.[38]

The only aggrieved group not included in this idyllic and very Brazilian picture were the slaveowners, and even they were remembered by having titles of nobility distributed to their leading spokesmen soon after the passage of the abolition. This was not enough. The response of their slaves to popular abolitionist enthusiasm had made them powerless to put up a harder fight against abolition. But they never forgave Isabel a Redemptora for her part in their defeat, more particularly for her failure to recommend that they should be compensated for the loss of their slaves. This was a cardinal factor in throwing them towards

[38] C. Nabuco, *Life of Joaquim Nabuco*, p. 168.

leading the coup which ended the monarchy in 1889.[39] Slavery brought down the Braganzas with it, and in this way also changed the course of Brazilian history. This single experiment with monarchy in the New World failed not because it was too reactionary for its setting, but because its representative was too anxious to get rid of the bitterly unjust institution on which Brazil's prosperity was founded.

Cuba's emancipation came in a very different way, largely because of the island's relationship to Spain. Here too, however, the abolitionists were fighting against an institution which was economically viable, and which became increasingly so during the course of the nineteenth century. We have already seen the way in which the sugar boom affected Cuba. Slaves in the coffee sector of the economy were tied to the growth of a similarly profitable crop. As in Brazil, the many slaves used in urban occupations and in domestic service, however redundant in relation to the economic life of the island as a whole, also bound their masters to the support of slavery. They represented a major investment in prestige and capital, and were important as a source of collateral for raising further money. Indeed the use of labourers as collateral is a feature of most unfree societies; this is the aspect of Russian serfdom brilliantly satirised by Gogol in *Dead Souls*. In Cuba, because of the demands of the sugar and coffee plantations, together with the difficulties of supply created by British interference, slave prices remained high. Again as in Brazil, the best index of the continuing support for slavery is the volume of nineteenth-century slave imports. Curtin calculates that 550,000 slaves were landed in Cuba from 1811 to 1870. Although there were eventually signs of a Creole revulsion against the trade, of the same sort as the Brazilian upsurge of 1850, the real factor which brought it to an end was the success of the British and Americans in suppressing it by force, and thus pushing the planters towards an increasing use of other forms of labour. Even in the 1860s, when co-operation between the British and American navies was assured, and the United States flag which had protected the traders for so long was no longer of any

[39] P. A. Martin, 'Causes of the Collapse of the Brazilian Empire', *Hispanic American Historical Review*, IV (1921) 4–48. On the empire as a whole, see C. H. Harding, *Empire in Brazil: A New World Experiment with Monarchy* (Cambridge, Mass., 1958).

use to them, an estimated 61,500 slaves were introduced.[40] Added to the interests of the slaveowners themselves, they were supported by the whole Spanish complex of merchants, bankers, shippers and mortgagees, who depended on them. Moreover, slavery in Cuba was protected by the colony's importance, real and emotional, to her mother country. Cuban wealth, or at least the opportunity of taxing it, was immensely important to the Spanish treasury. Perhaps even more crucial, the Latin American revolutions had left Cuba and her little sister Puerto Rico, also a slave island, as the last vestiges of Spain's magnificent empire in the Americas. Where the entire mainland had thanklessly reneged on its debts to Madrid, Cuba had remained true. She was the 'Ever-faithful Isle', 'the Pearl of the Antilles', 'the jewel in the Spanish Crown', the one relic of Spanish American grandeur and the last major source of Spanish American income. No Spanish government could lightly tamper with the settled institutions of this symbolic colony.

Yet neither Cuba nor Spain had escaped the very anti-slavery ideas associated first with the Enlightenment and latterly with the rise of European liberalism. Again, the rancorous divisions in colonial society left many interest groups who would be prepared to use the slave issue as a way of attacking men they disliked for other reasons. For instance Creoles conveniently denounced *peninsulares* as the men who had foisted slavery on the Cubans, and who used it to keep them loyal. Small planters in the backward eastern section of the island tended to see their grievances against the prosperous men of the western province as circulating around the slavery issue. Abolition was also used by liberals as an anti-clerical critique of a church which tolerated slavery and other social abuses. In the same way, in Spain itself, liberals at odds with the government expressed their grievances through complaints over the injustice of colonial slavery. At the same time, there was a great flexibility about the Cuban planters which made them entirely willing to use non-black workers whenever they could get them, and allowed them to experiment with all sorts of other sources of labour before they were seriously threatened by the abolitionists. One scholar believes that they had made so much progress in substituting other labourers for their slaves that the whole institution was 'dying' even before it was disrupted by

[40] Curtin, *Atlantic Slave Trade*, p. 234.

the Ten Years War from 1868 to 1878. The abolition of 1886 came to a system which 'had long ceased to play a vital part in any aspect of the economy'.[41] The imports of black slaves immediately prior to the war suggest that this claim may be slightly exaggerated. However, the adaptability the planters had shown in using rented slaves where possible, in experimenting with European and Yucatecan Indian contract labourers in the 1830s, and with indentured Chinese coolies in the late 1840s and thereafter, was an optimistic sign of willingness to meet changing conditions half-way. The same author also shows that the owners of the huge sugar estates of the western section were reorganising completely by the 1860s, consolidating into even larger *centrales*, and substituting cheaper forms of labour for their black slaves. The latter were sold off to provide capital for the new steam-driven machinery required for modern large-scale sugar production.[42] Although this does not necessarily imply any lowering of resistance to abolition among those who owned slaves – and there were still over 200,000 in the island at the end of the Ten Years War – it does suggest that the system was considerably weaker than it looked in the last decades of its life.

The nineteenth-century movement against Spanish slavery was almost exclusively secular. Unlike their Protestant fellows in Britain and America, the Catholic clergy seem to have done their best to remain aloof from discussion on the slavery issue. The situation of the Spanish abolitionists was additionally complicated, however, by the absence of any parliamentary forum through which they could exert pressure on the executive, and in which they could air their views. Neither Cuba nor Puerto Rico had representatives in the Cortes until the final stages of the debate. The censorship, which was unduly sensitive to the circulation of any ideas which might endanger the stability of the 'Ever-faithful Isle', also hampered anti-slavery efforts. These problems affected the abolitionists both in Madrid and in Cuba itself, where they had to hope for co-operation from successive indifferent royal officials. By and large, the Captains-General moved in the circles of their fellow *peninsulares*, and in intention if not always in practice tried to silence or exile these young

[41] H. S. Klein, *Slavery in the Americas: A Comparative Study of Virginia and Cuba* (Chicago, 1967) pp. 257–8.

[42] Ibid., pp. 256–7.

Creoles – like the opponent of the slave trade José Antonio de Saco – who became known for reformist views on slavery, the trade, or indeed anything else. In turn, Creole distrust of *peninsulares* was reinforced during the depression of the late 1850s, which also had the effect of widening the economic gap, and thus increasing the hostility between large and small planters, between underdeveloped east and expanding west. By this time it had become almost impossible for colonial officials to prevent widespread discussion of abolition. A further stimulus was given to the debate by the American Civil War, which had exactly the same effect as in Brazil in increasing the island's sense of isolation from the other civilised nations. At the same time, the great enthusiasm of the *peninsulares* for the victory of the South and the maintenance of slavery, which they equated with the *status quo*, in reaction drove the disaffected Creoles further towards Northern partisanship and acceptance of abolitionism.[43] This was as yet an abstract commitment, closely tied to hatred of Spain and not much connected to sympathy for the slaves, whom the Creoles themselves owned. Many of the Creoles also turned against slavery for anti-Negro reasons, either because of the security fears of a large servile population, or because their contempt for blacks was great enough to convince them that other material was needed to build a modern and genuinely civilised state. For instance the reformist Francisco de Friás y Jacott, Count of Pozos Dulces, felt that no technological change could come while the island relied on the 'dangerous brute force of the Negro and Chinese'.[44] Yet such feelings, whatever their origin, would eventually have their effect in bringing a general questioning of the whole system as it existed on the island. This was exactly what happened after Appomattox, when the realisation that slavery was now definitely ended in the United States brought a new flurry of speculation over ways in which the institution might be gradually abolished in Cuba, though the emphasis was always on gradualism and the end of the trade. No one seriously considered an immediate emancipation, but once again the Creole

[43] A. F. Corwin, *Spain and the Abolition of Slavery in Cuba, 1817–1886* (Austin, Tex., 1967) p. 142 and passim. My ideas on Cuba have been moulded principally by Corwin's work and by F. W. Knight, *Slave Society in Cuba during the Nineteenth Century* (Madison, Wis., 1970).

[44] Quoted in Knight, p. 147.

assumption was that, in so far as slavery was bad for Cuba, it was simply part of the network of tyranny through which the *peninsulares* and the Madrid government controlled the island.

At the same time, abolitionist demands were being made in Spain. At the end of 1864 the first real Spanish abolition society was founded, under the title of the *Sociedad Abolicionista Española*. It drew a great deal of support from Spanish liberals, but, strangely, the leading light behind it was a Puerto Rican Creole, Julio Vizcarrondo. His American wife, Harriet Brewster, founded a female auxiliary of the society, and it adopted the Anglo–American insignia of the supplicant slave. The first open debate on slavery in the Cortes was held in May 1865. This had the effect of crystallising the views of those in favour of slavery, and the debate was followed by a pamphlet war quite on North American lines.[45] The abolitionist sympathisers in the capital were still a tiny minority. Those who were talking in terms of emancipation in the foreseeable future were either unconnected with slave society, or came from Puerto Rico, where the vested interests in slavery were less dauntingly strong than in Cuba.[46] Yet the slavery issue could no longer be dodged. It bulked large in the discussions of the Colonial Reform Commission set up by the moderately liberal Leopoldo O'Donnell government in 1866. Before the Commission met, the *Sociedad Abolicionista* had been suppressed by the reactionary Narváez government which succeeded O'Donnell. Nevertheless, both Puerto Rican and Cuban delegates, incidentally exceeding their briefs from their constituencies, made proposals for definite outlawing of the slave trade. The Puerto Ricans came out for an immediate though compensated emancipation. While the Cubans would not go so far as that, they did suggest the beginning of gradual abolition through *vientre libre* legislation which would have liberated all children born of slave mothers after its passage. In fact, these recommendations were ignored. Indeed the failure of the

[45] Corwin, *Spain and the Abolition of Slavery*, pp. 153–71.

[46] On Puerto Rico, see S. W. Mintz, 'The Role of Forced Labour in Nineteenth Century Puerto Rico', *Caribbean Historical Review*, II (1951) 134–41; L. M. Díaz Soler, *Historia de la esclavitud negra en Puerto Rico* (Madrid, 1953). The latter work discusses the Puerto Rican abolition, pp. 269–380.

government to follow the Commission with any measures to reform its political and economic relationship with the colonies may be seen as the last straw which produced a true Creole movement for Cuban independence.

In either case, the whole situation was changed, and the abolition issue temporarily forgotten, with the 1868 liberal revolt which deposed Isabel II and drove the Bourbons from Madrid. The new government of General Juan Prim y Pratts was immediately faced with a new catastrophe in the outbreak of the Ten Years War in Cuba itself. The causes of the war were extraordinarily complex, but it is absolutely certain that it was not fought in the first instance over slavery. Rebellion was initially sparked off by Madrid's extraordinary tactlessness in imposing a range of heavy property taxes on Cuban holdings at a time when Creole society was expecting the implementation of reforms suggested by the Colonial Reform Commission. The result was a Creole conspiracy, centred on the backward eastern part of the island, where the new taxes were disproportionately burdensome to smaller planters who were being pushed to the wall owing to their inability to afford innovations in labour and equipment. On the discovery of the conspiracy, the eastern Creoles outlined their grievances in the so-called *Grito de Yara*, and established a provincial republican government under Carlos Manuel de Céspedes, a middling proprietor who, incidentally, freed his own slaves at the outbreak of the rebellion. The ending of slavery was not, however, a demand of the rebels. Many of them were themselves slaveholders, but slaveholders without the capital to adapt to other forms of labour if the system were changed. Nevertheless, in the early stages of the war the wealthy Creoles of the west remained at a distance from the rebels, largely because of fear that their indiscreet use of liberal principles would spread to the labouring population, slave and free, whom it was in the common interest of the planting class to keep down. Only the tactlessness of the 'Volunteer' government of *peninsulares* which took over from the Spanish authorities pushed a number of them towards the insurgents. In fact the war had relatively little effect in the west, where the sugar magnates continued to consolidate their plantations into larger units, with more modern and expensive equipment. At the same time, they slowly diversified the labour force to include various forms of contract workers as well as slaves – though it may well be that these were simply taking the place of the *bozal* blacks who would still have been imported if the Atlantic trade had not ended. In the eastern areas, however, the war had a direct effect on slavery. A number of masters voluntarily manumitted their slaves as a moral gesture of consistency with their liberal pronouncements. Both rebel and royalist troops liberated other individuals as a reward for military service, while the royalists also punished their enemies by setting their slaves free. A remarkable part was played in the rebel armies by free blacks, particularly the great patriot leader Antonio Maceo. Whatever the modern legend, atrocities were not confined to the *peninsulares* or the Spanish troops, but their extensive burning of crops and massacring of their enemies indirectly led to the break-up of many plantations and increased the difficulty of retaining their workers in slavery. By and large, the slave population did not rise up with the rebels, perhaps because of a justified suspicion of the racial views of the Creoles, but the dislocation of the war simply allowed numbers of them to walk away to freedom. The rebellion did not cause abolition, and it was not fought over it, but it did indirectly lessen the number of Cuban slaves, principally in the east.[47]

While the war was in progress, in fact, more important progress towards abolition was being made in Spain itself. Prim's liberal government, which came to office after Isabel II's deposition, was considerably more sympathetic to the abolitionists than its conservative predecessors. The great Puerto Rican abolitionist Julio Vizcarrondo, with several other prominent anti-slavery spokesmen, had actually been a member of the revolutionary junta behind Prim. The provisional government was headed by Francisco Serrano, an ex-Captain-General of Cuba who, perhaps because of his Creole wife, was one of the few to administer this office with any sympathy for the reformists. This was a situation very similar to the British one, where emancipation was engineered by responsible but committed men who represented the anti-slavery position within the ranks of the government. The provincial government came out in support of abolition in principle before the *Grito de Yara*. Both the British and American governments gave hints of seeing abolition as their price for non-

[47] P. Foner, *A History of Cuba and its Relations with the United States*, 2 vols (New York, 1963) II 174–275.

intervention.[48] By 1870 the abolitionist Segismundo Moret y Prendergast was Colonial Minister, and it was he who drafted and had passed the so-called Moret Law of that year. This secured gradual emancipation in Cuba and Puerto Rico. All slaves who had served meritoriously among the loyalist troops, and all slaves over sixty, were to be freed outright, with an indemnity for (loyal) masters in the former case. All children born of slave mothers were henceforward to be free, although they were to work for their master under a *patronato* system until the age of eighteen, and remain tied to him as wage labourers for another four years thereafter. It was stated that measures of total abolition would be considered once the war was over. Cuba and Puerto Rico had now reached the same point as Brazil was to reach with the Rio Branco Law in the following year, and the slave population, through the combined effects of the war and the Law, fell from 363,000 in 1869 to 228,000 in 1878.[49] As for the masters, although they at first opposed the Moret Law, they did see it as the writing on the wall, even in the heavily slave-owning west. They began to adapt increasingly to other forms of labour as part of the reorganisation in which they were already involved. Yet the Moret Law, like the Rio Branco Law, was unsatisfactory to abolitionists. After the war the government of the victor of the Ten Years War, General Martínez de Campos, secured a total abolition law, putting all the slaves under an eight-year *patronato*, so that slavery was scheduled to end formally in 1888. Since these eight years coincided with increased use of European and contract labourers, and with an appalling recession in the world sugar industry, the numbers of slaves held under the *patronato* declined steadily throughout the period. Against a background of continuing abolitionist agitation in the Cortes and growing planter apathy, the numbers of apprentices had fallen to 30,000 by 1886. These few remaining thralls were freed by royal decree on 7 October of that year.

Black plantation slavery in the Americas was thus officially ended except in Brazil, where the emancipation was delayed for another two years. In Cuba as in all the other post-emancipation

[48] C. J. Bartlett, 'British Reaction to the Cuban Insurrection of 1868–1878', *Hispanic American Historical Review*, xxxvii (1957) 296–312.

[49] Corwin, *Spain and the Abolition of Slavery*, p. 294. On the Moret Law, see Corwin, pp. 239–91; Knight, *Slave Society in Cuba*, pp. 171–6.

societies it left a bitter harvest of race hatred, not perhaps caused by slavery but certainly sharpened by the centuries of one people's domination over another. At a more immediate level, emancipation did nothing to soften Cuban grievances against Spain, and if anything worsened them. When the final War of Independence began, two of the leading elements among the rebels were rich Creoles aggrieved at the way the Spanish refusal to indemnify the abolition had disregarded their property rights, and poor Creoles horrified at Spain's cavalier disregard of their power and status for the sake of the blacks whom they hated. Madrid, like the Braganzas, and like Andrew Johnson, found that it was considerably more difficult to get rid of slavery in the nineteenth century than it had been to adopt it in the sixteenth or seventeenth.

11 Conclusion

MANY last words may be said on black slavery, although the gaps in our knowledge dictate a willingness to unsay them if anyone can provide better ones. One of the least mentioned aspects of the enslavement of Africans by Europeans is that it was only a new departure in the most limited sense. Even the racial component in this relationship has precedents, though no other slave society has ever been constructed along racial lines so close to rigidity as those of the various New World systems. Plantation slavery, too, had been in operation long before Columbus stumbled on the Bahamas, though seldom on so large and efficient a scale. What is not at all unique is the chattel component of black slavery. The great turning-point in human history comes not with the adoption of American slavery, but with the extraordinary decision to abandon it. Frederick Douglass, the greatest of black orators, was only too well aware of the countless ages through which slavery had existed without comment. He also knew that it had frequently bred the kind of prejudice from which his own race suffered in the United States:

> The misfortunes of my own race in this respect are not singular. They have happened to all nations, when under the heel of oppression. Whenever and wherever any particular variety of the human family have been enslaved by another, their enslavers and oppressors, in every such instance, have found their best apology for their own base conduct in the bad character of their victims. The cunning, the deceit, and the manifold vices and crimes, which naturally grow out of the condition of Slavery, are generally charged as inherent characteristics of the oppressed and enslaved race. The Jews, the Indians, the Saxons and the ancient Britons, have all had a taste of this bitter experience.[1]

[1] *Frederick Douglass' Monthly* (Mar 1862).

Douglass looks forward here to the tragic way in which these patterns would continue after slavery. But he also recognises that slavery's burden has descended on mankind as a whole, that the chattel relationship has long been part of the way of the world. Slavery may indeed be seen as the universal institution of pre-industrial societies. Partly because Japanese slavery took a household form, there is so far as I know no *haiku* which sums up the totality of this slave experience. It may therefore be excusable to substitute a line from Euripides:

> Scamandros echoes with endless cries of captured women,
> Assigned by lottery as slaves to various Greeks.[2]

The soul of the whole institution is here described by a classical playwright, whose characters were far removed in time and space from the events with which this book has dealt. The brutality, the unpredictability, the sexual element, the chattel status, even the racial hatred Euripides condenses are aspects of an institution whose American manifestations were only the final variations on a theme which has run right through human history. At the crudest level, the only unique characteristic of American slavery is that it was established to carry out American tasks.

With this qualification in favour of continuity, it is still hard to work out why the American colonists adopted slavery in the form they did and at the time they did. The British Prime Minister Lord Melbourne's habit was to distress benevolent Quaker delegations by having them explain their grievances while he belatedly shaved (and ignored them). His opinion of the slave trade was 'that religion, morality, law, eloquence, cruisers, will all be ineffective when opposed to a profit of a cent per cent and more'.[3] He was not misguided in seeing the close connection between the rise and fall of slavery and the slave trade and the rise and fall of profit. Black slavery was in the first instance an economic system, and it was black slavery which made the initial exploitation of the New World possible. It was its economic convenience – though not its economic necessity – which made the white colonists of the Americas use it as their predominant

---

[2] *Women of Troy*, ll. 26–7, in *The Bacchae and Other Plays*, trans. P. Vellacott (London: Penguin Books, 1954) p. 84.

[3] Quoted in Lord David Cecil, *Melbourne* (1939, 1954; reprinted London, 1965) p. 444.

labour system. Yet the continued existence of slavery was never entirely an economic matter. At some times and in some areas, where it had lost its profitability, it was preserved because the ownership of slaves was an index of social prestige, or because the ideological investment in the system was great enough to make its voluntary abandonment impossible. Here it might be preserved until a phase of economic inefficiency and weakness coincided with intellectual changes which called it into question. Nor were those who attacked slavery impelled by crude self-interest of the type described in *Capitalism and Slavery*, though they were children of their time in their belief in the economic world they hoped to put in the place of the slave system. It was only an ideological tradition which, whatever its economic attractiveness, had made the acceptance of slavery possible in the first place. The eighteenth-century abolitionist movement, too, was rooted in a series of profound intellectual changes which affected the whole of the Western world. Again, it was certainly change in slavery's economic importance which made the first abolitionist breakthroughs possible. But the nineteenth-century movement in its later phases was able to go on to free the slaves, by force or otherwise, even in areas where there was every economic reason for keeping them in thrall. Emancipation did not come because slavery had become unviable in the deep South, Cuba and Brazil, or because the free world was no longer willing to buy their produce. On the contrary, what gave the abolitionists their political strength was the momentum now gained by the idea of anti-slavery, by the religious and intellectual enthusiasm created by their earlier campaigns. The momentum of the economic system and the momentum of the idea are closely intertwined. The historian of slavery is wasting his time, and also being historically unrealistic, in attempting to separate them, or to deny that either aspect of this interaction was important. The two interplay constantly throughout the story of black slavery.

The black slave played a central part in the intellectual history of the modern West. Both the Christian and rationalist traditions gave ample rationalisation for enslavement, yet both had contradictions in which there was the potential for having it questioned and eventually overthrown. This potential went unrealised in the sixteenth century. The first Spanish needs for labour in the New World led to the decimation of the Indian population and the beginning of the massive Atlantic trade in black slaves. The Valladolid debates between Las Casas and Sepúlveda reflect a genuine pity for the former. They also show a doubt – which as yet affected few colonists – over the contradiction between slavery and the egalitarian message of the New Testament, although the inconsistency was not yet deeply enough felt to prevent the replacement of dead Indian labourers with more efficient black ones. The Portuguese in Brazil, in spite of their professed concern for saving souls, did not even have the scruples of the Spanish over enslaving the Indians. In the next century the English settlers moved towards the acceptance of black slavery as a labour system. Their hesitations over the use of forced labour were certainly not strong enough to deter them from enslaving aliens. But their discussions of the problem at least indicate the extent to which the contradiction in Christian assumptions on slavery was now being perceived. By the latter half of the eighteenth century the strain of comprising egalitarianism and hierarchy within one intellectual system had become intolerable. At the same time, the thought of the Enlightenment was eroding the classical and natural law assumptions in favour of slavery.

The emergence of a body of abolitionist writers and polemicists coincided with the weakening of the British vested interest in slavery. It was because of this that it brought the end of Britain's slave trade, and eventually of West Indian slavery. In North America a similar coincidence led to the liberation of the slaves in the Northern colonies. In Latin America, as a side-product of the Wars of Independence, slavery was removed from the whole continent barring Brazil and Cuba. Meanwhile other European powers, with the added stimulus of diplomatic pressure from London, also turned against slavery and the slave trade. As the nineteenth century progressed, the abolition idea gained support throughout the West, while the intellectual defence of slavery strengthened wherever it was still viable economically. The confrontation between the forces for and against the system produced the Civil War in the United States, and the tumultuous political aftermath of emancipation in Cuba and Brazil. With the laws of 1886 and 1888, black slavery was eradicated from the Americas. In nearly four centuries of existence it had presented European and American thinkers with one of their major intellectual problems. Few major philosophers or political theorists had written during this period without making direct or indirect reference to it, and it had been discussed at length by a host of polemicists and innumerable poets, dramatists and *littérateurs*. The shift in their attitude to slavery, and to some extent to race, has been one of the major changes in modern intellectual history. It was this change which the abolitionists reflected in their idea that it was no longer possible for civilised men or civilised nations to tolerate slavery.

Apropos of the abolitionists, it may be as well to defend them from two common accusations, which are often left unanswered in the modern historian's enthusiasm for finding revolutionaries in every anti-slavery society. The first accusation is that they ignored social abuses at home in their excitement over comfortably distant problems like slavery and foreign missions. The second is that they left their work undone, and gave up philanthropy (and the Negro) as soon as slavery had been legally ended. On the first count, many of the complaints are contemporary, frequently coming from working-class radicals intent on discrediting whatever evidence the bourgeoisie could give for its own good heart. The theme was also picked up, for instance, in *Bleak House*, where Dickens uses Mrs Jellyby's squalid home as a paradigm for the rotten society she allows to exist around her while occupied with her schemes on behalf of the natives of Borrioboola Gah. The popular American novelist Frederick Lippard was making the same point, though in relation to foreign missions, when he sneered at the Quaker city which

> every Sunday lifts its demure face to Heaven, and tells the Almighty God that it has sent missionaries to the Isles of the sea, to the Hindoo, the Turk, and the Hottentot; that it feels for the spiritual wants of the far-off nations, to an extent that cannot be measured by words, while it has not one single throb of pity, for the poor, who starve, rot and die, within its very eyesight![4]

There is also a good deal of bitter balladry on this subject. One example by Michael Sadler, for instance, tells of a factory girl dying in the street of starvation:

[4] F. Lippard, *The Monks of Monk Hall* (1844), ed. L. Fiedler (New York, 1970) p. 224.

That night a chariot passed her, while on the ground she lay,
The daughters of her master, an evening visit pay,
Their tender hearts were sighing as negro wrongs were told,
But the white slave lay there dying, who earned their father's
  gold.[5]

These pictures are unrealistic on three counts. In the first place, the central accusation is one of conscious hypocrisy. This implies deliberate deception, which would have been unthinkable for men and women with the value-system of the abolitionists. Alternatively, it may imply lack of confidence in one's values, which is a twentieth- and not a nineteenth-century problem. The abolitionists did not see the contradiction between their home and foreign attitudes, and when they did they tried to resolve them. Secondly, for many of them, for instance in Latin America, slavery *was* a home problem, more pressing than any others. Thirdly and most important, the abolitionists were quite alive to abuses other than slavery. According to their lights, they did what they could to combat them, either through slavery itself, which they genuinely saw as the key to *all* social evil, or by more specific action. It is impossible to find a single British or American abolitionist with no interest in other reform causes. Those in Dublin were popularly known as the 'anti-every-thingarians'. The French, Spanish and Brazilian abolitionists were the leading liberals of their time, for whom slavery was arguably the most horrifying, but only one among many social abuses they wished to remove.

As for the second accusation that the abolitionists stopped their work prematurely, as soon as slavery was dead, this too is untrue. Wilde's story about the philanthropist who almost died of *ennui* once his chosen cause had triumphed could not apply to the abolitionists, who had many other reforms in which they were interested, and which they (and their sons) pursued as soon as emancipation had been jockeyed through. Even on slavery, the British and French simply moved on to work for universal abolition once they had got rid of slavery in their own colonies. There is another argument, based mainly on the North American case, which condemns the abolitionists for failing to get rid of race

[5] Ballad by M. Sadler, n.d., quoted by K. Little, *Negroes in Britain: A Study of Race Relations in English Society* (London, 1948) p. 207.

tensions once they had got rid of slavery. This view takes the odd logical position of blaming the men and women who attacked slavery for the problems it left behind it. Added to this, there is the fact that many did what they could to protect and help the ex-slaves; the British were still doing so forty years after emancipation. If the abolitionists were not free from race prejudice, they were closer to being so than any of their contemporaries and most of ours. Admittedly, in the United States the abolitionists can be faulted for their 'failure' to follow black civil equality with black economic equality. With the gift of hindsight, divorced from the common assumptions of nineteenth-century social engineering, it is easy to pontificate about what should have been done in the reconstruction period. But to condemn the abolitionists for what they were not able to see should be done is to assume that nineteenth-century liberals had not only an obligation to go windmill-tilting in general, but a duty in particular to behave like twentieth-century radicals. In the United States, as in Latin America and Europe, the abolitionists were honest men with sensitive social consciences well ahead of their time. After overthrowing slavery, they dealt with the larger problem of race relations as best they could within the limits of their own world-picture.

No denial of abolitionist sincerity is implied in saying that one reason for the attention slavery attracted was its centrality to the economic development of Europe and the Americas. The New World would have been exploited much less efficiently if it had not been for the centuries of enforced and weary toil from black hands and backs. The brilliance of late sixteenth- and seventeenth-century Spain was based on wealth gathered by blacks who had replaced the miserable remnant of Las Casas's Indians. The Portuguese seaborne empire was heavily involved in providing Spanish America and their own poorer colony of Brazil with black manpower. After the confused commercial rivalries of the seventeenth century, England emerged as the leading power in European trade, secure in its control of the largest share of the Atlantic traffic and its own lucrative sugar islands. British profits from slaves, sugar and rum helped build the society which was to be the most prosperous of the next century. Some members of a new and powerful middle class built their fortunes directly or indirectly on the profits of the Guinea and West Indian trades.

In Africa, too, the structure of some societies on the Coast changed to meet the endless demand for black slaves. In the nineteenth century, slavery built the booming sugar and coffee industries of Cuba and Brazil, and indirectly the great European concerns which bought their exports. In the United States, the era of King Cotton saw new élites take the place of those who had climbed to the top of colonial society on the profits of slave-grown indigo, rice and tobacco. Cotton and its slaves dramatically altered the whole course of American economic history. This was so in the Black Belt, but also in the breeding states of the border South and the Northern mill towns which absorbed their share of the cotton crop. Even more important, United States cotton became the foundation of the vast Lancashire textile industry, which was one of the crucial areas of British investment and re-investment. Manchester cotton exports later became the instrument of British economic dominance in India, the Far East and, to a lesser extent, Africa. The wheel had indeed turned full circle when British abolitionist attention turned to East Africa on the eve of the scramble. The slave trade had first made possible the exploitation of North America, and an industry based on North American cotton was now to lay the foundations of British commercial greatness during a period when she was the power most conspicuous for opposition to the slave trade.

The cost of these contributions to European economic greatness at home and abroad has been dreadful. Curtin's figure of 8 million Africans carried across the Atlantic, or even the 15 million of the more traditional estimate, is a small total in the generations of man over four centuries. European guilt in this simple numerical sense is not much greater than that of the Arab world in similar enterprises, or indeed of many other civilisations. But this kind of figure takes no account of those who died before shipment to the Americas, of those killed in the violent business of amassing slaves, or through the dislocation of traditional societies. It also misses the white brutalisation and loss of life, much of it that of simple seamen, incidental to the trade. Above all, it ignores the countless millions of blacks who were born in the European colonies, only to rot out a short and miserable life as slaves. The sum of suffering involved in the shipping of these 8 million – a body of men and women four times the size of medieval England's whole population – is horrifying, but perhaps not so much so as the aftermath of violence and brutality which followed their introduction to the New World.

Slavery was by definition a system based on violence. In the end the wage of violence was more violence, and it was visited not only on the heads of the slaves but on the whole society which used their labour. The constant threat of slave revolts, and their relatively frequent incidence, would in themselves have been a high price to pay for slavery. The carnage of Haiti's revolution was only a scaled-up version of incidents which are scattered through the history of the Americas. Equally bad was the price paid in the corrupting effect of slavery on the masters themselves. Nothing is more true in Jefferson's perceptive comments on slavery than his bitter reflection that

> The whole commerce between master and slave is a perpetual exercise of the most boisterous passions, the most unremitting despotism on the one part, and degrading submissions on the other. . . . The parent storms, the child looks on, catches the lineaments of wrath, puts on the same airs in the circle of smaller slaves, gives a loose to the worst of passions, and thus nursed, educated, and daily exercised in tyranny, cannot but be stamped by it with odious peculiarities.[6]

His fears were echoed in the artist Charles Willson Peale's explanation of the great Virginian enthusiasm for swearing:

> One Reason . . . is the great number of Slaves which they have there, and being accustomed to tyranize and domineer over [them]. Even in their first Education they are suffered to Lord it over these unhappy Wretches. And by these Slaves are all laborious works performed, which makes them so n[ec]essary that every man who can possibly purchase Slaves does, and becomes Laisey themselves and of Course dissipated. Slaves doing the Labour, the poor White Labourer wants employment and Remains poor indeed – thurse the inequality of the inhabitants of the Country, being generally composed of very Rich and very poor, and but scarcely any of the middling class. . . . Where mankind are more dependent on each other,

---

[6] *Notes on the State of Virginia*, Query xviii.

and on greater equality, they [are] more circumspect in the[ir] Words and Actions.[7]

It is tempting to speculate that some of modern North America's complacency over violence stems from the free reign given to 'tyranny' in the slave era. The connection between slavery and war is uncanny. Apart from the bitter conflicts introduced to Africa by the slavers, and apart from the often-repeated abolition-ist argument that all slaveholders were automatically duellists and murderers, emancipation either came through violence or brought violence in its wake wherever slavery had not already run down as an economic system. This was true of Haiti, of the United States, and on a less spectacular scale of Cuba and Brazil.

Above all, slavery has left all the Americas to find a solution to the problems of racial hostility. Ghetto poverty and agrarian peonage, with the smouldering racial resentments they parallel, are the measure of the common failure to find such solutions. Though much is written or assumed about the idyllic race rela-tions of Brazil and other Latin American countries, the dark hand of slavery still lies over much of the hemisphere. The line between bond and free has been replaced by the line between white and black, for the abolitionists came from a generation which was unable to deal with the problem of race prejudice, or the eco-nomic inequalities left over from slavery which have done so much to reinforce it. It is asking too much of the abolitionists to expect them to have avoided the prejudices of their race, their class and their times. Nevertheless, the fact remains that the ending of slavery without finding a solution to race and class tensions left blacks as a subservient caste in those areas where they were not markedly in the majority over whites – and even there the substitute for a class system falling along the line be-tween white and black was one centred on the difference between black and mulatto. Setting aside the vexed question of the in-solubility or otherwise of problems of racial distrust, acceptance of the ex-slaves into society depended on their being given a measure of economic independence from their old masters. The fact that almost all the abolitionists shrank from calling for the

[7] C. W. Peale, *Diary*, entry for 13 Dec 1778, quoted in C. C. Sellers, *Charles Willson Peale*, 2nd ed. (New York, 1969) pp. 167–8. The punc-tuation in the quote follows Sellers.

kind of redistribution which would have made this possible – even if it crossed their minds – is a testimony to their place in the mainstream of the European intellectual tradition, which they were not prepared to desert. It is futile to see them as revolutionaries, except in the real sense that their destruction of a labour system which had survived for four centuries, and before this through most of recorded history, was in itself a revolutionary act of incalculable importance. The abolitionists had many of the conservative instincts of their century, and yet they presided over the greatest turning-point in the history of human society.

Slavery has not been entirely killed. There are still close to a million slaves in the world today, and the reformers determined to help them have become a handful. It is as if, as Wilde said, 'the nineteenth century has gone bankrupt through an over-expenditure of sympathy'.[8] Over-expenditure or not, the nineteenth century at least lifted the incubus of black slavery from the Americas. Even more fundamentally, the abolitionists, though they built upon concepts which had been extant for centuries, guided their contemporaries through to the rejection in principle and practice, of an oppressive institution which few earlier societies had done without. In doing this, they had wrought well, and achieved much.

[8] O. Wilde, *The Picture of Dorian Gray*, ed. H. Shefter (New York, 1972) p. 40.

Reading Suggestions

THIS very short bibliographical comment is by no means comprehensive. Used in conjunction with the more detailed references in the footnotes, however, it will provide a few titles to which the reader interested in any special area may turn to expand his knowledge. I have not mentioned any foreign-language works or primary materials here, and I have pointed to journal articles only when they are both centrally important and readily available. All these works should be available even in the most modestly equipped academic library.

Chapter 1

Unfortunately there is no full study which sets out to examine the sociological basis of slavery as a near-universal human institution, although there are many valuable insights in H. J. Nieboer, *Slavery as an Industrial System: Ethnological Researches* (The Hague, 1900). A modern approach to the problem of definition, stressing deracination as the essential component of the slave status, is M. I. Finley, 'Slavery', in *International Encylopedia of the Social Sciences*, 17 vols (New York, 1968) XIV 307–13. There is also a useful general essay on 'Slavery' in *Encyclopaedia Britannica*, 23 vols (London, 1969) XX 628–44. The obvious place to start reading on general Western attitudes to bondage, how-ever, is David Brion Davis's rich *Problem of Slavery in Western Culture* (Ithaca, N.Y., 1966), the first of a projected multiple-volume series on slavery and abolition. On the classical back-ground, M. I. Finley (ed.), *Slavery in Classical Antiquity: Views and Controversies* (Cambridge, 1960) is essential, and W. L. Westermann, *The Slave Systems of Greek and Roman Antiquity* (Philadelphia, 1955) most helpful. The medieval antecedents to New World slavery have been most fully explored in the volumin-ous works of Charles Verlinden, the most readily available of which is *The Beginnings of Modern Colonization: Eleven Essays*, trans. Y. Freccero (Ithaca, N.Y., 1970). The variants taken by the slave systems of the Americas are best distinguished through the excellent essays reprinted in L. Foner and E. D. Genovese (eds), *Slavery in the New World: A Reader in Comparative History* (Englewood Cliffs, N.J., 1969).

Chapter 2

The most useful work on the history of the slave trade is P. Curtin, *The Atlantic Slave Trade: A Census* (Madison, Wis., 1969). Although Curtin has been and will be questioned on some of his detailed deductions, all are agreed that he has made a masterly synthesis of research now available on the flow and volume of the trade. His figures may be fleshed out with the extraordinary collection of documents woven together in E. Donnan (ed.), *Documents Illustrative of the History of the Slave Trade to America*, 4 vols (Washington, 1930–5). The brutal Spanish experiments with Indian labour are examined in L. Hanke, *The Spanish Struggle for Justice in the Conquest of Latin America* (Philadelphia, 1949) and L. B. Simpson, *The Encomienda in New Spain: The Beginning of Spanish Mexico* (Berkeley, 1950). Neither work demonstrates the changes in Spanish labour organisation so well as the specialised account in W. Barrett, *The Sugar Hacienda of the Marqueses del Valle* (Minneapolis, 1970). The relation between Indian disease and black slaving is best pointed up in P. Curtin, 'Epidemiology and the Slave Trade', *Political Science Quarterly*, LXXXIII (1968) 190–216. A preliminary study of the equivalent period in Brazil is available in A. Marchant, *From Barter to Slavery: The Economic Relations of Portuguese and Indians in the Settlement of Brazil, 1500–1580* (Baltimore, 1942). As for the English, the finest starting-point on their adoption of slavery, especially on the mainland, is W. D. Jordan, *White over Black: American Attitudes toward the Negro, 1550–1812* (Chapel Hill, N.C., 1968). This gives references to most major articles on the controversy, although a recent and essential contribution is E. S. Morgan, 'Slavery and Freedom: The American Paradox', *Journal of American History*, LIX (1972) 5–29. The standard source on indentured servitude is A. E. Smith, *Colonists in Bondage: White Servitude and Convict Labor in*

America, 1607–1776 (Chapel Hill, N.C., 1947). England's island colonies are closely examined in R. S. Dunn, *Sugar and Slaves: The Rise of the Planter Class in the English West Indies, 1624– 1713* (Williamsburg, Va., 1972), a recent but already essential work. There is also a lot of helpful information in C. Bridenbaugh, *No Peace beyond the Line: The English in the Caribbean, 1624– 1690* (New York, 1972). There are few works on the French West Indies in English – or indeed in French – but the most useful is S. T. McLoy, *The Negro in the French West Indies* (Lexington, Ky., 1966). On the period of the sugar revolution as a whole, the most fruitful source is still N. Deerr, *A History of Sugar*, 2 vols (London, 1949).

Chapter 3

The legal formulation of the various American slave systems is also examined in many of the works mentioned above. Among the most interesting are the appropriate sections of Jordan, *White over Black*, and Foner and Genovese (eds), *Slavery in the New World: A Reader in Comparative History*. There is also more detailed material on specific English-speaking colonies in Dunn, *Sugar and Slaves*; E. V. Goveia, *Slave Society in the British Leeward Islands* (New Haven, 1965); and H. O. Patterson, *The Sociology of Slavery: An Analysis of the Origins, Development and Structure of Negro Slave Society in Jamaica* (London, 1967). A standard but exceedingly complex work on England's early mainland colonies is W. F. Craven, *The Southern Colonies in the Seventeenth Century, 1607–1689* (Baton Rouge, La., 1969), and there is also much valuable material on the early period in J. C. Hurd, *The Law of Freedom and Bondage in the United States*, 2 vols (Boston, 1858). The standard collection of printed sources and comment, although it deals primarily with more modern Afro-American history, is H. T. Catterall, *Judicial Cases Concerning American Slavery and the Negro*, 5 vols (Washington, 1926– 1937). On the agricultural organisation of early slave society, the sugar areas are best covered in Deerr, *History of Sugar*, while there is a general account of early mainland slave farming in L. C. Gray, *History of Agriculture in the Southern United States to 1860*, 2 vols (Washington, 1933). Detailed case studies of individual plantations are gradually being produced. Of these, the most important is M. Craton and J. Walvin, *A Jamaica Plantation: The History of Worthy Park, 1670–1970* (London, 1970). We know too little about black adaptation to the rigours of life in the Americas during the early period, but there is provocative and convincing material in G. W. Mullin, *Flight and Rebellion: Slave Resistance in Eighteenth Century Virginia* (New York, 1972). On the survival of African culture patterns among New World blacks, M. J. Herskovits, *The Myth of the Negro Past*, 2nd ed. (Boston, 1958) still provides a mine of information, though it is now clear that it relies too much on Caribbean and Brazilian evidence to prove a thesis on North America. A more modern study in this field is R. Bastide, *African Civilizations in the New World* (New York, 1972).

Chapter 4

Scholarship on the economic impact of the slave trade is currently in such a state of flux that it is impossible to cite definitive works on the field. Although Eric Williams, *Capitalism and Slavery*, 2nd ed. (London, 1964) has been severely criticised for its assumptions on the centrality of slaving profits to European industrialisation, its thesis has provided the conceptual approach for much modern research on the trade's position in the Atlantic business world. It should be read in conjunction with R. Anstey, 'The Volume and Profitability of the British Slave Trade, 1761–1807', a paper which will eventually appear in the published proceedings of the 1972 Rochester, N.Y., Comparative Systems of Slavery Conference. Useful points are also made in S. L. Engerman, 'The Slave Trade and British Capital Formation in the Eighteenth Century: A Comment on the Williams Thesis', *Business History Review*, XLVI (1972) 430–43, which only reached me when the present book was essentially finished. A useful paper which similarly shows the relatively low profitability of the French trade is P. Viles, 'The Slaving Interest in the Atlantic Ports, 1763–1792', *French Studies*, XXVI (1972). The profitability of British colonial ventures as a whole is challenged in R. P. Thomas, 'The Sugar Colonies of the Old Empire: Profit or Loss for Great Britain?', *Economic History Review*, 2nd ser., XXI (1968) 30–45. No similar work is yet available in English for the other seaborne empires, though it is probable that Thomas's findings would be mirrored in France at least. In domestic business organisation of the English trade, the fundamental work is K. G. Davies, *The Royal African Company* (London, 1957). It may be supplemented for the later period by G. Williams, *The Liverpool Privateers . . . with an Account of the Liverpool Slave Trade* (London, 1897). We do not yet have an adequate number of studies on the individual West India houses, but a brilliant pioneer venture is R. Pares, *A West India Fortune* (London, 1950). Political repercussions are examined in L. Penson, 'The London West India Interest in the Eighteenth Century', *English Historical Review*, xxxvi (1921) 373–92, and the growing difficulties of the planters in L. J. Ragatz, *The Fall of the Planter Class in the British Caribbean, 1763–1833* (New York, 1928). On the trade itself, the most readable short introduction is B. Davidson, *The African Slave Trade: Precolonial History, 1450–1850*, 2nd ed. (Boston, 1961). There is as yet no viable general study of slavery in African societies, but a great deal can be learned on the structure of the West African societies from which slaves were drawn from J. F. A. Ajayi and M. Crowder (eds), *History of West Africa*, vol. 1 (New York, 1972). The comparable background work for East Africa is R. Oliver and G. Mathew (eds), *History of East Africa*, vol. 1 (Oxford, 1963). Largely because of the disparity between different African societies, there is still much disagreement over the exact way in which they were affected by the trade. One key article by W. Rodney, 'African Slavery and Other Forms of Social Oppression on the Upper Guinea Coast in the Context of the African Slave Trade', *Journal of African History*, vii (1966) 431–443, implies that true chattel slavery was only introduced to Africa by means of the trade. J. D. Fage, 'Slavery and the Slave Trade in the Context of West African History', *Journal of African History*, x (1969) 393–404, makes a more general attempt to deal with the diverse experience of different parts of the Coast. The views of Rodney and Fage are examined in C. C. Wrigley, 'Historicism in Africa: Slavery and State Formation', *African Affairs*, lxx (1971) 113–24.

Chapter 5

The starting-point for all work on the growth of protest against slavery is Davis, *The Problem of Slavery in Western Culture.*

Unfortunately, however, there is no convenient work which covers the areas in which slavery's viability was weakening. Two useful works are A. O. Craven, *Soil Exhaustion as a Factor in the Agricultural History of Virginia and Maryland, 1606–1860* (Urbana, Ill., 1926), and Ragatz, *Fall of the Planter Class in the British Caribbean*. The early co-operation of American and European reformers is covered in M. Kraus, *The Atlantic Civilization: Eighteenth Century Origins* (New York, 1949). On the intellectual background, the most interesting approach is to begin with the relevant parts of *The Spirit of Laws* itself. F. T. H. Fletcher, *Montesquieu and English Politics, 1750–1800* (London, 1939) is a path-breaking work on Montesquieu's impact on the English-speaking world. At present, the only full work on the Scottish Enlightenment is G. Bryson, *Man and Society: The Scottish Inquiry of the Eighteenth Century* (Princeton, 1945), though it will soon be supplemented by the forthcoming work of N. T. Phillipson. W. Sypher, 'Hutcheson and the Classical Theory of Slavery', *Journal of Negro History*, xxiv (1939) 263–80, brilliantly shows the contribution of 'benevolism' to anti-slavery thought, while the influence of George Wallace has been picked up in D. B. Davis, 'New Sidelights on Early Anti-Slavery Radicalism', *William and Mary Quarterly*, 3rd ser., xxviii (1971) 585–94. There is a great deal of information on early French anti-slavery ideas in Davis, *The Problem of Slavery*. Other valuable English works in this field are Ruth Necheles, *The Abbé Grégoire, 1787–1831: The Odyssey of an Egalitarian* (Westport, Conn., 1971), and E. D. Seeber, *Anti-Slavery Opinion in France during the Second Half of the Eighteenth Century* (Baltimore, 1937). A fascinating study of early romantic protests is available in W. Sypher, *Guinea's Captive Kings: British Anti-Slavery Literature of the Eighteenth Century* (Chapel Hill, N.C., 1942), though the best way of exploring this field is simply by reading the literary works involved.

Chapter 6

Davis, *The Problem of Slavery in Western Culture*, is again the central work on early abolitionist propaganda. It can be usefully supplemented by T. E. Drake, *Quakers and Slavery in America* (New Haven, 1950). American Quaker philanthropy is more generally treated in S. V. James, *A People among Peoples: Quaker Benevolence in Eighteenth Century America* (Cambridge, Mass., 1963). There are few major biographies of early American abolitionists, but G. S. Brookes, *Friend Anthony Benezet* (Philadelphia, 1937) is useful, and D. Hawke, *Benjamin Rush, Revolutionary Gadfly* (New York, 1971) is a major contribution. The eighteenth-century American successes are charted in A. Zilversmit, *The First Emancipation: The Abolition of Slavery in the North* (Chicago, 1967). For the background of changing American ideas on slavery, it is useful to return to Jordan, *White over Black*. On the British fight against the slave trade, two nineteenth-century works are still exceedingly valuable. These are P. Hoare, *Memoirs of Granville Sharp, Esq.*, 2nd ed., 2 vols (London, 1828) and T. Clarkson, *The History of the Rise, Progress, and Accomplishment of the Abolition of the African Slave-Trade by the British Parliament*, 2 vols (London, 1808). The best political history of slave-trade abolition is D. H. Porter, *The Abolition of the Slave Trade in England, 1784–1807* (Hamden, Conn., 1970), though G. R. Mellor, *British Imperial Trusteeship, 1783–1850* (London, 1951) is also helpful. Williams, *Capitalism and Slavery*, is well worth reading, though its thesis that abolition came once slave-trade profits had made industrialism secure must be modified in the light of the findings of the papers by Anstey and Engerman cited above. Anstey summarises his alternative hypothesis in 'A Reinterpretation of the Abolition of the British Slave Trade, 1806–1807', *English Historical Review*, LXXXVII (1972) 304–32. On the Société des Amis des Noirs, it is essential to go to French-language works. The only convenient English information is what is available in Davis, *The Problem of Slavery*, and Seeber, *Anti-Slavery Opinion in France*.

Chapter 7

There is no recent political history of the campaign leading up to British West India emancipation, but the detailed story is well told in Mellor, *British Imperial Trusteeship*; in F. J. Klingberg, *The Anti-Slavery Movement: A Study in English Humanitarianism* (New Haven, 1926); and in W. L. Mathieson, *British Slavery and its Abolition, 1823–1838* (London, 1926). C. Lloyd, *The Navy and the Slave Trade* (London, 1949) will not be replaced as the standard work on British attempts at suppression by force. It is an incomparable essay in the combination of naval and civil history. Most studies on American suppression are somewhat out of date, but a recent valuable contribution is A. R. Booth, 'The United States African Squadron, 1843–1861', in J. Butler (ed.), *Boston University Papers in African History*, vol. 1 (Boston, 1964). Changing Western attitudes to Africa are examined in P. Curtin, *The Image of Africa: British Ideas and Action, 1780–1850* (Madison, Wis., 1966), but they may also be investigated by going straight to T. F. Buxton, *The African Slave Trade and its Remedy* (London, 1840), or H. H. Bell (ed.), *Search for a Place: Black Separatism and Africa, 1860* (Ann Arbor, Mich., 1969). The key change from gradual to immediate emancipation is explained in D. B. Davis, 'The Emergence of Immediatism in British and American Anti-Slavery Thought', *Mississippi Valley Historical Review*, XLIX (1962) 209–30. The best account of the British emancipation in its West Indian context is W. L. Burn, *Emancipation and Apprenticeship in the British West Indies* (London, 1937). There are short English accounts of French emancipation in S. T. McLoy, *The Negro in France* (Lexington, Ky., 1961) and idem, *The Negro in the French West Indies* (Lexington, Ky., 1966). These may be used in conjunction with material in Necheles, *Abbé Grégoire*, and the vivid account of violent self-emancipation in C. L. R. James, *The Black Jacobins: Toussaint l'Ouverture and the San Domingo Revolution*, 2nd ed. (New York, 1963). Emancipation in the Latin American republics has not been fully studied even by Spanish scholars, and next to nothing is available in English. A most useful recent work is J. V. Lombardi, *The Decline and Abolition of Negro Slavery in Venezuela, 1820–1854* (Westport, Conn., 1971). This will give an idea of the difficulties of emancipation even in a country where slavery was not an institution fundamental to national well-being.

Chapter 8

The connection between economic change and differences in slave societies is well argued in M. Harris, *Patterns of Race in the Americas* (New York, 1964). This must be read in conjunction with Stanley Elkins's seminal though much-worried *Slavery:*

A Problem in American Institutional and Intellectual Life
(Chicago, 1959), which stresses the cultural determinants of slave
conditions. Nineteenth-century slavery in North America is now
best approached through J. Blassingame, *The Slave Community:
Plantation Life in the Ante-Bellum South* (New York, 1972),
which fulfils the often repeated but seldom kept promise to write
black history from black sources. This does not exclude the careful
use of the traditional Southern work of U. B. Phillips, *American
Negro Slavery* (1918), ed. E. D. Genovese (Baton Rouge, La.,
1966). There is also much valuable data on the organisation of
plantation society in K. M. Stampp, *The Peculiar Institution:
Slavery in the Ante-Bellum South* (New York, 1956). The most
sophisticated recent contributions to the study of the ante-bellum
South are the many essays of E. D. Genovese, collected as *The
Political Economy of Slavery: Studies in the Economy and
Society of the Slave South* (New York, 1964); *The World the
Slaveholders Made* (New York, 1969); and *In Red and Black:
Marxian Explorations in Southern and Afro-American History*
(New York, 1971). Genovese brilliantly uses a Marxist framework
as a tool in the study of the relationship between the master class
and its labour force, though his conclusions have a flexibility
which is not always found in orthodox Marxism. Work on
Brazilian slavery in the nineteenth century is not readily available
in English, though a good point to start is with C. N. Degler,
*Neither Black nor White: Slavery and Race Relations in Brazil
and the United States* (New York, 1971), a valuable comparative
essay based primarily on secondary sources. The best introduction
to the early history of Brazil is C. R. Boxer, *The Golden Age of
Brazil, 1695–1750: Growing Pains of a Colonial Society*
(Berkeley, 1962). G. Freyre, *The Masters and the Slaves: A Study
in the Development of Brazilian Civilization*, trans. S. Putnam
(New York, 1956), though it has a racial bias and generalises
from one area of Brazil, is still essential. It has been criticised
more sensitively than usual in C. Vann Woodward, *American
Counterpoint: Slavery and Racism in the North–South Dialogue*
(Boston, 1971). One highly important area study in English is
S. J. Stein, *Vassouras: A Brazilian Coffee County, 1850–1890*,
2nd ed. (New York, 1970). The study of Cuba may be begun with
H. S. Klein's stimulating comparison with the Virginian case in
Slavery in the Americas: A Comparative Study of Virginia and

Cuba (Chicago, 1967). H. S. Aimes, *A History of Slavery in Cuba, 1511–1868* (New York, 1907) is still useful, but it has been largely replaced by F. W. Knight, *Slave Society in Cuba during the Nineteenth Century* (Madison, Wis., 1970). A. F. Corwin, *Spain and the Abolition of Slavery in Cuba, 1817–1886* (Austin, 1967) carefully traces Spanish and Cuban political responses to the rise and fall of slavery. Deerr's *History of Sugar* and Gray's *History of Agriculture in the Southern United States* are essential background works for this period.

Chapter 9

Because of its liberal, perhaps even radical, overtones, the anti-slavery movement has attracted a good deal of attention from historians intent on tracing the humanitarian lode in the American past. The literature is accordingly vast. The period prior to 1831 has been studied in A. D. Adams, *The Neglected Period of Anti-Slavery in America, 1808–1831* (Cambridge, Mass., 1908). There are valuable essays on the whole movement in M. B. Duberman (ed.), *The Anti-Slavery Vanguard* (Princeton, 1964). The standard narrative account of the movement is L. Filler, *The Crusade against Slavery, 1830–1860* (New York, 1960). Not a great deal has been written on the ideology and tactics of the abolitionists, but an essential contribution has recently appeared in A. Kraditor, *Means and Ends in American Abolitionism: Garrison and his Critics on Strategy and Tactics, 1830–1844* (New York, 1969). Lewis Perry, *Radical Abolitionism. Anarchy and the Government of God in Anti-Slavery Thought* (Ithaca, N.Y., 1973), is a major exploration of the ideas behind the divisions in the movement. The revivalist contribution to anti-slavery thought is best outlined in W. R. Cross, '*The Burned-over District': The Social and Intellectual History of Enthusiastic Religion in Western New York, 1800–1850* (Ithaca, N.Y., 1950). Abolitionism is set in context as part of the general reform impulse in C. S. Griffin, *Their Brothers' Keepers: Moral Stewardship in the United States, 1800–1865* (New Brunswick, N.J., 1960). W. Merrill, *Against Wind and Tide: William Lloyd Garrison* (Cambridge, Mass., 1964), by the co-editor of the Garrison papers, is an essential biography, as is J. Thomas, *The Liberator: William Lloyd Garrison* (Boston, 1964). On the conservative abolitionists, the best work is B. Wyatt-Brown, *Lewis Tappan and the Evangelical War against Slavery* (Cleveland, 1969). Black abolitionists have been given something of their rightful place in B. Quarles, *Black Abolitionists* (New York, 1969), but the best introduction to their work is to read any edition of Frederick Douglass's *Narrative*. No one has produced an acceptable generalisation on the motives of the abolitionists, and it is in response to this failure that W. H. Pease and J. H. Pease have demonstrated the total diversity of the movement in *Bound with them in Chains: A Biographical History of the Anti-Slavery Movement* (Westport, Conn., 1972). G. Sorin, *The New York Abolitionists: A Case Study of Political Radicalism* (Westport, Conn., 1971) argues that the commitment of the abolitionists was a commitment to what they genuinely saw to be right. D. B. Davis, *The Slave Power Conspiracy and the Paranoid Style* (Baton Rouge, La., 1970) stresses the importance of conspiracy fears in exacerbating tensions between the sections. Finally, *Uncle Tom's Cabin*, as the single most influential book of the ante-bellum period, is an essential source.

Chapter 10

J. H. Franklin, *The Emancipation Proclamation* (New York, 1963) is a standard short work on the Northern decision to end slavery. The most important work on continuing abolitionist agitation is J. M. McPherson, *The Struggle for Equality: Abolitionists and the Negro in the Civil War and Reconstruction* (Princeton, 1964). Abolitionist work in the South during the war is best explored through W. L. Rose, *Rehearsal for Reconstruction: The Port Royal Experiment* (New York, 1964) and W. S. McFeely, *Yankee Stepfather: General O. O. Howard and the Freedmen* (New Haven, 1969). An entertaining collection of freedmen's reminiscences of the period has been published in B. A. Botkin, *Lay my Burden Down: A Folk History of Slavery* (Chicago, 1945). The vast literature of reconstruction cannot be examined here, but it can be entered through K. M. Stampp and L. Litwak (eds), *Reconstruction: An Anthology of Revisionist Writings* (Baton Rouge, La., 1969). General problems of post-emancipation societies are assessed in W. Kloosterboer, *Involuntary Labour since the Abolition of Slavery* (Leyden, 1960) and in

Woodward, *American Counterpoint*. Later British contributions are the subject of C. Bolt, *The Anti-Slavery Movement and Reconstruction: A Study in Anglo-American Co-operation* (London, 1969) and M. Ellison, *Support for Secession: Lancashire and the American Civil War* (Chicago, 1972). British interest in the East African slave trade is fully examined in Lloyd, *The Navy and the Slave Trade*. The most important works in English on Brazilian abolition of the slave trade and slavery are P. A. Martin, 'Slavery and Abolition in Brazil', *Hispanic American Historical Review*, xiii (1933) 152–96, and the highly detailed monograph by L. Bethell, *The Abolition of the Brazilian Slave Trade: Britain, Brazil and the Slave Trade Question, 1807–1869* (Cambridge, 1970). An informative biography available in translation is C. Nabuco, *The Life of Joaquim Nabuco*, trans. and ed. R. Hilton (Stanford, 1950). R. Conrad, *The Destruction of Brazilian Slavery, 1850–1888* (Berkeley, 1973), not yet published at the time of writing, will be a useful addition to the English books on the Brazilian movement. For the Cuban case, there is much valuable material on the relative decline in slavery's viability in Klein, *Slavery in the Americas*. Knight, *Slave Society in Cuba*, is also useful, but the most highly detailed account of the vicissitudes of Cuban, Puerto Rican and Spanish anti-slavery is in Corwin, *Spain and the Abolition of Slavery in Cuba*. Few aspects of Latin American slavery and emancipation have been studied so thoroughly by an English-speaking scholar.

Postscript

Between the correction of the proofs of this book and its publication, three major books on slavery are scheduled to appear. One of them is Mr Genovese's new study of the slave experience in the United States, *Roll, Jordan, Roll*. Another is the second volume of Mr Davis's study of the Western response to slavery, to be entitled *The Problem of Slavery in an Age of Revolution*. Though complex, this will be an indispensable addition to the works I have recommended for reading on the anti-slavery impulse in the nineteenth century. Thirdly, 1974 is to see the publication, by a Boston firm, of a long-awaited statistical study of North American slavery, *Time on the Cross. The Economics of American Negro Slavery*, by R. W. Fogel and S. L. Engerman.

The 'cliometric' approach of this last work is revolutionary, and its conclusions will be unwelcome to many modern liberal historians. In short, they are that slavery was profitable and expansive right up to its forcible abolition; that slaves *did* work diligently, and adapted readily to industrial activities; that slave agriculture was more efficient than free northern family farming; that expropriation of income from slave labour was *lower* than the rate from northern free labour; that the slave's standard of material comfort was higher than that of the free northern worker; and that the slave family was a stable unit carefully protected by planters. These generalities, quite properly based on statistical averages, do obscure individual and regional cases which fail to fit them – and it is also true, in historical terms, that what the census says was happening in the Ante-Bellum South was less important than what contemporaries thought was happening. Not all Fogel's and Engerman's views, as it chances, are at odds with the more impressionistic ones presented in this book. In either case, their approach, though it will not provide new wards for all our imperfect keys to Southern history, is potentially most fruitful. This is not a book which should be set aside angrily because it seems to have holed many well-loved arks below the waterline. By the time this present book appears, two papers carefully assessing Fogel and Engerman's contribution will be available – C. Vann Woodward, 'The Jolly Institution', *New York Review of Books*, xxi no. 7 (1974) 3–6, and D. B. Davis, 'Slavery and the Post-World War II Historians', *Daedalus*, ciii (1974) 1–16.

Index